Manjushri's Innermost Secret

The material in this book is restricted. This book may be read only by those who have received a complete initiation into any highest yoga tantra practice.

In order to practice this material, it would be best if you have received a full initiation into either Guhyasamaja, Yamantaka, or Chakrasamvara.

LAMA CHÖPA THANGKA

MANJUSHRI'S INNERMOST SECRET

*A Profound Commentary of Oral Instructions
on the Practice of Lama Chöpa*

Kachen Yeshe Gyaltsen

Translated by David Gonsalez

Foreword by Ganden Tripa Lobsang Tenzin

Wisdom Publications
199 Elm Street
Somerville, MA 02144 USA
wisdompubs.org

Library of Congress Cataloging-in-Publication Data
Names: Tshe-mchog-gling Ye-shes-rgyal-mtshan, 1713–1793, author. | Gonsalez, David,
    1964–2014 translator. | Blo-bzang-chos-kyi-rgyal-mtshan, Panchen Lama I, 1570–1662. Bla
    ma mchod pai cho ga. English.
Title: Manjushri's innermost secret: a profound commentary of oral instructions on the
    practice of lama chopa / Kachen Yeshe Gyaltsen; translated by David Gonsalez.
Other titles: Bla ma mchod pai khrid yig gsang bai gdad rnam par phye ba snyan rgyud man
    ngag gi gter mdzod. English
Description: Somerville, MA: Wisdom Publications, 2019. | Includes bibliographical references and index. |
Identifiers: LCCN 2018039809 (print) | LCCN 2019011023 (ebook) | ISBN 9781614295884
    (e-book) | ISBN 9781614295631 (hard cover : alk. paper)
Subjects: LCSH: Blo-bzang-chos-kyi-rgyal-mtshan, Panchen Lama I, 1570–1662. Bla ma
    mchod pa'i cho ga | Guru worship (Rite)—Buddhism—China—Tibet Autonomous
    Region. | Buddhism—China—Tibet Autonomous Region—Rituals.
Classification: LCC BQ7699.G87 (ebook) | LCC BQ7699.G87 B553813 2019 (print) DDC
    294.3/923—dc23
LC record available at https://lccn.loc.gov/2018039809

ISBN 978-1-61429-563-1   ebook ISBN 978-1-61429-628-7

23 22 21 20 19   5 4 3 2 1

Diligent efforts were made in every case to identify copyright holders of the illustrations. The author and the publisher are grateful for the use of this material. The line drawings on pages 23, 68, 100, 181, 237, 315, 390, and 441 © 2015 Andy Weber. The chart on page 61 is courtesy of Yamantaka.org. The cover image of Arapachana Manjushri is courtesy of the Rubin Museum of Art, C2006.66.464 (HAR 925). Cover and interior design by Gopa & Ted2, Inc. Set in Perpetua MT Pro 12/14.5.

Contents

Foreword by Ganden Tripa Lobsang Tenzin ix

Publisher's Note to the New Edition xi

Preface to the New Edition from Wisdom Publications xiii

Translator's Introduction 1

A Biographical Account of the Author 5

PART I: A COMMENTARY ON LAMA CHÖPA

"A Treasury of Oral Instructions from the
Hearing Lineage Revealing the Innermost Secret" 9

Outline of the Commentary 381

PART II: RITUAL TEXTS

"Inseparable Bliss and Emptiness" 391

The Ganachakra Offering for Lama Chöpa 415

Appendix 1: *Fifty Verses of Guru Devotion* 425

Appendix 2: *"The Main Path of the Conquerors"* 433

Appendix 3: *Supplication to the Mahamudra Lineage* 443

Glossary 453

Bibliography of Works in English 463

Index 467

༄༅། བྱང་རྩེ་ཆོས་རྗེ་བློ་བཟང་བསྟན་འཛིན།

JANGTSE CHOEJE LOBSANG TENZIN

༄༅། དེ་ཡང་དུས་གསུམ་རྒྱལ་བ་ཀུན་གྱི་བགྲོད་པ་གཅིག་པའི་ལམ་བཟང་། རྒྱ་བོད་ཀྱི་མཁས་གྲུབ་

ཀུན་གྱི་ལྟགས་དང་གྱི་མཛེས། ཚོགས་གཉིས་རབ་འབྱམས་སྤྲུད་པའི་ལག་པ། ཐེག་པ་དང་སྡུང་བ་ཐམས་

ཅད་སྟེགས་པར་བྱེད་པའི་དུས་མཐའི་མེ་ལྡུ་བུ། མཆོག་མཆུན་མོང་གི་དངོས་གྲུབ་ཐམས་ཅད་སྩུར་དུ་འབྱུག་པའི་

ལྱགས་སླུ་ལྱུ་བུར། མདོ་རྒྱུད་དུ་མ་ནས་ལེགས་པར་བསྒྲགས་པའི་བླ་མའི་རྣལ་འབྱོར་འཛམ་མགོན་བླ་མ་ཚོང་

ཁ་བ་ཆེན་པོའི་ལྱགས་ཀྱི་བསྟུང་ལྱང་བ་ལྱུའི་གདུང་བ་ཟབ་མོ་གྲུབ་མཆོག་རྟ་མྱ་བཟ་ཡབ་སྲས་ཀྱི་གསུང་རྒྱུན་

ལྱུན་མོང་མིན་པ་བཏན་ཆེན་ཐམས་ཅད་མཐེན་པ་བློ་བཟང་ཚོས་ཀྱི་རྒྱལ་མཆན་གྱིས་མཛོད་པའི་ཟབ་ལམ་བླ་མ་

མཆོད་པའི་སྟན་བརྒྱུད་ཁལ་བཞེས་གསལ་བར་འབྱོད་པ་ཡོངས་འཛིན་ཡེ་ཤེས་རྒྱལ་མཆན་དཔལ་བཟང་པོས་

མཛོད་པའི་བླ་མ་མཆོད་པའི་ཁྲིད་ཡིག སསང་བའི་གནད་རྣམ་པར་ཕྱེ་བ་སྦྱན་རྒྱན་མན་ངག་གཏེར་མཛོད་

ཞེས་བ་དབྱེན་སྐྱད་ཕོག་འབད་ བརྩོན་ཆེན་པོས་ཟབས་བསྒྲུབ་བྱས་པ་འདིས་དེ་དུས་ཕར་ཕྱན་འཛོ་

སྐྱེད་གང་སར་པོ་བརྒྱུད་ དང་བསྒྱུན་འཐགས་ཕྱུལ་ན་ཡེ་ཐུའི་མཁས་པ་རྣམས་ཀྱི་བཞེད་སྲོལ་ལྱུན་མོང་མ་

ཡིན་པ་རྣམས་ལ་ དོ་སྣང་དང་རྣམས་ཡིན་བྱེད་མཁན་རྣམས་ལ་ཕན་བརྐྱབ་རྒྱ་ཆེན་ཡོངས་ལྱུར་རྗེས་སུ་

ཡི་རང་དང་འབྲེལ། འདིར་འབད་དགོ་བ་ཉིན་མོའི་འོད་ཟེར་དེས། ཁྱི་དགུའི་བློ་ཡི་སྲུན་པ་རབ་གསལ་ནས།

།རྒྱལ་བའི་དགྱེས་པའི་ལམ་བཟང་ཡོངས་རྫོགས་ཀྱིས། །འབྲས་བུའི་གོ་འཕང་མཆོག་ཏུ་དེས་འགྱུར་ཤོག

།ཅེས་པ་འདི་ཡང་རེ་བསྐུལ་ལྱང་དོན་བཞིན།

བྱང་རྩེ་ཆོས་རྗེ་བློ་བཟང་བསྟན་འཛིན་གྱིས་སྤྱོན་འདུན་དང་བཅས་ཤེས་པའོ། །

Foreword by Ganden Tripa Lobsang Tenzin

As the sole excellent path traversed by all the buddhas of the three times, this is the main spiritual practice of all the scholars and adepts of India and Tibet. As the infinite embodiment of the two accumulations, it incinerates all negativities and downfalls like fire at the end of time. It is like a hook that quickly summons all the common and supreme attainments. Guru yoga is like the heart-essence of the gentle protector Tsongkhapa the Great that is perfectly praised in numerous sutras and tantras. These profound instructions are from the uncommon lineage of teachings from the supreme siddha Dharmavajra and his spiritual son and were composed by Yongzin Yeshe Gyaltsen Palsangpo as an instructional manual on Lama Chöpa entitled *A Treasury of Oral Instructions from the Hearing Lineage Revealing the Innermost Secret*.

I rejoice that this text has been translated with great enthusiastic perseverance and pray that it will be of immense benefit to the practitioners of this modern era everywhere in this world, in both the East and West, who have had exposure to the Buddhist teachings of the Tibetan lineage that contain the uncommon tradition of the Nalanda scholars of India.

Through this virtuous endeavor that is [like] the light of day,
May the mental darkness of all living beings be dispelled
Through this complete and excellent path that delights the conquerors,
And may they definitely reach the supreme resultant state.

This prayer of aspiration was composed by Jangtse Chöje Lobsang Tenzin according to the request [of the translator].

Publisher's Note to the New Edition

It is a pleasure for Wisdom Publications to bring out the *Dechen Ling Practice Series*. Ven. Losang Tsering provided a great kindness to qualified practitioners when he made available in English these incredible texts, which combine the depth of Madhyamaka philosophy with the sophistication of Vajrayana practices, as found in Lama Tsongkhapa's rich tradition.

Some time ago, I expressed to Ven. Losang Tsering that these texts had been helpful in my own practice, and this led to conversations about Dechen Ling Press collaborating with Wisdom Publications. Not long before Ven. Losang Tsering passed, we both agreed that Wisdom Publications would be an excellent place to preserve the legacy of these books and make them available to practitioners throughout the world. I am very happy to see the fruition of our intentions. May this series be a support for practitioners under the guidance of qualified teachers.

Daniel Aitken

Preface to the New Edition from Wisdom Publications

Manjushri's Innermost Secret was one of the last books Venerable Losang Tsering translated and published. Though he often said the Dharma in total was "incredible," I was with him when he spoke of the very special and powerful place that this practice had for him—and could have for others who were inspired to practice it in its true form.

Venerable Tsering often said that the reason he practiced so hard and so diligently was for "mother sentient beings." In the light of his abiding wish that English-language practitioners might have the very best and authentic source material to practice the Holy Dharma, and specifically the Vajrayana, we are joyous at being able to partner with Wisdom and bring this book to Dharma practitioners around the world.

This will be the first book brought out in this partnership—but not the last. There have been some small changes made in this edition to spelling, punctuation, and word usage according to Wisdom's house style, and a few corrections and updates—for instance, the name of the foreword's author has been changed as he has been enthroned as the 104th Ganden Tripa since the original edition was printed—but otherwise the book is the same as the original.

May this work be of benefit to all sentient beings. May all beings never suffer, may they enjoy never-ending happiness, and may they reach unexcelled enlightenment as quickly as possible with no pain or harm.

Venerable Losang Tsering was my guru. I think he came to me in the form of a sick being because I have an overactive, critical, and negative mind. It would have been difficult for me to believe in a great being if the exemplification of them was a hale and hearty person, as I'd wonder if they were able to say grand things because everything was going well.

I witnessed as he practiced powerfully and long—for hours and hours every day and on many retreats—when he taught weekly for hours, and how in the last year and a half of his life he put out five books. He accomplished so much in each of these areas that you would think that any one was all that he did with his time. When he was on the throne I heard him bless the tumors in his liver, saying, "Without these, which I look at as Buddha's, I would not know the truth of impermanence." I watched as even the softest lined slippers would cause him immense pain. He'd grimace, then laugh as I hesitated for a moment to help him: "You think you are going to accrue bad merit for hurting the guru."

He taught me while I felt, to a greater or lesser degree, dazed. He taught me like someone in a hurry, a great hurry, and he taught me at such a level that I did not know what was going on; it has taken me years of studying, contemplating, and meditating to get to a point where some of his teachings could make sense to me, but those I do understand are profound. I just sat there like a person listening to something in another language: just nodding my head or trying to take notes on things that I had so little experience of I could not even ask a question. I tried to keep from having the three faults of the vessel, though I did not understand a great deal because of my lack of experience, my arrogance, and my laziness. Nevertheless, he kept pouring. He poured and poured, even while his illness waxed. One time he taught me while he sat on a gravity chair, with a bucket next to him, and he would explain, vomit into the bucket, wipe his mouth, and continue. Who can do this but a great being?

He was unique for me in another way. You see, I am technically Tibetan. My mother was of Tibetan nomadic stock, and my father was the son of a tulku and was a monk up until his late teens. However, I was raised in America. We were undocumented, poor, and without community. My mother did not speak English at all, and there was no way to function in America at that time if you only spoke Tibetan. My parents were deeply concerned that I would not be able to speak English well enough to do well in school. (As it turned out, language was not the reason I did poorly in school.) So all of their efforts were to make sure I learned English. As a result, I do not speak or read Tibetan. Therefore, a bulk of the teachings were not available to me. I had no access to Tibetan lamas, not really, and therefore I did not have access to any guru that could give me the time to teach me step by step, book by book. Even if I did, the language barrier would have been great. Still, he, they, found me; way over in the corner of the United States, the guru found me.

In *The Heart of the Path*, Lama Zopa Rinpoche states:

> In guru yoga, the essential point to understand is that all the buddhas are of one taste in the dharmakaya. The dharmakaya is the absolute guru, and this is all the buddhas. This is the very heart of guru yoga practice. Without understanding this there's no way to practice guru yoga comfortably. Even if we do the visualizations it won't be completely satisfactory because we'll be unclear as to how buddha is the embodiment of the guru and the guru is the embodiment of buddha. However, it will be extremely clear if we understand the very heart of guru yoga, that the guru is buddha and buddha is the guru.

The external guru leads one to the internal guru, the absolute guru, and thus we know that each and every guru is actually an embodiment of all the buddhas, for the Dharmakaya is all pervasive. The kindness of the guru, to lead one on this journey, is unmatched; I cannot overstate this. Without the path, nothing would have arisen but sorrow in my life. The only option would have been to try to ignore the suffering in any way possible, but a deep blessing I have had is that I am so weak; I cannot bear the slightest touch of suffering, fragile like a mass of foam, like a bubble . . . and so I sought a way out. And the guru was there.

I will conclude with two observations I had with him. Once, I made a comment of wonder at the enlightened activity of Lama Zopa by saying, "I can't imagine anyone can practice like that." Venerable Tsering looked at me quizzically and said, "That's funny, I never thought of him as practicing. He's a buddha," and I felt low and stupid. He said it was not bad that I said that, but that it was something that sounded so strange to him because it never arose in his mind that Lama Zopa was anything but a buddha. This is how he practiced guru yoga, the essence of the teachings and of this particular book specifically.

Another time someone had told him that spirits or demons may have caused his illness, and he said to me, "You know, they were my mother too. If these demons want me to die, then I'll die. It doesn't matter to me; it is only one life." This is an example of how to give even your life for mother sentient beings. In regard to this book, it demonstrates how he pushed so hard to get out the last four translations and then his biography, all the while managing his illness, which manifested immense pain in sores, no sleep, and other physical ailments. He said (this is not an exact quote but it is what I remember), "English-speaking beings will need these books in the years to come; they will need authentic sources to practice tantra; they'll need it to reach enlightenment for the sake of other sentient beings." He loved us all deeply. This love led him to put his very life on the line to serve us, not just in some individual practice, which he did even while nearly dead in the hospital (he practiced his *sadhana* in the hospital bed, and the doctor said, "You must really like that book"—and indeed he did). He did it in an individual and a wide-world way, in a way to give opportunities for everyone to end both their own and others' suffering—the true meaning of life. He gave these translations.

I am still so entangled in ignorance, and right now, it manifests as missing the guru.

May we never be far from the guru; may we always meet authentic sources and practice the holy Dharma and tantra purely and well until we reach the state of full enlightenment and skillfully end all suffering. Let us remember, in honor of the sacrifice of so many, that this is not only possible, it is inevitable with effort. Truly, what else could there be to do?

Guru Dorje

Translator's Introduction

It is well known that Lama Tsongkhapa had been in direct communication with Manjushri since the time of his retreat with Lama Umapa at Gadong, located about three miles from Lhasa, when Lama Tsongkhapa was around the age of thirty-five. It was from the time of this retreat onward that Manjushri acted as his direct guru, giving Lama Tsongkhapa many profound instructions. Because of this, the Gelug tradition contains many unique and unexcelled oral instructions. These lineages fall into two main streams, consisting of the Ensa tradition (stemming from Gyalwa Ensapa Losang Dondrup) and the Segyu lineage (stemming from Je Sherab Sengye). The teachings of Lama Chöpa come down to us through the Ensa lineage. The practice of Lama Chöpa contains all the most treasured and secret oral instructions within the Gelug lineage and was directly revealed to Je Tsongkhapa by Manjushri himself, who is the embodiment of all the buddhas' wisdom. Manjushri instructed Tsongkhapa to combine the teachings on the clear light and illusory body from the *Guhyasamaja Tantra*, the teachings on inner fire and the use of an action mudra from the *Chakrasamvara Tantra*, and the practice of Vajrabhairava, using these as a means of increasing wisdom and overcoming obstacles. With this as the foundation for his tantric practice he should establish a basis of *lamrim* and *lojong*[1] that is centered on the practice of guru yoga. Manjushri proceeded to give Tsongkhapa detailed teachings on all aspects of the aforementioned teachings and advised him to consolidate them all into a single practice. This was the impetus for the origins

---

1. Tib. *blo sbyong*, or mind training. In this instance the term *mind training* refers especially to the *Seven-Point Mind Training*, composed by Geshe Chekawa.

of Lama Chöpa. From these instructions there arose a very secret system of guru yoga that was transmitted orally from guru to disciple.

It was the very heart essence of practice for the greatest siddhas and scholars of the Gelug lineage such as Togden Jampal Gyatso, Baso Chökyi Gyaltsen, Chökyi Dorje, Gyalwa Ensapa, and many others on down to the First Panchen Lama, who compiled them into the ritual text known today as "Lama Chöpa." Later, the Third Panchen Lama, Palden Yeshe, requested Kachen Yeshe Gyaltsen to set in writing, for the first time, all of the detailed oral instructions with regard to the practice of Lama Chöpa. While there had been other commentaries prior to this, such as that by the Second Dalai Lama, they did not give details about the secrets of the oral lineage. Since the time of its composition, this commentary by Kachen Yeshe Gyaltsen has served as the foundation for all subsequent commentaries, making it similar to a "root text" with regard to the lineage of commentary, and it is one of the greatest literary contributions within the Gelug lineage.

Today many regard Lama Chöpa as a ritual that is performed on *tsok* days and nothing more. It saddens me deeply to see that one of the most treasured teachings of the Gelug tradition has been largely reduced to a ritual done twice a month. In fact, the practice of Lama Chöpa is the most skillful way to combine the practice of the three main deities of the Gelug tradition, established on the firm foundation of guru yoga and guided by lamrim and lojong. More specifically, it was traditionally used as a preliminary to the completion-stage practice. The great siddhas would streamline their practice by bringing everything into the practice of Lama Chöpa and then focus on the completion-stage practices that combine the essential features of Guhyasamaja, Chakrasamvara, and Vajrabhairava. There are even very secret oral instructions for practicing the completion stage based on the teachings that Manjushri revealed to Tsongkhapa, which Kachen Yeshe Gyaltsen briefly touches on in this commentary. For those who are interested I would like to suggest that you try to receive detailed oral instructions from your own guru.

When hearing that the practices of Guhyasamaja, Chakrasamvara, and Vajrabhairava are the three most important deities within the Gelug tradition, it may seem overwhelming to consider taking on all three of these practices. Yet the beauty of Lama Chöpa is that you can consolidate the essential features of all three of these deities, as well as guru yoga, lam-rim, and lojong, into a single practice. In this way we are not left with the task of filling our days with hours of recitations. Instead we can practice Lama Chöpa and focus on meditation, which is where the real transformation takes place. While receiving teachings on Lama Chöpa from Ribur Rinpoche, he mentioned that Lama Chöpa was Pabongkha Rinpoche's main practice and that Pabongkha would spend four hours every day meditating on Heruka–Lama Chöpa.[2] Someone asked Pabongkha if this were true and he replied, "Of course! Lama Chöpa is the very heart of everything taught in the Gelug lineage."

I had the good fortune to receive the oral transmission and commentary of this text from my guru, Gen Losang Choephel. I received the oral transmission of the ritual text from Geshe Khenrab Gajam, and later I received the oral transmission of the combined Heruka–Lama Chöpa from Ribur Rinpoche. While working on this translation I was repeatedly struck by the beauty and profundity of this commentary, and without the least bit of exaggeration I can safely say that this is the most inspiring commentary I have ever received.

I hope and pray that this translation will in some small way help raise awareness of and appreciation for the importance and profundity of this practice and will assist in elevating it from a ritual performed on tsok days to the heart practice of English-speaking practitioners.

Acknowledgments

First and foremost I must thank my kind guru, the abbot of Ganden Kachoe Monastery, Gen Lobsang Choephel, from whom I received the oral transmission and commentary. I would also like to acknowledge Geshe Khenrab Gajam, who gave me the oral transmission of the ritual text, as well as Ribur Rinpoche, who gave me the oral transmission of the combined Heruka–Lama Chöpa as well as a brief commentary.

I would also like to thank Sharpa Tulku, who made himself available on several occasions to go over my queries, and as always he was brilliant,

---

2. This is a version of Lama Chöpa that is combined with the practice of Heruka Chakrasamvara, a translation of which can be found at https://dechenlingpress.org/product/lama-chopa -heruka-sadhana/.

kind, humble, and extremely helpful. I am grateful for the kindness of Lobsang Thonden, who met with me one afternoon to address some of the difficult passages. I am also grateful to Keith Milton, who contributed his assistance with a few of the passages that posed certain challenges. I would also like to thank the members of Dechen Ling Buddhist Center who assisted me in accomplishing my various activities, such as Guru Dorje, and especially Kirk Wilson, who has not only kept Dechen Ling Press running on a day-to-day basis but has personally helped me in ways too numerous to count. I would like to thank the staff at Tibetan Buddhist Resource Center as well its founder, the late and great Gene Smith, for the constant support in providing me with texts needed for my various projects and the invaluable service that they provide. I would also like to extend my gratitude to Sidney Piburn, who has been an invaluable ally in bringing this and other books to fruition while constantly providing his unwavering support. I would like to thank Chris Banigan for his cover design and my editor, Steven Rhodes, for his dedication and expertise.

Finally, I would like to thank Susan and David Heckerman, who provided me with the support necessary to spend my entire life dedicated to meditation, study, translation, and a variety of other beneficial actions.

Special Acknowledgments

Dechen Ling Press would like to express our heartfelt gratitude to Lama Namdrol Tulku Rinpoche and Tekchen Choling Dharma Center in Singapore for generously funding this translation project. Their great kindness will bring immense benefit to English-speaking Vajrayana practitioners far into the future and go a long way in preserving this important lineage.

Dechen Ling Press would also like to extend our deep gratitude to all the other kind supporters of these final four publications. Together we have created something truly meaningful.

Losang Tsering (David Gonsalez)

A Biographical Account of the Author

KACHEN YESHE GYALTSEN was born in 1713 and died at the age of eighty in 1793. His early childhood was a difficult one, and he was often subjected to the quarrels of his parents. He entered Riku Monastery at the age of seven, where he learned to read and write. He entered Tashi Lhunpo Monastery at the age of nine and received ordination from the Second Panchen Lama, Losang Yeshe (1663–1737). Two of his other main gurus were Purchog Ngawang Jampa (1682–1762) and Drubwang Losang Namgyal (1670–1741). Drubwang Losang Namgyal is listed as his guru in the "Prayer to the Mahamudra Lineage Gurus." After receiving his *kachen*[3] degree from Tashi Lhunpo, Kachen Yeshe Gyaltsen began his studies with Drubwang Losang Namgyal in 1735, after which he spent more than twelve years in solitary retreat, where he reached the highest levels of spiritual attainment and mastered the teachings he received from his gurus on the Ganden Hearing Lineage. He was so poor during his retreats that he was often left with little or nothing to eat yet persevered in his retreat. His fame soon spread far and wide, even reaching the Potala, the residence of the Eighth Dalai Lama, who personally requested Kachen Yeshe Gyaltsen to become his tutor.

In 1751 Kachen Yeshe Gyaltsen traveled to Nepal, where he established Kyirong Samten Ling in 1756. He had many famous and highly realized disciples, including Konchog Tenpai Dronmé (1762–1823) and many others. His collected works are renowned for their profundity and accessibility, cover a wide range of subjects on sutra and tantra, and contain a

---

3. *Kachen* (Tib. *dka' chen*) literally means "great difficulty" and refers to the course of studies at Tashi Lhunpo. A kachen degree from Tashi Lhunpo is equivalent to a geshe degree at the three great monasteries of Ganden, Sera, and Drepung.

treasury of instructions on the Ganden Hearing Lineage. Among Tibetan lamas, Kachen Yeshe Gyaltsen is still held in the highest regard for his scholarship and practice as well as the peerless example he set, showing that spiritual realizations can be attained through diligence and unwavering determination.

PART I

A Commentary on Lama Chöpa

Lama Chöpa Field of Merit

Guhyasamaja Body Mandala

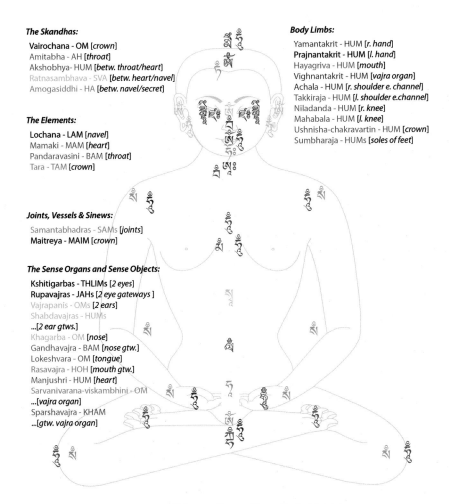

The Skandhas:

Vairochana - OM [*crown*]
Amitabha - AH [*throat*]
Akshobhya- HUM [*betw. throat/heart*]
Ratnasambhava - SVA [*betw. heart/navel*]
Amogasiddhi - HA [*betw. navel/secret*]

The Elements:

Lochana - LAM [*navel*]
Mamaki - MAM [*heart*]
Pandaravasini - BAM [*throat*]
Tara - TAM [*crown*]

Joints, Vessels & Sinews:

Samantabhadras - SAMs [*joints*]
Maitreya - MAIM [*crown*]

The Sense Organs and Sense Objects:

Kshitigarbas - THLIMs [*2 eyes*]
Rupavajras - JAHs [*2 eye gateways*]
Vajrapanis - OMs [*2 ears*]
Shabdavajras - HUMs
...[*2 ear gtws.*]
Khagarba - OM [*nose*]
Gandhavajra - BAM [*nose gtw.*]
Lokeshvara - OM [*tongue*]
Rasavajra - HOH [*mouth gtw.*]
Manjushri - HUM [*heart*]
Sarvanivarana-viskambhini - OM
...[*vajra organ*]
Sparshavajra - KHAM
...[*gtw. vajra organ*]

Body Limbs:

Yamantakrit - HUM [*r. hand*]
Prajnantakrit - HUM [*l. hand*]
Hayagriva - HUM [*mouth*]
Vighnantakrit - HUM [*vajra organ*]
Achala - HUM [*r. shoulder e. channel*]
Takkiraja - HUM [*l. shoulder e.channel*]
Niladanda - HUM [*r. knee*]
Mahabala - HUM [*l. knee*]
Ushnisha-chakravartin - HUM [*crown*]
Sumbharaja - HUMs [*soles of feet*]

Lama Losang Tubwang Dorje Chang Body Mandala

A Commentary on Lama Chöpa Entitled "A Treasury of Oral Instructions from the Hearing Lineage Revealing the Innermost Secret"

(bLa ma mchod pa'i khrid yig gsang ba'i gdad rnam par phye ba snyan rgyud man ngag gi gter mdzod)

I prostrate at the feet of, and go for refuge to, the Venerable Holy Guru who is inseparable from Tubwang Dorje Chang.[4] Please care for me with your great compassion at all times.

The sole agent that emanates and retracts
All the mandalas of the limitless conquerors,
The supreme guru-deity, protector of great bliss—
Eternally rest upon the anthers of the lotus of my heart.

I prostrate to the Buddha, together with your spiritual heirs—
The incomparable teacher Tubwang Dorje Chang,
Protector Maitreya, Manjushri,
The lord of secrets Vajrapani, and so forth.

I wholeheartedly bow to the scholars and siddhas of India who
Reached supreme attainments through this profound path,
Such as Indrabhuti the protector of bliss,
Saraha, Nagarjuna and his spiritual sons,
Mahasiddha Luipa, and Lalita,
Tilopa, Naropa, Atisha, and so forth.

I wholeheartedly bow to Jamgon and his spiritual sons,
Manjushri-Vajra Conqueror Tsongkhapa,
Khedrup and his brother, who accomplished the teachings of Manjushri,
Chökyi Dorje, who accomplished union, and others.

---

4. Today the principal of the field of merit is referred to as "Lama Losang Tubwang Dorje Chang." The term "Lama" refers to your own guru. "Losang" indicates that he is inseparable from, and appearing in, the outer aspect of Tsongkhapa, whose name is "Losang Drakpa." "Tubwang" refers to Buddha Shakyamuni, who is in the heart of Tsongkhapa. And "Dorje Chang" refers to Vajradhara, who is in the heart of Buddha Shakyamuni.

By worshiping the tip of the victory banner produced from the wish-fulfilling jewel of the Hearing Lineage of Losang's true intent, Ensapa sends down a rain of desires for the attainment of the three bodies, and King of the Dharma Panchen [Lama Chökyi Gyaltsen] raises the victory banner of Losang's Hearing Lineage Dharma to the peak of the palace of the complete teachings of the Buddha.

The great gentle protector of powerful speech[5] is the sole embodiment of the exalted wisdom of all the conquerors, the guide endowed with the eight powers of a sovereign lord with a magnificent mind of great excellence. Your love protects us lowly beings and your incomparable kindness and the nectar of your oral instructions restore us; therefore, I eternally make prostrations to those with incomparable kindness.

May the *dakinis* of the three places assist me to
Unveil this abode of the utmost secret
That is the supreme path to quickly accomplish enlightenment
    in one life
And is the heart essence of Losang Dorje Chang.

For that purpose I shall present the heart of all the scriptures of sutra
    and tantra
That is the path traversed by all the previous conquerors
And is the chief practice of all the holy scholars and siddhas of India
    and Tibet—
The oral instructions that extract the heart essence of the king
    of the Dharma Tsongkhapa the Great
And the tradition of the supreme siddha Dharmavajra and his
    spiritual sons.

The Dharma I shall explain is the yoga of the guru-deity as the complete embodiment of the profound path, which will quickly, quickly lead the fortunate beings to the ground of enlightenment. This has three sections:

---

5. In other words, Tsongkhapa.

1. An Explanation of the Source of These Instructions
2. An Explanation of the Greatness of These Instructions
3. How to Practice the Actual Instructions

An Explanation of the Source of These Instructions

The root text that is the basis for these instructions that I will be explaining was taught by the king of the Dharma Panchen Dorje Chang Losang Chökyi Gyaltsen and is known as *The Guru Yoga of the Profound Path That Completely Embodies the Path* or, in other words, *The Ritual of Lama Chöpa.*

These instructions were not fabricated in Tibet but find their source in the stainless teachings of the conqueror and were practiced by the holy scholars and siddhas of India. They were passed down orally in an unbroken lineage and arrived in Tibet. They were brought to fruition by the king of the Dharma Tsongkhapa and his spiritual sons and arrived in an unbroken line of accomplished beings.

For the sake of understanding the sentence "The scent of the blessings has not dissipated and has an authentic source," the Lama Chöpa [root text] begins:

In Sanskrit: Guru Puja Sya Kalpa Nama
In Tibetan: bLa ma mchod pa'i cho ga

I prostrate and go for refuge to the feet of the holy gurus,
    who have incomparable kindness.
Please care for me at all times and in every situation with your
    great compassion.

The wish-fulfilling jewel instantly bestows supreme bliss
Together with the supreme attainments upon
Whomever relies upon your three bodies.
In an instant you bestow the supreme wishes we desire.

By respectfully bowing to the lotus feet of the vajra holder
You accomplish every benefit and happiness for fortunate
    disciples,

Which is not surpassed by any means whatsoever.
It has sprouted from the lotus garden of the sacred oral
Instructions of sutra and tantra as a beautiful
Necklace of delightful flower garlands.

These verses reveal the authentic source of these instructions. Furthermore, although it is not necessary to state the Sanskrit title at the beginning of this text,[6] it is there for an extremely important reason, which is to indicate the correlation between the Tibetan and Sanskrit and reveal that these teachings were taught by the conqueror himself and that they come from an unbroken lineage of holy beings. We may wonder how that could be; therefore, I will give a short explanation since it is so very important.

The stainless tradition of Glorious Atisha and the king of the Dharma Tsongkhapa the Great states that the oral instructions must ultimately be traced back to the teachings of the conqueror. If someone claims that they have the ultimate innermost essence of the path, then they must find their source in the precious sutras and tantras that are the stainless teachings of the conqueror himself. If they are not in agreement with the teachings of the conqueror, then no matter how famous they may be it is not appropriate to place your trust in them.

Protector Maitreya said:

Because of that, there isn't a scholar in this world greater than the conqueror. His omniscient wisdom perfectly perceives the supreme suchness that is not [perceived] by the wisdom of others. For that reason, whatever the sage himself has set forth in the sutras is faultless. Because the teachings of [non-Buddhists] destroy the Buddha's teaching, they also bring harm to the holy Dharma.

If you wonder why the Hearing Lineage of oral instructions must abide in the teachings of the conqueror on the essential points of the path, it is because you are ignorant about the essential points of the path; therefore,

6. When a scripture was translated directly from Sanskrit into Tibetan, it was customary to begin by stating the title in Sanskrit in order to reveal its origins.

it is mandatory that the oral instructions of the Hearing Lineage possess them. If they don't [possess the essential points of the conqueror's teachings], although you may enter the conqueror's teachings without consideration, you will not be able to discover their intention and it will not be possible to make progress on the path. For example, although there may be a wish-fulfilling jewel in the ocean, you must rely upon a skilled captain with knowledge of the path, and once you have, you should follow such a captain and enter his boat with confidence and hold on tight. If you don't rely upon a captain and his boat, although you may haphazardly enter the ocean, not only will you not get the jewel, but you will be risking your life.

Thus, the *Explanatory Tantra Vajramala*[7] states:

> Reciting the king of mantras without the
> Oral instructions is the activity of fools.
> No matter what hardships one undergoes,
> It is like churning water, from which butter will never arise.
>
> Likewise, no matter how much beings persevere
> In mantra without oral instructions,
> They will never attain even the slightest
> Fruit from their recitations.
>
> A few ignorant men may
> Have a strong wish to cross the
> Four oceans and reach land,
> Yet they don't inquire about which path to follow.
>
> In the same way, the nature of the journey
> Is extraordinarily difficult
> For the practitioner without oral instructions.
>
> Because there are no results, although he may be wise,
> The practitioner will become angry.

---

7. bShad rgyud rdo rje phreng ba; *Vajramālābhidhānatantra*.

The moment he generates anger he will
Be reborn in the Wailing Hell.

Therefore, with all your effort,
Train with faith in the oral instructions
Transmitted by your guru.

And:

Instead of producing exalted wisdom,
Without being cared for by a protector
The boat will not even reach the other shore.
Likewise, despite being replete with good qualities,
There is no end to samsara without a guru.

For that reason, all the limitless enumerations of Dharma were taught by the conqueror after observing the disposition, intent, and capacity of his disciples. Therefore, although there are numerous instances where he taught the meaning of the essential points of the view [of emptiness] and so forth according to its interpretive meaning to some [disciples], there is not a single instance where any of his teachings contradict this teaching on the proper way to rely upon one's root guru. With one voice and one intention, [his teachings] proclaim that it is extremely important. Furthermore, the first gateway to entering the conqueror's teachings is going for refuge. Once you have commenced with that, you can receive the layperson's vows, the probationary monk's vows, the novice vows, and the full vows of ordination; all of which depend entirely upon the guru. At those times there are teachings on how to search for an abbot and master and how to rely upon them once found. Next, there is the tradition of searching for the master's abode for the sake of requesting what should be abandoned and adopted. The tradition of searching for a master of reading scriptures for the sake of listening, contemplating, and meditation and, once they are found, the way to properly rely upon them, showing respect for those lamas, as well as the proper way of offering service, the way to perceive the teacher, the way to rely upon them in thought, the way to offer respect to them with body and speech, and the way to rely upon them through practicing in accordance with his or her teachings are all extensively taught in the scriptures on the Vinaya. There are also extensive teachings on how to rely upon the guru and present offerings in sutra teachings of the Mahayana. In the *Avatamsaka Sutra*[8] it is taught how the bodhisattva Sudhana perfectly relied upon his spiritual master, after which it teaches that disciples also need to act in the same way.

The precious perfection of wisdom sutras state that discovering the profound meaning of the perfection of wisdom depends solely upon the virtuous friend, and after relying on the spiritual master we are taught the necessity of progressing on the path.

The *Perfection of Wisdom in Eight Thousand Lines*[9] states:

> The *bhagavan*, the bodhisattva, the great being taught how a beginner should abide in the perfection of wisdom, how he should train, and how to request it. The bhagavan addressed Subhuti in this way: "Subhuti, this great being, the bodhisattva who is a beginner and wishes to train in the perfection of wisdom should serve his spiritual masters; he should honor them with respect."

And:

> Those beings that are perfectly abiding in the pure superior intention that wish for buddhahood by completely actualizing the perfect unsurpassed complete enlightenment should serve their spiritual masters with devotion from the very beginning and honor them with respect.

Regarding the way to rely upon the guru, it is said that we should rely upon them in the same way as Sadaprarudita relied upon Dharmodgata. Sadaprarudita regarded the spiritual master as superior to all the buddhas and, through worshipping all the buddhas, once he perceived the great

---

8. *mDo sde phal po che; Mahāvaipulyabuddhāvataṃsakasūtra.*
9. *brGyad stong pa; Aṣṭasāhasrikāprajñāpāramitāsūtra.*

value in worshipping the spiritual master, he relinquished his body, life, and all his enjoyments without hesitation, after which he relied upon and worshipped his spiritual master Dharmodgata. Through the force of this he quickly progressed through the grounds and paths. I am concerned that if I cited all the sources for this, it would become too verbose; therefore, you should look into the precious sutras themselves and you will develop absolute conviction.

In short, the *Bodhisattva Section Sutra*[10] states:

> Obtaining and perfecting all the conduct of a bodhisattva and, likewise, the perfections, grounds, patience, concentration, clairvoyance, *dharani*, self-confidence, dedication, prayer, and attaining and perfecting all the Dharmas of the Buddha depend upon the guru. The guru is the root, the guru is the source, and the guru is the birthplace and the sense bases. Through the guru we are born, through the guru we grow. Rely upon the guru and the guru becomes their cause.

All of the good qualities depend solely upon the kindness of the guru; therefore, it is the intention of all classes of scripture within the Mahayana that you should practice guru yoga as the life of the path.

With regard to what is stated in the precious class of tantra, the lama himself is praised with extraordinarily high regard as the root of the path. All four classes of secret mantra rely upon receiving an empowerment and blessing to initiate your progression on the path of mantra. Next, protecting the commitments and vows is the indispensable basis of the path and among all the commitments, the commitment of the guru is principal. Once you are abiding in the commitments and vows, as you progress along the path it is said that you must progress along the path by establishing yourself in yoga where the supreme deity and the guru are inseparable. I am concerned that if I were to cite the sources for these teachings in each of the four classes of tantra, it would become too verbose; therefore, I encourage you to learn more from the precious tantras themselves.

In particular, the ultimate root source of these instructions is the root

---

10. *Byang chub sems dpa'i sde snod*; *Bodhisattvapiṭakasūtra*.

and explanatory tantras of Glorious Guhyasamaja. Furthermore, once you are established in the yoga of the guru and Vajradhara, the way of presenting the offerings to the guru and the mandala deity is presented in the *Guhyasamaja Root Tantra*. And although they have the complete methods for progressing on the two stages of the path, sealing with the ultimate and the four modes[11] are vajra knots that are very difficult to undo; therefore, the conqueror himself clarified their meaning for his disciples and "loosened" the seal of extreme secrecy by composing the explanatory tantras such as the *Vajramala* and so forth. Therefore, the essential points of this guru yoga come from the detailed presentation in the *Explanatory Tantra Vajramala*.

Initially the guru and disciple examine [each other's] qualifications. Then they are taught the proper way to rely on the guru, the system for viewing the guru as inseparable from the supreme deity, the system for meditation on the guru's body as the mandala, and the system for presenting outer, inner, secret, and suchness offerings to that [body mandala of the guru]. Next, the methods for meditating on the two stages are taught; yet, if I were to quote all the sources, I fear this text would become too wordy. Therefore, I shall leave it for the time being and explain a little more at the appropriate point during the actual commentary.

Thus, the conqueror gave extensive teachings on sutra and tantra in their entirety to Venerable Maitreya, Venerable Manjushri, the lord of secrets Vajrapani, and so forth, who then brought them to this world and revealed the teachings with complete mastery. Next, it was practiced by the mahasiddhas of India, such as the foremost great beings Nagarjuna and his spiritual sons, Asanga and his brother [Vasubandhu], King Indrabhuti, Mahasiddha Mahasukha Nath, Mahasiddha Saraha, Shawaripa, Luipa, Lalita, and so on. Furthermore, there were Tilopa, Naropa, and so on. They composed numerous texts and gave many oral instructions for the sake of future disciples. Mahasiddha Mahasukha Nath composed a commentary entitled *The Secret Accomplishment Clearly Revealing the Essential Meaning of the Root and Explanatory Tantras of Guhyasamaja*.[12] Within that he repeatedly stresses that this very method of guru yoga functions as the

---

11. The four modes are the literal (*tshig*), general (*spyi*), hidden (*sbas*), and ultimate (*mthar thug*).
12. *gSang 'dus rtsa bshad kyi snying po'i don gsal bar ston pa gsang ba grub pa.*

life of the path. Subsequent to that there were the other classifications of accomplishment such as "accomplishing exalted wisdom," "accomplishing suchness," and so forth as well as the famed *Essential Cycle of Teachings*,[13] such as the *doha* teachings of the great Brahmin [Saraha], which also repeatedly state that guru yoga functions as the life of the path. The great foremost being Nagarjuna composed his text on the five stages [of the completion stage] and arranged the five stages of the path based on the essential meaning of the root and explanatory tantras of Guhyasamaja. In that very text he also extensively explains that guru yoga is the life of the path and that one thereby makes offerings to all the buddhas, thus showing the great value of making offerings to the guru and so forth.

In short, this method of making guru yoga the life of the path is in agreement with the intention of all the mahasiddhas of India and is taught in all of our own texts and oral instructions. The sovereign lord of the complete oral instructions of all the mahasiddhas of India was Atisha. With regard to Atisha, he taught that the only way to progress through any of the grounds and paths of the Mahayana is through the kindness of the guru. Drom Rinpoche asked him, "Why is it that although there are many Tibetans who practice meditation, they haven't attained any special qualities?" Jowo [Atisha] replied, "Generating great or small qualities of the Mahayana are all developed in reliance upon the guru. You Tibetans regard the guru as an ordinary being; therefore, there is no way you can generate [such qualities]." Jowo Je [Atisha] himself practiced guru yoga as the essence of his practice and it is said that his enlightened actions spread all throughout India and Tibet because of the strength [of his guru devotion]. [Atisha also said], "Whatever good qualities I have with regard to kindheartedness are because of the kindness of Serlingpa." The root of all of Atisha's oral instructions is the *Lamp for the Path*,[14] which states, "I shall explain the perfect method / Taught by the gurus." Even the most subtle good qualities arc said to be due to the guru's kindness. Once you take guru yoga as the life of the path, it is as though the vast methods for training in the complete body of the Mahayana path have been clarified.

Thus, Je Rinpoche [Tsongkhapa] received the unbroken lineage stem-

---

13. *sNying po'i chos skor.*
14. *Byang chub lam gyi sgron ma; Bodhipathapradīpa.*

ming from Glorious Atisha from Drakor Khenchen and Lodrak Drubchen that in turn came from Tubwang Dorje Chang [Buddha Shakyamuni-Vajradhara] in a succession of lineage masters consisting of the holy scholars and siddhas of India down to Glorious Atisha. Furthermore, [Lama Tsongkhapa] received the lineage of Naropa that came from Lhodrak Marpa, a lineage of numerous Indian mahasiddhas that came from Je Go [Lotsawa], the lineage of the Pamtingpa brothers, and so on. In this way, Je Rinpoche received all the reliable oral instructions that came from India from Lama Kyungpo Lhäpa, Chöje Dondrup Rinpoche, Chenga Drakpa Jangchub, Jetsun Rendawa, and so forth. With regard to the uncommon oral lineage, initially Je Rinpoche received limitless teachings on the Dharmas of sutra and tantra from Jetsun Manjushri while Lama Umapa was acting as the translator. Later, he was able to directly perceive the face of Jetsun Manjushri himself and listened to the pith instructions on the paths of sutra and tantra in their entirety, and in particular [Manjushri] explained the ultimate intention of the conqueror as explained by Arya Nagarjuna with regard to the profound view of the Middle Way, whereby "through appearances the extreme of existence is dispelled and the extreme of nonexistence is dispelled through emptiness." He also received teachings on [Guhyasamaja], such as the essence of the five stages of the path, their enumeration, their structure, and so forth. Once again [Je Rinpoche] made limitless outer, inner, secret, and suchness offerings to Protector Manjushri and made extraordinarily powerful requests and supplications whereby Jetsun Manjushri bestowed the complete set of oral instructions of the Hearing Lineage on the complete body of the path of both sutra and tantra in its entirety. At that time he made a request to Jetsun [Manjushri] by inquiring, "What is the absolute quickest method for progressing to the state of Vajradhara?" To which Manjushri replied, "You must take as the life of the path this very yoga where the guru and deity are inseparable. Also, not everyone is capable of being a guru, for they must be able to lead one through the entire body of the path. Furthermore, you must also practice Heruka, Guhyasamaja, and Yamantaka without separation. As for Dharma protectors, you should rely upon Six-Armed Mahakala, Oath-Bound Dharmaraja, and Vaishravana. For companions, they must be in harmony with your guru, deity, and Dharma protector." At this point, Manjushri bestowed upon Je Rinpoche and Drubchen Jampal Gyatso, as well as a few fortunate gods, the complete oral instructions of the Hearing Lineage together with the *Great Emanation Scripture*.[15] This was the most extraordinarily secret set of teachings, which were not to be shown to just anyone. With regard to this uncommon guru yoga, they merely set to writing some of the key points by combining the sources from the tantras and composed commentaries on the *Fifty Verses of Guru Devotion*,[16] the *Explicit Commentary on Five Stages of the Completion Stage*,[17] and the *Practice Manual on the Six Yogas [of Naropa Entitled] "The Three Convictions,"*[18] while the detailed pith instructions had to be learned orally. Although the omniscient Je [Rinpoche] had a retinue of great beings like a collection of stars in the sky, when it came to the complete oral instructions of the Hearing Lineage, he only bestowed it upon the two "suns of speech,"[19] the powerful siddha Jampal Gyatso and his sole innermost heart-son, Khedrup Je. With regard to the *Great Emanation Scripture*, this was placed in the hands of the powerful siddha Jampal Gyatso. Because Mahasiddha Jampal Gyatso was the fountainhead of the Ganden Practice Lineage, he dwelt in an isolated place and practiced the oral instructions of the oral lineage in their entirety. He perfected the yoga of the profound two stages and gained knowledge of many hundreds of thousands of lives of himself and others. He continually perceived the face of the supreme deity Jetsun Manjushri and so forth and gained supreme realizations of the inconceivable secret and composed a compilation of oral instructions for fortunate beings. In particular, he bestowed the complete oral instructions of the oral lineage together with the *Emanation Scripture* upon Baso Chökyi Gyaltsen.

With regard to omniscient Khedrup, he dispelled all the defilements coming from the mistaken conceptions and doubts of those who lacked faith in the teachings of Je Lama and thoroughly removed any adulterations, like refining pure gold or a wish-fulfilling jewel on the peak of a victory banner, that were no match for his opponents. Although omniscient Je [Tsongkhapa] had already gone to the pure lands, [Khedrup's]

15. *sPrul pa'i glegs bam chen mo.* Often referred to as the *Kadam Emanation Scripture*, this text is said . to be the manifestation of Manjushri's omniscient wisdom, which is only perceptible to beings with extremely high realizations.

16. *bLa ma lnga bcu pa'i rnam bshad.*

17. *rGyud kyi rgyal po dpal gsang ba 'dus pa'i rdzogs rim rim lnga gdan rdzogs kyi dmar khrid.*

18. *Chos drug gi khrid yig yid ches gsum ldan.*

19. Tib. *smra ba'i nyi ma*, "sun of speech," is an epithet for Manjushri.

LAMA TSONGKHAPA

main practice was this guru yoga practice where guru and supreme deity are inseparable, whereby he had direct visions of [Je Rinpoche] five times who bestowed a vast number of prophecies and assurances. He spread the teachings of Je [Rinpoche] far and wide, and in particular he bestowed the oral instructions of the Hearing Lineage in their entirety upon Baso Chökyi Gyaltsen.

As for Baso Chökyi Gyaltsen, for the sake of practicing the oral instructions of Je [Rinpoche] and his spiritual sons' hearing lineage single-pointedly, he constantly maintained the intention to practice in isolated empty places, as in the liberating life story of Glorious Shawari.[20] According to dreams and prophecies he received directly from his guru and deity, [Baso Chökyi Gyaltsen] was told he should assume the throne at Ganden for the sake of upholding and preserving the teachings of Je Lama. When he was vastly propagating the teachings of Je [Rinpoche], and in particular when Mahasiddha Chö Dorje was eleven years old, he came to Ganden together with his parents. According to the prophecies that Baso Chökyi Gyaltsen had received from the dakinis, he presented numerous offerings to [Chö Dorje's] father and mother so that [Chö Dorje] could take ordination. At that time he gave him the name "Chö Dorje." For five years [Baso Chökyi Gyaltsen] then cared for [Chö Dorje] as his chief disciple and bestowed limitless instructions on sutra and tantra. In particular, he bestowed the oral instructions of the Hearing Lineage in their entirety together with the *Emanation Scripture*. [Chökyi Dorje] was told he should go to isolated places and accomplish its essential meaning and he was given the command of secrecy [and Baso Chökyi Gyaltsen told him], "In the future, there will be two fortunate beings to whom you should teach these oral instructions. To others you shouldn't even mention that you have oral instructions such as these."

Next, in accordance with the command of Baso Chökyi Gyaltsen, Mahasiddha Chö Dorje went to live in isolated places such as mountains, valleys, and forests and engaged in the essential practices to fulfill the command. Through this, one day he had a direct vision of Je Tsongkhapa the Great, who bestowed the common and uncommon instructions in their entirety. In particular, [Je Tsongkhapa] bestowed this practice with all the essential points of the paths of both sutra and tantra in conjunction with this guru yoga with the three nested beings.[21] Next, Mahasiddha [Chö Dorje] practiced this guru yoga single-pointedly, whereby he gained direct visions of countless buddhas and bodhisattvas, such as

---

20. Shawari was the disciple of Nagarjuna and Saraha and was the guru of Maitripa.
21. Tib. *sems dpa' sum brtsegs can*. In this practice this refers to the outer aspect of Lama Tsong-khapa as the commitment being, the inner aspect of Vajradhara as the wisdom being, and the secret aspect of a syllable HUM as the concentration being.

Avalokiteshvara and so forth. He sequentially gave birth to the realizations of the common and uncommon paths and attained the vajra body as the rainbow body.

Next, Mahasiddha [Chö Dorje] wondered to whom he should entrust these teachings on the Hearing Lineage of Je Lama, and when he looked with his exalted wisdom he realized that Gyalwa Ensapa would become the lord of the teachings of the Hearing Lineage. When Ensapa the Great had reached seventeen years of age, he was suffering from smallpox and was staying in Ensa when Mahasiddha Chö Dorje arrived in front of the door [to his retreat hut] and said, "I possess the complete oral instructions of the profound meaning." As a clue, he recited the *Praise to Dependent Relationship*[22] as though he were begging for alms. The moment Ensapa the Great merely heard his voice, his hairs stood on end due to his faith. Upon seeing him, [Ensapa] realized that this was someone who had attained supreme realizations. [Chö Dorje] appeared as a monk with a white mustache and goatee wearing the finest clothes and with a magnificent presence. When he examined him, he knew without a doubt that this was a supreme being, and once he understood that he was a mahasiddha holding the complete oral lineage of Je Lama, he requested him to take him into his care. With a delightful expression on his face, [Chö Dorje] told him to come to Mount Jomo Lhari[23] at a specific time. Next, when the specific time had arrived, Ensapa the Great went to Mount Jomo Lhari in accordance with Mahasiddha [Chö Dorje's] injunction. They met at Garmo Chözong on the slope of Mount Jomo Lhari. [Ensapa] presented offerings of everything he possessed as a *ganachakra*, together with a mandala. When he was receiving oral instructions, he was bestowed the complete Dharmas of sutra and tantra, but most importantly, the complete oral instructions of Je Lama's Hearing Lineage together with the *Emanation Scripture*.

Furthermore, from the time of his youth, Ensapa the Great himself had repeatedly received the blessings of directly perceiving the teacher Buddha Shakyamuni and Je Lama. In particular, one evening Je Lama gave him his hat and blessed him as the lord of the teachings of the Hearing

---

22. *rTen 'brel bstod pa.*
23. This is in Gromo Dzong, east of Phag Mountain on the border of Tibet, Bhutan, and Sikkim.

Lineage. When he reached the age of eight, one evening as the full moon was rising over Seg Mountain, he dreamt that he adorned himself with white silks and jeweled ornaments and, holding a vajra and bell, he sat on the moon and rang his bell, whose sound pervaded all worldly realms. This [dream] indicated that he would work to spread the oral lineage of Je Lama, which would fill the land of Tibet and produce accomplished beings. Ensa the Great remained in an isolated place in accordance with the command of Lama Mahasiddha [Chö Dorje] and, through his practice of guru yoga, he attained supreme realizations, thoroughly actualizing the stages of the common and uncommon paths. He was able to perform inconceivable activities that are expressed in his liberating life story, such as being able to understand many hundreds of thousands of previous lives of himself and others, reveal many magical transformations without obstruction, recite the *Perfection of Wisdom Sutra in Eight Thousand Lines* in Sanskrit, and so forth. He became the lord of the teachings of Je Rinpoche's Hearing Lineage.

Furthermore, Gyalwa Ensapa the Great himself said:

> In days of old there was Milarepa,
> Today there is Losang Dondrup.[24]
> With the exception of temporary food and clothes,
> I don't need any wealth or possessions.
>
> May I extract the essence of this leisure and endowment
> Abiding in an isolated place, abandoning attachment and hatred.
> By abiding in such excellent conduct may I
> Accomplish enlightenment in one life.

And:

> I who am called Losang Dondrup
> Am the supreme fortunate being of Tibet.
> By practicing this supreme path
> I attained enlightenment in this very life.

24. This is Ensapa's proper name.

And:

> In this day and age I am the sole
> Holder of the Hearing Lineage that is the essence
> Of the speech of this lama named Losang Drakpa,
> The supreme heart-son of Manjushri.

With regard to engaging in guru yoga that is the heart of practice, [Gyalwa Ensapa] stated:

> With great devotion I prostrate and supplicate Losang Drakpa, who is the essence of Tubwang Dorje Chang the Great, as well as the assembly of lineage gurus who are manifestations of Conqueror Losang Drakpa. Furthermore, I make single-pointed requests to Losang Drakpa, who is the nature of Tubwang Dorje Chang, who in turn is the nature embodying the wisdom and compassion of all the buddhas of the three times, as well as the root and lineage gurus, who are manifestations of Conqueror Losang Drakpa. This view is my way of understanding my religious tradition, which is a rosary of perfect precious jewels. Furthermore, in the beginning I relied on numerous guru-buddhas and placed their lotus feet on my crown. I received numerous pithy oral instructions that are the essence of their teachings, after which I sincerely applied myself to virtuous practice. Next, in the interim I utilized this special body of leisure and endowments by working toward the goal of swift enlightenment by combining the intention of the special oral precepts that encompass the essential meaning of all the scriptures of sutra and tantra with the special innermost essential nectar from the mouth of the guru, through which I obtained a unique experience of confidence in my practice. In this way, I made single-pointed requests to Conqueror Losang Drakpa, who is the essence of Vajradhara the Great, as well as the gurus who are manifestations of Conqueror Losang Drakpa.

And:

> By supplicating single-pointedly the guru-deity,
> I immediately apply whatever comes to mind.
> With my tradition I swiftly accomplish enlightenment
> With the tantric conduct similar to the urgings of a madman.

And:

> My tradition is to dwell alone in isolation.
> By single-pointedly supplicating the guru-deity,
> Once I abide in the tantric conduct of a madman,
> Whatever conditions arise for the most part appear as aids
>   to my spiritual practice.

In short, once you take guru yoga as the life of the path, the way to practice is to combine the complete body of the path from the teachings of both sutra and tantra, which is called "engaging in a combined practice" and is the sole property of the Hearing Lineage of Je Lama, which for the sake of comprehension [Gyalwa Ensapa] has set down here in writing:

> Namo, Tsongkhapa, the king of the Dharma, please care for me with your great compassion throughout all my lives.

> I prostrate to the feet of guru-Manjushri.

> Therefore, once you have initially trained in the common path you are a suitable [vessel] for tantra and you have pleased your guru, and you come to recognize that you are capable of practicing in dependence upon the profound path of a perfect empowerment, after which you must protect the commitments and vows. Next, you operate with high regard for the three sets of vows[25] that you took at that and other times.

---

25. The three sets of vows are the *pratimoksha* vows of individual liberation, the bodhisattva vows, and the tantric vows.

After establishing a foundation of perfectly protecting [your vows], you meditate on the first stage through the yoga of four sessions, which functions to ripen your roots of virtue for generating the extraordinary realizations of the completion stage. Next, once you generate the extraordinary levels of the completion stages, you then accomplish the body of union. Once you attain certainty by becoming a person with the necessary conditions for enlightenment with all the essential instructions of sutra and tantra, you will become a holder of the complete teachings of the Buddha and you will also be capable of disseminating them to others. This was composed by Losang [Dondrup] in accordance with the oral lineage of Dharmavajra.[26]

With regard to the meaning [of the above quotation], for the sake of proliferating the Hearing Lineage of Je Rinpoche, Gyalwa Ensapa the Great himself arrived to fulfill the wishes [of Chö Dorje]. Gyalwa Ensapa the Great gave the general oral instructions of the Hearing Lineage to many fortunate beings, and in particular he bestowed them in their entirety upon Khedrup Sangye Yeshe.

With regard to Khedrup Sangye Yeshe, he took this very guru yoga as his heart practice, and in dependence upon guru yoga completed all the essential paths of sutra and tantra. Relying on guru yoga he received prophecies as well as many visions. His extensive teachings emphasize that all of one's spiritual practice must be centered on guru yoga. I am concerned that if I were to cite all my sources to substantiate these points, this text would become too verbose; therefore, you should learn about this by referring to the collected works of Khedrup Sangye Yeshe.

Khedrup Sangye Yeshe bestowed the complete oral instructions of the Hearing Lineage upon the omniscient Panchen Losang Chökyi Gyaltsen. The great vajradhara Panchen Losang Chökyi Gyaltsen caused the Hearing Lineage of Je Lama to spread throughout every section of Tibet. In particular, once he composed this ritual of Lama Chöpa that contains the complete body of the paths of sutra and tantra, he bestowed it upon

---

26. Dharmavajra is Sanskrit for Chökyi Dorje, Gyalwa Ensapa's guru.

limitless fortunate beings. Through this, it spread from Dzalandhara in the west to the edge of the great ocean in the east and to every country and town. Because of this activity his kindness of spreading this supreme oral instruction is felt throughout the entire earth. Although Jetsun Losang Chökyi Gyaltsen had numerous powerfully accomplished heart-sons, the one who received the command to perform enlightened actions to proliferate this oral instruction was Dorje Zinpa Konchog Gyaltsen. Dorje Zinpa Konchog Gyaltsen made these very instructions his main practice and propagated them to others far and wide.

In particular, it was from my precious abbot, the omniscient Panchen Jetsun Losang Yeshe Palsangpo, that I received these very oral instructions in their entirety. This particular omniscient great being took this as his main practice and bestowed it upon countless fortunate beings. As for his command to proliferate [these teachings] through enlightened actions, this went to Dorje Zinpa Losang Rigdrol. This *dorje zinpa* [vajra holder] took these instructions as his main practice and bestowed them upon numerous fortunate beings. The powerful accomplished lama with incomparable kindness, Losang Namgyal, received the complete Dharmas of sutra and tantra from this very omniscient Panchen [Losang Yeshe], and in particular he received these instructions on guru yoga. However, it was Dorje Zinpa Losang Rigdrol who received the complete oral experiential commentary on this guru yoga that contains the complete body of the path. As for that great, powerfully accomplished, foremost lama [Losang Rigdrol], he took this very guru yoga that encompasses the entire path as his main practice. In dependence upon this, he reached the heights of the path. I myself received the kindness of this Dharma numerous times.

For that reason, Jetsun Losang Chökyi Gyaltsen said:

> With extensive backing of the sutras and tantras
> And mastery in the oral instructions,
> The uncorrupted lineage of blessing is
> Fleshed out by the qualified teachings of the Jetsun [guru].
>
> Although you may be a fortunate being wishing for liberation,
> If you wish to see the face of reality,
> Don't rely on dry superficial explanations of an abbot
> With little learning and without deep meditation.

Focus on the mind-essence of the famous Je [Tsongkhapa]
And continuously persevere in accumulation and purification.

From Tubwang Dorje Chang the Great until the present there hasn't been any break in this lineage of holy beings, and now that we have found these authentic trustworthy instructions that contain the complete body of the path that are so difficult to find, the wise wishing for liberation should enter the path that pleases the conqueror and train by following the perfect biographies of holy lamas of the Ganden Hearing Lineage.

An Explanation of the Greatness of These Instructions

The [Lama Chöpa] text itself states:

> Furthermore, this is the foundation for all of those wishing liberation, the root of all the limitless common and supreme attainments, and contains all the essential oral instructions practiced by yogis of the Supreme Vehicle. It reveals the unmistaken path for oneself that revolves around proper reliance upon the virtuous friend.

The *Blue Udder*[27] states:

> The primary embodiment of all instructions
> Is to not forsake the spiritual friend,
> From whom emerges faith, bodhichitta, and so forth—
> Who, as the source of all good qualities, bestows all.

The foremost omniscient being [Tsongkhapa] also stated:

> The root connecting all the excellent interdependence,
> Which accumulates excellence for this life and the next,
> Is striving with thought and action to properly rely upon the
> Holy virtuous friend who teaches the path.

---

27. *Be'u bum sngon po.* This is a very famous text on the stages of the path attributed to Geshe Potowa (1027–1105).

Seeing this, do not abandon him even at the cost of your life,
And please him by offering your practice of the teachings.
I, the yogi, practiced in that way;
You, who seek liberation, should do the same.

And:

Your kind guru is the root of all good qualities
Of virtue and excellence of this world and beyond.

The *Fifty Verses of Guru Devotion*[28] states:

Vajradhara himself said that
Attainments come from following the master.
Realizing this, you should thoroughly delight your guru
With all of your belongings.

And [another scripture states]:

Surpassing the qualities possessed by a jewel,
Good disciples should have devotion for their gurus
And they should always rely upon their wise gurus.
Why? Because the wise are the source of good qualities.

They will subsequently reveal the perfection of wisdom;
Therefore, rely upon the virtuous friends of the Buddhadharma.
The conqueror promised that they are the foremost of all
    good qualities.

For that reason the vajra master surpasses even all the buddhas as the field
within which the disciple is to accumulate merit and purify obscurations.

The *Samvarodaya Tantra*[29] states:

---

28. bLa ma lnga bcu pa; Gurupañcāśikā.
29. Dpal sdom pa 'byung ba'i rgyud; Saṃvarodayatantra.

He is the self-arisen bhagavan,
One with the supreme deity.
Because he is the best treasure for instructions
The vajra master surpasses [the deity].

In accordance with that reasoning, [Khedrup Sangye Yeshe] stated:

Meditating on guru yoga contains all the essential points of the path and is the supreme means of taking the essence of this life of leisure and endowments. Therefore, we should practice in accordance with this.

If I were to explain in detail each and every training and commitment listed above, I fear this text would become too verbose; therefore, in short, let me say that all the various forms of happiness, from the most subtle contaminated happiness while remaining in samsara up to the supreme bliss of unexcelled liberation, including all the good qualities of the resultant grounds and paths, emerge from the power of relying on and making offerings to your guru. Thus, not only do all the good qualities in general emerge from proper reliance upon the guru, but these instructions reveal the complete body of the path of sutra and tantra. Therefore, listening to this teaching contains all the essential points of the *Stages of the Path to Enlightenment* from "proper reliance upon the spiritual master" at the beginning up to "tranquil abiding and superior seeing," from which emerges these four greatnesses:

1. The greatness of realizing that all the teachings are noncontradictory.
2. The greatness of allowing all the scriptures to appear as personal advice.
3. The greatness of easily discovering the intention of the conqueror.
4. The greatness of preventing oneself from making the "great misdeed."[30]

---

30. Tib. *nyes spyod chen po*. This refers to regarding some of the Buddha's teachings as valuable and others inferior, which constitutes "disparaging the Dharma" and is the "great misdeed."

It also has the greatness of the mind training since it contains all the essential teachings of the *Seven-Point Mind Training*,[31] which states, "Like a diamond, the sun, and a medicinal tree," the meaning of which you should learn from the scriptures. It also states:

> This essential nectar of the lineage coming from Serlingpa.
> As the five degenerations proliferate,
> This becomes the path to enlightenment.

The same greatness also occurs in this teaching.

In addition to the essential points of the two stages of the [common] path, this also has all of the various good qualities and greatness of the two stages of highest yoga tantra combined in one teaching. Thus, if one is an intelligent person capable of distinguishing good and bad and desires the excellent and wishes to progress extremely quickly on the path of the Supreme Vehicle, the best thing one could do is persevere in profound instructions such as these. If one wonders, "How should I rely upon the practice of these instructions?" you must train your mind well in the common path and receive the four complete empowerments of highest yoga tantra of any suitable practice, such as Heruka, Guhyasamaja, or Yamantaka.

When you meditate on this guru yoga, you yourself perform deity yoga and imagine that you purify the world and its beings and transform them into the supporting and supported [mandalas], while visualizing that the principal of the field of merit is Lama Tubwang Dorje Chang as the three nested beings embodying the assembly of body mandala deities and surrounded by a mandala of the four classes of tantra. You then offer the extremely secret outer, inner, secret, and suchness offerings of highest yoga tantra. It also reveals the way to meditate on the two stages. To be able to listen, contemplate, and meditate on the ultimate secret of highest yoga tantra you must have perfectly obtained the four empowerments. If you haven't received an empowerment, it is inappropriate to reveal even

---

31. *bLo sbyong don bdun ma*. This is an extremely important and well-known mind-training text composed by Geshe Chekawa (1102–76).

the most subtle limbs of the path of mantra. When we enter the mandala we are issued a warning that states:

> Today you will receive the blessings of all the *tathagatas*. You must never speak of the tathagatas' mandala of supreme secrets to those who have not entered the mandala or to those who have no faith.

It also states:

> Today you have entered the lineage of all the tathagatas whereby I have generated the vajra-exalted wisdom within you. If [because of this] you will accomplish the attainments of all the tathagatas with that exalted wisdom, what need is there to mention other attainments? You should not speak of this mandala in the presence of those who have not seen it. If you do, you will defile your commitments. This is your vajra commitment. If you speak of this method to anyone at all, your head will split open.

Therefore, if you cannot even reveal the form of the mandala to the eyes of those who have not received empowerment without damaging your word of honor, what need is there to mention that it is inappropriate to reveal the ultimate secrets of mantra?

Thus, the *Explanatory Tantra Vajramala* states:

> Bestowing empowerment is principal,
> It is the eternal source of all attainments.
> I shall explain it just as it is;
> For its sake, listen well from the beginning.
>
> When the disciples are initially
> Bestowed empowerment by the wise,
> At that time they become receptacles
> For the completion-stage yogas.

Although the practitioners may understand the meaning of tantra
And they may perfectly bestow empowerment,
If they don't possess empowerment [themselves], both master
    and disciple
Will go to the great unbearable hell.

And:

Just as the milk of a snow lion
Should not be placed in an earthen vessel,
Likewise the tantra of the great yoga
Should not be given to unfit vessels.

At that moment the disciple will die
And this life and beyond will be ruined.

The *Drop of Mahamudra*[32] also states:

From the moment the disciple is first
Bestowed empowerments one time,
At that point explain the great secret,
For they have certainly become vessels.

Without empowerment there will be no attainments,
Just as you won't get butter from squeezing sand.

In this way, in the four classes of tantra there is a very strong oath set in place that it is improper to reveal the secrets of mantra to those who have not obtained empowerment. I fear that if I were to quote the sources from each of the tantras, this text would become too verbose; therefore, you should learn more by examining the tantras themselves.

Merely receiving an empowerment into the three lower tantras is not sufficient to make one a suitable vessel for this guru yoga that embodies the complete paths of both sutra and tantra. Instead, you absolutely must receive an empowerment into a mandala of highest yoga tantra. To

32. *Phyag chen thig le.*

perfectly receive an empowerment you must have properly trained your mental continuum in the common path. In the *Explanatory Tantra Vajra-mala* Vajrapani says to the teacher Tubwang Dorje Chang:

> If a disciple is replete with good qualities
> They become a suitable vessel for yoga tantra.

He then asks [Vajrapani], "What sort of good qualities do they need to enter the mandala of highest yoga tantra and receive empowerment?" To which he replies:

> With faith as well as devotion for the lama,
> Constantly abiding in virtuous actions,
> Having abandoned all negative thoughts,
> Having heard many scriptures,
> Having abandoned killing and violence,
> They always and perfectly strive
> With a mind of certainty for living beings.
>
> These and others are the good qualities
> Of good disciples with great faith.

Thus, [highest yoga tantra] is for someone who has elicited an experience by training their mind in the common path from the proper reliance upon the spiritual master up to training in the general conduct [of a bodhisattva]. In addition to that, it is especially necessary to have extremely strong faith in the guru and mantra. It is extremely important that you learn in detail the necessary preliminaries for the common path as explained in each and every word of the tantras. Yet, because I fear this text would become too wordy, the intelligent should attain certainty about these points by making a detailed analysis of tantra's meaning.

For these reasons, the supreme method for extracting the essence of this life is this very yoga of the guru-deity that embodies the entirety of all the essential points of the paths of sutra and tantra. Thus, you should search with great perseverance for the complete instructions for this guru yoga and then hold it as your primary practice.

How to Practice the Actual Instructions has two sections:

1. How to Engage in the Actual Session
2. How to Engage in the Session Breaks

How to Engage in the Actual Session has three sections:

1. The Preliminaries
2. The Actual Session
3. How to End the Session

The Preliminaries has two sections:

1. The General Preliminaries
2. The Extraordinary Preliminaries

The General Preliminaries has two sections:

1. How to Correct Your Motivation
2. How to Go for Refuge and Generate Bodhichitta

How to Correct Your Motivation

With regard to the place where one is going to practice, the twelfth chapter of the *Root Tantra of Glorious Guhyasamaja*[33] states:

> Practice in the location of an isolated mountain
> That embodies all attainments,
> In an area that is very secluded,
> Adorned with flowers, fruits, and so forth.

---

33. *dPal gsang ba 'dus pa'i rtsa rgyud; Guhyasamājatantra.*

The *Explanatory Tantra Vajramala* states:

> You should practice with diligence in a place
> Adorned with flowers, fruit, and water;
> At the peak of an isolated mountain
> You will gather all attainments.

And:

> A being in the isolated abode of the deity
> Will be free from the thorn of sound.
> The fortunate joyous being is without obstruction
> In the pleasure grove of great peace and happiness.
> Enjoy the five objects of desire and so forth whereby
> You will accomplish the superior attainments of mantra.

Furthermore, all the classes of tantra state that it is extremely important that you practice in an isolated place.

In particular, the *Tantra Requested by Subahu*[34] states:

> Prostrate and make offerings to gods and demigods
> In a delightful place endowed with merit such as
> Where the *pratyeka* buddhas and tathagatas were born
> And where the buddhas of old have lived.
>
> Through restoration and possessing vows
> You should joyously perform retreat.
> If you can't find a place such as this, you can also
> Stay in a place with a running stream or lake
> Adorned with lotuses and *utpalas*
> And utterly free from roaming people;
> With an abundance of delicious and appetizing water,
> Where terrible and harmful spirits don't live;

---

34. *dPung bzang gis zhus pa'i rgyud; Subāhuparipṛcchāsūtra.*

With clean flowers and fruit
And an abundance of medicinal trees and plants;
With an extremely clean place to sleep, set upon the ground,
Without tigers, leopards, or lions,
That is extremely pleasing and without thorns.
This is proclaimed as the place of attainments for beings.

Thus, the main places are where the tathagatas were born or where their feet have touched, as well as places that have statues or have been blessed by bodhisattvas, the great beings. Although you may not be able to find excellent places such as these, you should practice in a place that is extremely isolated and pleasing, with plenty of water, flowers, and fruit, and that has a minimum amount of disturbances from people roaming about. It should also not be a place where vicious nonhumans dwell but should be free from conditions that harm your body and life, while having groves of medicinal herbs. Additionally, it says that it is extremely important that it be a place where holy beings have lived and practiced as well as a land where the Buddha's teachings have spread and that is under the rule of a Buddhist king. [In such a place] there won't be harmful conditions to your body and life and it will be most agreeable. Furthermore, it is not appropriate to stay in just any town and so forth. Instead, it should be an extraordinary place that is isolated. The primary reason you should stay in an isolated place is because you will not have obstacles to your spiritual practice by things such as distracting activities. It also says that by staying in an isolated place, whatever virtue you undertake, such as prostrating, offering, and so forth, will have great power and the amount of ground you can cover on the path will greatly increase.

With a retreat hut, cave, and so forth, stay in an agreeable isolated place such as this and then clean, sweep, and sprinkle the place where you are going to stay, making it attractive and pleasing to the mind. Sprinkle it with the five cow products[35] and strew flowers, which should be done by utilizing the appropriate ritual texts. With regard to sprinkling and sweeping, there are many important points that come from the story of

---

35. The "five cow products" are five substances of a cow that are collected before they touch the ground. They are (1) urine, (2) dung, (3) milk, (4) butter, and (5) curd. You can obtain pills containing all five substances that are properly prepared.

how Sadaprarudita made offerings to Dharmodgata. As for anointing with cow products, the eighth chapter of the *Guhyasamaja Tantra* states:

> In peaceful places where the conqueror himself was born
> You should always anoint them with excrement, water, and so
>   forth
> For the sake of making offerings to the conqueror.

When making offerings to the guru and assembly of mandala deities, you should clean the place extremely well by anointing it with the five cow products.

Set out the four retreat markers in whatever place seems appropriate, such as in the four directions of the retreat house, in front of the door, upon the door, and so forth, and generate them as the four great kings.[36] Once you do, in that place request their assistance in your meditation practice with their enlightened actions to prevent unfavorable conditions while assembling all the favorable conditions. On an elevated support you should set out whatever representations you have, such as a statue of the teacher Buddha Shakyamuni, Venerable Manjushri, the foremost omniscient being [Tsongkhapa], and so forth, as well as a perfection of wisdom sutra, a tantric scripture, and so forth. In front of them set out beautifully arranged offerings that were honestly obtained. Beneath your seat draw a Buddhist swastika[37] upon which you should set untangled jointed grass.[38] Previously, out of his great compassion, the teacher sat upon a seat of jointed grass in front of the bodhi tree at Bodhgaya and subdued millions upon millions of demons with his concentration on love, whereby he actualized complete enlightenment, which is recalled in his liberating life story. To bring our own practice in alignment with the liberating life story of the teacher, we also utilize this as our seat and repeatedly contemplate, "I am going to subdue the demon of self-grasping together with samsara and perfect my practice of the profound path." Set a soft and comfortable cushion upon the jointed grass with its back slightly raised.

36. The four great kings are Vaishravana, Virudaka, Dhritarashtra, and Virupaksha.
37. Despite its strong negative association since the 1930s, the swastika is an ancient Indian symbol for inner strength, stability, and good luck.
38. Tib. *rtswa dur ba*.

If you are going to be practicing for a long time in that place, you should sit on something like a wooden bench, as explained in the Vinaya, so that your cushion doesn't rot.[39] If you can't obtain [such a platform], arrange your cushion so that there is a gap between it and the ground.

With regard to the essential physical postures for sitting on that cushion, you should sit in the sevenfold posture of Vairochana together with the elimination of [impure] winds, which makes eight essential physical postures. Both the *Collection of Spiritual Grounds*[40] of Asanga and the *Second Stages of Meditation*[41] of Master Kamalashila state that such physical postures are necessary when meditating on the two stages of mantra.

The *Explanatory Tantra Vajramala* states:

> Once the practitioner sits on a comfortable seat,
> His two eyes should be directed toward the tip of the nose,
> With the tip of the nose directly aligned with the navel.
> The two shoulders are even and the tongue is against the
>   palate,
> The teeth and lips rest at ease.
> The inhalation and exhalation of breath are relaxed
> And flow with very little exertion.
> With the inhalation and exhalation just right,
> Sit in the perfect vajra posture.

To exemplify this meaning, Gyalwa Ensapa the Great composed a summation that states:

> By combining the three—hands, feet, and spine—
> With teeth, lips, and tongue you get four.
> Together with the four of head, eyes, shoulders, and breath
> You get the eightfold posture of Vairochana.

---

39. This is in reference to a small wooden platform with holes for ventilation that prevent moisture from rotting your cushion.
40. *Sa sde*. This is one of five major treatises of Asanga.
41. *sGom rim bar pa*; *Madhyamabhāvanākrama*.

According to this there are eight essential points. Furthermore, according to the sitting posture of Venerable Vairochana, you should sit with your legs in the vajra posture, your two hands should be four finger-widths below the navel, with your left hand in the lowest position, with your right hand upon it and the tips of your two thumbs touching. Your shoulders should be level with each other. Your spine should be upright and straight. Your neck should be slightly bent. Your teeth and lips should remain natural. And the tip of the tongue should be touching your palate. Thus, all seven of these postures should be cherished as extremely important when practicing and regarded as indispensable.

Marpa Lotsawa said, "Even if you combine all the oral instructions of Tibet, they can't compete with Marpa Lotsawa's single instruction on sitting posture." And it is accepted as a uniquely profound bit of instruction that comes through the oral instructions of Je Lama's Hearing Lineage; therefore, we should hold it as an extremely cherished essential instruction. There are also reasons why we should engage in those essential bodily postures, what faults arise from not doing so, what benefits come from each one, and so forth. These points are extremely important and you should learn them in detail, yet I won't be able to write about them here; therefore, you should learn them from the mouth of your holy guru.

Thus, once you are seated with the sevenfold posture, you can either visualize the nine-round breathing meditation or reach a state of equanimity by examining the gentle movement of your breath. With regard to the way to dispel [impure winds] with the nine-round breathing, you inhale through your right nostril and exhale through your left. Then you inhale through your left and exhale through your right. Then you inhale through both nostrils and exhale through both nostrils. In this way you complete three rounds. When doing them, you imagine you exhale all of your mental faults and shortcomings and when you inhale, imagine you receive the blessings of the minds of all the buddhas.

As for the way to reach a state of equanimity by examining the gentle movement of your breath, you should recognize that you are under the influence of craving for the things of this life as well as attachment and anger and then contemplate, "Since beginningless lifetimes up to this moment I have been ruined by negative thoughts such as these. Even at this moment I am wasting this human life of freedom and endowment that I have obtained just this one time; therefore, right now I shall expel these negative thoughts on the spot!" With this thought, as you exhale you should imagine that the afflictive emotions within your mental continuum are expelled and purified, together with their seeds. As you inhale you should imagine all the blessings of the buddhas and bodhisattvas in the ten directions are collected into [yourself].

You should not exert yourself so strongly that your breath makes noise nor that your breath is uneven in length so that it disturbs your mind, but let it flow naturally and examine its slow and gentle outward and inward movement. Furthermore, once the winds flow outward and return back again, count that as one and continue up to seven such counts without letting your mind wander, and focus your mind to the best of your ability. Next, count another seven and focus your mind. Then again count another seven and focus. Once you have separated the defilements from the luminous nature of mind, you should rest for as long as possible within the sphere of awareness of the mind's luminosity.

It is extremely important that you commence your actions of the path with these important bodily features. And although it seems that I have given a rather extensive explanation of these points, it is because they are so important; yet, still I haven't written everything here because some of the main points have already been written about in the commentary on Ganden mahamudra entitled *Lamp Illuminating the Excellent Path of the Hearing Lineage: A Literary Commentary to Ganden Mahamudra*.[42] Thus, once you have settled the winds, investigate your mental continuum, and after correcting your motivation, you should generate a particularly virtuous state of mind.

Just as the Dharma begins with a heading in Sanskrit,[43] you should begin all your meditations by correcting your motivation once you investigate the state of your mental continuum. In *Questions of Pure Superior Intention*[44] [Je Tsongkhapa] asks, "What is similar to Sanskrit that initiates

---

42. *dGa' ldan phyag rgya chen po'i khrid yig snyan rgyud lam bsang gsal ba'i sgron me.*

43. When Tibetans translated works from Sanskrit they began by stating the name of the text in Sanskrit in order to reveal its origins.

44. *Dri ba lags bsam rab dkar.*

all meditation?" It was answered in [Losang Chökyi Gyaltsen's] text *Los-ang's Melodious Laughter*,[45] which states:

> It is asserted by the supreme incomparable lama
> That just like Sanskrit, the beginning of all meditations
> Should begin by perfectly
> Analyzing one's own mental continuum.

As this states, so it is also taught by Je Rinpoche himself. The meaning of *Questions of Pure Superior Intention* is meant to be applied to your own mental continuum.

Once you are in an isolated place with your body perfectly aligned, focus inward toward your mind, and when you have, contemplate:

> Since time without beginning I have been enmeshed in sam-sara and I will continue to be tormented by suffering, which is similar to that being produced by self-cognizer [in the Mind Only school].[46] From this day forward I must do what I can to prevent taking rebirth in such a place in the future.

You should feel this so deeply that if you don't act on it, it will be like experiencing a sharp pain in the kidney. Initially you should strive in the means to generate such feelings. This can be very difficult, and you may not be able to generate such an experience, and no matter how much your guru explains the profound methods for gaining liberation from samsara, it is like water flowing over ice. For example, it is like a person who remains still without making an effort to get a drink because they don't have the wish to drink water. Thus, remove such negative states of mind and approach your practice from within a clear and luminous state of mind.

You should continue to contemplate by thinking:

---

45. *bLo bzang bzad pa'i sgra dbyang.*
46. In the Mind Only school, all phenomena are seen as nothing other than appearances to the mind. Since the suffering of samsara is created by the mind, it is reminiscent of the view of the Mind Only school.

Although I have experienced uninterrupted suffering in samsara from beginningless time until the present, I have not become bored or weary of it even for a moment. My negative mind still thinks of samsara as the abode of manifest joy, yet because of it, I still must endure only unending boundless suffering just as before. However, at this moment, due to the kindness of the guru and the Three Jewels, I have obtained an excellent body of leisure. I have come under the care of the holy spiritual master who shows me the unmistaken path. I have met the complete precious teachings of the Buddha, which are so hard to find. I have obtained a small amount of wisdom that understands what to adopt and what to forsake. If I am able to practice from my own side, I will easily be able to attain the state of a buddha in this one short life in the degenerate age with such profound instructions as these. At this point, while I have the freedom to practice such a profound Dharma as this, if I don't work to attain stability, it will be extremely difficult to once again find such an excellent situation as this. I will find something like it only once and it doesn't last long, for it is quickly destroyed. I must certainly die and there is no certainty when I will die. When I die nothing except the Dharma is going to be of any benefit. Once I die, if I fall into the lower realms, I will have to experience unbearable harm and suffering, such as heat and cold, hunger and thirst, servitude and exploitation, stupidity and ignorance, and so on, and it will be difficult to even hear the sound of Dharma. Despite my searching, I also won't be able to find a refuge in such a place.

Even if I attain rebirth a hundred times in a higher rebirth, it will not transcend being anything but suffering. Human beings have the unceasing suffering of birth, aging, sickness, and death. The gods experience the suffering of falling from their statuses when they die and so forth. In short, no matter where I am born in any of the six realms, I am under the control of karma and afflictive emotions and wander without control while being afflicted by nothing but suffering. Just as I myself am tormented by suffering, so are all living beings tormented by suffering. All these living beings that are tormented by suffering are nothing other than my kind mothers. And they were not just my mother once, but acted as my mother countless times. And when they were my mother, their kindness was just like the kindness extended to me by my mother in this life; therefore, the kindness they have shown me is unbelievably great. Although these kind mothers wish for happiness, their behaviors of acceptance and abandonment are mistaken; therefore, they experience nothing but suffering, without even a moment's happiness making them [objects of my] compassion. How wonderful it would be if these mothers came to possess the most excellent happiness. How wonderful it would be if they were completely free from suffering.

With these thoughts, meditate on extremely powerful love and compassion. Continue by contemplating:

However, the burden of liberating all living beings from suffering has befallen me alone. Although [the responsibility] has fallen upon me, I am currently in the same situation; therefore, how can I possibly accomplish the welfare of all living beings? I am not even capable of perfecting the welfare of one living being! Not only that, even if I attain the two states of an arhat,[47] with the exception of some short-term benefit for living beings, I would not be capable of establishing all living beings in the state of perfect complete enlightenment. Who is capable of such a thing? A completely perfect buddha! For that reason, by all means, I too must attain the precious state of a completely perfect buddha for the welfare of all living beings.

With these thoughts, you should meditate on an extremely powerful bodhichitta motivation. You should investigate these points with the

47. The two types of Hinayana arhat are a pratyeka buddha and shravaka. The former is often translated as "solitary conqueror" and the latter as "hearer."

exalted wisdom of individual analysis and contemplate them repeatedly to transform your mind as much as possible. At the very least you should recite the words mentioned above [for setting your motivation] three times, and once you have wrapped your mind around those words, you should mix your mind with them as much as possible with bodhichitta.

Thus, you should begin by performing scanning meditation on the paths of a small and middling being. It is extremely important to cultivate bodhichitta at the outset of whatever spiritual practices you undertake. Once you have cultivated such a mind, whatever Dharma you undertake will become the Mahayana Dharma; yet, if you don't cultivate such a mind [of bodhichitta], no matter what you do, it will not become a Mahayana path. For that reason, the foremost omniscient being [Tsongkhapa] has repeatedly said that it is extremely important to cultivate the mind of bodhichitta at the beginning of your session.

The Kadam mind training also states, "There are two actions—one at the beginning and one at the end." It is saying that it is indispensable to adjust your motivation at the beginning of whatever spiritual practice you undertake. Once you understand the meaning of this, you understand the meaning of the statement made by Mahasiddha Ensapa and his spiritual sons that states, "It is imperative that you initiate whatever virtuous practice you undertake from within the state of this especially virtuous state of mind." These are powerful words that are extremely important; therefore, those beings with discriminating intelligence should establish certainty in this and act accordingly.

How to Go for Refuge and Generate Bodhichitta [Visualizing the Field of Merit]

With regard to visualizing the objects of refuge, in the sky directly before you is a tall and vast jeweled throne supported by eight great snow lions upon which are variegated lotus, moon, and sun mandala seats upon which is your kind root guru, Lama Tubwang Dorje Chang the Great. He himself is surrounded by an assembly of your direct and indirect gurus, personal deities, buddhas, bodhisattvas, heroes, dakinis, Dharma protectors, and guardians. In front of each of them is an immaculate throne, upon which is the scripture that they are teaching; these have the form of books of a luminous nature. The field of merit is revealing the aspect of being pleased with you. From your own side, your mind is in a state of great faith that recalls the good qualities and great compassion of the field of merit.

[Going for Refuge]

Surrounding you are all your mother and father sentient beings packed closely together like dust particles covering the earth. Contemplate how you and all father and mother sentient beings wander without control throughout samsara and are continuously tormented by suffering, whereby you cultivate a powerful mind of fear and trepidation [for samsara]. Next, contemplate, "No one other than the guru and Three Jewels has the power to protect us from this suffering; therefore, from this time forth until we attain enlightenment, I and all sentient beings will go for refuge to the guru and Three Precious Jewels from the depths of our hearts." With this thought, once you have imagined that you and all mother sentient beings are going for refuge, recite in unison, "I go for refuge to the guru" slowly one hundred times, one thousand times, and so on, seeking refuge with heartfelt trust.

With regard to the way you should visualize at this point, imagine Lama Tubwang Dorje Chang the Great is surrounded by your direct and indirect gurus. A stream of five-colored light rays and nectars descends from the gurus' bodies carrying the blessings of their body, speech, and mind. These [light rays and nectars] enter the bodies and minds of you and all other living beings, whereby all the negative karma that you have accumulated since beginningless time is purified. In particular, [the negative karma] of harming the body of your guru, disobeying his teachings, disturbing his mind, lack of faith, criticizing him, and so forth is purified. In short, all of the negative karma and obscurations created in dependence upon your guru are all expelled through the doors of your senses and hair pores in the aspect of smoke and soot, whereby you are cleansed and purified. Your body becomes luminous, clear, and the nature of light. All of your good qualities of life, merit, scripture, and realization are developed and increased.

Next, recite the refuge verse "I go for refuge to the Buddha" as many times as possible, whereby a stream of five-colored light rays and nectars descends from the bodies of Guhyasamaja, Heruka, Yamantaka, Hevajra, Kalachakra, the thousand buddhas of the fortunate eon, the thirty-five confession buddhas, and so forth. These [light rays and nectars] enter the bodies and minds of you and all other living beings, whereby your negative karma and obscurations are purified just like the visualization above.

Next, recite the refuge verse "I go for refuge to the Dharma" as many times as possible, whereby a stream of five-colored light rays and nectars descends from Dharma texts set before each of the objects of refuge and enters the bodies and minds of you and all other living beings, whereby your negative karma and obscurations are purified just like the visualization mentioned earlier.

Next, recite the refuge verse "I go for refuge to the Sangha" as many times as possible, whereby a stream of five-colored light rays and nectars descends from the bodies of the Sangha jewels, such as the bodhisattvas, hearers, solitary conquerors, heroes, dakinis, Dharma protectors, guardians, and so forth. [These light rays and nectars] enter the bodies and minds of you and all other living beings, whereby all of your negative karma and obscurations are purified just like the visualization mentioned earlier.

In particular, when the nectar descends from the bodies of the buddhas, it is the essence of the powerful blessings of the buddhas in the aspect of light rays and nectars. [When light rays and nectars descend] from the Dharma texts, they are the essence of their good qualities of abandonment and realization in the aspect of light rays and nectars. [When light rays and nectars descend] from the Sangha members, they are the essence of the blessings of their wisdom, compassion, and power in the aspect of light rays and nectars. You should combine the main visualizations for the negative karmas and obscurations accumulated in dependence upon various general and particular negative karmas and obscurations.

Next, recite the verses "I go for refuge until I am enlightened / To the Buddha, Dharma, and supreme assembly" as many time as possible, whereby a stream of five-colored light rays and nectars descends from the bodies of every object of refuge. It enters the bodies and minds of you and all living beings, whereby all the negative karma you have accumulated since beginningless time, and in particular all the negative karmas and obscurations you have accumulated in dependence upon the Three Jewels, are cleansed and purified. Your body becomes clear, luminous, and the nature of light. Your life, merit, and good qualities of scripture are developed and increased. In particular, all the blessings of the Three Jewels enter the body and mind of you and all living beings. You should imagine your commitment is strengthened by contemplating, "I have come under the protection of the Three Jewels. From now until I attain enlightenment I shall never forsake them as my refuge!"

[Generating Bodhichitta]

Next is the way of generating bodhichitta. For this we can recite "Through the virtues I collect by giving and so forth / May I attain enlightenment for the benefit of migrating beings." With this you are cultivating aspiring bodhichitta by thinking, "In dependence upon the roots of virtue that emerge from generosity, that emerge from moral discipline, that emerge from meditation, and so forth, may I quickly, quickly attain the state of completely perfect enlightenment for the welfare of all living beings." Next, strengthen your commitment by thinking, "Come what may, I must attain the precious state of complete enlightenment quickly, and even more quickly, for the welfare of all living beings. For that purpose I shall perfectly train in all of the conduct of the conqueror's children, such as the six perfections, the four ways of gathering, and so forth." In this way you delight Lama Tubwang Dorje Chang the Great through generating aspiring and engaging bodhichitta, whereby a duplicate [of him] emerges and dissolves into you, whereby your body transforms into the body of Lama Tubwang Dorje Chang the Great. With this transformation you should think, "I am Lama Tubwang Dorje Chang" and meditate on the divine pride. Light rays radiate from your body, appearing clearly as Tubwang Dorje Chang and going to the ten directions, purifying the negative karma, obscurations, and sufferings of all living beings. Furthermore, you should imagine that light rays radiate downward to the hot hells, touching the beings there with countless cooling light rays. By merely touching these beings' bodies their suffering of heat is pacified, establishing them in the state of bliss. Light rays the nature of warmth go to the beings in cold hells, pacifying their suffering of coldness. Countless light rays the nature of food and drinks radiate to the hungry ghosts and pacify their suffering of hunger and thirst. Light rays the nature of illumination go to the animals living in darkness in the depths of the oceans and between lands,[48] dispelling the ignorance within each of their mental continuums and pacifying their suffering of slavery and so forth. Countless light rays radiate to the gods, humans, and demigods, pacifying their individual suffering. Once again, countless light rays radiate to the ten directions, going from the peak of existence to the lowest hell, purifying all the negative karma and obscurations in the minds of all living beings, after which their minds become the truth body and their bodies that they have taken in the lower realms are transformed into the body of Vajradhara adorned with the signs and indications. Again, you should imagine that light rays radiate to the ten directions, whereby their environments are purified and are transformed into limitless purity.

Having purified the world and its beings in this way, imagine all living beings are established in the state of Tubwang Dorje Chang. Generate powerful divine pride by visualizing this transformation into supporting and supported [mandalas] of purity and joy. This is the way of engaging in the path of the resultant bodhichitta and is an uncommon oral instruction of Gyalwa Ensapa the Great. The previous holy beings have slogans such as "purify the abodes of the six classes of beings," "shake samsara to its depths," and so forth, making this oral instruction something special and profound that is not possessed by others and that is in accordance with the teachings of the omniscient Khedrup [Sangye Yeshe]. If from your own side you are incapable of practicing, [that is one thing,] but there is nothing whatsoever superior to these oral instructions of the Ganden Hearing Lineage. Thus, meditate on the method for engaging in the path of the resultant bodhichitta and place your mind in meditative equipoise for a moment.

Once you arise from that meditative equipoise, contemplate by thinking:

---

48. This is in reference to ancient Buddhist cosmology that describes our world system as consisting of Mount Meru in the center surrounded by a vast ocean with continents and subcontinents throughout.

From beginningless time until the present I and all father and mother living beings have been experiencing the various sufferings of samsara without control. What is the reason for this? I do not experience this suffering because of other beings. It is because of the demon of self-grasping within my own mental continuum, which causes me to have attachment for those dear to me and hatred for adversaries, and through the force of this I accumulate karma. Through the force of karma I experience the suffering of circling in samsara. Since that is so, how wonderful it would be if I and all mother living beings were to abide in equanimity free from attachment and hatred for those near and far. May they come to this state. I will work toward this aim. May the guru-deity bless me to be able to accomplish this. How wonderful it would be if all living beings were to have happiness and the causes of happiness. May they come to possess this. I will work toward this aim. May the guru-deity bless me to be able to accomplish this. How wonderful it would be if all living beings were to be freed from suffering and the causes of suffering. May they come to possess this. I will work toward this aim. May the guru-deity bless me to be able to accomplish this. How wonderful it would be if all living beings were never separated from their happiness and the causes of happiness. May they never be parted from this. I will work toward this aim. May the guru-deity bless me to be able to accomplish this.

Due to this request, a stream of five-colored light rays and nectars descends from the bodies of all the fields of merit,[49] entering the bodies and minds of all living beings, whereby all the negative karma and obscurations accumulated since beginningless time [are purified], and in particular cleansing and purifying all the sickness, harm from spirits, negative karma, and obscurations that interfere with the meditation that you and all living beings are performing upon the four immeasurables.

49. The phrase "fields of merit" is used by Kachen Yeshe Gyaltsen to emphasize that each being within the field of merit embodies all other beings in the field of merit.

Your bodies become clear, luminous, and the nature of light. Your life, merit, and all of your good qualities of scripture and realization develop and increase. In particular, imagine that you and all other living beings dwell in the peace of the four immeasurables.

[Generating Special Bodhichitta]

Next, with regard to how to practice the special meditations on bodhichitta, generate a powerful aspiration by repeatedly contemplating, "By all means I must attain the precious state of perfectly complete enlightenment quickly, and even more quickly, for the welfare of all mother sentient beings. For that purpose I am going to practice the profound path of the yoga of the guru-deity."

With regard to these methods for going for refuge and generating bodhichitta, it is extremely important for disciples of this day and age, who are novices, to make a sincere effort in the common path, and that is the reason for explaining it in this way. Once you have gained a perfect experience of the common path, the yogi should work hard with single-pointed focus on the path of mantra. Therefore, I shall present the uncommon method for going for refuge and generating bodhichitta within the state of deity yoga as follows:

The ritual text states:

> From the state of great bliss I arise as the guru-deity.

> Light rays emerge from my body appearing clearly [as the guru-deity] and radiate out to the ten directions, blessing all worlds and beings. With limitless purity and unique good qualities they become a perfect display of all things excellent.

> From within a completely pure mind of great virtue I and all mother sentient beings as extensive as space, from now until [we reach] the essence of enlightenment, go for refuge to the guru and Three Precious Jewels.

Recite three times:

Namo Guru Bhä
Namo Buddha Ya
Namo Dharma Ya
Namo Sangha Ya

Recite three times:

For the welfare of all mother sentient beings I will become
the guru-deity and lead all living beings to the supreme state
of the guru-deity.

You should perform this standard [Lama Chöpa] recitation in accordance
with the recitation and visualization described earlier.[50] There are different ways of practicing going for refuge depending on the mental development of the individual; however, this is something that should be learned
orally from your guru.

With regard to the extensive generation of special bodhichitta in
accordance with the teachings of Khedrup Sangye Yeshe, you recite the
following verses in accordance with the standard recitation:

For the welfare of all mother living beings, in this very life
I shall quickly, quickly become the primordial Buddha, the
guru-deity, and then liberate all mother sentient beings from
their suffering and establish them in the great bliss of the
Buddha-ground. For that purpose I will undertake the practice of the profound path of the yoga of the guru-deity.

With regard to the way of going for refuge and generating bodhichitta
once you have adjusted your motivation in this way, this comes from the
Lama Chöpa ritual text itself that states, "Furthermore, from within a
particularly virtuous state of mind we should begin by going for refuge,

---

50. The section prior to this that gave an extensive explanation is not part of the sadhana itself;
therefore, you should apply the explanation given over the last several pages to this section.

generating bodhichitta, and meditating on the four immeasurables." This is in accordance with the standard commentaries for recitation.

The *Root Text on the Precious Oral Lineage of Ganden Mahamudra That Is the Main Path of the Conquerors*[51] states:

> Since they form the gateway and main support for
> The teachings and the Great Vehicle,
> You should sincerely go for refuge and generate bodhichitta
> Without paying mere lip service.

From among the four great preliminary guides, this is the first great guide.[52] At this point the oral instructions on the Hearing Lineage very clearly set forth the complete teachings on how to practice [the four great preliminary guides]; however, their meaning is extremely vast and there are many quintessential oral instructions in accordance with the capacity and dispositions of the disciples. Therefore, once you have forsaken your obligations to this life, those with the desire to get to the very heart of the practice of essential meaning of the Ganden Hearing Lineage should get a detailed experiential commentary from their skilled spiritual master.

The Extraordinary Preliminaries has three sections:
  1. **Generating Yourself as the Deity**
  2. **Purifying the World and Its Beings**
  3. **Blessing the Offerings**

Generating Yourself as the Deity

At the end of your sincere process of going for refuge and generating bodhichitta, the field of merit collects sequentially from the edges and dissolves into Tubwang Dorje Chang. Once Tubwang Dorje Chang also melts into light, you should imagine he dissolves into the point between your eyebrows, whereby your mental continuum is blessed. Next, imagine that you also [dissipate] into unobservable emptiness, at which point you place your mind upon the view [of emptiness]. From within that

---

51. *dGa' ldan bka' rgyud rin po che'i phyag chen rtsa brgya.*
52. The four great preliminary guides are (1) going for refuge and generating bodhichitta, (2) mandala offerings, (3) Vajrasattva meditation and recitation, and (4) guru yoga.

state, imagine that you arise in the body of any supreme deity, such as Guhyasamaja, Heruka, Yamantaka, and so forth. Furthermore, if you take the deity Vajrabhairava as the primary example, you should imagine that you instantaneously arise in the body of glorious Vajrabhairava, with one face, two arms, holding a curved knife and skull cup, together with the mother. Furthermore, once the field of merit is collected between your eyebrows, recite the mantra OM SÖBHAWA SHUDDHA SARWA DHARMA SÖBHAWA SHUDDHO HAM / OM SHUNYATA JNANA VAJRA SÖBHAWA ATMAKO HAM. And: "Because I, the objects of refuge, the deity, and all other phenomena are dependently imputed, they are free from the four extremes of permanence, annihilation, and so forth, and transform into emptiness that is the nature of selflessness." Then you meditate on bringing death into the path as the truth body by way of the sequential withdrawal of subsequent destruction[53] and stabilize your correct belief, imagining that you have actualized the clear light of great bliss that is the truth body. From within that state of the clear light you instantaneously arise as Vajrabhairava together with the mother and bless your three places with the three syllables [OM AH HUM]. This roughly contains all the essential points of bringing the three bodies into the path.

If you take Guhyasamaja as your principal deity, you should imagine that you instantaneously arise from the state of emptiness as Vajra-Hatred, with a dark-blue-colored body and three faces that are dark blue, white, and red. You have six arms; your right hands hold a vajra, wheel, and lotus; and your left hold a bell, jewel, and sword. You embrace the goddess Sparshavajra, who has a similar appearance to you. Both of you are adorned with eight precious jeweled ornaments. The upper part of your body is draped in heavenly fabric and the lower part of your body is wearing a skirt made of heavenly silk.

If you are taking Chakrasamvara as your principal deity, from the state of emptiness you instantaneously arise as Heruka, with one face and two hands holding a vajra and bell while standing with your right leg outstretched. You embrace the red-colored Vajravarahi, who has one face and two arms holding a curved knife and skull cup.

53. This is a technical term that refers to dissolving the world and its beings into your body, after which your body too dissolves into the state of emptiness.

Furthermore, in general, although you can utilize the yogas of Heruka, Guhyasamaja, or Yamantaka, you should meditate in four sessions on the extensive generation stage until you have perfected the coarse and subtle generation stages. It is an extremely exalted and important pith instruction to meditate on guru yoga as a preliminary to either an extensive or concise generation-stage practice. Although those on the higher levels of tantra who have perfected the generation stage can rely upon a concise deity-yoga practice during their meditations on the path, for beginners it is absolutely essential that they meditate on a complete generation stage with all the essential points of bringing the three bodies into the path. This will protect you from outer and inner obstacles and swiftly bring the blessings of the supreme deity, you will easily complete your collections [of merit and wisdom], you will overcome ordinary appearances and conceptions, and so forth; thus, there are limitless reasons for its necessity. Primarily, it will purify birth, death, and the intermediate state, which are the basis to be purified; you will quickly accomplish the three bodies at the time of the path through ripening your roots of virtue; and you will quickly attain the three resultant bodies, all of which make it the supreme method and establish it as extremely important.

For that reason I will present the way to perform a concise meditation on the generation stage that contains all the essential points of bringing the three bodies into the path. This oral instruction for guru yoga was given to Je Chökyab Dorje by Gyalwa Ensapa: "Initially perform a scanning meditation on the common path and elicit a definite experience of renunciation, bodhichitta, and the profound view of the Middle Way. It is from within that state that you generate yourself as the deity in this way." While remaining in that state of yoga, imagine a blue syllable HUM at your heart the nature of light. Light rays radiate from the HUM at your heart going to the ten directions, whereby all worldly realms melt into light and dissolve into all living beings. All the living beings within those environments melt into light and dissolve into you. The guru also melts into light and enters through the crown of your head and dissolves into the syllable HUM at your heart. Just like breath on a mirror contracting toward the center, your body also melts into light from above and below and dissolves into the syllable HUM at your heart. The *shabgyu* of the HUM dissolves into the body of the HA. The body of the HA dissolves into the head of the HA. The head dissolves into the crescent moon, the crescent moon dissolves into the drop, the drop dissolves into the *nada*, and the *nada* dissolves into unobservable emptiness, at which point you recite OM SÖBHAWA SHUDDHA SARWA DHARMA SÖBHAWA SHUDDHO HAM.

All appearances are withdrawn and you place your mind single-pointedly on the clear light of emptiness. A blue HUM, a white OM, and a red AH emerge from within such a state of emptiness, from which emerge a sun, moon, and red lotus upon which are the three syllables OM AH HUM. They all blend into one and transform into a complete moon mandala upon which is a white five-spoked vajra marked by OM AH HUM. This completely transforms and emerges as the enjoyment body of Vajradhara, with a white-colored body, three faces that are white, dark blue, and red, as well as six arms. Your right hands hold a vajra, wheel, and lotus while your left hands hold a bell, jewel, and sword. Light rays radiate from that, whereby countless father and mother tathagatas enter into embrace and give birth to Akshobyas that fill all of space. Through their blessings all living beings attain bliss. They all merge into a single globular mass and enter into you, whereby you transform into the emanation body of Vajradhara, with a blue-colored body, three faces that are blue, white, and red, as well as six arms. Your right hands hold a vajra, wheel, and lotus and your left a bell, jewel, and sword. After this you engage in guru yoga according to the teachings.

Likewise, for Vajrabhairava, from the state of emptiness emerge the four elements stacked in sequence, together with the celestial mansion as the seat. Bring the intermediate state into the path as the enjoyment body and rebirth into the path as the emanation body. Generate yourself as the resultant vajra holder, complete with all faces and hands. Bless your three places and your sense bases. Invoke the wisdom beings. Bestow empowerment together with the sealing. Or, if you are conducting this in a brief fashion, do it in accordance with the preliminary for the meditation on the five stages [of the completion stage] composed by Jetsun Losang Chökyi Gyaltsen.[54]

54. For a complete translation of Losang Chökyi Gyaltsen's guru yoga for the completion stage of Chakrasamvara see *Source of Supreme Bliss* (Ithaca, NY: Snow Lion Publications, 2010).

Meditation/Visualization of the Eight Stages of Dissolution at Death

Stage 1
The whole universe, including the Vajrabhairavas and their mandalas, melts into light and dissolve into Yamantaka.
Earth element dissolves into water element.

Stage 2
The outer Vajrabhairava dissolves into the syllable HUM at the heart level.
Water element dissolves into fire element.

Stage 3
The lower part (*shabkyu*) of the syllable HUM dissolves into the HAM part of the HUM.
Fire element dissolves into consciousness.

Stage 4
The HA part (including the crescent, drop, and nada) of the syllable HUM dissolves into the head of the HA.
Wind element dissolves into consciousness.

Stage 5
The head of the HA dissolves into the crescent (and drop and nada).
Inner sign: Clear White Appearance.

Stage 6
The cresent dissolves into the drop (and nada).
Inner sign: Radiant Red Increase.

Stage 7
The drop dissolves into the nada.
Inner sign: Black Near Attainment.

Stage 8
The nada dissolves into emptiness.
Clear Light.

Once you have performed the yoga of the three purifications of Heruka, generate yourself as Heruka. Next, meditate on the guru yoga as taught in the guru yoga of Heruka. If you also perform the practice of bringing the three bodies into the path with all the essential features, practice the concise system in accordance with *Wish-Fulfilling*,[55] composed by the foremost omniscient being [Tsongkhapa], by bringing death into the path as the truth body through the sequential withdrawal of subsequent destruction, bringing the intermediate state into the path of enjoyment body by arising as the nada and sequentially generating the supporting and supported [mandalas], and bringing rebirth into the path of emanation together with the empowerment and sealing.

With regard to performing the extensive and concise generation stage, the eleventh and twelfth chapters of the *Guhyasamaja Root Tantra* both explain the extensive method for the four limbs of approaching and accomplishing[56] and the concise way to generate with the four vajras. Also, many of the mahasiddhas of India taught the concise and extensive generation stages. Regardless [of the method used], you definitely must practice deity yoga. If you don't practice deity yoga, you have no way of purifying the world and its beings, blessing the inner and outer offerings, emanating offering goddesses, or making the special outer, inner, secret, and suchness offerings. Not only that, but all the practices that come afterward, such as revealing the yoga of the two stages and practicing the two stages, all depend on deity yoga. What's more, the ultimate goal of practicing the path of unexcelled secret mantra is to accomplish the body of union of Vajradhara with the seven limbs of embrace, and to accomplish that you must accomplish union at the time of the path with a cause of a similar class. To accomplish that, you need the method of deity yoga as its uncommon cause, and so on. These are the ultimate secret pith instructions that are more secret than the greatest secrets; therefore, you should learn them in detail orally from your holy guru.

The teachings of [the Second Dalai Lama] Gyalwa Gendun Gyatso state that you should also bless the vajra and bell while performing this ritual of

---

55. bCom ldan 'das dpal 'khor lo bde mchog gi mngon par rtogs pa'i rgya cher bshad pa 'dod pa 'jo ba. This is Tsongkhapa's text on the generation stage of Heruka in accordance with the lineage of Luipa.
56. The four aspects of approach and accomplishment are (1) approach, (2) close approach, (3) accomplishment, and (4) great accomplishment.

Lama Chöpa, which is very important for protecting and being mindful of your commitments of mantra.

Purifying the World and Its Beings

An inconceivable number of light rays radiate from the joined organs and all parts of your body imbued with deity yoga. These [light rays] strike all worlds and their beings and, just like practicing "taking the essence,"[57] you instantaneously cleanse all impure worlds and beings. Stabilize your visualization by imagining all environments transforming into the celestial mansion and all beings becoming the nature of gods and goddesses, and everything is nothing but limitless purity. This is one of the four complete purities that are a special characteristic of secret mantra.[58] This is the "supreme activity of the conqueror"[59] that perfectly enacts the welfare of others and is equivalent to the stages of isolated body.[60] With regard to repeatedly radiating light rays from your heart, which purify all worlds and their beings, after which all worlds and their beings melt into light and dissolve into your heart, these are special methods that ripen your mental continuum for the exalted stages of the completion stage; therefore, they are held as cherished oral instructions.

Blessing the Offerings has two sections:
1. **Blessing the Inner Offering**
2. **Blessing the Other Offering Substances**

---

57. Tib. *bcud len*. Taking the essence is a practice where mundane objects are transformed through the practice of alchemy.

58. The four complete purities are pure (1) body, (2) abode, (3) enjoyments, and (4) deeds.

59. This is part of a threefold process included in extensive self-generation practices that consists of (1) the initial preparation, (2) the supreme conqueror of the mandala, and (3) supreme activities of the conqueror.

60. The completion stage of Guhyasamaja consists of five stages: (1) isolated speech, (2) isolated mind, (3) illusory body, (4) clear light, and (5) union. Isolated body was listed separately but many commentators subsequent to Nagarjuna listed isolated body as stage 1 prior to isolated speech, making six stages of the completion stage. It is during the practice of isolated body that you isolate your winds and mind from ordinary appearances of all forms, and this is equivalent to the supreme activity of the conqueror.

Blessing the Inner Offering has four sections:
1. Clearing
2. Purifying
3. Generating
4. Blessing

Clearing

If you are abiding in the yoga of Vajrabhairava, when you have an action vase cleanse the inner offering with water from the action vase while reciting [OM] KHANGA DHRIK [HUM PHAT] and imagine that the most subtle atoms of the vase water transform into a collection of Sword Yamantakas that chase away the obstructing spirits from the place where the inner offering substance is set. If you don't have an action vase, while you recite [OM] HRIH SHTRIH [WIKRITA NA NA HUM PHAT] countless wrathful Yamantakas emanate from your heart and chase away the obstructing spirits.

Purifying

Once you recite the SÖBHAWA mantra and recall its meaning, meditate in the state of natural purity.

Generating

From within that state of natural purity, from YAM emerges a wind mandala and from RAM emerges a fire mandala. Upon that, generate three moist human heads from AHs. Upon that, from AH emerges a broad and expansive skull cup that is white on the outside and red on the inside. Within that skull cup, in the east and the other three cardinal directions as well as the center are BHRUM, AM, DZRIM, KHAM, and HUM, from which emerge the five meats that are the nature of the five tathagatas and are marked by the first syllable of their names, GO, KU, DA, HA, and NA, respectively. In the four intermediate directions and in the center are LAM, MAM, PAM, TAM, and BAM, from which emerge the five nectars that are the nature of the five female tathagatas and are marked with the first syllable of each of their names: VI, RA, SHU, MA, and MU. In the sky above these substances are a blue HUM, a red AH, and a white OM, stacked one upon the other.

Blessing

Light rays radiate from the HUM at your heart, whereby the wind blows, the fire blazes, and the substances within the skull cup melt and boil. The nectars abiding in the ocean and so forth as well as the nectar of exalted wisdom of the buddhas and bodhisattvas in the ten directions are summoned. In particular, all the conquerors in the ten directions are summoned in the aspect of the three vajras, which then dissolve into the three syllables. The three syllables sequentially dissolve into the substance within the skull cup, whereby the HUM purifies the faults of color, scent, taste, and potentiality; AH transforms it into nectar; and OM causes it to greatly increase and expand.

If you are abiding in the yoga of Guhyasamaja, you should bless the inner offerings according to the sequence that they occur in the sadhana *The Pure Stages of Yoga*.[61] If you are abiding in the yoga of Heruka, you should bless the inner offering in accordance with the presentation set forth in *Luminous Great Bliss*.[62] Thus, blessing the inner offering is extremely important. The inner offering is the principal offering in highest yoga tantra; it is the special edible commitment substance, it [assists you] in quickly overcoming ordinary appearances and conceptions, it is praised as the supreme protection against interfering spirits, and it becomes the alchemical substances for the sake of accomplishing the immortal vajra body. It also brings together the special dependent relationship for quickly generating the higher paths of the completion stage that arise from penetrating the vital points of the vajra body. It also has symbolic significance that correlates to the way you generate the particular realizations for the various paths. Therefore, you must make a sincere effort to assemble the dependent relationship for quickly generating the special realizations of

61. *gSang 'dus sgrub thabs rnal 'byor dag rim.* This is Tsongkhapa's sadhana on the Vajrasattva Guhyasamaja system.
62. *'Khor lo sdom pa'i sgrub thabs bde chen gsal ba.* This is Tsongkhapa's sadhana on the Chakrasamvara system of Luipa.

the two stages in your mental continuum. It is not sufficient to merely skim through this; instead, you should make a sincere and concerted effort each time you do this ritual.

Blessing the Other Offering Substances

Cleanse and purify [the offerings] as previously explained [during the inner offering]. From the state of emptiness, from AH emerge broad and expansive skull cups equal to the number of offering substances. Within each of the skull cups are letter HUMs that are the essence of the exalted wisdom of inseparable bliss and emptiness. They melt and emerge as offering substances that are the nature of bliss and emptiness appearing in the aspect of the individual offering substances. They function as objects of the six senses that have the capacity to generate a special uncontaminated bliss. Thus, imagine that the flowers and so forth are endowed with these three special attributes.[63] They are blessed by supplementing their names with the three syllables [OM AH HUM].[64] If you don't have enough time to bless the inner offering and offering substances extensively, or if you wish to do it concisely, recite OM AH HUM and the rest of the section in accordance with [the Lama Chöpa ritual text].

Whatever offering substances you have prepared as the objects of observation that you are offering to the fields of merit, visualize a HUM in the lowest position above each of those offering substances, above that is an AH, and above that is an OM, stacked one above the other. Light rays radiate from the syllable HUM going in the ten directions, summoning the vajra mind of all the deities, which dissolves into the HUM. Imagine that the HUM dissolves into the offering substances, whereby all faults of bad color, scent, and taste are dispelled and they become pure like a crystal. Light rays radiate from the syllable AH going in the ten directions and summon the vajra speech of all the deities, which dissolves into the syllable AH. Imagine it dissolves into the offering substances, whereby the offering substances transform into a great ocean of uncontaminated nec-

63. The three special attributes are (1) they have the nature of bliss and emptiness, (2) they appear in the aspect of the offering substances, and (3) they generate bliss in the senses.
64. For instance, inserting the name for water for drinking, ARGHAM, between OM AH HUM, which results in OM ARGHAM AH HUM and so on.

tar. Light rays radiate from the syllable OM going in the ten directions and summon the vajra body of all the deities, which dissolves into the syllable OM. Imagine it dissolves into the offering substances, whereby it is vastly increased. You should strengthen your conviction that [the offerings] have become a great ocean of nectar, so that despite however much the fields of merit may partake of them they are inexhaustible.

Having blessed the offerings in this way, the offerings are the essence of the nondual exalted wisdom appearing in the aspect of the individual offering substances that have the capacity to generate a special exalted wisdom of uncontaminated bliss and emptiness in the six senses of all the fields of merit. Imagine that inconceivable precious and sacred clouds of outer, inner, secret, and suchness offerings cover the ground and completely fill the expanse of space.

These rounds of preliminary offerings are presented in the Lama Chöpa ritual text and should be learned orally; therefore, I won't explain them too extensively but provide little more than an outline:

> Furthermore, from within a particularly virtuous state of mind, go for refuge, generate bodhichitta, and meditate on the four immeasurables as a preliminary. Radiate rays of light from your own body endowed with the appropriate yoga of a supreme deity such as Guhyasamaja, Heruka, Yamantaka, and so forth. All worlds and their beings are cleansed of impurities. The worlds become the celestial mansion and the inhabitants become the nature of gods and goddesses so that there is nothing but limitless purity. Bless the inner offering and offering substances in accordance with any of the appropriate highest yoga tantra practices. Or, if you prefer to do it concisely, recite OM AH HUM, whereby they become the nature of exalted wisdom appearing in the aspect of the inner offering and individual offering substances. They function as objects of enjoyment of the six senses that generate a special exalted wisdom of bliss and emptiness, completely filling all the ground and the entire expanse of space with inconceivable clouds of precious and sacred clouds of outer, inner, secret, and suchness offerings.

TOGDEN JAMPAL GYATSO

The meaning of these words is arranged in detail according to the lineage of commentary for the oral instructions of the Hearing Lineage.

The Actual Session has four sections:
1. **Meditating on the Assembly of Guru-Deities in the Field of Merit**
2. **Presenting Them with the Offerings of the Seven Limbs and the Mandala**
3. **Making Supplications by Way of Your Great Faith and Devotion**

4. Training the Mind and Receiving Blessings by Way of
   Scanning Meditation on the Complete Body of the Path
   of Sutra and Tantra

Meditating on the Assembly of Guru-Deities in the Field of Merit has
two sections:
1. The Actual Way to Visualize the Assembly of Guru-Deities
2. The Way to Invoke the Wisdom Beings and Make Them
   Inseparable

The Actual Way to Visualize the Assembly of Guru-Deities

First, with regard to the place where you visualize [the assembly of gurus
and deities], in general there isn't a definite fixed position where you
should meditate on them. There are numerous options that depend on
your individual inclinations and disposition, and even the precious tantras
teach numerous possibilities. [In one system] you visualize the guru as
being inseparable from the principal of the mandala in the space before
you. [In another] you visualize the guru as the lord of the lineage [on the
crown of the principal deity]. [Another system states] that you visualize
the guru in the aspect of Vajradhara in the charnel grounds and so forth.
[In yet another still] the practitioner visualizes the guru at the crown of
his head, at his heart, and so forth. With regard to how we should proceed
in this case, in *Questions of Pure Superior Intention* the foremost omniscient
being [Tsongkhapa] asked the great meditators of Tibet, "Where should
you visualize the guru?" In *Losang's Melodious Laughter* [Losang Chökyi
Gyaltsen] responded by stating, "The place where you should visualize
the guru / Is before you, on your crown, or in your heart / Depending
on your individual inclination." Thus, you should meditate [on the guru]
in the space before you, on the crown of your head, or in your heart. It is
the latter two that we employ below and it is while visualizing the field
of merit that you visualize it in the space before you.

Regarding how to meditate once you establish the assembly of guru-
deities and how to visualize the principal of the field of merit upon them,
the ritual text itself states:

In the expansive heaven of inseparable bliss and emptiness in the center of a vast cloud of Samantabhadra's offerings on the peak of a wish-fulfilling tree with beautiful leaves, flowers, and fruit is a lion throne blazing with jewels upon which is an extensive lotus-, sun-, and moon-seat. Upon this is my root guru, who is kind in the three ways, the very nature of every buddha. He is in the aspect of a fully ordained monk with one face and two hands and with a radiant expression. His right hand is in the aspect of expounding Dharma and his left in the mudra of meditative equipoise holding a begging bowl filled with nectar. He wears the three saffron robes of a monk and his head is adorned with a golden pandit's hat.

Alternatively, you can skip from "the very nature of every buddha . . ." and continue:

At his heart is the pervasive lord Vajradhara with one face, two hands, and a blue-colored body. He holds a vajra and bell and embraces Vajradhatu Ishvari while delighting in the play of simultaneously born bliss and emptiness. He is adorned with a variety of jeweled ornaments and is draped in heavenly silken garments.

Once you have arranged it [i.e., the wording of the ritual text] according to your disposition, continue with the following regardless of which of the two systems you used:

Adorned with the signs and indications and blazing with a thousand rays of light, he sits in the vajra posture enveloped by five-colored rainbow lights. His aggregates are the five *sugatas*, his four elements are the four mothers, his senses, channels, and joints are in actuality bodhisattvas. His pores are the twenty-one thousand arhats. His limbs are the wrathful lords. His light rays are directional guardians and harm-givers. The worldly beings are cushions for his feet.

With regard to what you should keep in mind about that visualization, the practitioner should imagine that his or her own mind has become the nature of great bliss and is mixed inseparably with the object emptiness like water poured into water. In the space before you, amid a boundless heap of inconceivable cloud clusters of Samantabhadra's offerings, is a wish-fulfilling tree together with branches, leaves, flowers, and fruit that are all produced from a variety of precious jewels. Furthermore, the root of the wish-fulfilling tree is gold, the trunk is silver, the branches are lapis, the leaves are crystal, the petals are precious gems, the flowers are red pearls, and the fruit are emeralds. It is draped with various jeweled ornaments such as jeweled nets, half nets, tiaras, earrings, necklaces, and so forth. Whatever you can imagine, the attributes you desire—such as clothes, food, and so forth—all emerge from the branches. As the leaves are blown by the wind, they produce a melody that proclaims the essence of the Dharmas of sutra and tantra. Light rays radiate to the ten directions on the tips of which are countless emanations of buddhas and bodhisattvas. By seeing the tree, through experiencing the scent of the tree, through touching the tree, and through hearing the sound of the wind blowing the leaves of the tree, all of the sufferings of body and mind are pacified. Whatever one could possibly imagine is effortlessly accomplished. This is similar to what we find in the *Sutra Describing the Landscape of Sukhavati*.[65]

The peak of the jeweled tree is vast and extensive with flowers and leaves. Upon it are eight great lions that symbolize the four fearlessnesses[66] and the eight powers,[67] which support a precious throne that is high and expansive and upon which is a variegated lotus with an inconceivable number of petals. The lotus has eleven layers of petals with the lower petals just covering the edges of the lion throne. As it increases in height, the extent of the [tiers of petals] become increasingly smaller. At the center

65. *bDe ba can gyi zhing bkod kyi mdo.*
66. The four fearlessnesses are (1) fearlessness in asserting their own perfect realization, (2) fearlessness in asserting their own perfect abandonment, (3) fearlessness for the sake of others in revealing the path to liberation, and (4) fearlessness for the sake of others in revealing potential hindrances on the path.
67. The eight powers are (1) quality of body, (2) quality of speech, (3) quality of mind, (4) quality of virtuous energy, (5) quality of miracle powers, (6) quality of going everywhere, (7) quality of abode, and (8) quality of fulfilling wishes.

of its uppermost point is a four-petaled lotus with a heart and corolla upon which is a sun mandala symbolizing wisdom and a moon mandala symbolizing method, in the center of which is your root guru endowed with the three kindnesses.[68] He is in the aspect of the king of the Dharma, Tsongkhapa the Great. He has one face, two arms, and his complexion is white and tinged with a shade of red. He has a smiling, joyous expression. His right hand is at his heart in the mudra of teaching Dharma while his left hand is in the mudra of meditative equipoise holding a begging bowl that is filled with nectar. His two hands hold the stems of *utpala* flowers, whose tips reach the level of his right and left ears with blooming flowers. On the right is a wisdom sword blazing with light and on the left is a scripture that contains the essence of all essential instructions of sutra and tantra. On his head he wears a yellow-colored pandit's hat, and his body is beautified with the three sets of Dharma robes [of a fully ordained monk] as he sits with his feet in the vajra posture.

At his heart is Buddha Shakyamuni with a body like pure gold complete with an *ushnisha*. He has one face and two arms. His right hand is in the earth-touching mudra and his left is in the mudra of meditative equipoise holding a begging bowl filled with nectar. His body is beautified with the three sets of Dharma robes as he sits with his feet in the vajra posture.

At his heart is conqueror Vajradhara, who has a blue-colored body, one face, and two arms holding a vajra and bell and embracing the mother Vajradhatu Ishvari, who has a blue-colored body, one face, and two arms holding a curved knife and skull cup. They are both wearing jeweled ornaments and are draped in various silken fabrics. Their bodies are adorned with the signs and indications and are radiant, clear, and the nature of light. Countless light rays radiate from all three of their bodies going to the ten directions as they sit amid a circle of five-colored rainbow lights.

Visualize the following deities as the nature of your guru's five pure aggregates. At the crown of your kind root guru visualize a white Vairochana, at his throat is red Amitabha, at his heart is blue Akshobya, at his navel is yellow Ratnasambhava, and at his secret place is green Amoghasiddhi. Visualize the following as the nature of his four pure elements.

68. According to sutra the three kindnesses are bestowing (1) vows, (2) transmissions, and (3) commentaries. According to tantra they are bestowing (1) empowerments, (2) transmissions, and (3) oral instructions.

At the navel of your lama visualize white Lochana, at his heart is blue Mamaki, at his throat is red Pandaravasini, and at his crown is green Tara.

Imagine the following are the essence of his pure sources, sinews, and joints. At each of his two eyes visualize white Kshitigarbha embracing white Vajra Rupini goddesses. At each of his right and left ears are yellow Vajrapani embracing yellow Shaptavajra goddesses. At his nose is Akashagarbha embracing a red Gandhavajra goddess. At his tongue is red Lokeshvara embracing a green Rasavajra goddess. At his heart is red Manjushri. At his vajra is green Sarvanivarana-Viskambini embracing a blue Sparshavajra goddess. At all of his joints are green Samantabhadras. At his crown is white Maitreya.

Visualize the following deities as the nature of his respective limbs. At his right hand is wrathful black Yamantaka. At left is white Aparajita. At the opening of his mouth is red Hayagriva. At the opening of his vajra is blue Amrita Kundali. At his right shoulder is blue Achala. At his left shoulder is Takkiraja. At his right knee is Niladanda. At his left knee is black Mahabala. At his crown is Ushnisha Chakravarti. And at the soles of his two feet are blue Sumbaraja. The pores of his body are the nature of the twenty-one thousand Mahayana arhats. Imagine that the light rays generated from his body are also the nature of the directional protectors.

In short, the manifestations of your guru pervade all lands in the ten directions and every single conqueror and bodhisattva in the ten directions abides in the body of the guru. There are pure lands within each of his hair pores that are the abode of buddhas and bodhisattvas too numerous to count. You should stabilize your conviction that his nature is the embodiment of all objects of refuge.

Furthermore, once you conjoin this with the yoga of Vajrabhairava, you can meditate on Vajrabhairava at the heart of the principal of the field of merit. If so, you can recite, "Bhagavan Vajrabhairava is at his heart with one face and two hands embracing Vetali and delighting in the play of spontaneously born bliss and emptiness. He is adorned with the ornaments of a wrathful deity and has a gaping mouth, wrathful expression, and bared fangs. He has a radiant, wrathful black body and stands with his right leg bent and left outstretched." The explanation to meditate in this way comes from the teachings of Dorje Chang Losang Chökyi Gyaltsen compiled as notes by his secretary Taphug.

With regard to the outer aspect [of Lama Losang Tubwang Dorje Chang] as a fully ordained monk wearing saffron robes and the inner aspect as Buddha together with Vajradhara as the three nested beings, it is a unique feature that necessarily reveals ultimate essential instructions of the extremely secret path of Je Lama's Hearing Lineage. Also, if you wish, instead of having his external aspect as a saffron-robed monk, you can change it to Vajradhara, which is similar to the explanation in *A Practical Commentary on the Complete Seat of the Five Stages of Guhyasamaja*[69] by the omniscient foremost being [Tsongkhapa]. The oral instructions for this text also state, "Alternatively, [you can visualize him] as the pervasive lord Vajradhara" and so forth, stating that it is optional. If you proceed in that way, the system for meditating on Vajradhara is clear in that text. If you meditate on him as Yamantaka, you visualize him as Guru-Vajrabhairava with a complete set of faces and arms together with the mother. At his five places are the five lineages of Vajrabhairava, which are white, red, blue, yellow, and green. For this you visualize Ignorance Vajra and so forth with Lochana and so forth, and the sense powers, and the vajra body, [speech, and mind] at his three places and so forth.[70] This teaching comes from Gyalwa Ensapa the Great. If you wish to visualize Guru-Heruka, visualize your kind root guru as Glorious Heruka together with the mother. Imagine that his two outstretched legs completely transform into a wind mandala and so forth and meditate on the entire body mandala. Otherwise you can meditate on the body mandala of the guru by imagining that twenty-four places, such as his crown and so forth, are the abodes of the twenty-four places, and the channels and elements at those places transform into the twenty-four heroes and heroines, such as Khandakapala and Partzandi and so on, which is also a teaching of Gyalwa Ensapa the Great.

There is an ocean of oral instructions for this [Lama Chöpa] guru yoga that incorporates all the yogas of the guru-deity in relation to the four classes of tantra and, in particular, highest yoga tantra. Jetsun Losang

---

69. *gSang 'dus rdzogs rim rim lnga gdan rdzogs kyi dmar khrid.*
70. The entire Lama Chöpa Yamantaka sadhana as composed by Pabongkha Rinpoche states: "At his heart is the pervasive lord Vajrabhairava with nine faces and thirty-four arms . . . There are lotus-, moon-, and sun-seats at his five places of crown, throat, heart, navel, and secret place, upon which, in sequence, are white, red, blue, yellow, and green Vajrabhairavas with buffalo faces. They have one face and two hands holding a curved knife and skull cup while embracing their consorts with similarly colored bodies. There are various worldly beings that serve as cushions for their feet, such as Öser, Directional Protector, Harm Giver, and Guhya."

Chökyi Gyaltsen also composed methods for visualizing your root guru as Tubwang Dorje Chang, who is the essence of Heruka, Guhyasamaja, Yamantaka, and Hevajra. It is evident that it is the abode of limitless secret instructions of tantra; therefore, the holy upholders of the teachings should study it well.

This section of the guru yoga composed by Vajradhara Losang Chökyi Gyaltsen begins with "in the expansive heaven of inseparable bliss and emptiness" and reveals that these are unexcelled oral instructions extracted from the heart essence of the ocean of tantras. The *Guhyasamaja Root Tantra*, which is the embodiment of the essential points of all the precious highest yoga tantras, begins with the fourteen syllables that are the table of contents and are embodied in the two syllables E and VAM at the beginning. Those [two syllables] are the essence of all tantras and are the ultimate path to enlightenment in one lifetime, which is explained in the explanatory tantras such as *Vajramala* and so forth, which was attained through the diligence of numerous mahasiddhas of India.

If we condense the meaning of EVAM, there is resultant EVAM, which is the object of attainment; the path EVAM, which is the act of attaining; and the sign EVAM, which functions as a guide. The resultant EVAM, which is the object of attainment, is the resultant Guru-Vajradhara the Great together with his abode. Furthermore, the meaning of E is revealed by the sphere of space, the lion throne, lotus, and so forth, while the meaning of VAM is revealed by Lama Tubwang Dorje Chang.

The *Explanatory Tantra Vajramala* states:

> E is the secret sphere of space
> Or the *bhaga* phenomena-source lotus,
> Which is the seat of the lion, the yogi;
> It reveals the most wondrous and supreme.
> The vajra-VAM is Vajrasattva,
> The powerful lord Vajrabhairava,
> Heruka, Kalachakra, the
> primordial buddha, and so forth.

The path EVAM, which is the act of attaining, is the exalted wisdom of inseparable bliss and emptiness. The *Explanatory Tantra Vajra Mudra*[71] states:

> The mudra of the great king
> Is taught at the beginning of the tantras.

Thus the meaning of E from EVAM is the wisdom of emptiness, the meaning of VA is great bliss, and the anusvara[72] symbolizes inseparable bliss and emptiness. That very exalted wisdom of inseparable bliss and emptiness is the essential meaning of all the eighty-four thousand heaps of Dharma teachings, and it is said that there is nothing other than this as the ultimate quintessential point of the path; therefore, it is the mudra of the king of the Dharma and reveals that this exalted wisdom of inseparable bliss and emptiness is from where the means of attaining enlightenment in one short life in this degenerate age comes, and if it were not revealed, [enlightenment] would not be possible.

The *Explanatory Tantra Vajra Mudra* states:

> The table of contents of all tantras
> Embodies the meaning of all tantras as
> The indestructible emptiness and compassion.
> Wherever suchness is elucidated
> It is done with the two syllables E and VAM.
> Wherever these two are absent
> Is where suchness is absent.

As also quoted from the *Compendium of Conduct Tantra:*[73]

> This migrator is the nature of all five buddhas;
> He appears as a dancer or drawing;
> He is the only place called "great bliss"—
> A single vision with numerous emanations.

---

71. *bShad rgyud rdo rje kyi phyag rgya.*
72. This is the grammatical particle that denotes the *ma* sound. In Tibetan it is represented by a spherical drop at the top of the letter.
73. *sPyod pa bsdus pa'i sgron ma.*

The single exalted wisdom of the resultant Tubwang Dorje Chang the Great appears in various magical manifestations. During the path as well, whatever appears should all be viewed as manifestations of the exalted wisdom of simultaneously born great bliss.

The *Accomplishment of Secrets*[74] also states:

> I respectfully prostrate to all three realms
> In the perfect syllables E and VAM.
> The first abode of the tantra,
> The supreme essence surpassing the essence,
> The lord of the suchness of great bliss—
> It is called "the secret suchness."
> It is the source of bliss for buddhas,
> Bodhisattvas, and all living beings.
> It is the secret chapter of the king of tantras
> And the abode of glorious Guhyasamaja.

And:

> It is called "the realm of space,"
> Completely filled with tathagatas,
> Seen like a pod of sesame seeds
> Or as many sands of the Ganges River.
> The letters of suchness
> Reveal the method itself
> For attaining the unsurpassed state of
> The buddhas and bodhisattvas.

Throughout the entire body of the text of the mahasiddha [Saraha] there is an extensive praise for this very exalted wisdom of inseparable bliss and emptiness as necessary to attain enlightenment.

The mahasiddha Saraha also stated:

---

74. *gSang ba grub pa.*

Do not make two what is one;
Never make a distinction by dividing into types.

All things in the three realms without exception
Become one shade in the single great bliss of passion.

In it there is no beginning, middle, or end,
No samsara, and no transcending suffering.

In this supreme great bliss
Self and others do not exist

In front, back, or in the ten directions
To the extent that I witnessed the bliss of suchness.

On this very day, Protector, all such mistakes have been
    brought to an end;
Now I have no questions for anyone.

This very exalted wisdom of inseparable bliss and emptiness is
the ultimate essence of all paths; therefore, whatever appears
should only be viewed as the manifestation of great bliss. This
is the ultimate essential oral instruction; therefore, you should
put an end to all your doubts.

The entire body of the doha is accomplished by sincerely applying
yourself to the essence of the path, which is the exalted wisdom of simultaneously born great bliss. Therefore, the meaning of the resultant EVAM
refers to attaining the state of Lama Tubwang Dorje Chang the Great.
EVAM during the path is the exalted wisdom of inseparable bliss and
emptiness, and once we generate it through repeated effort, we should
regard whatever appears as a manifestation of that [bliss and emptiness].
To reach that we should learn its meaning led by the sign EVAM, which
is revealed by the deity yoga of meditating on the bodies of the father and
mother desire deities. This method is very difficult to realize; therefore,

it needs a detailed explanation. However, since I am concerned that this discussion will become too verbose, in addition to the fact that it is the abode of the ultimate secret, I have not elaborated beyond this short introduction.

In short, the foremost omniscient great being has repeatedly said, "It is indispensable that on the first stage [i.e., the generation stage] you regard everything that appears as the deity, and that on the second stage [i.e., the completion stage] you regard everything that appears as a manifestation of bliss and emptiness; therefore, you should apply yourself to this with all the strength you can muster." Vajradhara Losang Chökyi Gyaltsen said, "These are oral instructions as vajra words of the Hearing Lineage of the guru"; you should cherish this [advice]!

With regard to the phrase "clouds of Samantabhadra's offerings," the *Avatamsaka Sutra* contains teachings about the bodhisattva Samanta-bhadra, who emanated clouds of offerings for the conquerors and gained complete mastery over the method of enormously effective prayers. It is for that reason that we also meditate in accordance with the activities of Samantabhadra. However, since this teaching is primarily concerning the practice of mantra, we still use the term "Samantabhadra"; however, it is used to indicate the exalted wisdom of nondual bliss and emptiness. Furthermore, in the *Guhyasamaja Root Tantra* the term "Samantabhadra" is repeatedly used to denote exalted wisdom of nondual bliss and emptiness as the ultimate bodhichitta. This also accords with the explanation for the visualization for blessing the offerings at the beginning [of the ritual], where they are also regarded as the exalted wisdom of nondual bliss and emptiness appearing in the aspect of the individual offering substances.

The *Explanatory Tantra Vajramala* clearly explains the meditation for visualizing the guru's aggregates, sources, and elements as the conquerors of the five lineages and so forth. That tantra [i.e., the *Explanatory Tantra Vajramala*] states:

> The body of the conqueror sequentially abides
> In this body of the vajra master.
>
> First, the vajra body (Vairochana)
> Perfectly abides in his form aggregate.

> After that, the space vajra (Ratnasambhava)
> Abides in his aggregate of feeling.
>
> The bhagavan vajra speech (Amitabha)
> Abides in his aggregate of discrimination.
>
> The vajra of activities (Amoghasiddhi)
> Abides in his aggregate of compositional factors.
>
> The bhagavan vajra mind (Akshobya)
> Abides in his aggregate of consciousness.

Thus, this clearly explains how to meditate on the five aggregates of the guru as the five buddha families. The way to meditate on the elements as the four mothers is also explained in that very same tantra when it states:

> The earth element [of the guru], such as flesh and so forth, is also
> The abode of bhagavati Lochana.
>
> His water element, such as blood and so forth,
> Is the abode of bhagavati Mamaki.
>
> His fire element, such as warmth and so forth,
> Is the abode of Pandaravasini.
>
> His wind element, such as the unmoving,
> Is the abode of bhagavati Tara.

Thus, it clearly states that we meditate from the earth element dwelling in the guru's body as Lochana up to meditating on the wind element as Tara. With regard to meditating on the sources as bodhisattvas, that very same tantra states:

> At his two eye sense powers are
> The tathagata Kshitigarbha.

At his two ear sense powers are
The tathagata Vajrapani.

At his two nostrils are
The tathagata Akashagarbha.

Abiding at his tongue sense power
Is the tathagata Avalokiteshvara.

Abiding at his mind sense power
Is the tathagata Manjushri.

The globular masses that are the nature of his four elements
Are called "body."

His sex organ is the abode of the tathagata
Sarvanivarana Viskambini.

At all the joints of his body are
The tathagata Maitreya.

Thus, we visualize from "the guru's two eyes being Kshitigarbha" up to "all of his joints as Maitreya." Although there isn't a clear description for Samantabhadra at this point, the twenty-third chapter of this very same tantra states:

The characteristic of the individual channels[75]
Is the supreme basis of every bliss.
It is the nature of all things
And is explained as Samantabhadra.

Also, Rupavajra and so forth are not clearly explained at this point. However, the fifty-sixth chapter of this very same tantra states:

75. Tib. *rtsa*. This is sometimes translated as "vein," but because of the phrase "the supreme basis of every bliss" here I interpreted it to be "channel."

Once you have summoned Rupavajra,
The tathagata with three distinctions of form
Such as mudra, blue, and so forth,
You should offer her to Kshitigarbha.

Perfectly summon Shaptavajra,
The tathagata with three distinctions of sound
Such as songs and inexpressible melodies,
And offer her to Vajrapani.

Perfectly summon Ghandavajra,
The tathagata with three distinctions of scent
Such as saffron, aloe wood, and nutmeg,
And offer her to Akashagarbha.

Perfectly summon Rasavajra,
The tathagata with three distinctions of
Kissing, sucking, and the six tastes,
And offer her to Avalokiteshvara.

Perfectly summon Sparshavajra,
With three distinctions of a
Perfect lotus for uniting, garments, and embracing,
And offer her to Nivarana Viskambin.

In this tantra it also teaches that the consort of Manjushri is Vajradhatu. With regard to visualizing the wrathful deities at his limbs, the very same tantra states:

At the base of his right hand
Is the tathagata Yamantaka.

At the base of his left hand
Is the tathagata Aparajita.

Abiding on the lotus of his mouth
Is the tathagata Hayagriva.

Abiding at the abode of his secret place
Is the tathagata Amrita Kundali.

Abiding at his right shoulder
Is the tathagata Achala.

Abiding at his left shoulder
Is the tathagata Takkiraja.

Abiding at his right knee
Is the tathagata Niladanda.

Abiding at his left knee
Is the tathagata Mahabala.

Seated upon the crown of his head
Is the ushnisha Chakravarti.

Seated below his feet
Is the tathagata Sumbaraja.

Thus, we visualize from "Yamantaka on the right hand of the guru" up to "Sumbaraja at the soles of his two feet." In short, the guru's body is the abode of all the buddhas. That very same tantra states:

All the tathagatas abide in
Every part of this very body
And it is proclaimed as the "body mandala."
It is the very body of Vajrasattva.
The yogi will quickly attain
Nirvana in this rebirth
By regarding it as Vajrasattva,

The buddha body replete
With all the perfect buddhas.

Since all the buddhas abide in the
Body of the vajra master,
You should thoroughly offer your virtues.

If you see him it is indeed meaningful
And you will subsequently become a great being.

Therefore, all living beings should rely upon
Their guru with perfect diligence,
With offering substances of the deity.

This is extremely clear. This method is also taught in other tantras. The *Four Vajra Seats Tantra*[76] states:

If you ask, "How should I view the master?"
Listen! He himself is Vajrapani.
He has the characteristic of complete enlightenment,
His bodily parts are every buddha,
His limbs are the abodes of bodhisattvas,
His crown ornaments are the five buddha families.

With regard to meditating on the guru's hair pores as being in essence arhats, the light rays generated from this body as the essence of directional protectors, and the cushions under his feet as the worldly deity Mahabala, the *Four Vajra Seats* states:

His hair pores are arhats,
The worldly beings are cushions for his feet,
His light rays are secret harm-givers and so forth.
Thus, the yogi should always perceive
[The guru's] body as endowed with good qualities.

---

76. rDo rje gdan bzhi; Caturpīṭhatantra.

The thirty-second chapter of *Vajradaka [Tantra]*[77] explains in detail the characteristics of the master and at the end states:

> If you ask, "How should I perceive such a master?"
> His body is the nature of all the buddhas,
> His limbs are bodhisattvas,
> His hair pores are arhats,
> His ushnisha is the buddhas of the five lineages,
> Worldly beings are cushions for his feet,
> His light rays are secret harm-givers and so forth.
>
> Thus, his body is the nature of all good qualities.
> Those endowed with yoga should always
> Perceive him as possessing such characteristics.
> By understanding the signs, those endowed with exalted wisdom
> Will sincerely rely upon such a guru.

This is also extremely clear. The *Adorning the Essence of the Vajra Tantra*[78] also clearly explains the benefits of relying on the guru, the faults of not relying, what kind of lama you need, and the characteristics of the lama. With regard to how to view a lama that teaches the unmistaken path, that very same tantra [*Adorning the Essence of the Vajra Tantra*] states:

> Always respectful toward the guru,
> The disciples should view him in this way.
> The guru is equal to all the buddhas.
> He himself is the eternal source of Vajradhara
> And the precious tathagata.
>
> He is the great ocean of exalted wisdom,
> The benefactor of the precious wish-fulfilling jewel;
> He embodies all good qualities.
> Do not contemplate any faults with your mind.

---

77. *rDo rje mkha' 'gro rgyud*; *Vajraḍākatantra*.
78. *rDo rje snying po rgyan gyi rgyud*; *Vajramaṇḍalāmkāratantra*. Also known as the *Vajra Mandala Adornment Tantra*.

If you apprehend his qualities you will accomplish attainments;
By [seeing] faults your realizations will deteriorate.

In general you need to perceive your guru as the essence of all the buddhas. In particular, it says that you should view him as the nature of the
five buddha families. The *Heruka Explanatory Tantra Samvarodaya* states:

The master is the essence of all the buddhas,
His body is the nature of the deity,
He is the hero holding a vajra and bell.
Supplicate him together with the dakini.

Thus, it is very clear that you should meditate on him as the nature of all
the buddhas in the aspect of Vajradhara. The *Vajra Tent*[79] also states:

The guru is equal to all the buddhas,
Just like Protector Vairochana.

The conferring vajra holder is the lama himself,
Just like the great Akasha Samudra,
Just like Muni Samudra Dharma,
Just like Protector Sapta Raja—
These are proclaimed as the vajra master.

Thus, this clearly states that once you view the guru as equivalent to all
the buddhas, as well as being the nature of the five buddha families, you
should make offerings. With regard to these, I mentioned a few of the
main points, and since it is repeatedly taught in all four great classes of
tantra, the wise state that having seen that very tantra, disciples should
develop stable certainty in this ultimate oral instruction.

With regard to the phrase "worldly beings are cushions for his feet,"
this is exactly the same as the words of the tantra, and its meaning was
explained by Gyalwa Ensapa the Great when he said that the great worldly
gods such as Brahma, Shiva, Indra, and so forth support the lion throne.

---

79. *rDo rje gur gyi rgyud*; *Vajrapañjaratantra*.

The gurus' lineage of instruction states that the meaning is that it may be difficult to get the great worldly gods to place their jeweled tiaras at the lotus feet of Lama Tubwang Dorje Chang and yet they are worthy cushions for his feet.

I wonder what was meant in the tantra by having the great worldly beings pressed face down under the feet of Guru-Vajrabhairava the Great, or how the lord of the desire realm and his wife[80] are also being pressed down under the feet of Guru-Chakrasamvara? The wise should investigate this matter by looking into the meaning of the tantras by combining the root and explanatory tantras with the oral instructions.

With regard to visualizing the assembled retinue of deities, the text itself states:

> Sitting amid an ocean, he is surrounded in sequence by the lineage gurus, personal deities, a collection of mandala deities, buddhas, bodhisattvas, heroes, dakinis, and Dharma protectors.

As for the way to visualize this, light rays radiate from the heart of your kind root guru and go to the right. On the tips of those light rays are variegated lotuses and moons, upon which is Venerable Manjushri surrounded by the gurus of the lineage of profound view, such as Arya Nagarjuna and so forth. Light rays radiate in front of him, and on the tips of those light rays are variegated lotuses and a moon seat upon which is your kind root guru surrounded by all the gurus from whom you have directly received Dharma teachings. Light rays radiate above him, and on the tips of those light rays are the lineage gurus of the close lineage of blessings stacked one upon the other.[81]

On the lotus petal in front of your kind root guru is the bhagavan Glorious Guhyasamaja. He has a blue-colored body, three faces that are blue,

---

80. Ishvara and Kalarati.

81. Pabongkha Rinpoche introduced a system of visualizing five rows of lineage gurus behind Lama Losang Tubwang Dorje Chang. The lineage in the center begins with Vajradhara and contains all the lineage gurus of the Ganden Hearing Lineage of mahamudra. To the far right are the lineage gurus of Guhyasamaja and the right column closest to the center contains the lineage gurus of Yamantaka. In the column to the far left are the lineage gurus of Chakrasamvara and the left column closest to the center is the lineage of the sixteen-drop Kadam practice.

white, and red, and six arms. His first two right and left hands hold a vajra and bell. His lower right hands hold a wheel and lotus. His lower left hands hold a jewel and sword. His hair is tied up in a topknot. He is adorned with eight jeweled ornaments. The upper part of his body is draped in silken garments and he is wearing a lower garment. He sits in the vajra posture. He embraces his consort Vajra Sparsha, who has a blue-colored body, three faces colored blue, white, and red, and six arms. Her right hands hold a vajra, wheel, and lotus and her left hold a bell, jewel, and sword. They are complete with the entire supporting and supported mandalas.

On the lotus petal to the right is the bhagavan Glorious Vajrabhairava. He has a bluish-black body with nine faces, thirty-four arms, and six-teen legs. He embraces the mother Vajra Vetali. He is complete with the entire supporting and supported mandalas. On the lotus petal behind is the bhagavan Glorious Hevajra with a dark-blue body, eight faces, sixteen arms, and four legs. His central face is black, his right face is white, his left face is red, his upper face is smoke-colored, and the two extra faces to both the right and left are black. Each face has three eyes, bared fangs, and a changing expression. His eyebrows and moustache are orange and flashing. His hair is tied up on the crown of his head and is streaming upward, and its tip is adorned with a variegated vajra. He has a crown ornament of five dried skulls and a necklace of fifty moist heads dripping with blood. His sixteen hands hold sixteen skull cups while his first right hand holds a white elephant and his first left a yellow earth deity.[82] These two embrace the mother. In the second right hand is a green horse, in the third a donkey, in the fourth a red ox, in the fifth a gray camel, in the sixth a red human, in the seventh a blue eight-legged lion, and in the eighth a yellow cat. In the second left hand is the white god of water, in the third is the green god of wind, in the fourth is the red god of fire, in the fifth is the white moon god, in the sixth is the red sun god, in the seventh is the blue lord of death, and in the eighth is yellow Kuvera. Of his two front legs, the right legs are outstretched and the left are bent. His two rear legs are in the half-vajra posture. Vajra Nairatmya is blue with one face, two hands, and three eyes. Her right hand holds a curved knife aloft and her

---

82. The objects being described are within the skull cups.

left holds a skull cup with a *katvanga* in the crook of her elbow. They are complete with the entire supporting and supported mandalas.

On the petal to the left is the bhagavan Heruka Chakrasamvara. He has a blue-colored body, four faces, and twelve arms. His principal face is dark blue, his left face is green, his rear face is red, and his right face is yellow. Each face has three eyes, bared fangs, and his hair is streaming upward and tied up in a topknot with a variegated vajra marking its peak. The left side of his head is marked with a half moon. His head is adorned with five dried skulls and he wears a rosary of heads dripping with blood. His first two hands hold a vajra and bell and embrace the mother. His lower two hands hold an elephant skin, with his two outstretched hands in the threatening mudra. His third right hand holds a *damaru*, the fourth an ax, the fifth a curved knife, and the sixth a three-pointed spear. His third left hand holds a *katvanga* marked by a vajra, his fourth a skull cup filled with blood, his fifth a vajra noose, and his sixth a four-faced head of Brahma. He wears a lower garment of tiger skin. The mother Vajravarahi is red, has one face, and two hands. Her right holds a curved knife[83] and the left a skull cup, and she embraces the father. Both of her legs wrap around the father's thighs. They are complete with the entire supporting and supported mandalas.

On the lotus petal below that is the bhagavan Kalachakra. He has a blue-colored body and four faces. His principal face is black and wrathful with bared fangs. His right face is red and passionate. His rear face is yellow and dwelling in single-pointed concentration. His left face is white and very peaceful. Each face has three eyes. His hair is tied up in a topknot and is beautified with a variegated vajra and half moon. He has Vajrasattva as a head ornament and is adorned with the eight ornaments such as vajra jewel and so forth. His tiger-skin skirt is loosened. He has twenty-four hands. The first set of four are black [on the right and left], the second set of four are red, and the third set of four are white. The first of the four black right hands holds a vajra, the second a sword, the third a trident, and the fourth a curved knife. The first of the four red hands holds an arrow, the second a vajra hook, the third a naturally reverberating *damaru*, and the fourth a hammer. The first of the four white hands holds a wheel, the

---

83. The text says "vajra" but this is an editing error.

second a spear, the third a club, and the fourth a battle ax. The first of the four left black hands holds a bell with a vajra [handle], the second a shield, the third a *katvanga*, and the fourth a skull cup filled with blood. The first of the four red hands holds a bow, the second a vajra noose, the third a jewel, and the fourth a white lotus. The first of the four white hands holds a conch shell, the second a mirror, the third an iron chain, and the fourth a four-faced head of Brahma beautified with lotuses. He stands dramatically on the [gods of the] sun, moon, as well as Rahula, and Kalinga. His right red leg and his left white leg tread on Kamadeva and Raudra. The mother Vishvamata has a yellow-colored body. She has four faces that, beginning in front and going clockwise, are yellow, white, blue, and red. Each face has three eyes. Of her eight hands, the four right hands hold a curved knife, hook, reverberating *damaru*, and rosary. Her four left hands hold a skull, noose, white eight-petaled lotus, and jewel. Vajrasattva is her crown ornament. She is adorned with the five mudras. She stands with her left [leg] outstretched and enters into embrace with the bhagavan. They are together with the assembly of deities of the body, speech, and mind. Furthermore, there is a retinue of all the deities of highest yoga tantra, such as enemy, black, and red Yamantakas.

On the petal below that [are the yoga tantra deities headed by] Bhagavan Sarvavid Vairochana with a white-colored body, white face, and two hands in the mudra of meditative equipoise holding an eight-spoked wheel. All of his ornaments are jeweled ornaments. The upper and lower parts of his body are draped in silken wool. He has a peaceful gaze and sits in the vajra posture. Furthermore, he is surrounded by a limitless collection of yoga tantra deities.

On the petal below that is the bhagavan Vairochana Abhisambodhi with one face and two hands in the mudra of meditative equipoise. He has a yellow-colored body and is enveloped in a rosary of blazing light. He sits on a seat of white lotus. He has a crown ornament and a topknot. The upper and lower parts of his body are draped in silken wool. Furthermore, he is surrounded by a limitless collection of performance tantra deities.

On the petal below that is the bhagavan Trisamayavyuharaja, who has a body like refined gold. He is adorned with the thirty-two signs and the eighty indications of perfection. He has one face and two hands in the mudra of teaching Dharma. He is surrounded by an assembly of action tantra deities such as Vajravidarana and so forth.

On the petals below that are the thousand buddhas of the fortunate eon surrounded by other buddhas such as the thirty-five confession buddhas and so forth. On the petal below that are eight close disciples [of Buddha] surrounded by bodhisattvas. On the petal below that are the twelve solitary conquerors surrounded by a retinue of pratyeka buddhas. On the petal below that are the sixteen arhats surrounded by a retinue of shravakas. On the petal below that are a retinue of heroes and heroines of the twenty-four places. On the petals below that are a retinue of Dharma protectors and guardians, with the wisdom protector Six-Armed Mahakala in the front as well as outer, inner, and secret Oath-Bound Dharmaraja and so forth. On jeweled thrones in the four directions beginning in the east is Dhritarastra, in the south Virudaka, in the west Virupakasa, and in the north Vaishravana.

In front of each being in the field of merit is a throne made of the best substances, upon which are the scriptures of their respective teachings that are the nature of light in the aspect of books. Beyond the [beings in the field of merit] are an inconceivable array of magical emanations filling the ten directions in accordance with the disposition of those to be subdued.

All beings, the principal and retinue, have a white OM at their crowns that is the essence of the vajra body; a red AH at their throats that is the essence of the vajra speech; and a blue HUM at their hearts that is the essence of the vajra mind. Thus, this way of visualizing the field of merit with the principal guru of the field of merit in the aspect of the three nested beings together with the body mandala and so forth is arranged without embellishment in accordance with the intention of the tantras. Furthermore, as I have already explained earlier, every detail I have written here in this teaching is in accordance with the oral instructions that combine the root and explanatory tantras, which come from an unbroken lineage of holy beings. In particular, I have written this down in accordance with the ultimate oral instructions of the Hearing Lineage that were bestowed upon Conqueror Tsongkhapa the Great by Protector Manjushri, and Conqueror Tsongkhapa himself prophesied and bestowed them upon Gyalwa Ensapa the Great and Vajradhara Losang Chökyi

Gyaltsen.[84] There is also high praise given to this way of relying on the spiritual master in the *Questions of Pure Superior Intention* together with all the commentaries. In particular, [Tsongkhapa] poses the following questions to the great meditators: "If you are going to reveal great strength in the practice of guru yoga, explain the place to meditate on the guru, how to calculate the number of gurus, how to carry out the meditation on the actual guru yoga, the system of perceiving the root guru as inseparable from Vajradhara, and how to carry out emanating and retracting light rays." In response to this, *Losang's Melodious Laughter* states:

> The place where one should meditate on the guru
> Is in the space before you, on your crown, or in the center
>   of your heart,
> In accordance with each individual's disposition.

Also, the *Abhidhana Tantra* states:

> The kind guru can be visualized
> On the bodily parts such as
> The palm of the hand or the heart.
> That person will embody the
> Blessings of a thousand buddhas.

> With regard to calculating your gurus,
> How to actually meditate on [guru] yoga,
> The inseparability of Vajradhara,
> The deity radiating and retracting light rays, and so on,

> The way to perform the sequences
> Has been written elsewhere
> By your pure disciples of the snow mountains.
> The Hearing Lineage should be learned orally
> Through their own omniscient wisdom.

84. Gyalwa Ensapa and the First Panchen Lama, Chökyi Gyaltsen, were not direct disciples of Lama Tsongkhapa; therefore, the teachings must have been bestowed through a visionary experience.

The Way to Invoke the Wisdom Beings and Make Them Inseparable

The text itself states:

Invoking the Wisdom Beings

Their three places are marked by the three vajras. Hooking light rays radiate from the HUM and invoke the wisdom beings from their natural abodes in the same aspect as those visualized.

Although the nature of all phenomena is free from coming
   and going,
You manifest your enlightened actions of wisdom and
   compassion
According to the minds of those to be subdued;
Holy refuge and protector, please come to this place together
   with your retinue.

You are the source of all excellence, bliss, and everything
   supreme in the three times,
The root and lineage gurus, Three Precious Jewels,
And a collection of heroes, dakinis, Dharma protectors, and
   guardians;
Please come to this place through the power of your great
   compassion and remain firm.

With regard to the way to conduct this visualization, hooking light rays radiate to the ten directions from the hearts of all the fields of merit, but in particular your kind root guru in the aspect of the three nested beings, and invoke all the buddhas and bodhisattvas in the ten directions in the aspect of Lama Chöpa merit fields. Although there are numerous means of invocation, at this point you are invoking from the abode of the truth body. The wisdom beings invoked in this way are visualized as before, and they arrive at the crowns of the guru and assembly of deities. After you recite DZA HUM BAM HO you should imagine that they have been mixed inseparably and stabilized. With regard to what to visualize when proclaiming this mantra, as you recite DZA the wisdom beings come to the crowns of each of the commitment beings. As you recite HUM the wisdom beings dissolve into each of the commitment beings. As you recite BAM they mix and become inseparably one. As you recite HO you should imagine that they joyfully remain firm. If we extensively explain the meaning of the phrase "the three doors are marked by the three letters," it is taught that you should visualize that at the crown of each of the deities is the vajra body of Vairochana with an OM at his heart. At their throat is the vajra speech of Amitabha with an AH at his heart. At their heart is the vajra mind Akshobya with a HUM at his heart. If are you doing it in a concise fashion, you arrange the three syllables as explained earlier; we call those three syllables "the three vajras," which is explained in the *Cluster of Oral Instructions*.[85]

As for invoking the wisdom beings to the commitment beings at this point, it is for the sake of overcoming ordinary appearances and conceptions, which is also taught in the *Cluster of Oral Instructions*. Regarding the meaning of this, you arrange them on the body of Lama Tubwang Dorje Chang the Great; therefore, just as he abides in the space before you, he also pervades all pure realms. This is also seen in many historical accounts, such as when Arya Asanga attained [a vision] of Protector Maitreya and conversed with him, as well as numerous mahasiddhas of old who accomplished [the attainments of] supreme deities. Based on the conceptualizations that come from ordinary appearances and conceptions, we have the appearance of [enlightened beings] abiding in two differing places; therefore, to overcome these we invoke the wisdom beings and dissolve them into the commitment beings. With regard to the meaning of "commitment," the [Sanskrit] translation equivalent is "samaya," and if I were to explain the etymological meaning of the letters separately, I would use the *Cluster of Oral Instructions*, which explains its meaning as "the wisdom beings operate within the activity of coming and going." The Jamgon Lama [Purchog Ngawang Jampa] Rinpoche himself stated, "The guru's body is the assembly hall for all the buddhas in the ten directions."

85. *Man ngag snye ma.*

If you investigate this method, you will see that the absolute perfect treasure is the yoga of the guru. Thus, when it comes to viewing the guru as inseparable from Vajradhara, the *Mayajala Tantra*[86] states:

> Do not consider the guru
> And Vajradhara to be separate.

The same thing is said, not just once, but in countless texts of the tantra and of mahasiddhas. The lamrim text of Chayulwa also states, "If you propose that Vajradhara or your personal deity is separate from the guru, you will never receive attainments of that tantra." Also, in the historical accounts of numerous mahasiddhas of India as well as the historical accounts of many of the previous holy beings such as Marpa Lotsawa and so forth, although they perceived the guru as perfect, they prostrated to the personal deity prior to the guru and so forth and incurred massive misfortunes because of this mistaken dependent relationship. In the *Five Stages*[87] Protector Nagarjuna states:

> He is the self-arisen bhagavan,
> Utterly one with the supreme deity;
> Because he is the perfect source of oral instructions
> The vajra master is supreme.

Thus, this states that you should regard him as superior even to Vajradhara. Through these quotes and their sources you should strengthen your devotion that he is the nature embodying every single object of refuge and is the unsurpassed object of offering.

Presenting Them with the Offerings has two sections:
1. Contemplating the Reasons for the Greatness of Lama Chöpa
2. The Actual Way of Presenting Offerings to the Guru [and Assembly of Deities]

---

86. *sGyu 'phrul dra ba'i rgyud*; *Māyājālatantra*; *The Net of Magical Illusion.*
87. *Rim pa lnga pa*; *Pañcakrama.*

Contemplating the Reasons for the Greatness of Lama Chöpa

The Lama Chöpa text itself states:

> Then, as Protector Nagarjuna's *Five Stages* states:
>
>> You should completely forsake all [other] offerings
>> And commence with perfect offerings to the guru.
>> By pleasing him you will obtain the
>> Supreme exalted wisdom of omniscience.
>
> Once you have induced absolute certainty in these teachings, which state that making offerings to the guru is superior to making offerings to all other buddhas and bodhisattvas, you should offer the seven limbs, beginning with prostration.

In general the guru is very important for accumulating merit and purifying negative karma, and in particular, since we wish to become enlightened quickly, we should understand that he is the manifestation of skillful means, through which we quickly complete a great wave of merit and quickly purify obscurations. To accomplish that through the Perfection Vehicle you must accumulate merit through limitless ways for countless great eons. Here, in highest yoga tantra, you do not need to endure such austerities for such a long time. Instead, you should work to assemble all the causes to attain enlightenment in one short human life in this degenerate age. For that reason, by way of possessing the special method of deity yoga, you present limitless offerings of boundless purity to the assembly of mandala deities, who are inseparable from the guru as the ultimate field for accumulating merit, and in each passing moment you will be working to complete your great waves of merit as the causes of enlightenment. Furthermore, the *Chakrasamvara Root Tantra* states:

> Next, the practitioner [should]
> First please the spiritual master with all things.
> Desiring attainments and with strong concentration
> Make as many offerings to the guru as you are able.

And:

> Abiding perfectly in the body of the master,
> I, the hero, will accept the offerings
> From the practitioner.

And:

> Even the practitioner of little merit
> Will discover it by pleasing [me].

Accordingly, to swiftly achieve the supreme attainment of mahamudra you should make offerings to the guru and with that offering you will quickly complete your accumulations and quickly receive attainments. The meaning of the verse "Abiding perfectly in the body of the master . . ." and so forth is explained in the commentary to this tantra [composed by Lama Tsongkhapa] entitled *Clear Illumination of All Hidden Meaning*,[88] which states that in this degenerate age Heruka abides in the body of the master in order to accept the disciple's offerings. Also, although a person may have very little merit in the first part of his or her life, once they meet a fully qualified vajra master, if they rely upon him perfectly and make offerings, the conquerors will enter into the body of the master and that disciple will develop merit and quickly perfect the accumulations and accomplish supreme attainments in the latter part of their lives.

The *Vajra* [*Tent Tantra*] states:

> Requested by all the bodhisattvas,
> Our fathers and mothers should
> Reflect on the meaning of this.

> Why is that? Because
> It was proclaimed by the tathagatas.

---

88. *sBas don kun gsal.*

The attainments of Buddha Vajrasattva and
Vajra Dharma and Splendor
And the seven precious possessions of a king
Are therefore obtained without difficulty,

As well as the eye medicine, swift footedness,
The sword, going underground,
The pill, flight,
Invisibility, and alchemy.

You will quickly reach these attainments
By pleasing the wisdom-vajra.
Therefore, go into the presence of the master
And pay homage to the tathagatas.

Being thus, apprehend the form of the master.
By seeing him, living beings come under his care
And he abides in the body of ordinary beings.

The vajra master is all the buddhas; therefore, he is the abode of worship and, if you supplicate and make offerings to him, you will quickly accomplish all the common and supreme attainments.

The *Oral Instructions of Manjushri*[89] states:

For a few fortunate beings in this world
I will abide in his body and
Accept the offerings of other practitioners.
By delighting him with that, the
Obscurations of your mind will be purified.

Thus, this states that when the disciple makes proper offerings to the guru, all the buddhas of the ten directions enter into the body of that guru and accept the offerings.

89. *'Jam dpal zhal lung*; *Mañjuśrīmukhāgama.*

The *Accomplishment of Secrets* states:

> The guru and the vajra holder
> Should always be seen as inseparable.
> He authentically embodies all attainments;
> With him you will reach attainments in this life.

And:

> Through meditating on the guru himself as
> Vajradhara you will reach attainments.
> Although you may [meditate on] him otherwise,
> This will never result in attainments.

Thus, it states that once you meditate on the guru as Vajradhara, if you then make requests, you will reach supreme attainments of mahamudra. If you don't have faith in the guru, although you may understand the meaning of tantra you will not reach attainments.

The *Accomplishment of Exalted Wisdom*[90] states:

> Without a guiding protector
> Your boat will not reach the other shore.
> Although you may be replete with good qualities,
> Without a guru you will not put an end to samsara.

As it says, just as you will not be able to cross the water by relying on a boat if you only hear about freedom, in the same way, from the point when you first enter that path striving to attain the state of Vajradhara up to the final resultant attainment, all depends solely on the blessings of the guru and you will not reach attainments without [his blessings]. In short, the meaning of tantra is subsumed in the *Fifty Verses of Guru Devotion*, which states:

90. *Ye shes grub pa.*

BASO CHÖKYI GYALTSEN

Vajradhara himself said that
Attainments come from following the master.
Realizing this, you should thoroughly delight your guru
With all of your belongings.

Thus, it states that the supreme attainment of mahamudra comes after meditating with faith on the guru. If this is examined by someone with an understanding of the correct path, guru yoga is the most wonderful treasure imaginable. Furthermore, it is, for example, similar to the phrase "both the presence and absence of fire can be determined by [the presence or absence of] smoke"; smoke only arises in dependence upon fire, and without fire it is impossible that smoke will ever arise. Likewise, whatever good qualities of the grounds and paths together with the results that you ever attain come solely from relying upon the guru with faith, and without him you have no way of bringing them about. Examine these methods with the wisdom of individual analysis and repeatedly contemplate by recollecting his kindness until you generate great respect, and then make a sincere effort to make prostrations and offerings to the guru and assembly of deities.

The Actual Way of Presenting Offerings to the Guru [and Assembly of Deities] has three sections:
1. Making Prostrations
2. Presenting Offerings
3. How to Perform the Remaining Limbs

Making Prostrations has five sections:
1. Making Praises and Prostrations by Seeing the Guru as the Complete Enjoyment Body
2. Making Praises and Prostrations by Seeing the Guru as the Emanation Body
3. Making Praises and Prostrations by Seeing the Guru as the Truth Body
4. Making Praises and Prostrations by Seeing the Guru as the Nature Embodying All Three Jewels
5. Making Praises and Prostrations to All the Buddhas and Bodhisattvas in the Ten Directions by Seeing Them as Emanations of the Guru

Making Praises and Prostrations by Seeing the Guru as the Complete Enjoyment Body

The ritual text states:

> I prostrate to the lotus feet of my jewel-like guru,
> The vajra holder, whose compassion
> Can bestow in an instant even the supreme state of
> The three bodies, the sphere of great bliss.

This appears in numerous texts of the mahasiddha when it states:

> By whose kindness great bliss itself
> Is attained in an instant,
> I bow to the lotus feet of vajra holder,
> The jewel-like guru.

With the exception of a few minor differences, the words are the same. Furthermore, the attainment of the state of union in one short life in this degenerate age depends solely on the kindness of the guru. Otherwise, you need to practice for many countless eons, yet through the kindness of Guru-Vajradhara that supreme state can be accomplished in the brief instant of this momentary life in this degenerate age; therefore, he is the unsurpassed object of offering.

The *Heruka Samvarodaya Tantra* states:

> Completely forsake all other offerings
> And commence with perfect offerings to the guru.
> By pleasing him you will attain the
> Supreme exalted wisdom of omniscience.
>
> Whatever merit was not created
> By perfectly worshipping Vajrasattva
> Is effortlessly accomplished without hardship
> Through the unsurpassed practice of the master.

Through perfect offerings to the guru you will swiftly attain the exalted wisdom of spontaneously born great bliss; therefore, you should set aside making offerings to other buddhas and bodhisattvas and make offerings to the guru your primary activity. What is stated here in the *Samvarodaya Tantra* is exactly the same thing stated in Protector Nagarjuna's *Five Stages*. With regard to the need to view your guru as a wish-fulfilling jewel that is the source of all your wishes, the *Drop of Mahamudra* states:

Whoever bestows empowerment,
View him as Vajrasattva.
View the guru as an emanation of the conqueror,
View the guru as magnificent, like a flame,
View the guru as surpassing the Buddha,
View him as equivalent to a wish-fulfilling jewel,
With proper application and mantra.
With the king of emanation on your crown
You discover an immeasurable jewel.
Remove everything else from your head!

The first stage of the *Five Stages* states:

If someone falls from the peak of Mount Meru,
Although they may not think they are falling, they in fact
    are falling.
If you receive the benefit of transmission through the guru's
    kindness,
Although you may not think you will be liberated, you will
    in fact be liberated.

This teaches that you will quickly be liberated through the kindness of
Guru-Vajradhara by utilizing an example.

The second stage [of the *Five Stages*] states:

The great wonder of the emptiness of all,
The great exalted wisdom of luminosity and clarity—
By the kindness of the guru himself
You will subsequently perceive that clarity.

This states that through the kindness of the guru you will quickly manifest that clear light of great bliss.

The third stage [of the *Five Stages*] states:

Called "the stage of self-blessing,"
It reveals the conventional truth.
That is due to the kindness of the guru;
It cannot be attained anywhere else.

The stage of self-blessing
Cannot be found by just anyone.
Sutras, tantras, and investigation
Are meaningless hard work.

Attaining the stage of self-blessing
Comes from the principal, who is the nature of all the buddhas.
Have no doubt that you will attain the state
Of enlightenment in this very life.

Through the kindness of meeting the fully qualified vajra master you will attain the vajra body in this life. If you do not have perfect reliance and do not come under the care of the vajra master, no matter how much you train in the sutras or tantras, it will be utterly impossible for you to accomplish the supreme attainments. The *Accomplishment of Secrets* states that the ultimate cause of this supreme attainment, which is the exalted wisdom of simultaneously born great bliss, comes only from the kindness of the guru; therefore work to accomplish it through numerous and repeated efforts.

Mahasiddha Saraha also states:

If you carefully apply yourself to the guru's teachings,
Have no doubt that simultaneously born [bliss] will emerge.

This states that you will necessarily generate the exalted wisdom of simultaneously born great bliss only in dependence upon the kindness of the guru and repeatedly states that you will never find it anywhere else. The *Explanatory Tantra Vajramala* states that each and every one of the five stages of the path comes only from the kindness of the guru. I am concerned that if I quote more sources this text will become too verbose; therefore, the intelligent should develop conviction by looking into the tantras themselves.

Making Praises and Prostrations by Seeing the Guru as the Emanation Body

The ritual text states:

> I prostrate at the feet of the holy refuge and protector.
> As the exalted wisdom of all the infinite conquerors
> Displaying the aspect of a saffron-robed monk,
> Your skillful means appear according to the needs of your
>   disciples.

Regarding the teacher Shakyamuni's inconceivable emanations in general, the *Uttaratantra* (*Sublime Continuum*)[91] states:

> Through your great compassion you understand the world.
> Although you perceive the entire world,
> You do not waver from the dharmakaya,
> Yet the nature of your manifold emanations
> Is born in visible rebirths.

> Without ever wavering from the dharmakaya
> You transmigrate from Tushita,
> Enter the womb and take rebirth,
> Display the aspect of delighting in a queen and retinue,
> Develop renunciation and perform austerities.
> Moving to the heart of enlightenment
> You utterly destroy the host of demons,
> Turn the wheel of Dharma,
> Depart to nirvana,
> And reveal yourself until the end of time
> In the thoroughly impure environments.[92]

---

91. *rGyud bla ma; Uttaratantraśāstra.*
92. This is a reference to the twelve deeds of the Buddha, which are (1) descent from Tushita pure land, (2) entering his mother's womb, (3) taking birth in Lumbini Garden, (4) becoming skilled in various arts, (5) delighting in the company of royal consorts, (6) developing renunciation and becoming ordained, (7) practicing austerities for twelve years, (8) proceeding to the foot of the

Also, the *Ocean Cloud of Praises*[93] states: "From the limitless ocean of perfect accumulation of merit your unbelievably beautiful supreme body is born. Without ever reaching the ends of space it appears as a magical creation to the many living beings in all of the pure lands. For some, you take rebirth in various other lands, where your body displays the aspect of teaching the way to enlightenment. For the sake of every living being without exception, your wisdom transforms into this supreme manifestation and so many numerous others that I could not express them all."

In this world the guru reveals the way to nirvana while simultaneously taking rebirth in a pure land. For some he turns the wheel of Dharma and so forth, and he reveals all of these magical emanations simultaneously. With regard to displaying a multitude of emanations according to the karma and disposition of disciples, the *Meeting of Father and Son Sutra*[94] states:

> In the shape of Indra and Brahma,
> To some, in the shape of a demon,
> He works for the welfare of living beings;
> However, the worldly are incapable of understanding this.

> Undertaking deeds in the shape of a woman,
> He also reveals himself in the birthplace of animals,
> As well as the passionate and dispassionate,
> As the fearful and the fearless;
> He reveals himself as the ignorant and wise,
> As a madman and the sane,
> As a cripple and an able being.

> With these various emanations
> He works to subdue living beings.

Thus, from among the deeds of these limitless emanations, the most supreme is the supreme emanation body, which appears to us in a body adorned

---

bodhi tree, (9) overcoming the host of demons, (10) becoming fully enlightened, (11) turning the wheel of Dharma, and (12) passing into the sphere of nirvana.

93. *bsTod sprin rgya mtsho.*

94. *Yab dang sras mjal ba'i mdo; Pitāputrasamāgamasūtra.*

with the signs and indications in accordance with his great compassion, and which appears to us in human body in the form of a saffron-robed monk turning the wheel of Dharma. We ordinary beings are not fortunate enough to perceive his actual body adorned with the signs and indications, however, so he reveals the form of a saffron-robed monk performing the same actions by giving us the spiritual teachings; therefore, his kindness is incomparable. Not only is this a form of prostration, but because the conquerors abide in the body of the guru, you are performing a prostration and offering. With regard to this, the *Oral Instructions of Manjushri* states:

> For a few fortunate beings in this world
> I will abide in his body and
> Accept the offerings of other practitioners.

Many other tantras, such as the *Samvarodaya Tantra*, state the same thing. It is not only one conqueror involved in the practice of guru yoga, for it is repeatedly stated that the guru is the embodiment of the exalted wisdom of *all* the conquerors dwelling in the limitless pure lands of the ten directions. The seventeenth chapter of the *Glorious Guhyasamaja Tantra* states:

> Next, the tathagata Akshobya,
> The tathagata Ratna Shri,
> The tathagata Amitabha,
> The tathagata Amoghasiddhi,
> And the tathagata Vairochana.

> The vajra holder is called "vajra-observance of the samaya of attainments of all the vajra holders." Through the concentration of embrace he commands all the buddhas and bodhisattvas. All of you bodhisattvas listen up! Although any of the bhagavan buddhas dwelling in the ten directions are the source of the vajra-exalted wisdom of the three times, if you meet the master of Guhyasamaja, you should make offerings and prostrations. Why? Because he is the teacher, the bhagavan vajra holder, and the lord of the exalted wisdom of all the buddhas. Therefore, all of the bodhisattvas, the great beings,

supplicate all the tathagatas with these words. Where do the attainments of the body, speech, and mind of all the bhagavan tathagatas abide? It has been proclaimed by all the tathagatas that their three secrets of body, speech, and mind abide in the body, speech, and mind of the vajra master.

Making Praises and Prostrations by Seeing the Guru as the Truth Body

The ritual text states:

> I prostrate at the feet of the foremost supreme guru.
> Having uprooted all faults together with their imprints, you are
> An abundant treasure of precious good qualities
> And the sole gateway to all benefit and happiness.

His body is the nature truth body and wisdom truth body. The nature truth body is the ultimate sphere of reality that has abandoned the faults of the two obstructions together with their imprints. The wisdom truth body is the ultimate perception of reality of the two truths that has become the treasury of all good qualities and is the source of every benefit and happiness. Furthermore, this is the sole source of whatever benefit and happiness that may arise for embodied beings and the enlightened actions of all the buddhas. With regard to the agent of the enlightened actions of all the buddhas, it is well known that it is the state of omniscient wisdom. With regard to the treasury of good qualities of that state of omniscient wisdom, this accords with the extensive praise expounded in the perfection of wisdom sutras. With regard to perceiving the nature of those two bodies of the guru, it is taught that at the time of result, once the corporeal body of flesh and bones is exhausted, the body and mind become a single nature accomplished from the self-manifesting exalted wisdom. This method is very difficult to realize and is the ultimate secret abode. To understand all the essential points of this you should understand the essential points of union as presented in the *Five Stages*. To understand [union] you have to understand the illusory body of the third stage and the clear light of the fourth stage. These are the ultimate secrets that are very difficult to understand. With regard to viewing the nature of the truth body, this is also explained in the perfection of wisdom sutras. The *Vajra Cutter Sutra*[95] states:

> Whoever sees me as forms,
> Whoever regards me as sounds,
> They have entered the incorrect path;
> Those beings do not see me.

> The buddhas are the perception of the nature of reality,
> The guides are the dharmakaya.
> Because the nature of reality cannot be known,
> It is not possible to understand its attributes.

Making Praises and Prostrations by Seeing the Guru as the Nature Embodying All Three Jewels

The ritual text states:

> I prostrate to the kind gurus.
> In reality you are all buddhas and teachers, including the deities,
> The source of all eighty-four thousand pure Dharmas,
> Radiant amid the entire assembly of aryas.

With regard to viewing him as the nature of the Three Jewels, the *Explanatory Tantra Vajramala* states:

> He embodies all the characteristics of
> The Buddha, holy Dharma, and Sangha,
> The master, guru, teacher,
> Vajradhara, and disciple.

> His immaculate mind is the Buddha,
> The pure teachings of his speech are the Dharma,
> His body is called the Sangha,
> And he is the abode of the assembly of bodhisattvas.

---

95. *rDo rje gcod pa'i mdo; Vajracchedikāsūtra.*

The *Heruka Explanatory Tantra Samvarodaya* states as well:

> The guru is the Buddha, the guru is the Dharma,
> The guru is likewise the Sangha.
> The guru is the union of all the buddhas;
> He is the net binding the dakinis.
>
> Therefore, those wishing the state
> Of a buddha should please the guru.

It furthermore states:

> I prostrate to the gurus,
> Their bodies encompass all buddhas,
> They are the nature of the vajra holder,
> They are the root of all Three Jewels.

And:

> The guru is the Buddha, the guru is the Dharma,
> The guru is likewise the Sangha;
> I prostrate to the gurus.

These come from the tantras themselves and, with the exception of some slight differences in translation, they make the same point.

Making Praises and Prostrations to All the Buddhas and Bodhisattvas in the Ten Directions by Seeing Them as Emanations of the Guru

The ritual text states:

> With faith and devotion I sing a melodious ocean of praise
> And prostrate with emanated bodies equaling atoms
>   of the world

To all those worthy of prostration in the three times and the ten
directions,
Such as the guru and Three Precious Jewels.

It was Khedrup Sangye Yeshe who, through seeing the buddhas and bodhisattvas in the ten directions as emanations of the guru, composed verses
of prostration and praise utilizing phrases such as "Guru-Vajradhara,"
"Guru-Vajrabhairava," "Guru-Amitabha," and so forth. Vajradhara Losang
Chökyi Gyaltsen himself also composed a verse that states:

Glorious Vajrasattva, the pervasive lord
Of all mandalas of limitless conquerors,
Manifests as the guru endowed with three types of kindness,
Appearing as a saffron-robed monk according to [the disposition
of] disciples
For the welfare of beings without a protector in this degenerate age.

This states that Guru-Vajradhara is the essence of all the conquerors' mandalas. The same thing appears numerous times in the teachings of the
tantras of the mahasiddhas. Thus, just what should you do when prostrating to the guru and assembly of deities? You should prostrate with great
respect with your three doors. To prostrate with your body, imagine you
emanate bodies equal to the number of atoms in your body covering the
ground and that these bodies prostrate by touching their heads to the
soles of the feet [of the fields of merit]. To verbally prostrate, each and
every one of those bodies proclaims words of supplication in a web of
melodious song expounding the good qualities of their body, speech, and
mind. To mentally prostrate, with heartfelt faith and respect you promise
to place your trust in them and in no one else. If the conquerors in the ten
directions also act with veneration toward the vajra master, what need is
there to mention that you as the disciple should act with veneration by
making prostrations and presenting offerings?

Furthermore, the *Fifty Verses of Guru Devotion* states:

The tathagatas abiding in the worldly realms
Of the ten directions prostrate to the vajra master

From whom they received supreme empowerment
Throughout the three times.

The meaning of this is also expressed in the seventeenth chapter of the *Glorious Guhyasamaja Root Tantra*, which states, "If stated briefly, the moment all nurturing buddhas and bodhisattvas there are in the worldly realms of the ten directions appeared from the ten directions, all those tathagatas worshipped the master with perfect offerings; they departed to their buddha lands and extracted these vajra words: 'The father of all of us tathagatas, the mother of all of us tathagatas'; having spoken thus, he is called 'the teacher of all of us tathagatas.'"

Also, the *Cluster of the Ultimate Meaning*[96] states:

The children endowed with good qualities destroy samsara.
The teacher of all beings abiding in the realm of Brahma is the
    glorious guru.
There is nothing other than the glorious guru.
To him, the limitless buddhas also eternally present offerings,
And the buddhas and bodhisattvas abiding in the directions
    eternally bow.

The great being Nagarjuna compiled all the sutras and quoted the *Heap of Jewels Sutra*,[97] which states, "Ananda, if a bodhisattva sat in a chariot and enjoyed a feast with the five sense objects and enjoyed the presence of a woman, and there was no one else to pull his chariot, Ananda, the tathagatas would carry that bodhisattva's chariot on their heads." Likewise, numerous other sutras and tantras extensively state that all the buddhas and bodhisattvas praise and present offerings to the master who reveals the unmistaken path. It is taught that when you arrive at the exalted path of the completion stage, you don't need to rely upon prostrations and offerings to the buddhas and bodhisattvas in dependence upon body, speech, and mind; however, at that point you still definitely need to make

96. *Don dam nye ma.*
97. *dKon mchog brtsegs pa chen po'i chos kyi rnam grangs le'u stong phrag brgya pa las sdom pa gsum bstan pa'i le'u; Mahāratnakūṭadharmaparyāyaśatasāhasrikagranthetrisaṃvaranirdeśaparivartasūtra.*

prostrations and offerings to the guru, which is stated in numerous texts of the mahasiddhas such as the *Compendium of Conduct*, the *Accomplishment of Secrets*, the *Cluster of Oral Instructions*, and so forth. Therefore, those endowed with intelligence should examine these systems carefully. Vajradhara Losang Chökyi Gyaltsen said that we should view the guru as surpassing all the conquerors; therefore, these words should be deeply felt with certain conviction.

The Way of Presenting Offerings to the Guru and Assembly of Deities has five sections:

1. Outer Offerings Related to the Vase Empowerment
2. Inner Offering Related to the Secret Empowerment
3. Secret Offering Related to the Wisdom Empowerment
4. Suchness Offering Related to the Word Empowerment
5. The Way to Offer Medicine, Oneself as a Servant, and Uphold the Vows

Outer Offerings Related to the Vase Empowerment has five sections:

1. Offering the Four Waters
2. Offering the Close Enjoyment Offerings
3. Offering the Objects of Desire
4. Offering the Mandala
5. Offering Your Practice

Offering the Four Waters

With regard to what sort of special thoughts we should have while presenting offerings to the guru and assembly of deities, the [Lama Chöpa] ritual text itself says, ". . . you should present offerings once you have sealed them in the nature of the nonconceptual wisdom of inseparable bliss and emptiness of the three circles of the offerings." It is extremely important that you cleanse, purify, and bless the offerings as soon as you put them out. It is said that if you don't, and just leave them, the interfering spirits will rob the radiance of the offerings and the practitioner himself will be subject to harm. Furthermore, the negative force called Moving Like Water enters the water for drinking, the negative force

called Worldly Flowers enters into the flowers, the negative force called
Blackness is in the incense, the one called Single Topknot is in the lights,
Smell Eater is in the scented water, and Torma Eater is in the food. These
negative forces enter the substances and, once all the particular interfering spirits enter, they rob the scent, taste, and potentiality of those offerings. For the practitioner as well, they disturb the mind and so forth and
create a variety of obstacles. This has been taught in numerous tantras,
such as *The Tantra Requested by Subahu*, the *Supreme Knowledge Tantra*, and
so forth as well as numerous tantras of the mahasiddhas. I am concerned
that if I quote the sources this text will become too wordy; therefore, you
should learn about this from the tantras and their commentaries. Thus,
presenting the blessed offerings, you should bless them in accordance with
previous explanations for blessing the offerings. You should view (1) the
recipient of the offering, (2) the one presenting the offerings, and (3) the
offering substances appearing and empty of inherent existence while realizing that form is in emptiness and emptiness is in form, appearing like
an illusion. In particular, you should present the offerings after perceiving
them as nothing but the manifestation of inseparable bliss and emptiness. Furthermore, in general you should become intimately familiar with
your training in perceiving all phenomena as manifestations of emptiness.
Regarding this, the *Heart of Wisdom Sutra* states:

> Form is emptiness,
> Emptiness is form,
> Form is not other than emptiness,
> Emptiness is also not other than form.

Thus, it explains that all phenomena, such as form and so forth, are
emptiness and emptiness appears as these various phenomena. *Entering
the Middle Way*[98] states:

> Empty things such as reflections that depend
> Upon a collection are also not unknown.
> Just as reflections and so forth come from emptiness,

98. *dBu ma la 'jug pa*; *Madhyamakāvatāra*.

Likewise, the knowledge of their aspects is generated.
In the same way, although all things are empty,
They are perfectly generated from emptiness.

This and [other similar teachings] are extensively taught in the *Treatise on the Middle Way*. Vajradhara Losang Chökyi Gyaltsen made this very clear when he said:

Through the appearance of these nontruly existent entities
Both the extreme of truly existent appearances
And the extreme of nonexistence are dispelled.

The ability to dispel the extreme of nonexistence comes from
    the fact that
The appearance of phenomena is based in emptiness
As nontruly existent appearances.
Therefore, the extreme of nonexistence is dispelled because
    of existence.

Because of these reasons,
It is like creating emptiness from appearances,
It is like generating appearances from emptiness.

And:

Viewing emptiness as the nature of appearances
Is similar to generating the nontrue existence
Of appearances from appearances.

If we perceive them as coming from the side of appearance,
It functions to block the generation of appearances,
Which is similar to only generating appearances from
The lack of inherently existent appearances.

It has become the means of conventional truth
And is the outcome of the means of the ultimate truth.

Do not reinforce the conventional,
Do not empower conceptions of the ultimate;
Discover that emptiness comes from appearances.

If at the beginning you train in transforming emptiness into all appearances, such as the recipients of the offering, the offering substances, and so forth, you will be training in manifesting the inseparability of emptiness and great bliss, and you should stabilize your conviction that that very exalted wisdom of simultaneously born great bliss is appearing in the aspect of the various offering substances and so forth. This is the very heart of highest yoga tantra and is the heart practice of the mahasiddhas and is the supreme quick path to swift enlightenment. Someone as ignorant as myself finds it difficult to comprehend the tantras, and having a theoretical understanding is even more difficult. Now that you have met, this one time, the Hearing Lineage of the second conqueror Je [Tsongkhapa], even if you are mentally incapable of understanding the meaning of the words, at least establish as many imprints as you can through developing faith and devotion.

Having contemplated in that way, we offer the four waters. The ritual text states:

My refuge and protector, my guru together with your retinue,
I offer this ocean of clouds of various offerings;

From extensive radiant jeweled vessels perfectly arrayed
The purifying nectars of the four waters gently flow.

With regard to what you should be visualizing, countless offering goddesses emanate from your heart holding drinking water and present it to the hands of the fields of merit. You should imagine that, through offering it in this way, a special uncontaminated bliss is born in their mental continuum, after which the offering goddesses are reabsorbed into your heart. Likewise, sequentially offer water for the feet, water for the mouth, and water for sprinkling by emanating offering goddesses. When you are finished with the offerings, the offering goddesses are retracted into your heart. Furthermore, "water for the feet" is for washing the feet, "water for the mouth" is for rinsing the mouth, "water for sprinkling" is for sprinkling on the body. Regarding the way to offer the four waters, in the mandala rituals of Guhyasamaja, Heruka, and Yamantaka, the foremost omniscient being [Tsongkhapa] stated:

> This pure, stainless, and pleasing
> Supreme mantra-water-for-drinking
> I offer to you with a mind of faith;
> Accept it and bestow your kindness.

And:

> Offer with water for drinking, flowers, and so forth.

As for the water for drinking, the *Mandala Ritual Vajramala*[99] states, "For pacifying, white scented water should contain barley, milk, white flowers, *kusha*, sesame, puffed rice, and nectar." These are the famous seven substances for drinking water. There are different substances for increasing, controlling, and wrathful. I am concerned that if I explain in detail the way of accomplishing the four waters, what should be done while offering, how to make the mantras, mudras, and so forth, this text would become too verbose; therefore, you should learn about them elsewhere. However, I will explain a little about the meaning at this point; as for the "purifying agent," there are two: the common and uncommon. For the common, generally for water we use the term "the purifying agent," and in particular we should imagine it is the divine water of the River Ganges that possesses the eight limbs. Regarding the eight limbs, they are (1) cool, (2) delicious, (3) light, (4) soft, (5) clear, (6) pure, (7) not harmful to the stomach, and (8) not harmful to the throat.

Thus they are (1) cool, (2) delicious, (3) light, (4) soft, (5) clear, (6) pure, (7) beneficial to the stomach, and (8) not harmful to the throat. Regarding the uncommon, it is purifying ordinary appearances and conceptions and is common to all four classes of tantra. As for the uncommon way of purifying through highest yoga tantra, it is purifying

---

99. *dKyil chog rdo rje phreng ba.*

what is unharmonious to the exalted wisdom of great bliss and is called "mantra-water-for-drinking," where the ultimate meaning of "mantra" is mantra functioning as the exalted wisdom of inseparable bliss and emptiness. Therefore, that very exalted wisdom of inseparable bliss and emptiness arises in the form of water for drinking and is presented to the guru and assembly of deities. It has the power to generate the exalted wisdom of great bliss in their mental continuums, and although ultimately there isn't anything whatsoever to purify in the minds of the guru and the assembly of deities, from the perspective of us obscured beings, all of their impurities such as being afflicted with defilements and so forth are purified by merely touching the nectar water.[100] Proceed in the same way with the other three waters.

Offering the Close Enjoyment Offerings

The ritual text states:

> Beautiful flowers finely arranged as blossoming trees,
> Petals, and garlands filling the earth and sky.

> The lapis-colored smoke of sweet-smelling incense
> Filling the heavens like blue summer clouds.

> Light from the sun and moon, glittering jewels,
> And a mass of joyfully frolicking lamps
> Dispelling the darkness in a billion worlds.

> A vast ocean of scented water with the sweet scent of saffron,
> Sandalwood, and camphor swirling out to the horizon.

> A massive heap of delicacies of gods and men
> As food and drink endowed with a hundred flavors.

---

100. The point is that even though the guru and the assembly of deities don't have any defilements, by imagining they are purified we are purifying our own obscurations as well as impure appearances and conceptions.

From an endless variety of musical instruments
Emerges a symphony that fills the three worlds.

Regarding the way to visualize this, imagine that an inconceivable number of offering goddesses holding flowers emanate from your heart and present offerings to the guru and assembly of deities, whereby they offer flower garlands to the heads of the fields of merit as attire for the enjoyment bodies and appear in the sky above all the fields of merit with masses of flowers similar to canopies, garlands to wear as necklaces, and a variety of petals that they scatter covering all directions. Also, those flowers radiate light and emit a fragrant scent. When the flower canopies and garlands in the sky are stirred by the breeze, they naturally proclaim the melodious sound of the Dharma. The aroma of their sweet scent pervades every direction and so forth. These should be contemplated in accordance with the *Avatamsaka Sutra*, and once you have completed the offering, the offering goddesses are retracted into your heart.

Likewise, when offering incense, emanate countless offering goddesses from your heart holding vast jeweled incense containers made of gold, silver, and sapphire, inside of which is incense composed of a variety of substances such as aloe wood, juniper, and so forth as both single substances and composites. They completely fill the realms of space like summer clouds and are offered to the guru and assembly of deities. When the sweet scent merely reaches their nose, they generate a special uncontaminated bliss in their mental continuum, and once they are delighted by the offering, you absorb the offering goddesses back into your heart.

When offering lamps, emanate countless offering goddesses from your heart holding lamp containers made from jewels that are broad and expansive with lamps that radiate limitless rays of light. They fill the entire sphere of space and are beyond the imagination, exceeding the sun, moon, the precious wish-fulfilling jewel, and so forth. The light dispels the darkness of all worldly realms. It also dispels the darkness below the ground and between the four continents. The tips of the light rays from those jeweled vessels and lamps are as if intertwined in embrace and their webs and latticework create various designs of auspiciousness such as wheels, swastikas, endless knots, and so forth as well as a variety of other manifestations such as parasols, victory banners, and so forth. Thus, when [the fields of merit] merely see them with their eyes, they generate a special uncontaminated bliss in their mental continuum, after which you retract the offering goddesses.

When offering perfume, emanate innumerable offering goddesses from your heart. They hold vast and expansive jeweled vessels with a mixture of scented water with substances such as camphor, sandalwood, saffron, nutmeg, and so forth like a swirling ocean. The perfume is offered to the hearts of the guru and assembly of deities, whereby its sweet-smelling fragrance fills the entire realm of space. In dependence upon that, the guru and assembly of deities generate an uncontaminated great bliss in their mental continuums, whereby they are delighted, after which you reabsorb the offering goddesses into your heart.

When offering the food substances, emanate limitless offering goddesses from your heart. They hold broad and expansive jeweled vessels that contain a limitless ocean of nectar from the celestial realms as well as the human realm as special food and drink that are the embodiment of everything pleasing to the mind heaped like a mountain. You offer it to the guru and assembly of deities; they partake of the essence of the food and drink through their tongues which are straws of light, whereby they generate a special uncontaminated bliss in their mental continuum. Imagine they are delighted by the offering and reabsorb the offering goddesses into your heart. With regard to this food, it is barley flour, rice gruel, meat, and so forth. As for the drinks, they consist of substances such as peach, walnut, grapes, and so forth. The rest of the words are easy to understand. As for "a hundred flavors," they are six flavors: sweet, sour, astringent, bitter, hot, and salty. Each of those have divisions of six, such as sweet of sweet and so forth, which equals thirty-six combinations. For each one of those there are inferior, middling, and supreme, which equals 108.

When offering music, emanate limitless offering goddesses from your heart holding a variety of special musical instruments such as cymbals, guitars, flutes, conch shells, and so forth. After which, their songs and the sounds of their musical instruments pervade the expanse of space, filling it with melodious music. Those melodious sounds evoke the compassion of the guru and assembly of deities, and the melodious sound of Dharma is presented to each and every living being in the six realms in their own language and so forth. The vast expanse of music and so forth is just as it appears in the sutras. Once you imagine this, you offer it, whereby the guru and the assembly of deities generate great uncontaminated bliss in their mental continuum. The mode of existence of that bliss is placed inseparably within emptiness like water set in water, whereby they are delighted by this unexcelled offering. After imagining this, reabsorb the offering goddesses into your heart.

With regard to emanating and retracting after each of these offerings, the *Guhyasamaja Root Tantra* states:

> Having proclaimed the vajra-emanation,
> Once completed they should be completely reabsorbed.

As for the meaning of this, it has a special auspiciousness for quickly generating the exalted path of the completion stage in your mental continuum. These methods of presenting the offerings are in accordance with the eighth chapter of the *Guhyasamaja Root Tantra*, which discusses offering flowers and so forth to the guru and assembly of deities. The *Explanatory Tantra Vajramala* states:

> You should invoke Manjushri-Vajra
> And his perfect mandala.
> Summoned to the center of the mandala,
> Take your own separate seat
> And make perfect offerings.
> You should make offerings to the supreme mandala
> With offerings presented in sequence with their
> Individual mantras, divine flowers, and so forth.

In accordance with the meaning of this, the omniscient Je [Tsongkhapa] states in his mandala ritual texts for Guhyasamaja and Yamantaka:

> These sacred divine flowers
> Are for offering to the mandala.
> Protector, accept this offering
> And think of me with your compassion.

This continues with the close offerings together with music in accordance with the presentation for making offerings. According to the common interpretation, the phrase "divine flower" refers to the flower substance of the gods. The uncommon interpretation explains that the definitive meaning is that the exalted wisdom of inseparable bliss and emptiness appears in the aspect of a flower. When presenting these close enjoyment offerings together with music, you should offer them together with mantras and mudras as explained in the tantras, which also accords with what is taught in the mandala rituals of Heruka, Guhyasamaja, and Yamantaka of the omniscient Je [Tsongkhapa]. Regarding not performing these mudras and so forth at this point, this is for the sake of making it easy to comprehend for foolish and ignorant beings like me; therefore, you should perform them in a concise fashion. When you are performing a ganachakra in conjunction with Lama Chöpa, such as during teachings on the two stages and so forth, you should hold your vajra and bell and perform the mudras for each of the close offerings as usual.[101] The arrangement of these words for the close enjoyment offerings together with music reveals the concise essential points of the rosary of offerings for Guhyasamaja and Heruka. For that we say "divine flowers" and so forth, as mentioned above. [The extensive verse states]:

> Abundant emanations of goddesses held by the bliss of desire
> With beautiful bodies painted by the brush of concentration
> And youthful with figures as slender as fresh branches,
> Whose radiant faces are more beautiful than the moon.
> With blue eyes like *utpala* flowers and red lips
> Holding excellent, extensive garlands of flowers.
> For the sake of generating delight in the mandala deities
> I offer these close-enjoyment goddesses of bliss.

And likewise, in place of the flowers you have "goddesses holding vessels of sweet-smelling incense," "goddesses holding jewels blazing with brilliant lights," "goddesses holding supreme scents that pervade the three

---

101. During your daily recitations of Lama Chöpa, the offerings can be done in a concise way as presented in the ritual text. However, during important ceremonies the offerings should be made more extensively together with the hand mudras.

realms," "goddesses holding foods endowed with a hundred flavors," and "I offer a variety of melodious sounds arising from / Limitless pleasing musical instruments. / By hearing the sounds of these various melodies / The sufferings of body and mind are pacified." This is the condensed meaning of those verses. As for the "brush of concentration" verses of offering, these were sung by the goddesses of the three places during the construction of Nampar Gyalwai Ling[102] and were spoken while the omniscient Je [Tsongkhapa] was arranging the rosary of offerings for Heruka. These should generate a fresh realization in the mind of the guru and collection of deities, and although they in no way need to newly generate great bliss that they don't already have, it is for the sake of the practitioner's own completion of merit. And for that reason you should imagine that their uncontaminated bliss continuously increases. This is how we should offer the close enjoyment offerings that were mentioned earlier.

With regard to the way to present the inner close enjoyment offerings, the fifty-sixth chapter of the *Explanatory Tantra Vajramala* states:

> Likewise, the outer, inner,
> Both, as well as the unobservable.
> After fashioning the three into form,
> Offer them to the deities.

> The location is definitely the five objects
> And definitely occurs in the five states.
> Enjoy the five objects of desire
> Like a dream composed of energy wind.

> The practitioner attains the objects
> Through the path of the various senses.
> You should offer them all for the sake of
> Delighting great compassion.

> Through the perfect delight of the flower,
> The vajra-sun arises in the lotus and is
> Offered to the nature of the flower.

102. Tib. *rNam par rgyal ba'i gling*. This is another name for Ganden Monastery.

The supreme commitments of the three vajras
Are not the objects of conceptualization.

Thus, through the fire of *tummo*
The incense is definitely incinerated
And is offered to the mind of compassion.

The meaning of this is explained by the omniscient Je [Tsongkhapa], who composed a vajra song that states:

The extremely blue vajra-bee
In the sapphire-like secret chakra.
The red flower comes from the moving lotus
And is offered to delight Akshobya Vajra and the assembly
   of deities.

From the burning fire of *tummo* at the emanation wheel
The pleasing scent of camphor incense arises,
And the mind is satiated through this experience
And is offered to delight Akshobya Vajra and the assembly
   of deities.

Perfectly abiding in the center of the wheel of great bliss
Anointed by the pure jasmine-like scent,
It pervades the entire body and bestows supreme bliss
And is offered to delight Akshobya Vajra and the assembly
   of deities.

Like enjoying the objects of a dream
Emerging from the path of the various senses,
You are nourished by the enjoyments of those various objects
And offer them to delight Akshobya Vajra and the assembly
   of deities.

The joy emerging from enjoying union [and]
The sound of music of the supreme indestructible letter

Arises in the tone of the vowels and consonants
And is offered to delight Akshobya Vajra and the assembly
  of deities.

This explains the way to generate the supreme realizations of the completion stage in your mental continuum by penetrating the essential points
of your vajra body. These are the absolutely most secret teachings of all
the secret teachings.

Offering the Objects of Desire

The ritual text states:

And abundance of outer and inner goddesses as the objects
  of desire
Holding forms, sounds, scents, tastes, and objects of touch
  that pervade every direction.

Form goddesses emanate from your heart holding red double-sided mir-
rors in their hands, sound goddesses hold blue guitars, scent goddesses
hold conch shells filled with perfume in their hands, taste goddesses
hold nectar-food in their hands, and tactile goddesses hold silken fabrics
in their hands. They are countless in number. They offer these various
objects of desire to the guru and assembly of deities, whereby they generate a special uncontaminated bliss in their mental continuum, after which
the offering goddesses are reabsorbed into your heart. All these offering goddesses have one face and two arms. They are extremely elegant,
with a peaceful smiling expression, glancing from the corner of their
eyes and so forth, with beautiful aspects. These youthful maidens in the
bloom of youth frolic with delight in the five objects of desire such as
pleasing forms, melodious songs, wonderful spontaneously arisen scents,
extremely sweet and supreme tastes, and soft tactile objects. The sole
function of these objects is to generate a special uncontaminated bliss in
the mental continuums of the guru and the assembly of deities. Through
this way of offering the close enjoyments and the outer and inner objects
of desire, with the skillful means of mantra you are able to accumulate a

great wave of merit in each and every passing moment. It also becomes an agent ripening your virtuous roots for generating the supreme realizations of the completion stage, whereby you quickly accomplish supreme attainments and so forth. These and other limitless benefits are explained in the seventh and eighth chapters of the *Glorious Guhyasamaja Root Tantra*. The special definitive meaning of these offerings is extensively explained in the *Explanatory Tantra Vajramala*, the *Sandhi Vyakarana Tantra*,[103] and so forth.

Thus, when offering the four waters, the close enjoyments, and the objects of desire, you are not offering just a few. Instead, you have limitless offerings both set out and emanated by the mind. There are also limitless offerings in the pure lands of the ten directions that have arisen from the mind. You also offer inconceivable billowing clouds of Samantabhadra's offerings that completely fill all the realms of space.

With regard to how to offer the inner objects of desire, the omniscient Je [Tsongkhapa] states:

> Skilled in the sixty-four arts of love,
> Charming, beautiful maidens in the bloom of youth—
> These supreme mudras of form such as Padmini,
> I offer to please Akshobya Vajra and the assembly of deities.

> Glancing sideways and with a smiling appearance,
> The goddess Gauri and so forth skilled in song—
> These supreme mudras of song such as Padmini,
> I offer to please Akshobya Vajra and the assembly of deities.

> A spontaneously arising and anointed sweet scent
> Constantly arises from their bodies—
> These supreme mudras of scent such as Padmini,
> I offer to please Akshobya Vajra and the assembly of deities.

> Through the experience of melting the bodhichitta
> The honey of your lower lip is red like a bimba fruit;

---

103. *dGongs pa lung bstan pa'i rgyud*; *Saṃdhivyākaraṇatantra*; the *Tantra That Prophesies Realization*.

These supreme mudras of taste such as Padmini,
I offer to please Akshobya Vajra and the assembly of deities.

Through the mutual meeting of tips of their secret places
This tactile experience arouses the inner fire—
These supreme mudras of touch such as Padmini,
I offer to please Akshobya Vajra and the assembly of deities.

The rosary of offerings of Heruka states:

All forms that exist throughout limitless realms
Completely transform and arise as goddesses;
I offer these Rupavajra goddesses
With a lovely smile and displaying a beautiful body.

Through the force of all appearing forms
Arising as Rupavajra goddesses
May I have unchanging great bliss
And complete the supreme concentration of bliss and
    emptiness.

The remaining verses combine the other objects of desire in the same way.
    The following comes from the seventh chapter of the *Guhyasamaja Root Tantra*, which states:

Having understood the three aspects of form,
Which function as offerings, you should make offerings.
That itself is the assembly of bhagavans
And the basis of Buddha Vairochana.

And:

You should always conjoin forms,
Sounds, tastes, and so forth with the mind;
This is the concise essence of the secret
Of all the buddhas.

This elucidates the meaning of the *Explanatory Tantra Vajramala*. Once you view all of the objects that appear to your six senses as the nature of gods and goddesses—such as meditating on all forms as Rupavajra goddesses and so forth—you then offer them to the guru and assembly of deities, as well as expanding the bases for the senses of yourself visualized as the deity. In short, working with the means of increasing the great bliss of everything that appears is the ultimate essence of highest yoga tantra. The extent to which you can increase simultaneously born great bliss is proportionate to the extent that you will be able to increase a powerful consciousness ascertaining reality. And the extent that you are able to increase bliss and emptiness is proportionate to the degree to which you will sever the root of samsara. And once you increase your capacity to destroy mistaken dualistic appearances and their imprints, you will quickly become enlightened. Once you understand the meaning of this, the omniscient Je [Tsongkhapa] said, "You should work to establish whatever imprints you can by making a sincere effort to regard whatever appears, right down to mental events, as being the manifestation of bliss and emptiness."

Offering the Mandala

The ritual text states:

> My refuge and protector, great treasure of compassion,
> The supreme field of merit, I offer to you with a mind
>   of faith
> A hundred million of the four continents, Mount Meru, and
> The seven major and minor precious possessions of a king—
> A collection of perfect worlds and beings that generate
>   every joy
> As a great treasure of desired enjoyments of gods and men.

With regard to the substance of the mandala kit, the best is composed of gold and silver; the middling is composed of bronze, copper, and so forth; and the least is composed of wood and so forth—any of which are acceptable. If you can't even afford that much, it is even acceptable to use a round or square slab of stone. When, following the advice of Jetsun Manjushri, the omniscient Je [Tsongkhapa] and his retinue abandoned all worldly pursuits and went to Olga Chölung to engage in practices of accumulation and purification, Je Rinpoche used a stone slab with a very stable base and a flat surface and used his forearm to make the mandala offerings, and numerous mahasiddhas of India did the exact same thing. Furthermore, this kind of thing is for ascetic yogis who have abandoned all their possessions and, having forsaken their belongings, are without any resources. If you have resources but are incapable of mentally letting go of them in that way, or you have such resources and are incapable of using grains or seeds and instead use split stones and so forth, you are only cheating yourself! Geshe Potowa said that if someone goes and picks foul-smelling herbs[104] for scenting a conch shell with perfume saying, "It is water with sandalwood and camphor," it is like a blind person trying to confuse those with perfect sight. Therefore, if you have a great deal of resources, the best would be gold, silver, and so forth. The middling would be conch shells, shells, and so forth mixed with grains. At the very least you should have clean grains. Also, if you have forsaken your belongings as explained above and so forth and therefore can't afford grains, white crushed stones would also be acceptable.

The ritual for the mandala offering in *Victory over the Enemy*[105] states:

> Offering feces of a cow together with water
> And rubbing perfectly is moral discipline,
> Removing worms and ants is patience,
> Applying yourself without becoming weary is perseverance,
> Focusing that momentary cognition
> Is concentration, and wisdom is visualizing the design.
> With this as the mandala offering of the *muni*
> One attains the six transcendent perfections.

Once we mentally recall this meaning, we anoint the mandala with the five cow products and saturate the grains with perfumed water and the

---

104. Tib. *spang spos. Nardostachys chnensis batal.*
105. *dGra las rnam rgyal.*

five nectars. There are various amounts of heaps of mandalas, such as the twenty-three, thirty-seven, and so forth. This twenty-three-heap system was practiced by numerous mahasiddhas of India such as Panchen Naropa, Master Abhyakara, and so forth and was the personal practice of the omniscient Je [Tsongkhapa]. In accordance with the personal practice of Conqueror Tsongkhapa, Ensapa and his spiritual son [Khedrup Sangye Yeshe] also used this twenty-three-heap system. Here, in the Lama Chöpa ritual, we also utilize the twenty-three heaps. With regard to these twenty-three heaps, they are (1–4) the four continents, (5–12) the eight subcontinents, (13–19) the seven precious substances, (20) the great treasure vase, (21) the sun, (22) the moon, and (23) Mount Meru.

With regard to how to offer the twenty-three-heap mandala, recite OM VAJRA BHUMI AH HUM, which is the great and powerful golden ground. Then recite OM VAJRA REKHE AH HUM, which is the external encircling rim of iron mountains. Place a heap of grains[106] in the center mixed with the perfume and nectar and recite OM HAM SUMA BHYA MAI RA WE NAMA, which represents Mount Meru in the center. Set flowers in the east and recite OM YAM BURWA VIDHEHA YA NAMA for Videha in the east. Set out the substance in the south and recite OM RAM DZAMBU DVIPA YA NAMA for Dzambuling in the south. Set out substances in the west and recite OM LAM APARAGODANIYA for Aparagodaniya in the west. Set out substances to the right and left of the southern continent and recite OM RAM UPADRIPAYA NAMA twice for Chamara and Upachamara. Set out substances to the right and left of the western continent and recite OM LAM UPDRIPHAYA NAMA twice for Shatha and Uttarmantrina. Set out substances to the right and left of the northern continent and recite OM VAM UPADRIPAYA NAMA twice for Kurava and Kaurava.

Next, set out substances on the inner side of the continent in the east and recite OM YAM GADZA RATNAYA NAMA for the precious elephant. Set out [substances] in the south and recite OM RAM PURUSHA RATNAYA NAMA for the precious householder. Set out in the west and recite OM LAM ASHVA RATNAYA NAMA for the precious horse. Set out in the north and recite OM VAM STRI RATNAYA NAMA for the precious queen. Set out in the southeast and recite OM YAM KHADGA RATNAYA NAMA for the precious general. Set out in the southwest and recite OM RAM CHAKRA RATNAYA NAMA for the precious wheel. Set out in the northwest and recite OM LAM MANI RATNAYA NAMA for the precious jewel. Set out in the northeast and recite OM VAM MAHA NIDHI RATNAYA NAMA for the great treasure vase. Set out in the inner east and recite OM SURYAYA NAMA for the sun. Set out in the inner west and recite OM CHANDRAYA NAMA for the moon. As you do, accurately visualize each of their aspects. Visualize clouds of Samantabhadra's offerings and a pure land completely filled with various jewels. In particular, imagine your own body and enjoyments of the three times together with your virtuous accumulations and imagine you are actually offering them in a variety of various forms set out upon the mandala and recite the words from the ritual text that state:

> My refuge and protector, great treasure of compassion,
> The supreme field of merit, I offer to you with a mind of faith
> A hundred million of the four continents, Mount Meru, and
> The seven major and minor precious possessions of a king—
> A collection of perfect worlds and beings that generate every joy
> As a great treasure of enjoyments and desires of gods and men.

While reciting this you should imagine that you are offering the mandala to the guru and assembly of deities.

Although you may not be able to practice the extensive method with the offering mantras, when you are only utilizing the verses in conjunction with the Lama Chöpa ritual you should follow the system of arranging the heaps during these verses. Regarding the phrase "a hundred million," upon a single massive wind mandala that functions as the lower support is a water mandala. Upon that is the golden base. Upon that golden base are the four continents and each one has an ocean. Those four continents have eight subcontinents [in total]. There are seven golden mountains in the center surrounded by seven alternating oceans with a square Mount Meru in the center that is halfway submerged below the surface of the water and halfway protruding from the surface of the water and is the nature of the four precious substances.[107]

On the four tiers [of Mount Meru] are the abodes of the four *yakshas*: (1) Lagna Zhongthog, (2) Trengthog, (3) Tagnyo, and (4) the four great kings in ascending order. Upon Mount Meru is the heavenly abode of the thirty-three. In the center is the celestial mansion of Indra called Complete Victory and endowed with inconceivable heavenly enjoyments. Regarding the "three thousand worlds," the first "thousand" comprises one thousand similar sets of the four continents together with Mount Meru. The second "thousand" is calculated by counting the first "thousand" a thousand times [which would equal one million]. The third "thousand" is calculated by counting the second "thousand" a thousand more times [a billion]. That is how we calculate the "hundred million of the four continents and Mount Meru." They are all in their three-dimensional aspects and set atop the mandala. And this is not all there is [to imagine], for the *Guide to the Bodhisattva's Way of Life* states:

> On a clean foundation anointed with incense
> And strewn with flowers that please the mind
> I offer to those whose nature is compassion
> A celestial mansion with delightful melodious song
> And beautified with hanging ornaments of precious pearls
> With infinite radiance that illuminates space.

These are generated by the mind and pervade the limitless sky of all worlds and are set upon the mandala and offered.

Regarding the seven jewels, they are (1) the precious wheel, (2) the precious jewel, (3) the precious queen, (4) the precious minister, (5) the precious elephant, (6) the precious supreme horse, and (7) the precious householder.

The precious wheel is produced from gold and has a thousand spokes. It is five hundred leagues[108] in width. It is not made by a blacksmith but is produced through the force of the merit of the *chakravartin* king. It moves

---

107. Gold, silver, ruby, and crystal.
108. Tib. *dpag tshad*. Known as *yojana* in Sanskrit, this is an Indian measure of distance equal to 16,000 cubits, or about 4.5 miles (7.4 km).

through the realms of space like the sun and travels a hundred thousand leagues in a single day. Through the power of the wheel, the chakravartin king and his four branches of soldiers are able to travel through the four continents and the heavenly abodes of the four great kings. Anything that he can imagine is able to be produced by the wheel.

The precious jewel is produced from lapis lazuli. It is eight-faceted and radiates five-colored lights for a hundred leagues and illuminates the night as if it were day. Its light rays cool you when you are hot and warm you when you are cold. Wherever the jewel is placed is a place where sickness and untimely death will not occur. Through the power of the jewel whatever the king imagines is spontaneously accomplished. The precious queen is born into the royal family. She has a beautiful figure. She is not too tall or too short. She is neither too fat nor too thin. She has an auspicious manner and is lovely to behold. Her body has a naturally pleasant scent of sandalwood, camphor, and so on. The scent of *utpala* flowers emerges from her mouth. In whatever land she dwells is a place without hunger and thirst and suffering is dispelled. Merely touching her body bestows supreme bliss and pacifies all physical illnesses and afflictive emotions. She is free from the faults of ordinary women and possesses all good qualities.[109] She is like a mother to all the beings that live in that land. She possesses these and numerous other good qualities.

The precious minister has forsaken all harm and non-Dharmic activities in his relationships with others. He is skilled in all worldly conventions and is without faults. He knows all the wishes of the chakravartin king without needing to be told and fulfills them. In particular, he is empowered and skilled in all the activities of the four branches of the army as well as where to go, where to overthrow, and where to stay. In short, he performs all the activities of the king.

The precious elephant has seven limbs. He is white in color, massive, and is like a traveling great snow mountain. He is endowed with the natural strength of a thousand elephants. If the king commands him, he can circle the world three times in a day. His body emits a naturally sweet scent. He is so wise that he can be led by merely a thread. When traveling

109. This is not to say that women have faults and men don't. Everyone in samsara with afflictive emotions has faults regardless of their sex.

he causes no discomfort to his rider. He moves gently so as not to harm other living creatures. He is victorious over the disputes of all opponents.

The precious horse is white in color. It is adorned with numerous ornaments such as heavenly jewels and so forth and is also adorned with numerous auspicious designs. He is so wise that he protects his rider from all harm. His body is without the faults of sickness and so forth and can circle the world three times in a single day. He does not agitate the body of his rider and is endowed with every beauty.

The precious householder is the royal treasurer for the chakravartin king. He fills the royal treasury with all types of supreme jewels, such as gold, silver, and diamonds. Furthermore, he fills the lands in every direction with a variety of precious jewels, causing their riches to greatly increase and stabilizing them so that they are never depleted. He is utterly free of deceit and never harms other beings. He cares for all beings in his land like a father, and by merely seeing him your mind becomes extremely joyful.

The seven minor precious possessions are (1) the precious sword, (2) the precious hide, (3) the precious bedding, (4) the precious garden, (5) the precious house, (6) the precious garment, and (7) the precious shoes.

Regarding the precious sword, whatever disputes arise against the chakravartin king are dispelled by sending the sword to the place of conflict; without causing any harm to living beings and by merely seeing the sword, they are all brought under his control.

The precious hide is the hide of a great *naga* who lives in the ocean. It is five leagues wide and ten leagues in length. It cannot be burned by fire, it cannot get wet in the rain, and when it is cold it makes you warm. By merely wearing it on your body you are endowed with supreme bliss. Its illumination is vast like the rays of the sun and the moon.

The precious bedding is extremely soft and does not develop depressions but immediately regains its original shape. If you meditate [while sitting] on that bedding, you quickly attain concentration and your intelligence will become very lucid. Whatever afflictive emotions arise, such as attachment and so forth, those afflictive emotions will be pacified by merely sitting on the bedding.

As for the precious garden, if the chakravartin king goes to the garden, every divine enjoyment will emerge from that garden while numerous daughters of the gods are engaged in playing various musical instruments. Only virtuous actions are practiced in that garden.

Regarding the precious house, if the chakravartin king stays there at night, light radiates as if it were day. If you are looking inside from the outside, it is transparent, and if you are looking outside from the inside it is also transparent. It is adorned with various precious jewels. There are many sons and daughters of the gods making offerings. There is never any harm whatsoever from pain, mental suffering, and so forth. It is endowed with immense supreme joy and is the most exalted and special dwelling.

With regard to the precious shoes, they are jeweled shoes that are produced from the merit of the chakravartin king. Once they are put on the feet, he can travel on the water without sinking. If he wishes to go somewhere, he can quickly travel five hundred leagues during which time his body will not become the least bit tired.

Once you visualize the precious jewels upon the mandala in that way, you present them to the guru and assembly of deities. This is a special method for completing a great wave of merit.

For the mandala there are three: (1) the outer mandala, (2) the inner mandala, and (3) the secret and suchness mandala. The way to present the outer mandala was just explained. As for how to present the inner mandala, the parts of your body transform into the various heaps of the mandala, such as the four continents, Mount Meru, and so forth.

Vajradhara Losang Chökyi Gyaltsen stated:

> Your skin is placed upon the beautiful golden ground,
> Your blood is nectar that is used for sprinkling,
> Your flesh and blood are heaped masses of flowers,
> From your limbs emerge the four continents,
> The minor parts of your body are the eight subcontinents,
> Your chest is mountains of stacked jeweled particles,
> Your head is the beautiful celestial palace,
> Your two eyes are the sun and the moon dispelling darkness,
> Your heart is a precious wish-fulfilling jewel,
> And your sense organs and internal organs completely transform
> Into the most excellent and splendid objects of desire of gods
>   and men.

If this excellent mandala, as an ocean of all that is desired,
Is perfectly offered to the root and lineage gurus, Three Jewels,
Buddhas, bodhisattvas, heroes, and yoginis,
Together with an ocean of protectors of the teachings,
Once they accept with their compassion
They will bestow the blessing of attainments.

[Secret and Suchness Mandala]

Visualizing yourself as the father and mother desire deities, you generate the special exalted wisdom of bliss and emptiness. Or, if you are not able to do that, once you imagine you generate it, you then imagine that [the exalted wisdom of bliss and emptiness] appears as the various offering substances, such as the four continents, Mount Meru, and so forth. This is a highly praised method for completing your collection of merit.

The eighth chapter of *Guhyasamaja Root Tantra* states:

This land and the seven types of jewels
Are completely filled by the wise
For the sake of bestowing all desired attainments
And are offered with wisdom every day.

For those wishing to attain the supreme attainment of the mahamudra, it is stated that they should fill the three thousand worlds with the seven types of jewels and offer them repeatedly.

The *Fifty Verses of Guru Devotion*, which presents the fundamental meaning of the tantra, states:

With a mandala and flowers in the palm of your hands
Respectfully honor your teacher-guru
And prostrate with his feet on your head.

Thus, each and every day you should prostrate to your guru and deity. Offering the mandala is also taught as one of the commitments of mantra; therefore, it is extremely important. Having understood this point, the previous lamas gave separate profound commentaries on the mandala as one of the preliminary guides.[110] This very commentary on the mandala offering for accumulating merit is one of the "four great preliminary guides" for Ganden mahamudra.

Offering Your Practice

The ritual text states:

> From the purity of samsara and nirvana, both set out and
>   imagined,
> I offer this delightful garden to please the venerable guru.
> On the banks of an ocean are offering substances that arise
> With a broad thousand-petaled lotus—the source and nature
>   of all mundane and supramundane joy,
> Blooming with flowers that are the virtues of the three doors
>   of myself and others,
> With a hundred thousand scents of Samantabhadra's offerings and
> Endowed with the fruits of the three trainings, the two stages,
>   and the five paths.

With this, whatever virtuous accumulations that you have amassed in the past as well as those that you will accumulate in the future take on the form of pleasure groves that you then offer. Furthermore, you offer your virtues that you actually have presently, such as the moral discipline of your vows and so forth, as well as those that you don't presently have in your mental continuum and those that will arise in your mental continuum in the future by training in the common path together with the path and the result of the uncommon generation and completion stage. They all assume the aspect of visual objects that you then offer. This is taught as a special pith instruction of dependent relationship. You are not only offering your own roots of virtue but the virtues of all ordinary and superior beings as well, which are mentally created into form and offered.

---

110. This is referring to the preliminaries such as refuge and bodhichitta, Vajrasattva recitation, mandala offerings, and so on.

This is a very important skillful means of magical transformation of the Mahayana.

The *Sutra of King Prasenajit's Instructions*[111] states:

> If such a great king as yourself, with many deeds and many activities, is incapable of training in the perfection of generosity up to the training in the perfection of wisdom in every possible aspect of every possible time of day and night, yet you, great king, aspire for perfect complete enlightenment with faith and diligence, then whether you are sending forth benedictions, whether you are standing, whether you are sitting, whether you are lying down, whether you are eating, or whether you are drinking, you should rejoice by always retaining in your mind and always being mindful in your daily actions of the merits of the buddhas and bodhisattvas, the arya shravakas, the pratyeka buddhas, each and every living being, as well as your past, future, and present roots of virtue, which are all consolidated, analyzed, and calculated.
>
> The supreme form of rejoicing is like the sky and such a rejoicing is equal to nirvana. Once you have rejoiced, you should present offerings to all the buddhas, bodhisattvas, arya shravakas, and the pratyeka buddhas. Once they are offered, they are joined together with [the merits of] all living beings. Next, up to the attainment of omniscience, and until you perfectly complete all the teachings of the Buddha, you should dedicate [these merits] toward unsurpassed perfect complete enlightenment during the three times each day.
>
> Great King, if you conjoin [your merit] in that way, you can also engage in your royal duties without your royal activities degenerating and you will also perfectly complete your accumulations for enlightenment. Great King, you will also ripen your roots of virtue for the perfect and complete mind of enlightenment, whereby you will be reborn many times as a god, you will be reborn many times as a human, and when

111. *gSal rgyal la gdams pa'i mdo.*

you take rebirth as a god or human you will act as a ruler. What's more, Great King, your roots of virtue for the mind of perfect complete enlightenment will also never decrease. However, Great King, if the roots of virtue that come from a single mind of completely perfect unsurpassed enlightenment focusing on the liberation of all living beings, focusing on the [future] liberation of all living beings, focusing on relieving the suffering of all living beings, focusing on the complete liberation of all living beings are innumerable and so forth, what need is there to mention someone engaging in many such [aspirations for enlightenment]?

Thus, once you have arranged the virtuous roots of yourself and others, offer them to the guru and assembly of deities, whereby the guru and assembly of deities give birth to an immeasurable special unsurpassed bliss in their mental continuums that is inconceivable and beyond description. Furthermore, they perfect the abandonment and realizations of the buddhas and completely perfect all of their good qualities. Although they are utterly without the need to attain new good qualities, for the sake of yourself as the practitioner completing your collection of merit, you are training your mind by imagining that they give birth to immeasurable great bliss in their mental continuums that they did not previously possess, whereby their minds are extremely pleased. This is praised in the Mahayana sutras. The dedication of Dorje Gyaltsen in the *Avatamsaka Sutra* contains an extensive explanation of how all the virtues of the three times in general, and whatever appears to each of your six senses in particular, are all visualized as offering substances and offered to the buddhas. With regard to how to imagine that the buddhas are delighted by that offering, the same sutra [*Avatamsaka Sutra*] states:

> Through this thorough dedication may those buddha tathagatas also come to possess inconceivable bliss and abide in the state of enlightenment. Through that incomparable bliss of the buddhas' concentration may they perfectly grasp the incomparable bliss of a buddha's concentration. May they perfectly stabilize the limitless bliss of a buddha. May

they come to possess the immeasurable bliss of a buddha's liberation. May they perfectly grasp the limitless bliss of a buddha's miraculous emanations. May they perfectly grasp the inconceivable bliss of a buddha dwelling in a state free of attachment. May they perpetually find the bliss of a bull-like buddha's perfect power that is difficult to obtain. May they come to have perfect bliss through the limitless bliss of a buddha's power. May they come to unchanging bliss through the pacification of all feelings and nonproduction. May they come to have immutable bliss without having to apply the two types of mental stabilization through constantly abiding in the nonattachment of a tathagata. In this way, bodhisattvas thoroughly dedicate the roots of virtue of the tathagatas.

In the same way, by offering your roots of virtue to the bodhisattvas, you should imagine that the fields of merit generate immeasurable bliss in their mental continuum, whereby you are creating the conditions for quickly completing the grounds and paths. Likewise, by offering [your roots of virtue] to the shravakas, they generate bliss in their mental continuum and, once they purify the subtle defilements of their individual abodes, they enter the Mahayana. There are extensive explanations regarding how this creates the conditions to quickly complete the grounds and paths. I am unable to expound on them all here; therefore, those possessing intelligence should learn about it from the precious sutras themselves. Furthermore, the way the practitioner presents the offerings is extremely easy to understand and is clearly expressed.

> Hearing is an ocean of drinking water swirling in every
>   direction;
> My good qualities are flowers; moral discipline is clouds
>   of incense;
> My wisdom is a lamp; faith is a lake of perfume;
> My concentration is supreme nectar-food;
> Singing songs of praise produces the sweet sound of music;
> My sharp intellect of universal compassion
> Is hoisted umbrellas, victory banners, and pendants;

My body is a storied celestial mansion fully adorned.
May the Dharma-lord remain forever
As the drop in the center of the lotus petal in the center
    of my heart
Upon its vast petals to receive my offerings.
Through my supplications made with a mind of intense
    yearning,
May the guru of migrators be eternally pleased,
May the king of the Dharma be eternally pleased.

And:

From the roots of extensive learning of the great scriptures
Amid a great ocean of pure moral discipline
With a hundred thousand vast limbs of stainless reasoning
And scattered flowers born from certain knowledge that does
    depend on others
The honey-nectar forms from the stamen of the three principal
    paths,
The grounds and paths of earth, gold, moon, and so forth[112]
Are unimaginable pleasure groves adorned with perfect fruit;
I offer these for the sake of pleasing the kind and supreme gurus.

I offer a swirling ocean of refreshing drinking water of the
    seven abandonments,[113]
Faith as flowers and moral discipline as sweet-smelling incense,
Hearing as a lamp and giving as scented water,
The pliancy of concentration as nectar-food,

The three wisdoms as a variety of music,[114]
Self-respect and modesty as a variety of desirable objects;

112. This is in reference to the twenty-two types of bodhichitta, such as the earth-like, gold-like, moon-like, and so forth. For a complete description, see Geshe Acharya Thubten Loden, *Path to Enlightenment in Tibetan Buddhism* (Melbourne: Tushita Publications, 1993), 512–21.
113. The seven abandonments are the three nonvirtues of body and the four of speech.
114. The three wisdoms are listening, contemplation, and meditation.

These ocean-clouds of completely pure offerings
I present to please the assembly of root and lineage gurus.

It would be extremely excellent if—once you have arranged your good qualities, such as the three higher trainings as well as listening, contemplating, and meditating in the aspect of forms—you present these offerings to the guru and assembly of deities. Furthermore, even if you don't recite these words and instead recite the section from the ritual text that states, "On the banks of an ocean are offering substances that arise . . ." you visualize these things at that time and then offer them with the visualization.

Inner Offering Related to the Secret Empowerment

The ritual text states:

I offer this drink of China tea endowed with the glories
Of a hundred flavors and with an excellent scent as
The five hooks, the five lamps, and so forth,
Purified, transformed, and increased into an ocean
    of nectar.

Regarding the phrase "I offer this drink of China tea," there is a tradition of explaining it by subsuming it within the outer offering, yet I wonder if there would be any contradiction in subsuming it within the inner offering. It would be most appropriate to use China tea as the basis of your inner offering liquid, and the previous holy beings that were the custodians of this system of the precious Ganden Oral Lineage[115] have stated numerous times that the [moral discipline of] the pratimoksha is the foundation of the teachings and is cherished as being extremely important; therefore, it appears that they used tea as the liquid basis for their inner offering. In any case, with regard to drinking tea, it is considered the drink of sages and is explained in the Vinaya scriptures as one of the

115. Tib. *dGa' ldan bka' rgyud rin po che*. Sometimes the "bka' rgyud" section of this phrase is interpreted as referring to the Kagyu tradition of Tibetan Buddhism; however, by reading the following sentences it becomes clear that it is in reference to the Gelug lineage.

eight drinks of sages. Regarding apple, the fruit of a banana tree, juniper tree, winter cherry plant,[116] udumbara lotus,[117] a forest,[118] grape juice, and dates,[119] these are praised by the *rishis* of old. And the Buddha gave his permission to drink them at the appropriate time. In addition to drinking tea, the *rishis* also praised extracting the essence of the other parts [of the plant], such as the leaves.[120] By doing so, your mind becomes clear, enunciation is easy, you can walk quickly, and when engaging in virtuous actions your awareness will be sharp and lucid, and so forth. Many of the previous holy beings have sung its many praises. In particular, Glorious Atisha was extremely pleased and said that it is acceptable to drink tea in the afternoon like they do in Tibet and that the ordained Tibetans have great merit to be able to drink it.

Regarding the way to present the offering of tea, this is in accordance with the well-known system, or in accordance with the oral precepts that offer it in conjunction with the secret system of mantra composed by Khedrup Sangye Yeshe, which states:

> This ocean of tea offering of perfect great bliss
> I offer to please my venerable root guru
> From within the state of expansive spontaneous great bliss;
> Grant your blessing that our minds may mix as one.

You should imagine you are presenting the offering in this way and are receiving blessings.

As for how to present the inner offering, you cleanse, purify, generate, and bless by purifying, transforming, and increasing the inner offering substances that consist of the five meats, the five nectars, and so forth. You should emanate countless Rasavajra goddesses from your heart that scoop up [the inner offering] as an ocean of nectar with skull cups and offer it to the guru and assembly of deities, whereby you imagine they generate a

116. *Physalis flexuosalin.*
117. Tib. *u dum ba ra*; *Ficus glomerata.*
118. Tib. *rtsub 'gyur.*
119. Tib. *'bra go.*
120. For more on the appropriate food and drink for the Sangha, see Jamgön Kongtrul Lodrö Tayé, *Buddhist Ethics* (Ithaca, NY: Snow Lion Publications, 1998), 140.

special uncontaminated bliss in their mental continuums. The five meats are called "the five hooks" and the five nectars are called "the five lamps." There are also reasons for addressing them in this way. When you purify, transform, and increase the five meats and the five nectars and offer them to the guru and assembly of deities as well as taste them yourself, you quickly summon all attainments and illuminate all the attainments. Furthermore, if you enjoy these special secret substances once they have been blessed by mantras, it will give strength and stamina to your vajra body, you will live a long time, and these special substances will bless your channels, winds, and drops, whereby they will become serviceable. You will be able to penetrate the vital points of your vajra body, which will become the cause for attaining the highest realizations of the profound completion stage in this life. For these reasons the five meats are praised as "the five hooks" and the five nectars as "the lamps." Applying the conventional designations to the five meats and the five nectars with this meaning contained in the terms "hooks" and "lamps" comes from the *Heruka Explanatory Tantra Samvarodaya*, which states:

> Flesh, fat, and likewise blood
> Should be apprehended by the wise.
> The practitioners who desire attainments
> Should address all that exists as "the five lamps."
> Or, in this case it is killing that is primarily explained;
> If that is perfectly obtained, capture it.

> Bull meat, horse meat,
> Elephant meat, and likewise
> Human flesh and dog meat
> Should be apprehended by the wise.

> The well-known term transmitted
> By Vajrasattva was "the five lamps."

This clearly explains the process of identifying the substances and addressing them as "the five hooks and the five lamps."

The *Cluster of Oral Instructions* by Master Abhyakara also states:

> These "hooks" are likewise for the sake of drawing the objects that one deeply desires near and are therefore called "hooks." The five exalted wisdoms are in the aspect of the perfectly pure exalted wisdoms and so forth. For the sake of these we are capable of works of great importance; therefore, they are great exalted wisdoms. We imagine these aspects as the five tathagatas that are the nature of the five exalted wisdoms, and they are called the "five lamps and the five hooks."

This plainly explains how the substances are the nature of the five exalted wisdoms and why they are called "the five hooks and the five lamps."

If we are unable to acquire all of the actual five meats and five nectars as the substances of the inner offering, the seventeenth chapter of the *Guhyasamaja Root Tantra* clearly explains what to do by stating that once you obtain a properly produced nectar pill, it is also completely appropriate to place it in the basis for your inner offering such as beer, and if you can't get even that, you just use beer. Otherwise, if you are uncomfortable because you feel it is imperative not to use [alcohol], you can use a tea broth or at the very least water. This is explained in the *Cluster of Oral Instructions*.

Whatever basis you use for your inner offering, it is that very [substance] that should be imagined as the five meats and the five nectars. Once you do, it is suitable to accomplish. The *Guhyasamaja Root Tantra* states:

> Although you may be without all of the meats,
> You should impute them all with the imagination.

This is very clear.

Thus, presenting the inner offering to the guru and assembly of deities once you properly accomplish it is highly praised. The fourth chapter of the *Guhyasamaja Root Tantra* states:

> Feces, urine, semen, blood, and so forth
> Should be offered to the deities;
> Having done so, the very famous
> Buddhas and bodhisattvas are delighted.

It is also stated during the "offering to the guru" in the eighth chapter of the [*Guhyasamaja*] *Root Tantra*:

> Having contemplated the mudra of the lord,
> In the center of the buddha mandala
> With a mind inclined toward desire
> You should offer the contact of union to the Buddha.
>
> You should meditate on the mandala that
> Is displayed amid the sphere of space.
> And with the body of the tathagata
> Offer feces and urine to the guru.

This clearly states that you should offer both the inner offering and the secret offering to the guru.

With regard to these verses for offering, the mandala ritual of Guhyasamaja takes from the teachings in the *Explanatory Tantra Vajramala* which states:

> This food of the five nectars,
> It is the supreme activator of all attainments.
> I present it as an offering to the mandala.
> Protector, please accept this offering and keep me
> In your thoughts with your mind of compassion.

The meaning of these verses has been arranged here [in Lama Chöpa] as oral instructions.

When you are giving a commentary on the two stages, as well as at special times and so forth, you should perform a ganachakra at this point during the inner offering. Numerous mahasiddhas of India also taught a variety of ways to present the ganachakra in the mandala rituals.[121]

Regarding the ganachakra, it compensates for your broken and defiled

---

121. "Mandala rituals" refers to rituals that utilize a mandala, such as self-initiation and extensive offering ceremonies.

commitments, it performs the function of delighting the heroes and dakinis, it quickly engages the blessings of the guru and assembly of deities in general, and it functions to quickly generate realizations of the higher paths. For these reasons, it is taught in numerous tantras and texts of the mahasiddhas that you should repeatedly perform the tsok offering.[122] In particular, how to perform a ganachakra is explained in the sixteenth chapter of the *Guhyasamaja Tantra*, and it states that if you perform the ganachakra properly, you will quickly reach attainments. The *Explanatory Tantra Vajramala* provides an extensive explanation on how to perform a ganachakra, what sort of tsok substances you need to perform the ganachakra, the tsok for the vajra master, [the characteristics and qualification of] the action-vajra, what sort of characteristics each of the members of the tsok are required to have, how to perform the ritual, and so forth. These are all extensively explained in the *Guhyasamaja Explanatory Tantra Vajramala* as well as in the *Heruka Explanatory Tantra Samvarodaya*, the *Ocean of Dakinis*,[123] and so forth. In particular, the *Ocean of Dakinis* states that for your commitment, the best thing is to offer a ganachakra every day and if that is not possible, once a month, and at the very least you should offer a ganachakra once a year. I won't be able to set forth how to [perform a tsok offering] in detail because this text would become far too verbose. However, I will set forth a brief presentation of the most necessary things to know when performing the ganachakra.

You should set out clean ganachakra substances and the appropriate articles for practice. You need an assembly of practitioners who have received a highest yoga tantra empowerment and properly maintain their commitments. If you are performing it at this point during Lama Chöpa, since you have already blessed [the various offering substances] earlier, there is no fault if you don't do it again at this point. Also, for the sake of visualization, if you bless the environment and so forth, you should recite the section from the [ganachakra] ritual text that states:

---

122. There are two different terms being used here. One is *tshogs mchod*, which I am translating as "tsok offering," and the other is *tshogs 'khor*, for which I am providing the original Sanskrit term as "ganachakra."

123. *mKha' 'gro rgya mtsho.*

EH MA HO: Great manifestation of exalted wisdom,
All lands are vajra-lands
And all abodes are great vajra-palaces with
A radiant ocean of clouds of Samantabhadra's offerings.

An abundance of glorious enjoyments,
All beings are actual heroes and heroines.
Without even the mistaken imputation "impurity"
There is only limitless purity.

The [two verses above] bless the environment. Next, you bless the tsok substance like you do the inner offering with [the four stages of] clearance, purification, generation, and blessing. Next, for the actual ganachakra offering, you recite the section from the [ganachakra] ritual text that states:

HO: This ocean of tsok offering of uncontaminated nectar
Blessed by concentration, mantra, and mudra
I offer to delight the assembly of root and lineage gurus.
OM AH HUM
Satiated by this glorious display of all that is desired,
EH MA HO
Please send down a great rain of blessings.

HO: This ocean of tsok offering of uncontaminated nectar
Blessed by concentration, mantra, and mudra
I offer to delight the assembly of yidams and mandala deities.
OM AH HUM
Satiated by this glorious display of all that is desired,
EH MA HO
Please send down a great rain of attainments.

HO: This ocean of tsok offering of uncontaminated nectar
Blessed by concentration, mantra, and mudra
I offer to delight the assembly of Three Precious Jewels.
OM AH HUM

Satiated by this glorious display of all that is desired,
EH MA HO
Please send down a great rain of holy Dharma.

HO: This ocean of tsok offering of uncontaminated nectar
Blessed by concentration, mantra, and mudra
I offer to delight the assembly of dakinis and Dharma protectors.
OM AH HUM
Satiated by this glorious display of all that is desired,
EH MA HO
Please send down a great rain of enlightened actions.

HO: This ocean of tsok offering of uncontaminated nectar
Blessed by concentration, mantra, and mudra
I offer to delight the assembly of mother sentient beings.
OM AH HUM
Satiated by this glorious display of all that is desired,
EH MA HO
Please pacify mistaken impure appearances.

Next, the action-vajra holds up the first select portion and recites:

EH MA HO
You who have followed the path of the sugatas of the three times,
By realizing that you, the great hero,
Are the source of all attainments,
I forsake the mind of conceptualization;
Continuously partake in this circle of tsok.
A LA LA HO

After which [the action-vajra] offers it to the hands of the vajra master.
Next, he sequentially offers it to all the practitioners. Next, they all hold
the tsok substance in their hands and the master recites:

OM: With a nature inseparable from the three vajras
I appear clearly as the guru-deity.

AH: This uncontaminated nectar of exalted wisdom,
HUM: Without wavering from the mind of enlightenment,
I partake to satiate the deities dwelling in my body.

AH HO MAHA SUKHA

There are ways of practicing that incorporate the outer, inner, secret, and suchness ganachakra; therefore, you should at least train your mind through mere imagination to establish whatever imprints you can.

Next, you collect the leftover tsok offering substances and place them in a clean container such as a copper basin and bless them as you would the inner offering. Invoke the assembly of oath-bound field protectors and recite:

HO: This ocean of remaining tsok offering of uncontaminated
   nectar
Blessed by concentration, mantra, and mudra
I offer to delight the assembly of oath-bound field protectors.
OM AH HUM
Satiated by this glorious display of all that is desired,
EH MA HO
Please accomplish appropriate actions for the yogi.

HO: By offering this ocean of remaining tsok offering
To the remaining guests and their retinue,
May the precious teachings flourish.

May the holders of the teachings, the benefactors, and
I, the yogi, and those in my retinue
Be free of sickness, obtain a long life, power,
Glory, fame, good fortune,
Vast enjoyments, and all attainments.
Please bestow the attainments of
The actions, such as pacifying, increasing, and so forth.
Those who possess the commitments, please protect me,
Bestow assistance in all attainments,

Eliminate bad times, death and sickness,
Harm from interfering and harmful spirits,
Eradicate bad dreams, bad signs,
And bad actions.

May there be happiness in the world
And excellent years,
May our crops increase and the Dharma flourish,
And may peace and excellence and everything supreme
Arise according to my wishes.

Recite whatever other dedication prayers are appropriate.

Secret Offering Related to the Wisdom Empowerment

The ritual text states:

I offer beautiful, voluptuous, illusory-like consorts,
A host of messengers born from mantra, places, and
    spontaneously born,
With slender figures, in the bloom of youth,
And skilled in the sixty-four arts of love.

Regarding the visualization to keep in mind, emanate an inconceivable number of magically created field-born, mantra-born, and spontaneously born messengers from your heart. Among those three you primarily emanate countless mantra-born dakinis as lotus-shaped, conch-shaped, elephant-shaped, and deer-shaped messengers. They have beautiful and pleasing colors and shapes, with the countenance of a sixteen-year-old maiden. They glance with desirous eyes and are adorned with numerous precious jewels. In particular, they have hanging garlands of pearls, their breasts are voluptuous, and they have narrow cleavage. Their garments are slightly loosened to reveal the beautiful lower parts of their bodies. They sing melodious vajra songs and a sweet scent spontaneously emerges from their bodies, and they are endowed with an amazing sweet taste similar to honey. They are soft to the touch, they have extremely slender waists, and their wide navels swirl to the right. Their lower parts and genitals are thick. They move slowly and gracefully and are skilled in the sixty-four arts of love. They appear as precious women that are magically created by an illusionist; they lack inherent existence and fill the realms of space. They all dissolve into Vajradhatu Ishvari, the Mother of Lama Tubwang Dorje Chang, who is the principal of the field of merit. Because of this, he gives birth to a special exalted wisdom of simultaneously born great bliss in his mental continuum, whereby he is delighted and satiated. Since all the beings of the field of merit are manifestations of Lama Tubwang Dorje Chang, imagine that they are all satiated and delighted by uncontaminated great bliss.

Regarding being skilled in the sixty-four arts of love, in general there are many skillful arts. The Vinaya scriptures speak of the sixty-four skillful arts such as shooting arrows, a protection wheel of swords, and so forth, which are different special unique qualities of an ordinary being. Regarding the skilled arts in this teaching, they are similar to those in the treatises that explain the arts of intercourse and have aspects that are similar to the sixty-four arts of love. Furthermore, the commentary on the *Vajradaka* explains them as embracing, kissing, biting, scratching, perfect movement, making erotic noises, the woman acting like a man, and lying on top; these are the eight primary arts. Each one of those eight has an internal division of eight, thereby equaling sixty-four. If you are wondering what they are for, through the power of these skillful arts the yoginis generate numerous aspects of the most exalted simultaneously born great bliss in the practitioner.

To whatever degree you increase spontaneously born [bliss], to the same extent you will be free from the extreme of conceptual elaborations and your mode of apprehending emptiness as the mode of existence will exponentially increase. To whatever degree that increases, to that extent you will quickly destroy self-grasping and its imprints, which are the root of samsara, after which you will become enlightened with unprecedented swiftness. It is for that reason that they are called "messengers." As you can see, the only similarity this bears to the treatises that explain the arts of love is its name. Their meaning is utterly different. The arts of love explained in the treatises on sex are the means for increasing your afflictive emotions, whereas what is explained here is the method used to abandon afflictive emotions. Furthermore, in the Perfection Vehicle, until you have the full capacity of completion, maturation, and cultivation, it is inappropriate to put all your energy into abandoning afflictive emotions and you should instead primarily apply yourself to the accumulation of merit, whereas here in the highest yoga tantra vehicle there are occasions where it is permissible to put all your energy into abandoning afflictive emotions [by bringing them into the path]. Furthermore, having seen that the entirety of samsara is like a mass of blazing fire, you overcome your attachment and cultivate powerful renunciation. And once you see that your old mothers, who are as pervasive as space, have fallen into the dreadful ocean of samsara, you next elicit an extremely powerful mind of bodhichitta for an extremely long period of time and generate the profound view of the Middle Way in your mental continuum that is capable of destroying the view grasping at the signs [of true existence] so that not even an atom [of inherent existence] remains. You then combine these [qualities mentioned above] with exalted wisdom of simultaneously born great bliss while perfecting the yoga of the first stage and perfecting the three isolations[124] of the second stage. Many of the tantras and texts of the mahasiddhas state that it is permissible to carry out your practice in this way. In particular, the *Lamp for Compendium of Practice Elucidating the Meaning of the Five Stages*[125] also explains that there is a definite order of the path from the preliminaries up to—if you fully realize the generation of the exalted wisdom of the ultimate isolated mind—the practice of combining the exalted wisdom of simultaneously born clear light.

If you don't develop an understanding of the essential points of the path in that way, saying, "I engage in the path of the desirable object of secret mantra" will be mere words, and being fascinated with this you will drink alcohol, eat in the afternoon,[126] and shamelessly engage in your desires. In this way, you will be deceiving yourself and will be accomplishing the causes for the unbearable hell realms. The vajra-dakinis will punish you

---

124. The three isolations are isolated body, isolated speech, and isolated mind.

125. *Rim lnga'i don 'grel spyod bsdus sgron ma.* This is a famous text by Aryadeva entitled *Caryāmelāpakapradīpa* in Sanskrit.

126. Here, Kachen Yeshe Gyaltsen is addressing fully ordained monks who have vowed not to eat after noon.

with their wrath and in this life numerous harmful afflictions will plague your aggregates, such as contagious diseases, harm from spirits, and so forth. There are immeasurable damages that are spoken of, such as the great harm caused to the root of the Conqueror's teaching.[127] The *Glorious Guhyasamaja Explanatory Tantra That Prophesies Realization*[128] states:

> Beings of the future
> Will run after the eight worldly concerns;
> Dwelling in mistaken views
> They will indulge in any and all desires.
> Some will delight in singing and dancing
> And pursue laughing and flirting,
> Delighting in scents and garlands
> And likewise delighting in obscene language.
> Ignorant, some are angry and
> Likewise pursue foolishness.
> Some likewise grasp with attachment,
> Aware of others they become desirous.
> Fish, flesh, and likewise beer,
> Ordinary beings cover up
> Feces, urine, semen, and blood, and devour them.
> While proclaiming the Dharma of nihilists
> They have intercourse with those with whom they should
> Not have intercourse, such as their mothers and sisters.
> They kill their fathers and mothers as well
> And likewise kill other living beings.
> The very words they speak are lies.
> In particular, they also steal and
> Make advances toward another's wife
> While engaging in criticizing others.
> Some abandon the holy Dharma
> And likewise perform the [five] heinous actions.
> Although they engage in a variety of negative actions
> They still wish for the attainments of mantra.

127. The pratimoksha.
128. *dGongs pa lung bstan pa'i rgyud; Saṃdhivyākaraṇatantra.*

In this day and age, once you have intertwined your faults with mantra, you shamelessly engage in the objects of desire, and in particular you delight in sexual intercourse and wrathful actions that inflict harm and injury upon other beings while drinking beer and eating in the afternoon without restraint. You claim, "all phenomena are mistaken appearances" and fixate on the view of nihilism and so forth. These bad conducts and views that we now possess were all clearly prophesied.

What's more, in this day and age these various bad actions are for the most part appearing as prophesied, and once you intertwine your faults with mantra and engage in crude behavior, you have ruined both this life and your future lives. This very same tantra [the *Tantra That Prophesies Realization*] states:

> Painful illnesses, poison, and poison potions—
> Once these various overwhelming
> Illnesses become unbearable,
> You desire their pacification.
> Yet rejecting [the correct path] out of ignorance
> And performing terrible negativity,
> You pursue mistaken views
> And travel to the three lower realms.

The *Accomplishment of Secrets* also states:

> That very lord of precious jewels
> Abandons all disputes.
> Yet once he forsakes the excellent methods
> And then practices something different
> That contradicts his commitments and so on,
> He will lament while he roasts [in the fires of hell]
> And is set ablaze in such flames.
> When he enters [hell], the heaps of roots
> And trees will become ash
> And sprouts and so forth will not grow,
> And that itself will be as if nonexistent.
> Producing such incredible events,
> He will abide there for as long as space exists.

After death he will go to hell
And meet a variety of poisonous snakes.
Without the aid of medicine, mantra, and so on,
Whatever he enjoys is the nature of ignorance.
As he considers going to the abode of Yama,
In such an endless ocean
He will enter many other boats;
But without a method and support,
In an instant he will die.

Likewise, the tantra ending in the word DZA
Has thoroughly forsaken the use of intercourse.[129]
Having performed such vile and base actions,
You will go to the Avici Hell.

Having attributed your faults to mantra, you shamelessly engage in actions such as drinking beer, eating in the afternoon, having sexual intercourse, and so forth, through which you will experience inconceivable karmic effects, such as having to remain in hell for as long as space exists and so forth.

Examining the shapes of those messengers' bodies, the places from where they come, the special actions they perform, what special characteristics they possess, and so forth are all given special detail in the *Heruka Root Tantra*[130] and its explanatory tantras, such as the *Samvarodaya*, *Vajradaka*, and so forth, where they are clearly explained. They can also be found in the texts of Guhyasamaja in the Jnanapada tradition, such as the *Oral Instructions of Manjushri*, and in *A Lamp for the Compendium of Practice* in the Arya Tradition.

129. I was unable to ascertain the tantra being referenced to as "DZA"; however, Sharpa Tulku explained that this is taking the other extreme with regard to the use of intercourse on the path to enlightenment. The previous verses reveal the extreme of abusing the use of intercourse in the practice of tantra, whereas here the tantra ending in DZA has made the error of forsaking it entirely.
130. For a translation of the *Chakrasamvara Root Tantra*, see David Gonsalez, trans., *The Chakrasamvara Root Tantra* (Seattle: Dechen Ling Press, 2010).

Suchness Offering Related to the Word Empowerment

The ritual text states:

> I offer you the supreme ultimate bodhichitta
> Beyond words, thoughts, and expressions;
> The sphere of reality; all phenomena free from the
> Elaborations of inherent existence as the great exalted
>   wisdom of
> Spontaneous bliss liberated from obstruction.

Through the force of having previously offered those special messengers, the guru and the assembly of deities give birth to the unsurpassed ultimate bliss that is the spontaneously born exalted wisdom that is free from obstruction and is inseparable from emptiness as the fundamental nature of reality, through which you imagine that their minds are satiated by the offering of suchness. Through the power of the inconceivable compassion and blessing of the guru and the assembly of deities—that never wavers from that ultimate unsurpassed bliss—you should stabilize your conviction that you yourself attain the very same extraordinary simultaneously born exalted wisdom and the body of union.

Thus, this way of presenting the inner offering, secret offering, and suchness offering is repeatedly taught in the *Glorious Guhyasamaja Root Tantra* and in particular in the eighth chapter, on offering to the guru and assembly of deities, which states:

> Those wishing for enlightenment eternally worship by
> Commencing with an ocean of offerings consisting of
> The five objects of desire,
> Precious garments, and so forth.

> You should eternally delight the deities
> With the five supreme aspects of offering
> And supreme young girls that are Ratnasambhava
> And are adorned with various supreme jewels.

> For the sake of accomplishing siddhis in all your lives
> You should present offerings to all the buddhas.

This clearly states that in general you should present offerings of everything you possess, and in particular you should present offerings of the messengers. As for the phrase "You should present offerings to all the buddhas," this is explained in the commentary to mean that you offer to the guru, who is the nature of all the buddhas. If we think about this excellent method, we will understand what an absolutely great treasure guru yoga is.

I have already cited the fourth chapter of the [*Guhyasamaja*] *Root Tantra* as the source for how to present the inner offering. When presenting the secret offering you should imagine that from the most subtle particles of the father and mother's bodhichitta emerge conqueror fathers and mothers that fill the realm of space. They enter into embrace [with the guru], whereby their minds are satiated by simultaneously born bliss and are delighted by the secret and suchness offerings. The fourth chapter of the [*Guhyasamaja*] *Root Tantra* states:

> Having emanated buddhas from the abode of peace,
> They perfectly adorn the sphere of space.

And:

> If you practice in that way, the buddhas
> And bodhisattvas will be delighted.

The *Explanatory Tantra Vajramala* states:

> The age of their slender bodies is that of a sixteen-year-old,
> They are adorned with form and good fortune,
> Their pale green eyes are broad and look
> With compassionate thoughts and perfect longing;
> They have a melodious voice and have obtained
>   empowerment
> With superior devotion for yoga tantra.

Once [this text] has explained the many enumerations of the characteristics of the messengers, it explains that in that way you should imagine presenting an offering of those messengers to Guru-Vajradhara and concludes with "You should offer them to the guru." Although this makes nothing more than a mention of their mere illustrations, they are taught in all the highest yoga tantras and not just once either. To understand all the essential points of all four offerings of outer, inner, secret, and suchness, the first thing to know is the system for properly establishing the seeds of the four bodies at the time of the empowerment; then, which empowerment functions on which path; then, understanding just how each of the uncommon commitments of each empowerment correlates with those [paths]; then, during your practice, you should understand how to generate within your mental continuum the various stages from the path of the generation stage of the vase empowerment up to union of the fifth stage of the fourth empowerment without diverging from the meaning of the four empowerments.[131]

If you develop such an understanding, you will attain an uncommon faith and confidence in Vajradhara Jetsun Losang Chökyi Gyaltsen's vajra words of oral instructions on the Hearing Lineage of Conqueror Tsongkhapa and come to hold these as the supreme instructions.

The Way to Offer Medicine and Oneself as a Servant[132]

The ritual text states:

> I offer numerous types of excellent medicine
> That destroy the illness of the 404 delusions,
> And to please you, I offer myself as your servant;
> Please hold me as your disciple for as long as space exists.

---

131. The generation stage is related to the vase empowerment, the secret empowerment is related to the illusory body, the wisdom mudra empowerment is related to the clear light, and the word empowerment is related to the union of the clear light and illusory body.

132. Here the headings diverge slightly from the outline. At this point there is a separate heading for offering medicine and oneself as a servant, while the section for upholding the vows comes next with its own separate heading.

You offer all the special medicine in existence for dispelling the illnesses that are produced from the corresponding nonvirtuous actions of living beings in general and in particular offer yourself as a servant to Lama Tubwang Dorje Chang. The *Explanatory Tantra Vajramala* states:

> Once you offer gold, jeweled garments,
> And various flower garlands
> Set before the guru,
> The disciple speaks thus:
> "From this day forth, I am your servant;
> Principal, please accept my offerings."
> After which you should please him with expressions
>   such as
> "I will always worship the guru,
> The guru is in essence Vajradhara,
> Therefore, I perfectly worship the guru."

Thus, this clearly states that in general you should offer everything you have in worship of your guru and in particular offer yourself as a servant. The *Heruka Root Tantra* also states:

> [Then make excellent offerings to the guru.
> For the teachings of the tathagata offer]
> One hundred thousand gold [coins]
> And a variety of precious things,
> A hundred pairs of clothing,
> Horses, elephants, and the kingdom,
> Earrings, and bangles,
> Necklaces, and excellent rings for the fingers,
> A sacrificial thread made of gold,
> Your excellent wife and daughter herself,
> Male and female servants, and [even] your sisters.
>
> After making prostrations offer [these].
> Thus, according to the teachings the disciple
> Should thoughtfully offer themself to the guru,
> As well as all other offerings.

> From that time forth, you become a servant [of the guru],
> [Saying,] "I offer myself to you as your servant."

In general you present offerings to the empowering guru, and in particular you offer yourself as a servant, which accords with the teaching mentioned earlier. The same thing is taught in many other tantras, such as the *Samvarodaya* and so forth. There are also many teachings in the lower classes of tantra and the sutras that state the essential thing is to offer yourself as a servant. The *Guide to the Bodhisattva's Way of Life* states:

> Now and always, I offer my body to
> The conquerors and bodhisattvas;
> May the supreme heroes thoroughly accept me.
> Out of respect I will become your servant.
>
> When I come under your care
> I will be fearless of samsara and benefit living beings;
> I will perfectly purify my previous nonvirtues
> And from then on I will not perform nonvirtues.

The Heruka sadhana states:

> For the sake of liberating migrating beings
> From the ocean of samsara that is difficult to cross
> I offer my momentary self to
> The buddhas.

Once you have offered yourself as a servant to the guru and assembly of deities you must act in accordance with whatever the wishes of the guru-deity are, and as far as the guru and assembly are concerned, there is nothing to do other than working for the welfare of living beings; therefore, you should stabilize your intention by thinking, "I will not come under the influence of afflictive actions even for an instant, and until samsara is empty I will work for the welfare of living beings without ever becoming weary or discouraged." The *Arrangement of the Three Commitments Tantra*[133]

---

133. *Dam tshig gsum bkod pa'i rgyud; Trisamayavyūhatantra.*

states that it is the essential point of the bodhisattva vow to offer oneself [as a servant].

Regarding the meaning of the phrase "the illnesses of the 404 afflictive emotions," there are four root illnesses of wind, bile, phlegm, and their combination. Each one of those has a division of a hundred limbs, making 404. There are 404 bad actions that are the origin of those illnesses. There are 404 afflictive emotions that create the accumulation of those karmic actions. Once we nourish those karmic actions, there are 404 afflictive emotions that function as the condition to directly produce the illnesses.

Thus, presenting the outer, inner, secret, and suchness offerings as well as offering yourself as a servant to the guru and assembly of deities is taught in the tantras. The *Fifty Verses of Guru Devotion*, which is a summation of the meaning of the tantras, states:

> Vajradhara himself said that
> Attainments come from following the master.
> Realizing this, you should thoroughly delight your guru
> With all of your belongings.
>
> Desiring the inexhaustible,
> Whatever is even slightly pleasing
> Becomes the most special;
> It is what you should offer to the guru.
>
> That generosity becomes an eternal
> Generosity to all the buddhas.
> That offering is the accumulation of merit;
> Through accumulation you accomplish supreme siddhis.

This explains the [various offerings] together with the reasons [for offering them]. The *Secret Accomplishment* also states:

> With all of his belongings,
> For as long as is pleasing to the master,
> Steadfast in body, speech, and mind,
> The stainless disciple
> Delights him for a long time

With perfect offerings of the best quality.
Through the kindness of the honorable guru
He will reach attainment without obstruction.

And:

Even more than practicing method and wisdom,
With profound respect in the three times
Prostrate with your head to his feet,
And without regard even for your own body
You should offer a mandala as a preliminary.

Next, through the kindness of the guru he will bestow
The teachings of the buddhas of the three times.
That holy being will be without obstruction
And the disciple will reach attainment.

Thus, all the texts of the mahasiddhas and the tantras state that if you make offerings to the guru in this way, you will quickly attain the supreme attainment of the mahamudra.

[Maintaining the Bodhisattva and Tantric Vows]

At this point it is taught that we should take the bodhisattva vows and the tantric vows; therefore, I shall present the method for doing so. Having visualized the guru and the assembly of deities and performed the uncommon refuge as the preliminary, take the oath of aspiring bodhichitta and the engaging bodhisattva vows, for which you imagine that you are reciting the following verse after it is spoken by Lama Tubwang Dorje Chang:

I go for refuge to the Three Jewels
And confess each and every nonvirtue.
I rejoice in the virtue of migrating beings
And hold in my mind a buddha's enlightenment.[134]

---

134. The phrase "hold in my mind" is a poetic way of saying you promise to attain enlightenment and you will never let go of that determination.

You recite this verse three times. Simultaneously with the end of the third recitation you should imagine that you have received perfectly pure bodhisattva vows that are the embodiment of the aspiring and engaging bodhichitta. Although through this procedure you don't obtain new bodhisattva vows that you haven't already received, those that you have previously received will be further increased. This system for taking the vows is in accordance with the intention of the tantras. Many of the mahasiddhas, such as the great scholar Siddha Shantipa, Master Abhyakara, and so forth, have used these verses for taking aspiring bodhichitta and engaging bodhichitta at the beginning of empowerments. There are various teachings that are both concise and extensive for taking the aspiring and engaging bodhisattva vows in numerous texts of the mahasiddhas and tantras, such as the *Vajra Tent*; therefore, this is definitely not the final word on the subject. Yet the way I have presented it here is in accordance with the intention of Master Abhyakara. This is the way that those disciples of sharp faculties take the vows once they have trained their mind in the path; therefore, once you properly contemplate the common and uncommon methods for going for refuge and have imagined each aspect of the visualization, you should contemplate:

> I vow that until I attain enlightenment I will never forsake the uncommon Three Jewels, I will look upon all migrating beings with a pleasing, loving attitude as though they were my only child, and I shall generate extremely powerful compassion that is unable to bear the slightest torment of migrating beings that dwell in samsara. With those two factors of love and compassion I myself shall alone liberate all of these mother sentient beings and establish them in the state of enlightenment. For that purpose I am going to attain the state of enlightenment.

Having imagined the generation of bodhichitta, continue with your contemplation by thinking, "I shall not forsake that mind of enlightenment until I attain enlightenment." Set your motivation with aspiring bodhichitta and contemplate, "I shall perfectly train in all the practices of a bodhisattva." This is taking the engaging bodhisattva vows.

[Taking the Tantric Vows]

To take the tantric vows recite the following verses three times:

All buddhas and bodhisattvas,
Please listen to me.
I, whose name is . . . [say your secret name],
From this time forth
Until the essence of enlightenment
Shall generate the unsurpassed sacred bodhichitta,
Just as all the protectors of the three times
Have ensured their enlightenment.

I shall uphold firmly each of the
Three moral disciplines:
Moral restraint,
Accumulating virtuous Dharmas,
And working for the welfare of living beings.

From today onward I shall uphold
The vows arisen from the buddha yoga—
The unsurpassed Three Jewels of
The Buddha, Dharma, and Sangha.

I shall uphold purely
The vajra, bell, and mudra of
The great, supreme vajra family,
And I shall uphold purely the master commitment.

I will always make the four types of gifts
Six times each day—
The pleasing commitments of
The great supreme jewel family.

For the pure, great lotus family,
Arisen from great enlightenment,

I shall uphold each of the holy Dharmas
Of the outer, the secret, and the three vehicles.

For the great, supreme karma family
I shall uphold purely each of the
Vows I am endowed with,
And make as many offerings as I am able.

I shall generate the holy, unsurpassed bodhichitta,
And for the welfare of all living beings
I shall uphold all of my vows without exception.

I shall liberate those not liberated,
Deliver those not delivered,
Give breath to those breathless,
And lead all beings to nirvana.

You should imagine that you receive the extraordinary tantric vows simultaneously with the completion of the third recitation. Furthermore, you should base the tantric vows upon having completely pure bodhisattva vows. The four lines that state, "Just as all the protectors of the three times . . ." reveal how the aspiring and engaging bodhichittas are limbs of the tantric vows. I have already explained the visualizations for the aspiring and engaging bodhichittas. Imagine receiving aspiring bodhichitta and engaging bodhisattva vows by generating a very powerful aspiration by thinking, "[The aspiring and engaging bodhichittas] are the sole path traversed by all the buddhas of the three times; therefore, until I attain enlightenment, I as well will never forsake the precious minds of aspiring and engaging bodhichittas." Thus, once you have prepared yourself by receiving the aspiring and engaging bodhichittas, make a promise to perfectly protect the general and individual vows of the five buddha families without forsaking them until you attain enlightenment.[135] It should also

---

135. The phrase "until enlightenment" is used repeatedly in Buddhism and is slightly misleading. It is not saying that once you attain enlightenment you forsake bodhichitta or your vows. Instead, it implies that once you attain enlightenment you are the perfect embodiment of all good qualities and there is no need to make a conscious effort to maintain bodhichitta or keep your vows.

be stated that it is inappropriate to merely recite the words; instead, you should understand the underlying cause for whatever commitments and vows you are promising to keep. Once you do, and you have generated a powerful aspiration and have penetrated the respective visualizations [for aspiring and engaging bodhichitta], you should promise to protect them just as you have promised.

Concerning the individual commitments of the five buddha families, for the lineage of Vairochana there are six commitments not to be forsaken until the attainment of enlightenment that are (1–3) the promise to train in the three types of moral discipline[136] and (4–6) to go for refuge to the Three Jewels. For the lineage of Akshobya there are four commitments: (1) the commitment of the vajra, (2) the commitment of the bell, (3) the commitment of mudra, and (4) the commitment of the master. For the lineage of Ratnasambhava there are four commitments that are to be trained in during the six times [of the day]: (1) giving material things, (2) giving fearlessness, (3) giving Dharma, and (4) giving love. There are the three commitments of Amitabha: (1) upholding the outer [tantric] lineages of action and performance, (2) the secret yoga and highest yoga tantras, and (3) the holy Dharma embodied in the three vehicles; in short, upholding all the Dharmas of the three vehicles and the four classes of tantra. There are two commitments of Amoghasiddhi: (1) to protect all three types of vows and (2) the commitment of offering. Thus, although there are limitless divisions of the individual [commitments], they can be subsumed under the nineteen commitments.

For the general commitments of the five buddha families there are the commitment of eating, the commitment of safeguarding, and the commitment of reliance. You are promising to protect all of those commitments at the cost of your life. I will not be able to write more about them individually in detail since this text would become very lengthy.

Although you will not obtain new tantric vows that you have not previously received, those that you have received will be increased and become an extraordinary offering of practice. Furthermore, the only wish of the guru and assembly of deities is to extract living beings from the state of

---

136. The three types of moral discipline are the moral discipline of restraint, accumulating virtuous Dharmas, and working for the welfare of living beings.

samsara; therefore, if you extract even one living being from the abodes of samsara, they are extremely pleased. You are promising from the depths of your heart, "I will not merely liberate myself from the abodes of samsara, but I alone shall liberate all living beings as extensive as space from the abodes of samsara." You are also promising, "I shall protect the commitments and vows of highest yoga tantra, which is the method for attaining swift enlightenment for the welfare of all living beings just as I have sworn to do." Therefore, that also makes them very pleased. In that way it becomes the supreme offering of practice in accordance with the teachings.

This ritual for taking the vows of the five buddha families is taught in the *Vajra Peak Tantra*,[137] the *Vajradaka*, the *Samputa*, and so forth and is primarily used as a way of taking them when an empowerment is being given. It is also explained in the texts of mahasiddhas such as Avatar and so forth as a way of taking them when presenting offerings to the guru and assembly of mandala deities, and the omniscient Je [Tsongkhapa] also taught that we should take these vows either during the sadhanas and mandala rituals of Guhyasamaja, Heruka, and Yamantaka or when presenting offerings to the guru and assembly of deities. Having understood their significance, the mahasiddha Ensapa and his spiritual son [Sangye Yeshe] held that taking the two higher vows at this point in the guru yoga is very important.

[How to Perform the Remaining Limbs]

Confession and the Remaining Limbs has five sections:
1. **How to Perform Confession**
2. **How to Rejoice**
3. **How to Request Them to Turn the Wheel of Dharma**
4. **How to Request Them Not to Pass into Nirvana**
5. **How to Perform Dedication**

---

137. *rDo rje rtse mo rgyud*; *Vajraśekharatantra*.

How to Perform Confession

Thus, once you have taken the vows you should make confession. Ensapa and his spiritual sons said that once we have examined our mental continuums to determine whether or not we are defiled by the faults of having transgressed the boundaries of our three vows, we should make confession. For this you should examine whether or not you are defiled by a downfall of the pratimoksha training in your mental continuum through either extensive or concise binding words of our teacher [Shakyamuni]; you should examine whether or not you are defiled by any root downfalls or transgressions through the verses for the twenty vows and root downfalls of bodhichitta; and you should examine your mind to see whether or not it has been defiled by faults through the *Fifty Verses of Guru Devotion*, the verses for the fourteen root downfalls, and the eight secondary downfalls. You can use either the well-known verses for the root and secondary downfalls or the verses that appear in the mandala of Vajrabhairava that were composed by Khedrup Sangye Yeshe, which state:

> Do not criticize your master.
> Do not transgress the words of the tathagata.
> Likewise, do not proclaim the faults of
> Your [vajra] siblings out of anger.
> Absolutely under no circumstance should you
> Ever abandon the mind of love for living beings.
> Do not abandon the mind of enlightenment.
> Do not criticize the Dharma of yourself or others.
> Do not reveal the very secrets to those
> Living beings who are not thoroughly ripened.
> Do not abuse your own aggregates.
> Do not renounce the nature of phenomena.
> Always abandon malevolent kindness.
> Do not grasp at the extremes of phenomena.
> Do not deceive faithful living beings.
> Always rely upon the commitments.
> Do not proclaim the faults of
> Women, who are the nature of wisdom.

You should examine your mental continuum to see whether or not you are defiled by any of the root downfalls mentioned in these verses which come from the *Red Yamari Tantra*.[138] There are also ways of reciting verses for the secondary downfalls whose words are few and the aspects of visualization are clear. It is extremely important that you try your best to practice in this way since those who are making the most sincere effort on the path of tantra consider protecting the vows and commitments as the foundation and their protection is therefore absolutely essential. Once you have examined your mental continuum in that way to see whether or not you are defiled by faults and transgressions, you should confess each of the three sets of vows, in accordance with how they appear in the texts, for the sake of purifying whatever faults and transgressions you have incurred. At the very least you should confess your downfalls through the prayer "Lama Dorzinma."[139] For the sake of purifying your natural nonvirtues you should make a sincere effort in confession and restraint through the *General Confession* while making prostrations. The *Root Text on the Precious Oral Lineage of Ganden Mahamudra That Is the Main Path of the Conquerors*[140] states:

> To perceive the ultimate nature of the mind
> You should rely on accumulating merit and purifying obscurations.
> Make confession with at least one hundred thousand
>   hundred-syllable mantras,
> And as many prostrations as possible.

We have a huge amount of obscuring karma that makes it difficult for us to generate any good qualities in our minds; therefore, it is a sacred bit of instruction that we purify our obscuring karma through confessing our downfalls. The omniscient Je [Tsongkhapa] and his disciples made a hundred thousand prostrations[141] together with the *General Confession* with

---

138. *gShin rje'i gshed dmar po'i rgyud*; *Raktayamāritantra*.
139. This refers to the *General Confession* (*sPyi bshags*) that begins "u hu lag bla ma rdo rje 'dzin pa."
140. *dGa' ldan bka' rgyud rin po che'i phyag chen rtsa ba rgyal wa'i gzhung lam*. A translation of this text can be found in Appendix 2.
141. Lama Tsongkhapa actually made one hundred thousand prostrations to each of the thirty-five confession buddhas, making a total of three and a half million prostrations.

great enthusiasm, whereby they gained direct visions of many buddhas and bodhisattvas while giving birth to masses of extraordinary realizations on the path of sutra and tantra; therefore, those who have a deep heartfelt desire for practice should train by following the peerless deeds of Je [Tsongkhapa] and his disciples.

Regarding the words of confession that come from the ritual text itself, they state:

> In the presence of the greatly compassionate ones I confess
> with regret
> The nonvirtues and negative actions I have accumulated
> Since beginningless time, caused others to do, or have
> rejoiced in,
> And promise to refrain from such actions again in the future.

With regard to their meaning, they must be practiced with all four opponent powers to purify negativities and downfalls; therefore, this way of making confession through the practice of Lama Chöpa contains all four opponent powers and contains all the meaning of these teachings. Furthermore, if the four opponent powers are complete, we will be able to purify even the most grave transgressions and downfalls; if we don't have them all we won't be able to. Therefore, we need all four opponent powers to purify negative karma and downfalls. Regarding this, the *Sutra Declaring the Four Qualities*[142] states:

> If a loving bodhisattva, a great being, possesses these four qualities, the negativities he committed and accumulated will become overpowered. What are these four? They are the righteous conduct of destruction, the righteous conduct of the opponent, refraining from faults, and the power of reliance.

With regard to how to apply all four powers in this instance, we begin by reciting the section from the ritual text that states:

---

142. *Chos bzhi bstan pa'i mdo; caturdharmanirdeśasūtra.*

> I confess the nonvirtues and negative actions I have
>   accumulated
> Since beginningless time, caused others to do, or have
>   rejoiced in.

By contemplating "Since beginningless time until the present, I have directly engaged in negative actions such as the natural nonvirtues,[143] have caused others to perform them, and have rejoiced in the faulty conduct of others" you should generate powerful regret while keeping all of these and whatever else may exist in mind. This is the power of destruction. The phrase "In the presence of the greatly compassionate ones" is the power of reliance and the power of righteous conduct of the opponent. Go for refuge by thinking, "I place my hopes in no one other than the Lama Tubwang Dorje Chang and the assembly of deities, who are the natural embodiment of all Three Jewels, and I myself will actualize such a state for the welfare of living beings," which is the power of reliance. Making the request once you have evoked their great compassion by addressing them as "the greatly compassionate guru and assembly of deities" is the power of the righteous conduct of the opponent. With strong regret you are saying, "I confess and promise to refrain from such actions again in the future," which is the power of refraining from faults. These words are easy to understand.

Since it is said that if you make a sincere effort in confession and restraint with all four opponent powers you will be able to purify even your greatest faults that are certain to ripen, what need is there to mention being able to purify the subtle faults that are not certain to ripen? In particular, regarding the ability to quickly purify extremely grave faults such as the four defeats [of a monk] and the five actions of immediate retribution by those practicing deity yoga though perfectly protecting their vows and commitments after entering the path of mantra, the fifth chapter of the *Guhyasamaja Root Tantra* states:

---

143. There are two broad classifications of nonvirtues: natural and prescribed. Natural nonvirtues are actions that are naturally harmful, such as killing. Prescribed nonvirtues are actions that violate a prescribed set of moral discipline.

> Although sentient beings have engaged in great acts
> Of nonvirtue such as the five heinous actions,
> In this life, they will attain siddhis of the Supreme Vehicle,
> Through the great ocean of the Vajrayana.

From out of these we see that this yoga of the guru-deity has great power to utterly purify negative karma and downfalls. The *Drop of Mahamudra Tantra*[144] states:

> Just as wood is burned by fire
> And turned to ash in an instant,
> If, in the same way, you please your guru,
> Your negativities will be instantly incinerated.

The *Empowerment of Vajrapani Tantra*[145] also states:

> For example, the wise desire the worldly
> Eyes of the sun and the moon;
> Likewise, these beings also desire
> A master who is like eyes.

> For example, through the fire element
> All the firewood becomes incinerated;
> Likewise, you should realize that through the master
> The firewood of your ignorance is incinerated.

The *Oral Instructions of Manjushri* states, "For some people this is meaningful . . ." As I cited earlier, when the disciple worships the guru, all the buddhas enter the body of that guru and accept the offering. Through the power of that their obscuring karmas are purified. The same thing is also taught in many other tantras, such as the *Heruka Root Tantra* and so forth. In short, if you take guru yoga as the life of the path, you will become enlightened very quickly, which is in agreement with all the tantras and

---

144. *Phyag rgya chen po'i thig le'i rgyud; Mahāmudrātilakatantra.*
145. *Lag na rdo rje dbang bskur ba'i rgyud; Vajrapāṇyabhiṣekatantra.*

the texts of the mahasiddhas. As for "swift enlightenment," this occurs because we swiftly complete our collection of merit and swiftly purify our negative karma and obscurations. It is for this reason that guru yoga has such great power for purifying negative karma and obscurations and is perfectly established through scripture and reasoning. We can also come to know this through the historical accounts of the former holy beings. Panchen Naropa diligently made offerings and worshiped Mahasiddha Tilopa, whereby he quickly purified his obscuring karma and accomplished the supreme realization of mahamudra. Drom Rinpoche cleaned Atisha's feces with his hands, whereby he purified his obscuring karma and suddenly gained such vast clairvoyance that he could understand the subtle thoughts in the minds of living beings down to the ants and other creatures that were many hundreds of leagues away. In the earlier part of his life, Jetsun Milarepa accumulated enormous nonvirtue by killing many living beings and countless minute creatures through black magic and hail. However, once he met Lama Marpa he quickly purified his great store of negative karma and obscurations through his sincere efforts in worshiping and serving his guru, after which he attained the highest realizations. There are many other such stories in the biographies of the previous holy beings who sincerely worshiped and served their gurus, whereby they purified their negative karma and obscurations and attained numerous good qualities.

How to Rejoice

The ritual text states:

> Although dreamlike phenomena are free from
> The signs of inherent existence,
> We sincerely rejoice in all the pure white virtues and
> Whatever bliss and joy that arise for ordinary and arya beings.

The *Bhadracarya Pranidhana*[146] states, "You should rejoice in the virtues of the five types of persons." As for these "five" they are (1) buddhas,

---

146. *bZang spyod.*

(2) bodhisattvas, (3) pratyeka buddhas, (4) shravakas, and (5) ordinary beings. It is stating that you should rejoice in all the roots of virtue of these five types of beings. There aren't any living beings whatsoever that are not included in those five types of beings; therefore, there are also not any roots of virtue that are not included within those. Once you have included both ordinary and arya beings within these five, you rejoice in their virtues. In short, you rejoice in all the roots of virtue of yourself and others.

Furthermore, in accordance with the perfection of wisdom sutras, we should rejoice in whatever amount of virtue there exists in all the buddhas of the past, all those that will become enlightened in the future, and all those buddhas who are currently residing in the worldly realms of the ten directions, from the time they initially generated the mind of enlightenment up to their final enlightenment. We should rejoice in whatever deeds the buddhas performed by turning the wheel of Dharma from the time of their enlightenment. We should rejoice in all the Dharma conduct of the disciples of those teachings who abide in listening, contemplating, and meditating, such as all the possible bodhisattvas that appeared in dependence upon those [teachings], all the possible shravakas that appeared, and all the possible pratyeka buddhas that appeared, up to all those conquerors who abide in the teachings after attaining nirvana. We should rejoice in all the possible roots of virtue that are produced by gods and humans with stupas of holy relics and whatever roots of virtue exist through each and every ordinary being who presented offerings to the conquerors and bodhisattvas and whatever ripened effect of happiness that occurred in their minds through the power of those virtuous roots as well as whatever higher good qualities they generated and so forth. Thus, we should take all the roots of virtue that are the source of temporary and ultimate benefit and happiness, mentally collect them, analyze them, and then rejoice.

The sutras state that once we assemble all their essential points, "We should rejoice with a pure mind in whatever completely pure joy and happiness that arise for all ordinary and superior beings." It is extensively taught in the perfection of wisdom sutras that our wisdom should comprehend the complete purity of the three circles that does not grasp at the signs of true existence of the happiness that we are rejoicing in. Here as well, the ritual text states:

> . . . dreamlike phenomena are free from
> The signs of inherent existence.

Regarding the act of rejoicing in the virtues of all ordinary and superior beings through comprehending them with the wisdom realizing the complete purity of the three circles, it is said that the merit from this is far greater than the merit gained from making offerings to the conquerors for the extent of an eon.

With regard to this system of rejoicing, the great beings, the bodhisattvas who abide on the [higher] spiritual grounds, also take this as the most fundamental practice. It is a vast accumulation of merit that is so highly praised for accomplishing the state of enlightenment, and the perfection of wisdom sutras extensively sing its praises. Je Tokjo[147] also stated:

> With the supreme act of rejoicing in virtue
> A vast amount of merit is accumulated with little effort.
> In particular, if you generate delight without pride
> When rejoicing in your former virtuous deeds,
> Your former virtuous deeds will increase further.
> It would be excellent if you generate such a joyous mind
>   by seeing
> That there are numerous other needs for the sake of
> Accomplishing the teachings of the conqueror.

How to Request Them to Turn the Wheel of Dharma

The ritual text states:

> Please send down a rain of vast and profound Dharmas
> From the multitude of clouds of your wisdom and compassion
> So that the jasmine garden may nurture, sustain, and
>   propagate
> The benefit and happiness for limitless sentient beings.

147. Tib. rJe'i rtogs brjod.

Evoke the compassion of Lama Tubwang Dorje Chang and the assembly of deities. All of these migrating beings that fill all of space wish for nothing other than to be happy and to not experience suffering. The temporary happiness and all the subsequent benefit all come from nothing other than that holy Dharma. As for where this Dharma comes from, the Dharma of the teacher depends upon the guru. Furthermore, the *Commentary on Valid Cognition*[148] states:

> When the outcome of the method is hidden,
> It is difficult to explain.

If you don't know what to adopt and what to reject, you can't teach others; therefore, the Dharma teacher should learn exactly what to adopt and reject. A Dharma teacher must have perfected his compassion for all of his disciples with impartiality. Lama Tubwang Dorje Chang himself is endowed with a mind of perfect wisdom and compassion; therefore, we make requests with powerful longing by requesting him to continuously turn the wheel of Dharma of the profound and vast teachings so that we may generate roots of virtue and the Dharma may remain for a long time, as well as increase. We can also make a request at this point in accordance with the teachings of Khedrup Sangye Yeshe, which state:

> Losang, the primordial buddha vajradhara, please
> Reveal your all-pervasive, outer, inner, and secret bodies.
> Think of beings with compassion for as long as space exists,
> And turn the outer, inner, and secret wheels of Dharma.

When you perform extensive rituals, such as during a ganachakra, you can also make the following request to turn the wheel of Dharma of the five buddha families:

> Reveal your body of the all-pervasive Buddha lineage
> As the display of the great mirror-like exalted wisdom;

---

148. *Tshad ma rnam 'grel*; *Pramāṇavārttika*.

Think of beings with compassion for as long as space exists,
And turn the outer, inner, and secret wheels of Dharma.

Reveal your body of the all-pervasive Padma lineage
As the display of the great exalted wisdom of investigation;
Think of beings with compassion for as long as space exists,
And turn the outer, inner, and secret wheels of Dharma.

Reveal your body of the all-pervasive Vajra lineage
As the display of the great exalted wisdom of dharmadhatu;
Think of beings with compassion for as long as space exists,
And turn the outer, inner, and secret wheels of Dharma.

Reveal your body of the all-pervasive Ratna lineage
As the display of the great exalted wisdom of equality;
Think of beings with compassion for as long as space exists,
And turn the outer, inner, and secret wheels of Dharma.

Reveal your body of the all-pervasive Karma lineage
As the display of the great exalted wisdom of accomplishing
    activities;
Think of beings with compassion for as long as space exists,
And turn the outer, inner, and secret wheels of Dharma.

This is for the sake of generating, remaining a long time,
    and increasing.

Regarding these teachings, the *Lamp Illuminating the Five Stages*[149] states
that it is not acceptable to listen to these instructions merely once. We
need to listen to them repeatedly. In particular, when training in the path
of the five stages [of the completion stage], as you become very close to
generating a direct experience of the paths in your mental continuum, you
present outer, inner, and secret offerings to your guru, as well as mandala

---

149. *Rim lnga gsal sgron.*

offerings and so on, after which you make requests. Then you should listen
to the instructions on the meaning of the teachings.

How to Request Them Not to Pass into Nirvana

The ritual text states:

> Although your vajra body knows neither birth nor death
> But is a vessel of the powerful conqueror's union,
> Please remain according to our wishes
> Without passing away until samsara ends.

Until you attain the state of enlightenment you need to rely upon a guru
to teach you the unmistaken path. If you don't have a guru, you will not
be able to progress to the higher paths. Once you consider this, you make
requests through your powerful devotion for the guru. It is his mind of
self-manifesting exalted wisdom of nondual bliss and emptiness appearing
as the immortal vajra body with signs and indications of a fully enlightened being that manifests as a coarse form body to our subjective ordinary
appearances and is like a jeweled casket. It is this [coarse body] that we
are requesting to remain. It is also this coarse form body that we request
to not reveal the aspect of passing into nirvana until the attainment of
enlightenment and to remain as our refuge, protector, and companion.
Imagine that through making requests in this way, as well as evoking
them [the gurus] to turn the wheel of Dharma, your guru is very pleased
and accepts your request. This indicates a special profound meaning of
dependent relationship.

The explanation of this term "vajra body" is the ultimate essential
meaning of the root and explanatory tantras of Guhyasamaja. Initially,
you complete the first [i.e., generation] stage; then, through the force of
penetrating the essential points of the vajra body during the completion
stage, you bring the extremely subtle wind and mind under control and
attain the example clear light, and from there the illusory body of the
third stage. Next, by purifying that [impure] illusory body and clear light
you attain the pure illusory body. That body is separated from your corporeal body of flesh and bones and is a body similar to a rainbow. That body

is adorned with the thirty-two excellent signs and the eighty indications and fills the limitless worldly realms with rays of light and pervades the limitless pure lands with its emanations. Even Indra and Brahma are not capable of seeing it, and it remains continuously for as long as space exists. That is what we call the "vajra body" and is also referred to as the "body of union." From the continuum of that body emerges the completely pure enjoyment body endowed with the five certainties.[150] This is the object of our devotions and it is this very complete enjoyment body possessing the five certainties that we are supplicating.

By perfectly contemplating in this way you should have complete trust in these supreme instructions, which are vajra words that have been arranged according to the writings of the oral instructions of Vajradhara Losang Chökyi Gyaltsen's Hearing Lineage that extract the essence of the ocean of tantras. When requesting the guru to have a long life in conjunction with a ganachakra, we should recite this verse of request three times.

How to Perform Dedication

The ritual text states:

> I dedicate this collection of pure white virtue that I have
>   produced
> So that throughout all my lives I may never be separated
> From the venerable guru who is kind in the three ways;
> May I always come under his care and attain the union
>   of powerful Vajradhara.

As for what you should be imagining at this point, establish an extremely strong aspiration by contemplating:

> Now that I have obtained this excellent body of leisure, I have
> met the guru-buddha, and I have the causes for practicing the

---

150. The five certainties are attributes of the enjoyment body: (1) the certainty of place, (2) the certainty of body, (3) the certainty of time, (4) the certainty of teachings, and (5) the certainty of retinue.

profound holy Dharma to utilize this meaningful life of leisure; by all means I must practice the instructions transmitted by the guru-buddha to attain the state of the guru-buddha in this very life. For that purpose I dedicate that in dependence upon the force and capacity of these roots of virtue, through presenting offerings and supplications to the guru and assembly of deities, may I never be separated even for an instant from the guru-buddha throughout all my lives and receive a continuous stream of teachings. Through the force of that, once I swiftly complete all the good qualities of the grounds and paths, may I swiftly attain the state of Vajradhara the Great.

This way of dedicating, to be cared for by the guru, is a teaching of Ensapa the Great.

CHÖKYI DORJE

Next, once you have visualized in this way, you should present an extensive mandala and make a request for the three great purposes: that you may (1) swiftly generate in your mental continuum the common path and the uncommon path of the two stages; (2) put an end to all mistaken minds and opposing factors, such as disrespect for your spiritual master; and (3) make very powerful supplications that there are not any outer and inner obstacles that interfere with generating them in your mental continuum and that you have a complete set of favorable conditions so that you will quickly generate the complete path in your mental continuum.

All seven of these limbs are great binding factors for the practice of the Mahayana, and if we condense them even further they are subsumed under accumulation, purification, and increasing. They can be further condensed into accumulation and purification. Each one of the seven limbs functions to purify whatever interfering obscurations there are to generating [realizations] as well as to create the cause for accomplishing the various good qualities of the higher paths. They are also very necessary and important for accomplishing the various temporary and ultimate benefits; however, I am not able to write about them all at this point. Instead, you should learn them from the oral explanatory tradition during the extensive commentaries on the path. There are also many unique features when [the seven limbs are] conjoined with the uncommon practice of mantra.

Making Supplications by Way of Your Great Faith and Devotion has four sections:

1. **How to Make Supplications through Contemplating the Faults and Benefits and Evoking His Mental Continuum through Reciting His Name Mantra**
2. **How to Make Supplications through Recollecting His Good Qualities and Kindness**
3. **How to Make Supplications through Recollecting His Outer, Inner, Secret, and Suchness Qualities**
4. **How to Make the Supplication of Planting the Stake and Taking the Four Empowerments of Concentration**

How to Make Supplications through Contemplating the Faults and Benefits and Evoking His Mental Continuum through Reciting His Name Mantra

The Lama Chöpa ritual text states:

> Next, the *Vajrapani Empowerment Tantra* states:
>
> > Apprehend your master's good qualities.
> > Never focus upon his [apparent] faults.
> > If you apprehend his qualities, you receive attainments.
> > If you focus on his faults, you will not accomplish
> >   attainments.
>
> Thus, you should repeatedly rely upon introspection by thinking, "I will not let my mind look for flaws in my guru." Once you do, you should properly contemplate the sacred teachings of the sutras and tantras that repeatedly discuss the benefits of relying upon the guru and the faults of not relying upon him or her. In particular, merely hearing the name of your root guru robs the lower rebirth of its fear and merely contemplating him dispels the suffering of samsara. If you make requests to him, all attainments are bestowed with ease. Rely upon him with fervent devotion without placing your hopes in any other and contemplate that he is the very nature embodying the nondeceptive Three Jewels. While contemplating in this way, make as many requests as you can with prayers such as the "Migtsema" and so forth.

Regarding the benefits of relying upon your spiritual master, if you properly rely upon your spiritual master, you delight all the buddhas and bodhisattvas of the ten directions. You quickly purify your obscuring karma. You will not be damaged by outer and inner harms. With each passing moment you complete a great wave of merit. And you will quickly accomplish the higher extraordinary good qualities. You will not fall into lower realms in your next life and you will be able to do whatever you set your mind to. There are limitless other benefits such as these. Primarily, you quickly accomplish the state of enlightenment. Furthermore, the *Heruka Root Tantra* states:

> I will perfectly dwell in the body of the master
> And accept offerings from practitioners.

Thus, when the disciples with pure commitments make perfect offerings to their guru, Heruka and other deities will dwell in the body of the guru, and by accepting the offerings, the practitioner will quickly complete their accumulation of merit. The *Oral Instructions of Manjushri* also states the same thing by saying, "Jetsun Manjushri will abide in the body of the guru and accept the offerings of disciples, whereby they will quickly complete the accumulation of merit and quickly purify their negative karma and obscurations." I have already quoted this earlier. Many other tantras also state basically the same thing. Furthermore, it is not as though only a particular deity dwells in the body of the guru, for when a disciple who purely maintains his or her commitments makes offerings to their guru who teaches the unmistaken path, *all* the conquerors in the ten directions definitely enter the body of that guru. The *Explanatory Tantra Vajramala* states:

> Through that, all the conquerors dwell
> In the body of the vajra master.
> Listen! He is meaningful to behold;
> In future lives you will be a great hero.
>
> Because of that, rely upon the guru
> With all the divine substances
> Of all living beings.

This explanation is extremely lucid.

The *Kalachakra Tantra* also states:

> For the beings who live in this world I am the glorious vajra
> holder who is without negativity. The living beings that cause

him harm will definitely go to hell, where there is nothing wondrous. By pleasing him, I am pleased; by getting angry with the guru it is "great anger" (i.e., the worst kind of anger). The guru himself is worthy of prostrations and worthy of offerings because he bestows the resultant state of the bliss of liberation upon those very living beings.

If you perfectly rely upon your guru, you will delight all the conquerors and quickly accomplish attainments. If you are mistaken in your reliance, there is no doubt that it will be disastrous. The *Drop of Exalted Wisdom Tantra*[151] states:

> The guru is the teacher, the guru is the protector,
> The guru is the vajra holder himself.
> Through the kindness of the guru's presence
> You will discover the supreme state.
>
> There is no doubt that you will discover
> The attainment of mahamudra in this life
> And become a powerful lord of the ten grounds.
> This is the kindness of the guru!
>
> Therefore, how could there be another
> Great teacher that surpasses the guru?

If you rely properly upon the guru you will quickly attain the supreme attainment of the mahamudra, and there is no other object of offering that surpasses your guru. Although these writings are nothing more than mere illustrations, they are taught extensively on numerous occasions in the four classes of tantra. Protector Nagarjuna's *Five Stages* also states:

> The stage of self-blessing
> Is the teaching of relative truth.
> Through nothing other than the kindness of the guru

---

151. *Ye shes thig le'i rgyud; jñānatilakatantra.*

You will reach attainments.
The stage of self-blessing
Will not be discovered by those with
Superstitions about sutra and tantra,
For whom it becomes meaningless hard work.

Since the principal is the nature of all the buddhas
You should have no doubt that you will
Accomplish the stage of self-blessing and
Attain enlightenment in this very life.

If you rely properly upon your guru, you will accomplish the body of union through his kindness. Once you understand this, you will reach attainments in this life. If you don't rely upon your guru, whatever effort you put into things such as listening to and contemplating the sutras and tantras will never become the means of accomplishing supreme attainments. Aryadeva also states in his *Purification of Mental Obscurations*:[152]

You should apprehend his good qualities
And never his faults.
The guru is the supreme deity;
You should sincerely make offerings.

He is the perfect abode for the actual
Form of the king of vajra holders,
Just as a jewel is purified of all impurities
By [placing] in pure water;
In the same way, the clear jewel
Purifies the mind into the aspect of a jewel.

This teaches, together with an analogy, that if you act with proper respect for your guru, you will quickly give rise to realizations. The *Secret Accomplishment* also states:

---

152. *Sems kyi sgrib pa rnam par sbyong ba'i rab tu byed pa; Cittāvaraṇaviśodhaprakaraṇa.*

From among all the commitments,
Worshiping the guru is supreme;
He is the jeweled treasure of the Buddha
Who teaches Glorious Guhyasamaja and others.

Although you may not say so,[153]
He is the perfect abode [of the buddha], and his blissful
Body, speech, and mind work for the welfare of all sentient
  beings.
You should bring to mind that he is referred to as "the mind
  of enlightenment";
Without conceptualization and without fixed location
He is pure and without self-nature.

Through the kindness of the honorable guru
You will quickly reach attainment.

And:

Through delighting the vajra-guru
All the best attainments are bestowed.

And:

For that sake you should make every effort
To respectfully worship your guru.

Thus, through properly worshiping your guru you will quickly manifest
the exalted wisdom of simultaneously born great bliss. If you don't rely
upon your guru, there is no way to accomplish exalted wisdom; therefore,
you should make a sincere effort to worship your guru. The *Accomplishment of Exalted Wisdom* also states:

153. This is stating, "Although it doesn't matter whether you think of the guru as a buddha or
not, . . ."

Wherever the kind guru exists,
That very place becomes a reliquary.
Out of ignorance the childish [worship] elsewhere
For a long time and become delusional.

The guru becomes the Dharma, the Buddha,
And likewise the Sangha;
Through his kindness you become wise.
Thus, he is the Three Jewels.

And:

Although you may practice nonduality,
There is nothing greater in the three realms than the master.
Through his kindness
You will reach numerous attainments;
He is the heroic vajra holder.

Although you prostrate to all the buddhas,
Worshiping the master is unsurpassed.
You should offer him whatever you can.

The texts of the mahasiddhas in general state in numerous ways that the guru is the root of all excellent accumulations and, in particular, once we enter the practice of mantra, accomplishing the supreme attainment of mahamudra in this life is accomplished solely through relying upon the kindness of the guru. In short, the omniscient Je [Tsongkhapa] stated, "The source of all happiness and excellence from generating a single good quality in the mind of the disciple and removing the obscuration of a single fault on up are due to the holy spiritual master. Therefore, it is extremely important that you rely upon him from the outset." And, "In all the vehicles in general, and this vehicle in particular, you should work at not defiling your commitments to your guru and make offerings through viewing him as the Buddha. You should please him with everything pleasing and abandon what is displeasing. Striving sincerely in this way is the real practice." You should definitely keep these benefits deep in your mind.

Regarding the faults of not relying on your guru, these are extensively discussed numerous times in all the sutras and tantras, as is how once you rely upon your spiritual master, if you rely upon him improperly in this life, you will be harmed by a plethora of illnesses and afflictions. In your next life, once you fall into the lower realms, it will be very difficult to get free, and even when you do get free, and since the result is similar to the cause, you will find it very difficult to meet a spiritual master and so forth. As the ripened effect of that karma you will experience atrocious and terrifying suffering with endless screams of anguish. This is the thought behind the sutras and tantras as well as all of their commentaries and is taught numerous times. If you make a mistake in this way in relying upon the guru as the root of the path, although you may bear hardships, such as performing austerities of listening to and contemplating the sutras and tantras, exerting yourself in practice and deity yoga, and so on, it will be utterly impossible for you to generate realizations of the higher paths. The *Guhyasamaja Root Tantra* states:

> Although you may practice, if you
> Criticize your master from the heart,
> You will never reach attainments.

Directly commenting on that, the *Clear Lamp* states, "By being close friends with defiled commitments, you will not reach attainments." Like a pus-ridden frog, you will bring ruin to yourself and all of your companions. Thus, once you have analyzed the benefits and faults with the wisdom of individual analysis, you should repeatedly contemplate them and generate absolute certainty. If you don't induce certainty, your faith, devotion, offerings, supplications, and so forth will be mere words and you will be doing nothing more than merely imitating others and will never be capable of producing blessings. These methods were also held as very important in the biographies of the previous holy beings. Furthermore, the bodhisattva Sadaprarudita viewed his guru as superior to all the buddhas, and although he directly perceived numerous buddhas, that was not sufficient; he sought out his spiritual master Dharmodgata and relied upon him without any regard for his body, life, and enjoyments whatsoever, and through his worship he progressed in a few short years from the stage of accumulation to the first bodhisattva ground, which would have otherwise taken many eons to accomplish. Drom Rinpoche said that making requests to Atisha brings greater blessings than supplicating any enlightened support (of body, speech, or mind). Jayulwa sincerely worshiped and venerated Chengawa and assiduously served him by fetching water, building his fire, and sweeping the ashes. At one time, when Jayulwa was carrying Chengawa's spittoon through the doorway to throw it out, he suddenly developed concentration like climbing the steps of a ladder. He developed a vast awareness that could directly perceive numerous superior deities. He said, "Although these spiritual masters give instructions to others, these days those geshes do not understand that Dharma means serving your guru." He also said, "If one asserts that Noble Vajradhara or some personal deity exists separate from the guru, such a person will never accomplish attainments in his mental continuum." These are repeatedly stating that all the realizations of the stages of the path to enlightenment must be attained through the kindness of the guru. Jetsun Sakya Pandita diligently served Jetsun Drakpa Gyaltsen as his nurse while he was ill, whereby he directly perceived guru-Manjushri, through the force of which he accomplished all the supreme attainments. Gyalwa Ensapa the Great said:

> In short, whether great or small realizations come from
>   meditating
> Depends on whether you have great or small faith.
>
> Contemplate the good qualities and don't look for faults
> In the kind lama, the source of all attainments.
>
> Hold his instruction as your main practice;
> May there be no obstructions to perfecting this oath.

This is stating that all good qualities must be generated solely in dependence upon faith and respect for your guru. The tantras and texts of the mahasiddhas sing great praise for the yoga of the holy guru as the life of the path; therefore, you must come to understand this by inducing certainty about such things. If you don't, saying, "I see the guru as the buddha" will be nothing more than mere words and you will not be able to realize the essential points of the path through merely exerting yourself in some insignificant cycle of visualizations. Je Rinpoche said, "Therefore, you should understand that the former instructions are also known as the practice of 'guru yoga.' However, nothing will come from it by training in its meditations for only a single session." Therefore, once you repeatedly contemplate the meditations regarding the benefits of relying upon your spiritual master and the faults of not relying on him or her, you train with fierce faith and devotion. In particular, merely hearing the name of that very guru who is endowed with the three types of kindness robs the fear of the lower realms, and by merely recalling him, the suffering of samsara is dispelled. Make supplications to him with a powerful mind of trust and confidence without placing your hopes in anyone else and contemplate how he is the embodiment of the nondeceptive Three Jewels as your source of refuge; when you supplicate him, he will easily bestow all attainments. Furthermore, supplicate the gurus of the close-lineage of blessings of Ganden mahamudra as well as make supplications to your guru, who is kind in the three ways according to the traditional practice of recitation. In particular, recite a hundred supplications with:

Ngo Drup Kung Jung Tubwang Dorje Chang
Mig Me Tse Wai Ter Chen Chenrezig
Tri Me Kyen Pai Wang Po Jampalyang
Du Pung Ma Lu Jom Dzai Sangwai Dak
Gang Chen Kay Pai Tsug Gyen Losang Drak

Kyab Sum Kun Du Lama Sangye La
Go Sum Gu Pai Go Nay Sol Wa Deb
Rang Shen Min Ching Drol War Chin Gyi Lob
Chok Dang Tun Mong Ngodrup Tsal Du Sol

Losang Drakpa, the crown ornament of scholars of the
    land of snows,
You are Shakyamuni and Vajradhara, the source of all
    attainments,
Avalokiteshvara, the great treasure of unobservable compassion,

Manjushri with powerful stainless wisdom,
And Vajrapani, destroyer of a host of demons.
Guru-buddha, the embodiment of the Three Jewels,
With my three doors I respectfully make requests;
Please bestow your blessings to ripen and liberate myself
    and others
And bestow the common and supreme attainments.

Throughout this supplication a stream of purifying nectar descends from the heart of Lama Tubwang Dorje Chang, as well as a stream of purifying nectar from the bodies of all others in the field of merit. Furthermore, a stream of five-colored light rays and nectars descends from the bodies of the guru and assembly of deities and enters the body and mind of yourself and all other living beings, whereby all of your negative karma and obscurations that you have accumulated since beginningless time, and in particular all the harm you have caused to the glorious guru's body—not heeding his teachings, disturbing his mind, speaking of his faults due to a lack of faith, and so forth—are purified. In short, all the negative karma and obscurations you have accumulated in your dependence upon your guru are expelled through the doors of your senses as smoke, soot, and liquid ash, as well as through your pores, whereby you are cleansed and purified. Your body becomes radiant, clear, and the nature of light. Your life, merit, and good qualities of scripture and realization all increase and flourish. In particular, imagine that all the blessings of the body, speech, and mind of the glorious guru enter the body and mind of all living beings.

Regarding this recitation of the omniscient Je [Tsongkhapa's] name mantra, this performs the same function as all the profound secret mantras taught in the tantras. By way of this you evoke the mind of the guru and assembly of deities and your sickness, harm from spirits, negative karma, and obscurations are pacified and your life, merit, and good qualities of scripture and realization flourish and so forth, whereby you accomplish limitless pacifying, increasing, controlling, and wrathful actions, as well as causing rain, protecting from hail, accomplishing [treasure] vases, developing the essence of the earth, and so forth. Up to this current era this has been the practice tradition of holy beings of the precious Ganden Oral Lineage; therefore, the beings of the land of snows rely upon the power of this supplication for their benefit and happiness. In particular, Protector Manjushri bestowed the uncommon instructions upon Je Lama, which state:

> Cleanse impurities and dispel ignorance.
> Great with a body and clear with speech,
> Swift with seeds, profound with hand symbols,
> And expounding, debating, and composing with
> A scripture, sword, and a scripture and sword.[154]

This explains how to practice with special techniques for developing wisdom through this process, in accordance with the well-known seed-syllable HUM at the heart of Lama Tubwang Dorje Chang the Great and a syllable MAM marked by a HUM as the uncommon seed-syllable at the heart of Omniscient Je [Tsongkhapa]. The reason for this arrange-ment comes from the *Manjushri Root Tantra*; during its prophecy about Je Rinpoche it states, "The first syllable of intelligence is MA,"[155] and in accordance with this prophecy, the first syllable of [Je Rinpoche's] name mantra is MA. Primarily, this guru yoga functions to evoke the mind through making supplications with this name mantra and was given by Omniscient Je [Tsongkhapa] himself individually to Mahasiddha Jampal Gyatso, Omniscient Khedrup Je, and Baso Chöje and sealed in secrecy. Later on, it was bestowed directly by Je [Rinpoche] himself upon Maha-siddha Chö Dorje [through a direct vision]. In general, Omniscient Je [Rinpoche] spread the complete teachings of the muni in this northern land and his activities are just like the deeds of Buddha Shakyamuni himself; therefore, his kindness is incomparable. He is Jetsun Manjushri appearing in human form and, as everyone knows, was clearly predicted in the *Manjushri Root Tantra*. [Lama Tsongkhapa] is also the essence of both Arya Avalokiteshvara and Vajrapani; therefore, he is the sole embodiment

---

154. This verse refers to the seven types of wisdom, which are developed by imagining various objects: (1) great wisdom with miniature Manjushris, (2) clear wisdom with Manjushri's mantra, (3) quick wisdom with DHI syllables, (4) profound wisdom with scriptures and swords, (5) the wisdom of exposition with texts, (6) the wisdom of debate with wheels of swords, and (7) the wisdom of composition with books and wheels of swords.

155. This is in reference to the "Migtsema" prayer, which begins with the syllable "MA."

of the three lineages in one. This is clearly explained in the *Kadam [Emanation] Scripture*; it is for that reason that we make this request with [Tsongkhapa's] name mantra, for which there is the explanation that the outer aspect should be similar to their inner qualities and to the three supreme deities [of Avalokiteshvara, Vajrapani, and Manjushri] in their secret [aspects], as well as how they all possess inseparable entities. In dependence upon these we establish the outer accomplishment, inner accomplishment, and secret accomplishment, which have three divisions each, whereby we get the cycle of nine that are in the uncommon sadhana. Furthermore, for these there is a phrase that states, "The peaceful is the holder of the white lotus" and so forth, which comes from the cycle of teachings of Manjushri, for which there are numerous unique collections of ritual actions. The peaceful should be learned orally from your spiritual master.[156]

How to Make Supplications through Recollecting His Good Qualities and Kindness has two sections:

1. Making Supplications by Training in Faith as the Root by Contemplating His Good Qualities
2. Making Supplications through Recalling His Kindness

Making Supplications by Training in Faith as the Root by Contemplating His Good Qualities has three sections:

1. Making Supplications by Contemplating the Good Qualities of Your Guru as Explained in the Vinaya
2. Making Supplications by Contemplating the Good Qualities of Your Guru as Explained in the Common Mahayana
3. Making Supplications by Contemplating the Good Qualities of Your Guru as Explained in the Vajrayana

---

156. There are numerous secret practices associated with the "Migtsema." You can find some of them in volume 2 of Pabongkha Rinpoche's *Collected Works* in a text entitled *dGa' ldan lha brgya ma'i rnal 'byor nyams su len tshul snyan brgyud zhal shes man ngag rin chen gter gyi bang mdzod*.

Making Supplications by Contemplating the Good Qualities of Your Guru as Explained in the Vinaya

The ritual text states:

> I make requests to the foremost second buddha,
> A great ocean of moral discipline, the source of all good
>   qualities,
> Replete with a treasury of much learning,
> In saffron robes, the elder and upholder of the Vinaya.

The *Three Hundred Verses of the Vinaya*[157] states:

> Praise a guru who has knowledge of the ritual of the Vinaya
>   and is endowed with moral discipline,
> Has compassion for the ill, and a pure retinue;
> He is diligent in benefiting with the Dharma and material
>   things
> And gives teachings at the appropriate times.

The foundation of all good qualities is pure moral discipline. In general, the guru is endowed with extensive learning in the three baskets,[158] and in particular he has knowledge of the three key features of acceptance and rejection and explains their procedures. In general, he is of great benefit to his disciples and, in particular, has compassion for the ill, has a pure retinue, is skilled when he teaches Dharma, and so forth. Contemplating these good qualities explained in the Vinaya, you should train in faith and make supplications.

Regarding the term "elder,"[159] this is a fully ordained monk who has kept his vows purely without interruption for ten years. In the Vinaya an elder is someone who is endowed with the fivefold good qualities, such as being skilled in the trainings and their applications. The Vinaya scripture

---

157. *Dul ba sum brgya* (*gSum brgya pa / gzhi thams cad yod par smra ba'i dge tshul gyi tshig le'ur byas pa*). Composed by Shakyaprabha.

158. The three baskets are Vinaya, Sutra, and Abhidharma.

159. Tib. *gnas brtan*.

Lifetime Vows[160] states, "Skilled and maintains [the vows] for ten years." Regarding the phrase "the second Buddha," the conqueror himself praised the elders upholding the Vinaya by stating that their actions are just like his. The Vinaya scripture states:

> The person who upholds the Vinaya possesses five benefits. A retinue of four are arranged in his presence. The instructions and subsequent teachings are all not dependent upon others. They are the inner treasury guarded by the perfectly complete buddhas of the past, the future, and those that presently exist. They sit on the crown of fully ordained monks and Brahmins. They dwell in bliss for the sake of abiding in the holy Dharma and the trainings; thus, they benefit numerous beings.

And:

> He perfectly protects his moral discipline and is modest about his [pure] discipline. He invites the retinue of four to be actually present and becomes the teacher for those beings who develop regret [for their previous nonvirtuous actions]. He dwells, and not just for a short while, among the Sangha. Through the factors congruent with the Dharma [such beings] annihilate adversaries.

And:

> I see light and luminosity in the direction of the Vinaya holder's abode, the generation of clarity and the creation of radiance. I have minimum concerns for those abiding in that situation; I see that situation is not without value.

Regarding the verses presented here [in Lama Chöpa] that state, "A great ocean of moral discipline, the source of all good qualities . . . ," the Vinaya scriptures state that the abbot and the resident lama should have the five

160. *Bar sdom.*

sets of good qualities and that among those they must absolutely possess the two good qualities of support and skill. These two are most essential, but if I explain them it would become very extensive. With regard to the Vinaya holder being the lord of the teachings, Glorious Atisha said, "Even if some tasks suddenly emerge, we Indians do not place great importance upon it. It is said that once you assemble the holders of the three baskets, you should not obstruct the three baskets or interfere with the three baskets." Once you reach a definite conclusion, you should settle firmly upon it. In addition to that, Kamalashila said that once someone engages in the conduct of a bodhisattva, we should not obstruct them nor should we interfere with their activities on the path and [those activities] should be conducted in accordance with the holder of the Vinaya.

Thus, as explained in the Vinaya, it is inappropriate for the guru to have only one pure moral discipline; he must have numerous good qualities, such as being endowed with extensive learning of the three baskets, he must not have transgressed the robes indicating he is ordained, he must understand the ritual actions of the Vinaya, and so forth. For that reason, when you are initially searching for a guru, you should not settle for just anyone who comes along, but seek out someone who is fully qualified and then request his kindness in bestowing vows and precepts. Next, you should consider that in terms of his continuous teaching and revealing the precepts he is kinder than even the Buddha. You should make powerful requests with a vivid faith that understands your great good fortune in having met such a spiritual master endowed with the good qualities extolled in the Vinaya during a degenerate age such as this and that repeatedly contemplates the special good qualities explained in the Vinaya.

Making Supplications by Contemplating the Good Qualities of Your Guru as Explained in the Common Mahayana

The ritual text states:

> I make requests to you, the Mahayana virtuous friend,
> Lord of the Dharma, successor of all the conquerors,

Endowed with the ten qualities required to
Teach the path of the sugatas.

Regarding the qualifications of a Mahayana spiritual master, the *Ornament for Mahayana Sutras*[161] states:

Rely upon a friend who is subdued, pacified, thoroughly pacified,
Has superior good qualities, is enthusiastic, has a wealth of
    scriptures,
A realization of suchness, is skilled in speaking,
Has a compassionate nature, and has abandoned weariness.

Thus, your spiritual master should have the following ten qualities:
1. "Subdued" through his training in moral discipline.
2. "Pacified" through his training in concentration.
3. "Thoroughly pacified" through his training in wisdom.

These first three are in reference to the three higher trainings.
4. Possesses good qualities of scripture and realization superior to your own.
5. Has great diligence in accomplishing the two aims.
6. Has a wealth of scripture through listening to numerous teachings on the three baskets.
7. Has a realization of suchness concerning the mode of existence of phenomena.
8. Is skilled in explaining instructions to his disciples.
9. Has great compassion for living beings in general and disciples in particular.
10. Does not grow weary of working for the welfare of his disciples.

A qualified spiritual master should possess these ten good qualities. If I were to explain these in detail, this discourse would become far too verbose; therefore, you should consult the *Great Exposition on the Stages of the*

161. *mDo sde rgyan*; *Mahāyānasūtrālaṃkāra*.

Path to Enlightenment.[162] Drom Rinpoche said, "When a Mahayana guru gives an explanation, he creates limitless understanding [in the minds of his disciples]. When they are putting the teaching into practice, they must demonstrate what is beneficial at a time when the teachings are declining and what is useful in the present situation." Furthermore, the *Verses about Friends*[163] states:

> Relying upon an inferior, your dignity becomes impure;
> Relying upon your equals, you stagnate;
> Relying upon your superior, you attain saintliness;
> Therefore, rely upon [a master] who is superior to yourself.

Therefore, you should rely upon someone with qualities superior to your own. Furthermore, it is not sufficient that they are superior in terms of a few minor qualities; they should surpass you in terms of major qualities. It is indispensable that a superior operates with high regard for the prescribed rules of the Vinaya, possesses the complete set of instructions for the path of the Mahayana, and engages in as many of their practices as possible. If they don't have such [good qualities] and don't understand the Mahayana path, they will teach a mistaken path. If you encounter such a teacher, you will fall into a mistaken path; and once you become defiled by bad behavior, you will be ruined. Furthermore, through your intimacy with such persons your conduct will defile the Dharma. The bad smell of garlic and so forth will cause the container to smell. While whatever you place in that container, such as camphor, saffron, and so forth, will become imbued with their good scent, as is directly evident. A guru who reveals the unmistaken complete path of the Mahayana is the heir of all the conquerors and accomplishes the deeds of all the conquerors. As I have already explained, if all the conquerors in the ten directions respectfully honor such a guru, what need is there to mention his disciples? Therefore, initially perform careful examination and conduct a thorough search for a fully qualified spiritual master who reveals the unmistaken path of the

---

162. For a translation of this text see Tsong-kha-pa, *The Great Treatise on the Stages of the Path to Enlightenment*, 3 vols. (Ithaca, NY: Snow Lion Publications, 2000–2004).
163. *Tshoms; Mitravarga.*

Mahayana and request his kindness in teaching the Dharma. Next, you should perfectly rely upon him and cherish him more than your life. In particular, once you evoke a powerful mental experience by repeatedly contemplating the qualifications of your spiritual master as taught by Jet-sun Jamgon [Tsongkhapa], you should meditate and make supplications of great intensity.

Making Supplications by Contemplating the Good Qualities of Your Guru as Explained in the Vajrayana

The ritual text states:

> I make requests to you, principal holder of the vajra;
> Your three doors are perfectly subdued, you have great
>   wisdom and patience,
> And without pretense or deceit, with knowledge of mantras
>   and tantra,
> You are endowed with the two sets of ten qualities
> And are skilled in drawing [mandalas] and explaining them.

Concerning the qualifications of a Vajrayana guru, the *Fifty Verses of Guru Devotion* states:

> Stable, subdued, and wise,
> Patient, honest, and nondeceptive,
> Knowledge of mantras, tantras, and [ritual] actions,
> Compassionate and skilled in the treatises.
>
> He possesses the two sets of ten qualities,
> He is skilled in drawing the mandalas,
> Has knowledge of the activities of explaining mantra,
> Perfect faith, and subdued senses.

He is perfectly restrained by employing mindfulness of his body, speech, and mind. He has vast wisdom. He is endowed with the three types of patience: (1) patience toward those who cause harm, (2) patience toward the hardships of practice, and (3) patience of profound Dharma. Toward all living beings he is honest and nondeceptive.[164] Through explaining mantra and tantras he is capable of overcoming interferences through the use of medicinal rituals and so forth. He has compassion for living beings. He is skilled in all sciences in general and he is skilled in the inner sciences of the three baskets in particular. He is endowed with both sets of ten qualities. He is skilled in the activities of drawing sand mandalas. He is skilled in explaining the path of mantra to his disciples. He is endowed with stable faith and devotion for the Mahayana in general and mantra in particular. He is subdued through restraining the doors of his senses with introspection. A [Vajrayana guru] should be endowed with these good qualities.

Regarding the two sets of ten qualities, *The Vajra Mandala Adornment Tantra* states:

> The rituals of the two reversals.
> The rituals of secret and wisdom-exalted-wisdom [initiations]
> And uniting and separating.
> Torma, vajra recitation,
> The ritual of accomplishing the wrathful as well as
> Consecrating and accomplishing mandalas.
> These are the ten secret [qualities].
>
> Mandalas, concentration, and mudra,
> Ritual dances, sitting postures, and proclaiming mantras.
> Burnt offerings, offerings, ritual actions,
> And retracting the aspect of [deities] once again.
> These are the ten outer [qualities].

These are the ten inner qualities and the ten outer qualities. Regarding the ten inner qualities, they are

1. skill in expelling through meditating on the protection circle,
2. skill in expelling through drawing mandalas and binding them to the body and so forth,

---

164. In this instance, "nondeceptive" means not hiding one's faults and shortcomings.

3. skill in bestowing the vase empowerment and the secret empowerment,
4. skill in bestowing the wisdom-exalted-wisdom empowerment and the fourth empowerment,
5. skill in separating enemies from their protectors and separating the conjoined,
6. skill in torma rituals,
7. skill in the various types of recitation, such as mental recitation, vajra recitation and commitment recitation, palanquin recitation, fierce recitation, wrathful recitation, heap recitation, and so forth,
8. skill in the means of performing wrathful actions of dispersal when they cannot be accomplished properly,[165]
9. skill in ritual of consecration,
10. skill in making ritual offerings to the mandala.

The ten outer qualities are

1. skill in how to draw the outer mandalas and how to meditate on the inner mandalas,
2. skill in the concentrations, such as the initial preparation and so forth,
3. skill in the hand mudras,
4. skill in the ritual dances, such as with his right leg outstretched, left leg outstretched, circular, equal posture, and so forth,
5. skill in sitting in the vajra posture, the posture of Vajrasattva, and so forth,
6. skill in proclaiming mantras,
7. skill in burnt offerings,
8. skill in the offering rituals,
9. skill in ritual actions,
10. skill in requesting [the buddhas] to depart and summoning them back.

---

165. Here, "properly" means through other means, such as peaceful actions.

It is said that the master needs all ten of the outer qualities in the lower classes of tantra while the vajra master of highest yoga tantra must have all ten of the inner qualities. The fifth chapter of the *Explanatory Tantra Vajramala* states:

> Openly praise such a guru who is
> Skilled in the actions of pacifying and so forth,
> Has knowledge of mantra and yoga rituals and is
> Trained in the twenty ritual actions.
>
> Has pure moral discipline and generosity,
> Is endowed with patience and supreme diligence,
> Is accustomed to meditation during both day and night,
> And endowed with wisdom and skilled in creating.
>
> With a collection of good qualities of an outer guru
> He is proclaimed "glorious master."
> Inwardly he delights in Guhyasamaja
> With the outer conduct of a shravaka.
>
> With such oral instructions he sequentially
> Trains his disciples and followers,
> Whom he teaches thoroughly.

Thus, this is stating that a vajra master of Glorious Guhyasamaja trains in the vast wave of the bodhisattva's way of life and, by maintaining perfectly the prescribed rules of the Vinaya, he should nurture the yogas of the two stages of Glorious Guhyasamaja. The eighth chapter of the *Vajra Tent* states:

> The mantra thoroughly taught by
> The fully qualified vajra master
> Will be accomplished in the practitioner!
> He has stability and profound Dharma,
> Is skilled in all sciences,
> Has knowledge of burnt offerings, mandalas, and mantras,

Consecrations, tormas, and departing,
And knows the ten qualities.

Protecting the conduct of a shravaka,
Devotion for the stages of the mantra vehicle,
Delighted when seeing form bodies,
Skilled in recitation and drawing mandalas.

He has thoroughly destroyed downfalls from the root,
And through the practice of mantra and tantra
He bestows bliss upon the worldly.
Once you actually encounter such a guru
You should not degrade him, no matter what.

This accords with the previous explanation about the qualification of a vajra master and states that, in particular, he should not be defiled by a root downfall of mantra. The phrase [in Lama Chöpa] that states, "Your three doors are perfectly subdued, you have great wisdom and patience" is taught in numerous tantras, such as the *Web of Illusion Tantra*,[166] *The Vajra Mandala Adornment Tantra*, and so forth, when describing the qualifications of the vajra master and [the verses in Lama Chöpa] are arranged in a condensed form in the *Fifty Verses of Guru Devotion* and, other than a few minor differences, they are exactly the same as the words of these tantras. You should come to a decisive understanding of these words as they are explained in the tantras and you should develop an extremely vast understanding of the meaning of the tantras by consulting the commentaries as explained by the mahasiddhas. Therefore, when you initially wish to enter mantra, the *Explanatory Tantra Vajramala* states:

Just as you polish a jewel and
Burn, cut, and examine gold,
In the same way the disciple
Should examine [a potential guru] for up to
    twelve years.

---

166. *sGyu 'phrul dra ba'i rgyud; Māyājālatantra.*

For that purpose there should be
Such mutual examination at all times.

You should not rely upon just anyone who happens to appear, as though you are a dog happening upon a scrap of lung. Instead, you should examine [your potential guru] well and make supplications to he who is fully qualified. Furthermore, the *Cluster of the Ultimate Meaning* states:

> Through the power of the degenerate age the faults and good
>   qualities of the guru mix.
> There is no one who is without nonvirtue in every respect.
> Therefore, after a thorough examination, the disciples should
>   come to rely
> Upon whoever has a dominance of good qualities.

Due to the force of place and time it is very difficult to meet someone who is fully qualified in accordance with the explanations set forth in the tantras; therefore, we should seek out someone who has at least some of the qualifications. Furthermore, the *Commentary on Valid Cognition* states:

> If one does not have knowledge of all the
> Procedures and means as well as the qualifications
> Regarding the objects of abandonment,
> Yet has the wish for such authenticity,
> It does not matter if he has clairvoyance
> As long as he has the desire to realize such qualities.

You should accept someone who teaches the unmistaken boundaries of acceptance and abandonment with regard to the three sets of vows. Although he may have clairvoyance and miracle powers, if he doesn't teach the means of acceptance and abandonment, it is totally improper to have confidence in such claims. The *Fifty Verses of Guru Devotion* also states:

> The wise disciple should not accept as a guru
> Someone who lacks compassion, is hostile and angry,
> Arrogant, attached,
> Lacking restraint, or boastful.

For the wise that have a heartfelt desire to enter mantra it is unacceptable to rely upon just any guru. In particular, it is completely unacceptable to rely upon someone who has no regard for protecting the prescribed boundaries of his vows. The same thing has been taught in numerous tantras. Therefore, although you may get the impression that the guru has limitless good qualities, according to these instructions it is an extremely important point that he has the good qualities of the three sets of vows. Numerous tantras, such as the *Vairochana Abhisambodhi Tantra*[167] and the *General Secret Tantra*,[168] state that to enter the path of mantra we should rely upon someone who possesses the pratimoksha vows. The *Explanatory Tantra Vajramala* states:

> Thus, a fully ordained vajra holder
> Who has knowledge of twenty rituals
> Is known as the lord of beings.

This is stating that the empowering master should be a fully ordained vajra holder. To quote the *Commentary on the Kalachakra Empowerment Chapter*:[169]

> Among those with knowledge of the ten qualities,
> A fully ordained monk is supreme,
> A novice is middling,
> And a layperson is least qualified.

Thus, this states that a fully ordained monk is the very best. During a Kalachakra empowerment there is a special distinction made with regard to the height of empowerment platforms for the fully ordained monk, a novice, and a layperson. Also, during the actual empowerments, great emphasis is placed on making a distinction between these statuses, such as the number of activities and so forth. The *Great Commentary Stainless Light*[170] states that if a fully ordained vajra holder is staying in the same region it is improper for a lay vajra holder to bestow empowerment, per-

---

167. *rNam snang mngon byang*; *Vairocanābhisambodhitantra.*
168. *gSang ba spyi rgyud*; *Sarvamaṇḍalasāmānyavidhīnāṃguhyatantra.*
169. *Dus 'khor dbang le'i 'grel.*
170. *'Grel chen dri med 'od*; *Vimalaprabhā.*

form consecration rituals, and so forth and that a fully ordained vajra holder should not prostrate to a lay master, and so forth. [The *Great Commentary Stainless Light*] states in numerous ways the great importance of revering the pratimoksha as the foundation of the teachings. I am going to leave this point here because I am concerned that if I quote too many sources from the other tantras it will become too verbose.

In the *Great Exposition on the Stages of the Path to Enlightenment*, when the omniscient Je [Tsongkhapa] praises the greatness of Atisha, he primarily praises the greatness of the purity of his three vows. If the wise contemplate these points, they will gain great certainty on the essential points of the complete teachings. You should repeatedly contemplate the good qualities as I explained them earlier and, once you cultivate stable confidence and faith, you should make extremely powerful supplications.

Making Supplications through Recalling His Kindness

When reciting the verse that begins, "I make requests to you, my compassionate refuge and protector . . ." you should develop great respect by contemplating, "In general, although countless buddhas have already appeared, they were unable to subdue me, and although there have been other buddhas who appeared in this fortunate eon, with regard to teaching the good path of the conqueror to ignoble disciples like me during this era of the five degenerations who have been abandoned out of trepidation, it is my guru who is more kind and compassionate than all the buddhas." With this we should make a very powerful request by reciting:

> I make requests to you, my compassionate refuge and protector;
> You perfectly reveal the path of the sugatas for those
> Migrators of these degenerate times so difficult to tame
> Who were not subdued by the countless buddhas of the past.

Furthermore, the thousand buddhas of this fortunate eon generated the mind of enlightenment in the presence of the tathagata Ratna Garbha. When they were laying claim to their various realms, there was no one who was capable of assuming the responsibility of this age of strife when the lifespan is one hundred years. However, the bhagavan Shakyamuni had taken rebirth as the Brahmin Samudrarenu and, due to his compassion, was unable to bear this; therefore, he said, "I alone will subdue these ignoble beings that have been forsaken by all the other buddhas and I shall attain enlightenment during the age of strife when the lifespan of beings is only one hundred years." Thus, after generating the mind of enlightenment and making five hundred great prayers, he was born in this world. You should contemplate, "I was not able to see the compassionate teacher directly; however, it is my compassionate guru, my refuge and protector, that is the sole embodiment of all the conquerors' compassion, and even if all the buddhas appeared directly before me and taught the entire path of sutra and tantra, this could not compare to the compassion and kindness of my guru." You should think along these lines with faith and devotion until the hair pores of your body quiver and you are moved to tears.

Next, recite:

> I make requests to you, my compassionate refuge and protector;
> As the sun of the Buddha's teaching is setting
> So many living beings are without a refuge or protector,
> Yet you perfectly accomplish the deeds of the conquerors.

You should generate extremely powerful devotion by contemplating as follows: "Even the compassionate bhagavan Shakyamuni was not able to subdue me by revealing the path to nirvana. After him came the two great charioteers[171] who were prophesied by the conqueror, as well as countless scholars and siddhas and so forth that were all unable to subdue me. And now that things have become increasingly degenerate so that there are ignoble beings like me who are so difficult to tame, it is my guru who accomplishes the deeds of the conqueror. Furthermore, among all the deeds of the conqueror, it is his activity of teaching that reigns supreme. Since it is my refuge and protector, my kind guru, that teaches all the essential points of the paths of sutra and tantra that were taught by the conqueror in their entirety, there is no way that I could ever repay his kindness."

171. Nagarjuna and Asanga.

While meditating by faithfully recalling his great kindness at this point, Omniscient Je [Tsongkhapa quotes the *Array of Stalks Sutra*] which states:

I have come to this place after single-pointedly contemplating,
"My spiritual masters who teach the Dharma
Thoroughly reveal the good qualities of phenomena
And then reveal the bodhisattva's way of life in its entirety.

Because they generate [these qualities] they are like a mother,
Because they give the milk of good qualities they are like wet
     nurses,
They thoroughly train me in the limbs of enlightenment,
These spiritual masters expel the aspects of harm.

They are like doctors that free me from old age and death,
They send down a rain of nectar like Indra, the lord of gods,
Like the full moon they cause the virtuous Dharma to flourish,
Like the illuminating sun they reveal the way to peace.

Toward friends and enemies they are like mountains,
Their minds are unassailable like an ocean,
They completely protect me like a boat."
Thinking in this way, I, Sudhana, have come here.

These bodhisattvas have developed my mind,
They have produced my enlightenment as a son of the buddhas;
I praise these spiritual masters as buddhas.
With these virtuous thoughts I have come here.

By protecting the world, they are like heroes,
And have become my captains, protectors, and refuge.
They are eyes that produce happiness in me;
With such a mind I honor these spiritual masters.

In accordance with the way in which Youthful Sudhana made supplications through the kindness of his gurus, you should exchange the name

"Sudhana" with your own and, using a melodious chant, generate as much devotion as you can for the kindness of your spiritual masters and recite these verses until you are moved to tears. Even if you don't actually recite them, you should develop faith by recalling his kindness by contemplating the meaning of this request. Vajradhara Losang Chökyi Gyaltsen said:

> We have been left behind by many buddhas of the past,
> And those who are buddhas who are currently living
> In the worldly realms of the ten directions
> Have been unable to subdue the beings of the degenerate age,
> Who are left without a refuge or protector.
> Recalling the kindness [of my gurus], I, Jetsun Losang Chökyi
> Gyaltsen,
> Supplicate those who accomplish the deeds of the omniscient
> conqueror.

And:

> For the sake of the meaning of each Dharma verse
> You should endure such hardships as the buddhas of old,
> Such as jumping into a pit of blazing flames and
> Piercing yourself a thousand times with iron spikes and so forth.

> Yet these days no one has such great perseverance.
> Father, through your great kindness I have obtained
> Many vast and profound Dharmas of sutra and tantra.
> Until I attain the essence of enlightenment there is no way
> I could repay your kindness, which is the cause of omniscience.

> Listen with your mind of compassion and joyously accept these
> Enjoyments and collection of virtue of my three doors that I offer
> For the sake of producing delight in you, the foremost being.

> Since beginningless eons of old, you, my father,
> Have repeatedly protected me with your compassion.
> And again even now, until the essence of enlightenment,

I seek no refuge other than you as my foremost guru
Regardless of the time and situation.

My foremost guru, think of me with your wisdom,
With all the happiness and suffering, qualities and faults of
    myself, the lowly practitioner,
And hold me with the hook of your compassion.

May I never generate even the slightest wrong view
Toward whatever deeds my foremost guru manifests.
May I accomplish my eternal aim
Through the profound path of guru yoga.

We should also contemplate the meaning of these words.

Next, the ritual text states:

I make requests to you, my compassionate refuge and protector;
Even just one of your hair pores
Is praised as the perfect field of merit, superior to
All the conquerors of the three times and the ten directions.

We should meditate with faith and devotion by contemplating, "Although from the perspective of good qualities there isn't any superiority among the conquerors or distinctions between higher and lower qualities, such as those of abandonment and realization, as it states here even one hair pore of my guru surpasses all the conquerors in the ten directions as my own field for accumulating merit." And, "If, from my own side, I am able to make requests, I will receive blessings from all the buddhas in the ten directions and, although it requires many countless eons to accomplish the supreme state, through the power of my compassionate guru I will be able to quickly accomplish realizations; therefore, there is nothing that compares to the kindness and compassion of my guru." Thinking in this way you should make powerful supplications. As a field for the disciples' accumulation of merit, even one pore of the guru is superior to all the buddhas. The seventeenth chapter of the *Guhyasamaja Root Tantra* states:

In this way, for example, child of the lineage, however many bhagavan buddhas there are dwelling in the ten directions and however many heaps of merit produced from the vajra body, speech, and mind of those bhagavan buddhas, they are all surpassed by the merit of a single pore of the master. Why? Because, child of the lineage, bodhichitta is the essence of the wisdom of buddhahood, from transforming one's place of birth up to being the source of the wisdom of omniscience.

The *Samputa Tantra* states:

> Those abiding in the ten directions make offerings to the intelligent master, whom the conqueror worships. Because he sees that the tip of just one pore of the master's hair has the merit of a perfected buddha or bodhisattva, therefore a buddha will be seen making offerings to a master, a bodhisattva.

Another translation of the *Samputa Tantra* states:

> Because a single pore of the guru is superior
> To the merit of the buddhas
> And bodhisattvas of the ten directions,
> Therefore, the buddhas and bodhisattvas
> observe offerings made to the master.

To make this plain and simple: if even the conquerors consider the vajra master who reveals the unmistaken path as an object of worship, what need is there to mention [the guru's] disciples! There are other teachings such as this mentioned in numerous tantras.

How to Make Supplications through Recollecting His Outer, Inner, Secret, and Suchness Qualities has four sections:
1. **How to Make Supplications by Proclaiming His Outer Qualities**
2. **How to Make Supplications by Proclaiming His Inner Qualities**

3. How to Make Supplications by Proclaiming His Secret Qualities
4. How to Make Supplications by Proclaiming His Qualities of Suchness

How to Make Supplications by Proclaiming His Outer Qualities

Recite the verse from the ritual text that begins, "The ornamental wheels of your three sugata bodies . . ."[172] There are numerous ways in which these lines have been explained by lamas. Beginning with the previous verse, "Who were not subdued by the countless buddhas of the past . . . ," up to this point you are making supplications by proclaiming his outer qualities. The verse "Your aggregates, elements, . . ." is a supplication by proclaiming his inner qualities. The verse "The manifestation of omniscient exalted wisdom . . ." is a supplication by proclaiming his secret qualities. The verse "The manifestation of spontaneous joy free from obstruction . . ." is a supplication by proclaiming his qualities of suchness. In another system the verses from "Who were not subdued by the countless buddhas of the past . . ." up to the verse "All the conquerors of the three times and the ten directions" are related to his outer qualities. The two verses "The ornamental wheels of your three sugata bodies . . ." and "Your aggregates, elements, sources, and limbs . . ." are related to his inner qualities. The verse "The manifestation of omniscient exalted wisdom . . ." is related to his secret qualities. The verse "The manifestation of spontaneous joy free from obstruction . . ." is how to make supplication through his secret qualities. Yet another system states that "the ornamental wheels of your three sugata bodies . . ." is related to his outer qualities. The two verses "Your aggregates, elements, sources, and limbs . . ." and "The manifestation of omniscient exalted wisdom . . ." are related to his inner qualities. And the verse "The manifestation of spontaneous joy free from obstruction . . ." is making supplications through expressing both his secret and suchness qualities.

---

172. The sequence of the lines in the ritual text is arranged slightly differently throughout the following section.

Thus, as you can see, although there are many ways of explaining these verses of supplication expressed through the devotion of various disciples, their meaning is similar. Nevertheless, for those with vast intelligence there appear to be numerous ways of generating an understanding of the composition with the essential points of the paths of sutra and tantra in general and the two stages of the path of mantra in particular in dependence upon the way the meaning of these verses is explained. No matter how you do it, regarding how to make the supplication, meditate with devotion by thinking, "For the sake of caring for the living beings such as myself and others like me in this time of the five degenerations who do not have the good fortune to be able to encounter the Buddha in person, for the sake of those with fortune equal to my own, all the buddhas dwelling in the pure lands in the ten directions emanate bodies as an ordinary being who leads us to the Buddha-ground through teaching us the quintessential points of the oral instructions in their entirety; therefore, his compassion is immeasurable."

The verse from the ritual text states:

> I make requests to you, my compassionate refuge and protector;
> From your charming, graceful web of magical emanations
>   and skillful means
> The ornamental wheels of your three sugata bodies
> Manifest in ordinary forms to guide living beings.

With regard to the phrase "The ornamental wheels of your three sugata bodies," when the conquerors manifest complete enlightenment, they spontaneously accomplish the truth body, enjoyment body, and emanation body simultaneously. As a symbolic representation of those three, their bodies are adorned by a white OM of the vajra body, a red AH of the vajra speech, and a blue HUM as the vajra mind. During the practice of highest yoga mantra, the vajra speech functions as the enjoyment body and so forth and begins with the secret offering. There are so many ways of explaining this yet I won't elaborate. The phrases "Presently, your inexhaustible ornamental wheels of your three bodies" and "The inconceivable secrets of your body, speech, and mind" have similar meanings. Regarding the phrase "inconceivable secrets of your body," it is stated that "being embraced by the power of the previous bodhisattvas who conquered the enemy of the worldly realm of the east," which is in reference to their fortitude in coming into this worldly realm to make offerings to Buddha Shakyamuni and listen to the holy Dharma. If, for the sake of seeing the extent of the body of the tathagata and the tip of his ushnisha, they manifest their own body eighty-four thousand leagues and perceive six million eight hundred thousand bodies of the tathagata, they still could not perceive the extent of his body. With regard to being unable to perceive the tip of his ushnisha, through the bodhisattva Vegadhari's generation of magical powers he went to more buddha lands above than there are grains of sands in one trillion Ganges Rivers and, when he arrived in the worldly realm called Padma Chen, he looked and the tathagata's body was as vast as the sky, yet he still could not see his ushnisha. Thus, it is not possible to measure the extent of his body.

Next, [Vegadhari] asked a tathagata named Padma Shri Raja Garbha (the Essential King of the Glorious Lotus), who lived in that same pure land, to what extent he could perceive the Bhagavan Shakyamuni's body and if [he could see] the tip of his ushnisha, to which [Padma Shri Raja Garbha] replied that he could not perceive it even to the ends of space and said:

Whatever is the extent of space
Is the extent of the Buddha's body.

Yet the ushnisha of the lord of the world
Is equal to realms of space.

For as far as space pervades,
His body pervades to the same extent.

To whatever extent his body pervades,
Light rays pervade to the same extent.

To whatever extent the light rays pervade,
His speech pervades to the same extent.

To whatever extent his speech pervades,
His mind pervades to the same extent.

There are vast explanations of the good qualities of his body.

Regarding the inconceivable secrets of his speech, for the sake of examining the extent of the melodious Brahmin speech of the tathagata, Maudgalyayanaputra went to the peak of Mount Meru, to the outer iron ring of mountains, and so on yet could still hear his voice as before. Next, through the force of his magical powers he went to more buddha lands in the western direction than there are grains of sand in seven hundred and seventy billion Ganges Rivers. When he arrived in the worldly realm called Öser Gyi Gyaltsen (Victory Banner of Light Rays), he listened [to the Buddha's speech] and it was no different than when he was in the presence of the Buddha and listened to his speech at Vulture's Peak. In that realm resided a tathagata called Öser Gyi Gyalpo (the King of Light Rays). His body was only one league [in height] and the bodies of his bodhisattvas were only half a league in height; however, Maudgalyayanaputra walked around the rim of the begging bowls of those bodhisattvas and sat down. Those bodhisattvas touched Maudgalyayanaputra with their hands and said with complete wonder, "What sort of living being is this tiny creature that is walking around the rim of the begging bowl and assuming the form of a fully ordained monk in this way?" When they asked the tathagata Öser Gyi Gyalpo, the tathagata said, "This supreme emanation of the shravaka is from the world of unbearable suffering[173] of the teacher Shakyamuni; therefore, don't disparage him." Next, Maudgalyayanaputra displayed his miraculous transformation and caused his body to pervade that pure land with a single cross-legged posture and supplicated the teacher to come to this realm. This story is explained in detail in the *Sutra of the Inconceivable Secret*.[174]

Regarding the inconceivable secrets of his mind, if all the roots and trees of the worldly realms equal to the number of grains of sand of the Ganges River were burned by fire and their ashes equaling the number

173. Saha world. Our world system is known as the "world of endurance" because the living beings here endure unbearable suffering.
174. *gSang ba bsam gyis mi khyab pa'i mdo*; *Tathāgatācintyaguhyanirdeśasūtra*.

of grains of sand of the Ganges River were poured into a great ocean and mixed up for a thousand years and were then removed and the subtle atoms of each of those ashes filled the worldly realm, and if you asked the tathagata, "From which region did this ash come and from where did this root come?" the Buddha could instantaneously perceive this with his unobstructed wisdom and could identify each and every atom of ash by proclaiming, "This came from this worldly realm, this came from this region, this is grass and this is tree; this is the ash of a root, this is from the trunk, this is from the branches, this is from the leaves, this is from the fruit" and so on while identifying each particle without mixing them. Furthermore, in the sutras the conqueror himself explained how his knowledge operates by using similes with regard to what is incapable of being calculated in *In Praise of the Praiseworthy*,[175] which states:

> Only your exalted wisdom
> Pervades all objects of knowledge.
> For everyone other than you
> There are still objects to be known.

Regarding the wisdom of the Buddha simultaneously pervading all objects of knowledge of the three times, beyond merely saying, "Objects of knowledge are equal to the extent of space," among both migrating beings and gods there isn't anyone capable of calculating the wisdom of a buddha. Regarding the exalted wisdom understanding all aspects of a buddha's mind, it pervades all objects of knowledge, and even the direct nonconceptual realizations of the great beings, such as the shravakas and pratyeka buddhas and the great bodhisattvas dwelling on the great grounds, cannot calculate it. In short, the omniscient Je [Tsongkhapa] states:

> However much they are examined, the secrets of your
> Body, speech, and mind are not objects
> For the bodhisattvas, shravakas, or pratyeka buddhas.
> Therefore, what need is there to mention Brahma, Indra,
>   and so forth?

175. *bsNgags 'os bsngas bstod*; *Vanarahavarnastotra*.

Contemplate:

> Thus, not only are the inconceivable secrets of his body, speech,
> and mind not within the sphere of our comprehension, we
> do not have the good fortune of those ordinary beings with
> pure karma on up that are suitable to perceive his supreme
> emanation body adorned with the signs and indications. How-
> ever, out of his immeasurable compassion and skillful means
> of magical transformation he revealed himself as an ordinary
> being with fortune similar to our own in a body of flesh and
> bones and revealed the aspect of giving teachings.

After which you should meditate with faith and devotion and make supplications. Regarding this point, the *Explanatory Tantra Vajramala* states much
of the same thing when it says, "Outwardly he safeguards the conduct of a
shravaka." Numerous tantras, such as the *Hevajra Tantra Entitled "The Two
Examinations"*[176] as well as the *Vajra Tent* and numerous sutras, such as the
Meeting of Father and Son Sutra, mention the Buddha assuming an ordinary
form in this degenerate era. Such means of teaching are widely renowned.
Instead of having too many doubts about these qualities discussed in the
previous subject matter, we should generate certainty. Previously, during
the life of the Buddha, he revealed numerous forms as ordinary beings
in accordance with the thoughts and inclinations of his disciples. For the
sake of subduing Angulimala, the Buddha revealed himself as an ordinary
monk, and to subdue King Kapina he emanated as a chakravartin king.
Maudgalyayana emanated as a great minister. For the sake of subduing
the king of smell eaters, Perfect Joy, [Buddha] emanated himself as an
ordinary smell eater and so forth. [Enlightened beings] assume these ordinary forms and work for the welfare of living beings. There are numerous
stories such as these in the sutras.

176. *rTag gnyis.*

How to Make Supplications by Proclaiming His Inner Qualities

The ritual text states:

> I make requests to you, supreme guru, the nature of the
>   Three Jewels;
> Your aggregates, elements, sources, and limbs
> Are the nature of the fathers and mothers of the five buddha
>   families,
> The bodhisattvas, and the wrathful powerful deities.

Regarding the inner aggregates, elements, and sources of your guru's body, who is kind in the three ways and assumed the aspect of an ordinary being with a fortune similar to that of us ignorant and foolish beings, you should think, "He is in fact not an ordinary being but is the nature embodying all Three Jewels, such as the fathers and mothers of the five buddha families, the eight bodhisattvas, the ten wrathful deities, and so forth," and supplicate him with great faith and devotion. I have already explained these points in detail during the visualization of the field of merit.

How to Make Supplications by Proclaiming His Secret Qualities

The ritual text states:

> I make requests to you, protector of the primordial union;
> You are the ten million circles of mandalas,
> The manifestation of omniscient exalted wisdom,
> The principal vajra holder, pervasive lord of a hundred
>   lineages.

We should make supplications with intense devotion by contemplating, "Whatever mandalas were taught in the four classes of tantra are all dominated by, emanations of, and the nature of my kind root guru, who is kind in the three ways." In short, we ascribe the epithet "All-Pervasive Lord Vajradhara" [to our guru], who is the sole embodiment of the compassion and exalted wisdom of all the conquerors and bodhisattvas dwelling in the limitless pure lands in the ten directions.

Regarding how the protector of the primordial union was established, the omniscient Khedrup stated:

> I prostrate to the protector of the primordial union,
> The deity that arises from the sky-realm of the clear light
> As the crystal jewel of the extremely subtle life-supporting
>   wind
> In a body embraced by ten million white rays of moonlight.

By penetrating the essential points of the inner vajra body, the root and branch winds are collected into the central channel; and from their dissolution, the example clear light and the meaning clear light arise in sequence; and then, from the great bliss that is the spontaneously born exalted wisdom, along with this mount [the very subtle winds], the body of union is accomplished. What we call the "protector of the primordial union" comes from the same continuum as that body and is the complete enjoyment body endowed with the five certainties. From its mind emerges the display of the hundred lineages and so forth. As for these "hundred lineages," there are twenty lineages of the lineage of Vairochana, the twenty lineages of Ratnasambhava, the twenty lineages of Amitabha, the twenty lineages of Amoghasiddhi, and the twenty lineages of Akshobya; these are the hundred lineages. All one hundred of those lineages can once again be reduced to the five lineages. They can be further subsumed under the three secrets. All three secrets can be further subsumed into Vajradhara—the sole lineage of the great secret. Regarding these methods, they are the abodes of the most tightly kept secrets that reveal the innermost essence of Glorious Guhyasamaja; therefore, this way of supplicating is "secret supplication."

How to Make Supplications by Proclaiming His Qualities of Suchness

The ritual text states:

> I make requests to you, actual ultimate bodhichitta,
> The manifestation of spontaneous joy free from obstruction,
> The all-pervasive nature of all things stable and moving,
> Free from beginning and end, the pure nature of Samantabhadra.

This is also called "How to meditate on the definitive meaning of the guru." Regarding the meaning of this, the omniscient Khedrup states:

> Dissolving conceptual elaborations of dualistic appearances
>   into the sphere of reality,
> You cut the moving wind of the wheel of existence.
> I prostrate to the truth body of great bliss,
> The supreme joy of simultaneously born "all empty."

To comprehend these points in detail, you must understand that self-grasping is the root of samsara, and to overcome that you need the wisdom realizing the mode of existence. Without letting the means of attaining liberation through familiarity become mere words, you need to achieve profound certainty without letting that wisdom become separated from the limbs of familiarity. In addition to that, you need the uncommon explanation of highest yoga tantra regarding the way in which the energy winds function as the root of all of samsara and nirvana, and how dissolving the movement of conceptual winds severs the root of samsara. Also, you should understand how the winds function to [allow one to] attain the state of omniscience by stopping the flow of the moving wind of conceptualization, and through the force of that you accomplish the truth body of great bliss. This presentation is the pinnacle of all tantras and is the essential meaning of the root and explanatory tantras of Guhyasamaja and explains the hidden meaning from among the six limits and the four modes.[177] This

---

177. The six limits and four modes are indispensable keys for unlocking the meaning of the

is the essential meaning of the ultimate explanation; therefore, you should become well acquainted with highest yoga tantra in its entirety upon the realization of this abode of extreme secrets, and in particular the meaning of the root and explanatory tantras of Glorious Guhyasamaja.

With regard to the truth body of the guru, it is not only praised in the perfection of wisdom sutras, but as already cited earlier, it is clearly expressed in the *Diamond Cutter Sutra*. It is taught in many other sutras as well. Ensapa and his spiritual sons repeatedly use the terms "truth body guru" and "definitive meaning guru"; therefore, these terms are not my own fabrications and this meaning is taught by the conqueror himself in the sutras and tantras. The perfection of wisdom sutras state:

> Subhuti, the perfection of wisdom itself is the bodhisattva, the great being, the spiritual master. Subhuti, all six perfections are the bodhisattva, the great being, and the spiritual master. All six of these perfections are your teacher. The six perfections are your illumination. The six perfections are your light. The six perfections are your protection. The six perfections are your attainment. The six perfections are your abode. The six perfections are your companion and defender. The six perfections are your temple. The six perfections are your mother. The six perfections are your knowledge, realization, and dwelling for the meaning of engaging in the unsurpassed, perfect, complete enlightenment.

And from the *Chapter That Focuses Completely on the Six Perfections*:

> Ananda, in short, just as I am your teacher, in the same way the perfection of wisdom is your teacher.

This is taught extensively [in the perfection of wisdom literature].

Not only must you perceive the resultant perfection of wisdom that is the exalted wisdom of omniscience as your guru and teacher, but you

---

tantras. The six limits are the views of (1) the interpretive meaning, (2) the definitive meaning, (3) the implied, (4) the not implied, (5) the literal, and (6) the not literal. The four modes are (1) literal, (2) general, (3) hidden, and (4) ultimate.

[must] also perceive the six perfections at the time of the path as your guru and teacher. We call these our "inner teachers," which is well known in the perfection of wisdom scriptures. The root and explanatory tantras provide extensive explanations of the six limits by using terms such as "the definitive guru," the "definitive deity," and so forth. The exalted wisdom of simultaneously born great bliss is lord of all things stable and moving and itself pervades all things stable and moving, and so forth. These teachings are extremely difficult to realize, yet if you don't realize them, you will not discover the life of the path of highest yoga tantra. There is great value in realizing these points that contain the ultimate essential meaning of tantra, and even though they require an explanation to cut the root of doubt, the only reason foolish and ignorant beings like myself can even give a brief explanation of these ultimate secrets is by merely repeating what my own holy guru has said. Therefore, study and analyze these vajra words in detail through the guidance of a holy being that has actualized the meaning of the tantras. Therefore, you will never be able to comprehend even a mere portion of such profound secret points by taking refuge in merely the scriptures themselves or through the logician's use of clever reasoning. You will only ever succeed through the kindness of a holy guru. The *Hevajra Tantra in Two Chapters Entitled "The Two Examinations"* states:

> Simultaneously born bliss is not expressed by others,
> And you will also not find it there.
> It should be learned when, through your merit,
> The guru reveals the way.

Vajradhara Losang Chökyi Gyaltsen also said:

> Simultaneously born bliss is not expressed by others,
> And you will also not find it there.
> Through serving you and listening to your teachings,
> Combined with your incomparable kindness of direct
>   realization,
> I, Jetsun Losang Chökyi Gyaltsen,
> Supplicate your three doors with devotion while
> Recalling from my heart your immense kindness.

Grant me your blessing that I may quickly generate
Simultaneously born inseparable bliss and emptiness free
    from obstruction.

How to Make the Supplication of Planting the Stake and Taking the Four Empowerments of Concentration

The ritual text states:

You are the guru, you are the yidam, and you are
The *daka* and Dharma protector.
From now until I attain enlightenment I will seek no refuge
    other than you.
In this life, the intermediate state, and in all future lives
Please hold me with the hook of your compassion,
Liberate me from all fears of samsara and nirvana,
Bestow all attainments, be my constant companion, and
Protect me from all obstacles. (3x)

Make three extremely powerful supplications in this way. Regarding the visualizations that should be undertaken at that time, once you have observed that your kind root guru, who is endowed with the three types of kindness, is the embodiment of all three refuges, you should then make single-pointed supplications with the entirety of your mind that places your hopes in no other. At that point you should imagine that you grasp the feet of your guru and touch your head [to his feet] while reciting the supplication. Furthermore, with regard to the kind root guru, having realized that he is the sole embodiment of the exalted wisdom of omniscience and compassion of all the conquerors in the ten directions, you should contemplate:

It is through the guru's generosity that he lifts me out of the great abyss of the miseries of samsara and the lower realms and then guides me along the path of liberation and omniscience in accordance with my fortune. Therefore, until I attain enlightenment, I will place my hopes in no other; please lead me along the path until I attain the state of enlightenment. I supplicate you who are the sole embodiment of all Three Jewels appearing as my guru; quickly protect me from all the fears of samsara and peace. I supplicate you who are the sole embodiment of all personal deities; please quickly bestow the common and supreme attainments. As well as all the heroes and dakinis of the three places, you, Guru-Vajradhara, are the manifestation of the great exalted wisdom of great bliss; therefore, you are the sovereign lord of the dakas and the nature embodying all the dakinis. I supplicate you; be my companion and assist me to quickly traverse the path until I attain enlightenment. You are the magical display of Guru-Vajradhara's enlightened actions appearing as all the Dharma protectors and guardians abiding in the eight charnel grounds and the twenty-four places. I supplicate you who are the nature embodying all Dharma protectors to protect me from all interfering unfavorable outer and inner conditions that prevent me from attaining enlightenment. In short, at all times, in this life, my next life, and in the intermediate state, I will never place my hopes in anyone other than you, Guru-Vajradhara. Please hold me with the hook of your compassion without ever being apart and grant me your blessings.

Make this supplication with intense yearning and devotion.

Having made intense supplication by "planting the stake,"[178] the ritual text describes the way of taking the four empowerments of concentration:

> Through the force of requesting three times in this way,
> White, red, and blue light rays and nectars
> Arise sequentially and collectively
> From the guru's body, speech, and mind and
> Descend sequentially and collectively into my three places.

178. The verse that begins "You are the guru, you are the yidam, . . ." is called "planting the stake" because you repeatedly make the request out of faith and devotion as if pounding a stake further and further into the ground.

> My four obstructions are purified;
> I receive the four empowerments and attain the four bodies.
> My guru is pleased; a replica dissolves into me,
> And I receive his blessings.

Regarding what you should be visualizing, through the force of making three supplications out of your extremely fierce devotion you should imagine that Lama Tubwang Dorje Chang is delighted from the depths of his heart, whereby a stream of white nectar descends from the OM at his crown. It dissolves into your crown, purifying all the negative karma and obscurations you have accumulated with your body and your ordinary appearances and conceptions in particular. You receive the vase empowerment and establish the potential to accomplish the emanation body.

A stream of red nectar descends from the AH at the throat of your guru. It dissolves into your throat, purifying all the negative karma and obscurations you have accumulated with your speech and your ordinary appearances and conceptions of grasping at your energy wind and mantra as being separate in particular. You receive the speech empowerment and establish the potential to accomplish the enjoyment body.

A stream of white nectar descends from the HUM at the heart of your guru. It dissolves into your heart, purifying all the negative karma and obscurations you have accumulated with your mind and the stains that prevent you from embracing whatever appears as bliss and emptiness in particular. You receive the wisdom-exalted-wisdom empowerment and establish the potential to accomplish the truth body.

Streams of white, red, and blue nectar descend simultaneously from the OM, AH, and HUM at his crown, throat, and heart. They dissolve into your three places, purifying all the negative karma and obscurations you have accumulated in common with your three doors. You receive the fourth empowerment, the precious word empowerment, and establish the potential to accomplish the resultant union. Thinking in this way, you should stabilize your conviction. This is merely the concise way of receiving the blessing of the four empowerments.

If you would like to take each of the four empowerments in a more elaborate way so that you are sure to receive all the symbolic meanings of each of the four empowerments, make the three supplications as before in a very powerful way. Establish your conviction by thinking, "Since I wish to quickly attain the body of union, once I enter the path of mantra I am going to make a respectful supplication for the special four empowerments that are the ripening agent for attaining my goal," and contemplate, "I am respectfully requesting the vase empowerment in particular." Due to this powerful supplication, light rays radiate from the heart of Lama Tubwang Dorje Chang the Great to the ten directions and they invoke all the father and mother conquerors in the ten directions in the space before you. Lama Tubwang Dorje Chang the Great sets the intention to bestow the empowerment. Lochana and so forth together with knowledge goddesses dwell in the space before you holding umbrellas, victory banners, and so forth above you. They sing, dance, and play musical instruments while sending down a rain of flowers, such as saffron and so forth. They hold vases in their hands filled with white bodhichitta that they tilt slightly and bestow the empowerment. Rupavajra goddesses and so forth sing songs of auspiciousness and proclaim auspicious verses. The wrathful deities chase away obstructing spirits in the cardinal and intermediate directions. They bestow the empowerment through the crown of your head with a flood [of nectar] while reciting OM SARWA TATHAGATA ABHISHEKATA SAMAYA SHRI YE HUM. Your body is filled with nectar-water and all of the negative karma and obscurations you have accumulated through your body since beginningless lives, such as taking what is not given, sexual misconduct, and so forth, and in particular all the stains of ordinary appearances and conceptions that grasp at your body as being ordinary, are purified. Your body becomes clear, luminous, and the nature of light, which you visualize clearly as the deity body. The excess water overflows onto the crown of your head and Akshobya becomes your crown ornament, which you recognize as being the nature of your guru. Through this you have received the vase empowerment. Primarily, the three types of stains associated with your body from the past are purified and you promise to refrain from them in the future. Through washing away the stains of ordinary appearances and conceptions that grasp at your ordinary body you are cleansing your vajra body. You should imagine that you are empowered to meditate on the generation stage, together with its limbs. You establish the special capacity to accomplish the resultant emanation body. You should imagine that the empowering goddesses dissolve into you, whereby your mental continuum is blessed.

Next, make supplications through your extremely powerful faith and devotion for Tubwang Dorje Chang the Great while thinking, "Please bestow the secret empowerment upon me." Due to this, Lama Dorje Chang the Great enters into embrace with the Vajradhatu Ishvari. Light rays radiate from their joined organs and his heart and go out to the ten directions invoking the father and mother conquerors of the ten directions and enter into the crown of the head of your guru. Their bodhichitta melts and a stream of red and white nectar emerges from the joined organs of Guru-Vajradhara Father and Mother the Great, as well as an immeasurable stream of nectar from all parts of their bodies that dissolves into your body, whereby your entire body is filled with nectar. In particular, an immeasurable amount of red and white bodhichitta enters the area of your throat, whereby all the negative karma and obscurations you have accumulated through your speech, such as lying, harsh speech, idle gossip, and so on, are purified, especially all the stains of grasping and conceiving of your energy wind and mantra as being separate. Your body becomes clear, luminous, and the nature of light. In particular, your channels, winds, and drop-elements are blessed, whereby you are empowered to meditate on the pure and impure illusory bodies and you establish a special potential to accomplish the resultant enjoyment body. Meditate with joy, thinking, "I have attained the secret empowerment."

Next, make supplications through your extremely powerful faith and devotion for Tubwang Dorje Chang the Great while thinking, "Please bestow the wisdom-exalted-wisdom empowerment upon me," through which duplicates of the mother Vajradhatu Ishvari emerge from Guru-Vajradhara Father and Mother the Great that dissolve into the mother of yourself visualized as the desire father and mother deities. Through embracing with her you sequentially attain the joy, supreme joy, extraordinary joy, and simultaneously born joy. During the simultaneously born joy, the movement of the winds that give rise to conceptualization cease, all elaborations are completely pacified, and you place your mind in single-pointed meditative equipoise upon emptiness as the fundamental nature of reality. At this point you should stabilize your conviction of having manifested the truth body that is the clear light of great bliss. Regarding this clear light of great bliss, this single mind is capable of producing both the form body and the truth body and is the special substantial cause for accomplishing union in this very life as the uncommon path of highest yoga tantra. The omniscient Je [Tsongkhapa] said:

> It is best if you are able to generate simultaneously born bliss; however, if you are unable to, if you can generate bliss through melting [the bodhichitta] during the generation stage, you should meditate on that. However, if you are unable to, at the very least you should try to establish as many imprints as possible for the profound path of mantra by mentally evoking the experience in dependence upon intellectual understanding of how it works.

In this way you have received the wisdom-exalted-wisdom empowerment. All the negative karma and obscurations that you have accumulated since beginningless lives with your mind, such as covetousness, malice, wrong views, and so on, are purified. In particular, defilements that prevent you from perceiving whatever appears as the manifestation of bliss and emptiness are purified. You are empowered to meditate on the clear light of the path. In particular, you establish the potential to accomplish the resultant truth body of great bliss. Thinking in this way you should meditate with joy.

Next, you make another powerful request of faith and devotion to Lama Tubwang Dorje Chang the Great and imagine that you are requesting him with great respect to bestow the fourth empowerment, the precious word empowerment. Through this mental supplication Lama Tubwang Dorje Chang the Great says:

> When you received the third empowerment you imagined your body to be the deity body and your mind to be simultaneously born joy, whereby you ascertained the true meaning of suchness as existing equally in both. By continuing to meditate on their meaning in this way you will ultimately accomplish the complete enjoyment of exalted wisdom accomplished from your mere wind and mind embracing the body of a knowledge goddess. Simultaneously with that your mind of simultaneously

born joy and emptiness will become one taste with the all-empty clear light. As these two become inseparable you will manifest the state of union of nondual exalted wisdom. This object of accomplishment is the meaning of the fourth empowerment.

For the fourth empowerment you identify the meaning of union and Lama Tubwang Dorje Chang the Great is extremely pleased, whereby a duplicate of his body emerges and dissolves into your body, whereby all the negative karma and obscurations you have accumulated with your three doors since beginningless time are purified. In particular, all the mistaken dualistic appearances and their imprints are purified and you enter into the sphere of the clear light of emptiness. You then instantaneously emerge from that clear light like a fish jumping from the water and instantaneously arise in the body of the primordial protector of union. You should stabilize your conviction that your three doors have become inseparably unified with the body, speech, and mind of Lama Tubwang Dorje Chang the Great and place your mind in meditative equipoise to the best of your ability. Through that you have received the fourth empowerment, the precious word empowerment. The negative karma and obscurations, together with the imprints of your three doors, are purified. You are empowered to meditate on the path of union. You should meditate with a mind of joy, thinking, "I have established a special capacity to quickly accomplish Vajradhara's resultant body of union."

This is how you take the four empowerments in an elaborate way. It can be done in conjunction with the yogas of Heruka, Guhyasamaja, or Yamantaka. Alternatively, you can also practice this in a somewhat generic way. In particular, if you are combining it with the words of the yoga of Vajrabhairava, you can switch the aspect of the principal into Vajrabhairava. You should know how to take the four empowerments, such as the vase empowerment and so forth, by imagining the five buddha families emerging from the five lineages of Vajrabhairava that are dwelling in the body of Guru-Vajrabhairava the Great,[179] which are arranged according to Gyalwa Ensapa the Great's teachings on the guru yoga of Vajrabhairava.

179. The sadhanas for the practices of Heruka and Yamantaka Lama Chöpa are available at https://dechenlingpress.org/product/lama-chopa-heruka-sadhana/ and https://dechenling press.org/product/yamantaka-lama-chopa/, respectively.

If you wish to practice in conjunction with Guhyasamaja, once you switch the principal of the field of merit to Akshobya-Vajra, you should take the four empowerments as explained above or take the four empowerments by extracting them from the Guhyasamaja mandala ritual. Regarding the uncommon way of taking them, you should follow Vajradhara Losang Chökyi Gyaltsen's Guhyasamaja guru yoga.

If you wish to practice in conjunction with Chakrasamvara, once you switch the principal of the field of merit to Chakrasamvara and you wish to take the four empowerments in an uncommon way, you should base it on the guru yoga of Heruka composed by Gyalwa Ensapa the Great. Mahasiddha Ensapa and his spiritual sons wrote out the oral instructions of the Hearing Lineage of Conqueror Tsongkhapa the Great for taking the four empowerments of concentration; therefore, we should have confidence that they are in actuality the teachings of Conqueror Tsongkhapa the Great. Ensapa and his spiritual sons had high words of praise for these instructions for taking the four empowerments of concentration through guru yoga that came from Conqueror Tsongkhapa the Great. My own holy guru also said that this is extremely important and in fact indispensable for establishing imprints on the path of mantra and repeatedly stated its necessity by proclaiming, "At the very least, they should be done every day without break."

Thus, once you have taken the four empowerments of concentration, you should recite the mantra from within the state of having transformed yourself into Vajradhara, the primordial protector of union. You can also imagine that your guru comes to the center of your heart and becomes inseparable from your extremely subtle wind and the mind of Vajradhara the Great. In his heart is a sun mandala upon which is a syllable HUM surrounded by the mantra rosary standing upright and circling clockwise like an assembled rosary of butter lamps. The mantra naturally proclaims its own sound. Light rays radiate from the mantra rosary and syllable HUM traveling to the ten directions, which strike all worldly environments, cleansing all impurities, and all environments transform into the celestial mansion. Light rays once again radiate to the ten directions, striking every living being in the six realms, purifying the negative karma and obscurations of each one, whereby they transform into the body of Vajradhara. At the heart of you and all living beings visualized as the deity is a mantra rosary from which light rays radiate and retract. You should recite the mantra while visualizing the blessings of the buddhas and bodhisattvas descending.

As for the mantra to be recited, you should initially recite the name mantra of your guru; therefore, I will give the mantra of my own holy guru: OM AH GURU SUMATI GYANA SIDDHI HUM HUM.[180] You should teach this visualization to your disciples as well.[181] I not only recite this name mantra during the actual four sessions, but during the session breaks as well. Next,[182] recite OM MUNI MUNI MAHA MUNAYE SÖHA, which is the name mantra of Shakyamuni and should be recited as many times as possible. Next, recite OM AH VAJRADHARA HUM HUM, which is the mantra of Vajradhara and should also be recited as many times as possible. Next, recite the mantra OM AH HUM as many times as possible.

Reciting the name mantra of the guru has unbelievably great power to bestow blessings. Khedrup Sangye Yeshe said, "If you recite the guru's name mantra and make supplications, it brings greater blessings than supplicating all the buddhas," which can also be seen in historical accounts of the previous holy beings. Furthermore, the degree of blessing that comes from the guru's name mantra depends upon the disciple's own faith. If, from the side of the disciple, he has uncontrived faith and devotion, and from the depths of his heart he views his guru as the nature embodying all the buddhas, that disciple will receive the blessings of all the buddhas regardless of the actual status of the guru's mental development. Also, supplicating the guru will bring swifter blessings than supplicating all the buddhas. However, if the disciple doesn't have faith and devotion, even if the guru is an actual buddha, they won't receive any blessings whatsoever. In the *Blue Scripture* Geshe Potowa said:

> The blessings of the guru are not really
> Great or small; they depend upon oneself.
> If you don't recall their kindness and you don't have faith,

180. This is the name mantra of the Second Panchen Lama, Losang Yeshe.
181. At this point you can replace this name mantra with the mantra of your own guru.
182. In other commentaries it is suggested that you recite the name mantra of Lama Tsongkhapa, OM AH GURU VAJRADHARA SUMATI KIRTI SIDDHI HUM, at this point.

Although you may directly perceive Manjushri or Avalokiteshvara,
It will never become meaningful.
Even if the guru does not have a full set of qualities,
If you have faith, devotion, and repay his kindness,
You will receive his blessings.

This is illustrated by an old woman that had faith in an arhat from the
distant past and someone gave her a dog's tooth, telling her that it was
the tooth of the arhat. Because of the old woman's faith, she continuously made offerings and single-pointed supplications. After some time
that tooth began to produce relics, light rays, and so forth, and that old
woman reached attainments. This story is given in numerous narratives.
After considering these historical accounts we should generate conviction.
We should also recite the mantra of Buddha Shakyamuni since the sutras
state that it purifies many tens of thousands of eons of negative karma and
obscurations. The mantra of Vajradhara has been extensively praised in
the root and explanatory tantras of Glorious Guhyasamaja as the means
of accomplishing supreme attainments. The three syllables OM AH HUM
are the essence of the body, speech, and mind of all the buddhas. This
mantra has the power and capacity of all the special and profound mantras that are taught in the tantras. It is capable of producing all of the
pacifying, increasing, controlling, and wrathful actions of all the other
mantras. Not only that, when a yogi on the generation stage attempts
to accomplish the various pacifying, increasing, controlling, and wrathful actions yet isn't successful, if he practices evoking the minds of all
the buddhas and bodhisattvas with three syllables, he will most certainly
succeed; this is taught in the tenth chapter of the *Guhyasamaja Root Tantra*. For those completion-stage yogis that are working at bringing their
winds into the central channel, they will not only be able to accomplish all
the pacifying, increasing, controlling, and wrathful attainments through
these three syllables, but through the force of combining them with their
winds through vajra recitation they will also be able to quickly accomplish
the supreme attainment of mahamudra. The thirteenth chapter of the
Guhyasamaja extensively praises this and states, "Vajra recitation with the
three syllables is the 'King of Secret Mantra' and is called the 'precious
recitation that bestows whatever common or supreme attainments you

desire.'" [Vajra recitation with OM AH HUM] is the essence of this guru yoga; therefore, lamas should explain the pith oral instructions in detail. If you examine in detail the teachings of Ensapa and his spiritual sons, as well as Vajradhara Losang Chökyi Gyaltsen, you will see that there are numerous extraordinary pith oral instructions regarding this point; and for those who wish to accomplish the essence of the oral instructions of Jamgon's [Tsongkhapa's] Hearing Lineage, you should not be satisfied by merely reciting the Lama Chöpa ritual text, and you should not merely undertake your practice through clinging to your intellectual investigation of the ultimate essential points of the oral instructions. Instead, you should meditate once you have cultivated stable certainty induced through the path of scripture and reasoning.

I make respectful prostrations to the holy venerable guru, who is endowed with great unobservable compassion. Please care for me with your great compassion.

Training the Mind and Receiving Blessings by Way of Scanning Meditaiton on the Complete Body of the Path of Sutra and Tantra has two sections:

1. The Way to Rely upon the Spiritual Master as the Basis of the Path
2. How to Train the Mind through Such Reliance

The Way to Rely upon the Spiritual Master as the Basis of the Path

Contemplating this way while in this state of meditation on the guru-deity, you will quickly accomplish the state of enlightenment through your proper reliance upon the virtuous friend, who reveals the unmistaken path. Temporarily, you will not be harmed by sickness, the spirits, and so forth and you will accomplish whatever you wish. With regard to whatever benefits that are explained in the teachings of the conqueror and [what happens] if you act improperly in your reliance, such as showing disrespect for your lama and so forth, it is said that the maturation will be greater than even the [five] actions of immediate retribution, whereby you will have to wander in the unbearable lower realms and in this life you will be harmed by multiple afflictions, such as illness, harm from spirits, and so forth. In this and all future lives you will continue to decline. You should repeatedly contemplate all the ways these faults are taught and, once you develop stable determination, you should develop the aspiration to blend this with your intention to rely properly upon your virtuous friend. Next, you should actualize the good qualities and faith, moral discipline, concentration, wisdom, and so forth, and furthermore, direct your mind toward such good qualities by repeatedly contemplating the good qualities taught in the sutras. In short, you should not let your mind be distracted by any shortcomings, and instead contemplate that [your guru] is the completely perfect Buddha appearing as your spiritual guide for the sake of guiding us wretched beings. Generate these thoughts through contemplating his good qualities utilizing numerous avenues and meditate until you generate a mind of pure faith. Next, meditate until you develop great respect by contemplating in accordance with the sutras, which explain his kindness in benefiting you in the past and how he will benefit you in the future. Next, contemplate in accordance with Je Rinpoche's advice in which he stated:

> May I plant the seeds of unceasing bliss and excellence in the sacred ground during all four seasons, from which emerges all excellent accumulations of this life and the next, which one plows with faith, whereby the fields of merit are sown. As stated in the sutras, it would be an extremely great loss if you didn't engage in the activities of cultivating [this field]. When we listen we don't remember the words, when we contemplate we don't understand the meaning, and when we meditate we don't generate [realizations] in our mental continuum; it is at times like these, when your mind has very little power, that you should rely upon such a powerful field. You should contemplate, "While I have met such a most excellent field of merit as this, if I don't cultivate the seeds of virtue for the sake of establishing the root of bliss and excellence, but instead abandon it, this would be so stupid that it must mean that my heart is rotten.

The virtuous friend is an actual buddha and is the foundation of all good qualities, the root of all bliss and excellence, the field of all benefit and happiness; therefore, you should use your body to respectfully honor him, use your speech to recite praises and supplications, use your actual possessions to make offerings, and please him by practicing in accordance with his teachings. Make very powerful supplications by reciting, "Venerable guru, please delightfully care for me with your great compassion until I also attain the state of enlightenment."

The ritual text states:

> Through the force of having made respectful offerings and requests
> To you, the venerable and holy guru, the supreme field of merit,
> I seek your blessings, protector, the root of all bliss and excellence;
> Please joyously take me into your loving care and grant me
>   your blessing.

Due to this request, a stream of five-colored light rays and nectars descends from the bodies of the guru and the assembly of deities. It enters the body and mind of yourself and all other living beings, whereby all the negative karma and obscurations you have accumulated since beginningless time—and in particular the negative karma and obscurations that interfere with your proper reliance upon the virtuous friend through thought and deed—are purified. Your body becomes luminous, clear, and the nature of light. Your life, merit, and good qualities of scripture and realizations develop and increase. Imagine that through the power of viewing the guru-buddha with faith while recalling his kindness with respect and devotion you and all living beings generate special realizations in your mental continuum.

How to Train the Mind through Such Reliance has two sections:
1. How to Train the Mind in the Common Path
2. How to Train the Mind in the Uncommon Path of the Vajrayana

How to Train the Mind in the Common Path has three sections:
1. How to Train the Mind in the Path Common to a Being of Small Capacity

GYALWA ENSAPA

2. How to Train the Mind in the Path Common to a Being
   of Medium Capacity
3. How to Train the Mind in the Path Common to a Being
   of Great Capacity

How to Train the Mind in the Path Common to a Being of Small
Capacity has two sections:
1. Generating a Mind Striving for a Future Life in the World
2. An Explanation of the Method for Happiness in a Future Life
   in the World

Generating a Mind Striving for a Future Life in the World

Here [in Lama Chöpa], the two contemplation rounds of the leisure and endowments are conjoined with impermanence into a single round of contemplation, which is composed in accordance with the tradition of uncommon oral instructions that Omniscient Je [Tsongkhapa] received from Protector Manjushri. Furthermore, the teachings that Protector Manjushri bestowed upon Omniscient Je combined all the scriptures into a summary of oral instructions as "The Three Principal Aspects of the Path," which are renunciation, bodhichitta, and the profound view of the Middle Way. There are two methods of implementation when meditating on renunciation: overcoming attachment for this life and overcoming attachment for the next life. With regard to the means of overcoming attachment to this life, there are two lines that state:

> Overcoming attachment to this life through familiarizing
>   the mind
> With the urgency that this life of leisure and endowments
>   is difficult to find.

It is taught that the way to meditate is to combine the pair of contemplation rounds for leisure and endowments with impermanence. With regard to the great and small lamrims that arrange the rounds of contemplation on leisure and endowments separately, the great being Nagarjuna combined them into a single body of literature for practicing all the scriptures by composing the *Compendium of Sutras*,[183] and the bodhisattva Shantideva assembled them into a single body of literature for practicing all the scriptures by composing the *Compendium of Trainings*[184] and *Guide to the Bodhisattva's Way of Life*. In all three of those texts, the round of contemplation on leisure and endowments is presented separately as a preliminary, which is in agreement with the texts of the great charioteers. Nevertheless, unifying the two rounds of contemplation does not contradict their meaning and comes down to the same intention, which is clearly

---

183. *mDo kun las btus pa*; *Sūtrasamuccaya*.
184. *bsLab bdus*; *Śikṣāsamuccaya*.

explained in the *Great Exposition on the Stages of the Path to Enlightenment*.
With regard to this oral instruction of Vajradhara Losang Chökyi Gyaltsen
that unifies the two rounds of contemplation, it is the ultimate intention of Je Rinpoche and should also be learned from his *Songs of Spiritual
Experience*,[185] which states:

> This body of leisure surpasses even a wish-fulfilling jewel.
> We will find a body like this only once.
> Hard to find, and easily destroyed, like a bolt of lightning
>   in the sky.
> Contemplating this, you will come to realize
> That all worldly actions are like a husk of grain,
> And that day and night you must take its essence.
> I, the yogi, practiced in this way;
> You who seek liberation should do the same.

These points are difficult to realize. The phrases "the great value of leisure" and "quickly destroyed" are not difficult to understand. It has been
stated that it is extremely difficult to correctly understand and establish
the proper imprints through sustaining the individual visualizations with
their enumerations and degrees of the path. I have written just a small
fragment for the intelligent to analyze so that they will attain confidence
in this uncommon oral instruction of Vajradhara Losang Chökyi Gyaltsen.
A more extensive discourse should be provided by your holy virtuous
friends.

   With regard to practicing the actual contemplations for this, you
should contemplate in this way while absorbed in the meditation on the
guru-deity. Contemplate the following and elicit as much of a mental
transformation as you can:

> Since beginningless time I have circled through the three
> realms of samsara in general and the three lower realms and
> so forth in particular. Without any freedom I have wandered
> repeatedly in darkness through the continents without ever

185. *Nyams mgur.*

attaining a body such as this and never meeting the complete path of sutra and tantra. In contrast, at this moment, through compassion of the holy guru, I am capable of understanding what to adopt and forsake with regard to virtue and nonvirtue and I have obtained such a state of leisure with the opportunity to practice Dharma. I have the endowment of having completed all the outer and inner conditions that are absolutely necessary to practice Dharma. I have obtained a special rebirth with such leisure and endowments. This human body is extraordinarily meaningful. Temporarily, I can accomplish a body of a human or god as well as all the excellent things that could possibly exist within samsara with this human body. It also has ultimate meaning because I can accomplish the state of liberation and omniscience with this human body. By relying upon this human body, complete with the leisure and endowments, I can accomplish the vajra body of union in this short life. Therefore, although it might be difficult to find enough wish-fulfilling jewels to fill the three realms to the brim, this human life far exceeds even that. Therefore, this metaphor is incapable of expressing the extraordinary great meaning of this human life. Right now, at this moment I have obtained [such a life] just once and if I do not make a sincere effort at this point in time, it will be extremely difficult to obtain a life like this again. Obtaining this human life is more difficult than balancing a mustard seed on the tip of a needle or throwing peas at a glass surface and getting them to stick. It is not possible to obtain a human life such as this that is replete with all the conducive conditions for practicing Dharma from anywhere else among the six classes of beings in the three realms. Furthermore, the primary cause for attaining a human life such as this is completely pure moral discipline and, what's more, there must be numerous causes. With regard to my own abilities, if I am not even capable of developing the pure desire to protect my moral discipline, what need is there to mention pure moral discipline? Right now, I have obtained this one time a human body of leisure and endowments, and if I don't make a sincere effort while I have it, I will not be able to attain a life like this again.

Having contemplated in this way, you should develop an extremely powerful aspiration by thinking:

I will not waste even a moment of this human life with a vajra body replete with the leisure and endowments that I have attained this one time and instead I shall extract its essence. The way to take its essence is to rely upon the guru as inseparable from the Buddha and practice the essence of the teachings of the Supreme Vehicle, whereby I will easily attain the state of enlightenment in one lifetime.

Furthermore, think:

If I don't make a sincere effort from this very moment, because this human life does not last long and it is certain I will die, and I am also incapable of overcoming whatever outer and inner conditions [there are that contribute to my death], I cannot add even one moment to my life and it is quickly exhausted with each passing moment. And while I am alive there are a variety of outer and inner distractions that leave no time for Dharma practice. In general, a life in this world is uncertain, the conditions for death are numerous, and the conditions for life are few. This body is very feeble; therefore, there is the danger of dying even this very day. If I die on a day like today, even my friends, body, and enjoyments will all be of no benefit, and when I die it is certain that only the Dharma will be of benefit; therefore, I must practice right now. Furthermore, I am going to practice the essential instructions of the profound path of the yoga of the guru-deity, which embodies the essence of the Supreme Vehicle. Guru-deity, please grant your blessing that I may be able to act in this way.

The ritual text states:

> Having found this leisure and endowment just once,
> And realizing how quickly it is destroyed and how difficult
> it is to find,
> I seek your blessing that I may extract the essence of this
> endowment
> Without becoming distracted by the meaningless activities
> of this life.

Recite this verse and make a very powerful supplication, whereby a stream of five-colored light rays and nectars descends from the bodies of the guru and assembly of deities and enters the body and mind of yourself and all other living beings, whereby the unique obstructions are purified and, in particular, the various realizations are developed in the minds of yourself and all living beings.

An Explanation of the Method for Happiness in a Future Life in the World

While remaining in a state of meditation on the guru and assembly of deities [continue] contemplating by thinking:

> I have obtained this one time a human body with its leisure and endowments yet it is quickly destroyed, and when I die I have no control over where I will take rebirth. Instead, I must take rebirth through the force of my virtuous and nonvirtuous karma. Because of my enjoyments I have not transcended the karma appropriate to take rebirth in the lower realms. If I take rebirth in the lower realms I will have to endure unbearable torments, such as heat, cold, hunger, thirst, enslavement, and so forth, and the suffering of being trapped amid a mass of blazing fire. In that place I will not find any refuge whatsoever; therefore, I must seek a refuge right now that can protect me from such horrors. Other than the Three Precious Jewels there is no other refuge whatsoever in samsara that can protect me from that.

Go for refuge from the very depths of your heart by entrusting yourself in whatever you do to the guru and Three Precious Jewels without placing your hopes in anyone else, whether things are going well or going poorly. Once you have gone for refuge, you must undertake the precepts and protect them without forsaking them even at the cost of your life. In particular, if you don't make a sincere effort to adopt and forsake virtue and nonvirtue in accordance with the teachings of the Buddha, he will not be able to liberate you from the fear of the lower realms; therefore, you must employ mindfulness with your three doors and properly apply yourself to abandoning nonvirtue and practicing virtue. Therefore, think, "Guru-deity, please grant your blessings so that I may be able to conduct myself in this way."

Make the following request from the ritual text that states:

> Being terrified by the blazing fire of lower realms' suffering,
> From the depths of my heart I go for refuge to the Three Jewels
> And seek your blessing that I may strive earnestly to
> Accomplish the complete collection of virtue and abandon
>   negative actions.

Through this very powerful supplication a stream of five-colored light rays and nectar descends from the bodies of the guru and assembly of deities and enters the body and mind of yourself and all other living beings, whereby the particular obstructions are purified and, in particular, the various realizations are developed in the minds of yourself and all living beings.

How to Train the Mind in the Path Common to a Being of Medium Capacity has two sections:
1. Generating a Mind Striving for Liberation
2. How to Train in the Path Leading to Liberation

Generating a Mind Striving for Liberation

While remaining in a state of meditation on the guru and assembly of deities, [continue] contemplating by thinking, "If I go for refuge to the Three Jewels and make a sincere effort to adopt virtuous actions and abandon nonvirtue, I will indeed be liberated from the abyss of the lower realms and attain a body as someone in the fortunate realms; however, this will not transcend the nature of suffering, whose transcendence comes from complete liberation from samsara." No matter where you are born, from the peak of samsara to the lowest hell, by coming under the influence of the afflictive emotions you lack any independence and are incessantly oppressed by the suffering of suffering, the suffering of change, and all-pervasive suffering. And whatever actions you undertake do not transcend the nature of suffering; therefore, you must overcome your attachment and develop aversion for this great ocean of existence that is without bottom or boundary. You must generate an intensely powerful mind wishing for liberation that is just like a person who wishes to attain freedom from prison. Furthermore, merely cultivating revulsion for the suffering of suffering is something that even animals possess. As for growing weary of the contaminated pleasant feelings that is the suffering of change, this is something that even the non-Buddhist sages possess; therefore, merely these thoughts alone do not constitute a fully qualified wish for liberation. For that reason, you must cultivate sincere aversion and detachment for this feeling of equanimity that is still influenced by karma and afflictive emotions, whereby you perceive even something like the mind of meditative stabilization of the peak of samsara[186] as the nature of suffering. Therefore, think, "Guru-deity, please grant your blessing that I may develop an extremely powerful mind wishing for liberation by perceiving the whole of samsara as a pit of blazing fire."

Make the following request from the ritual text that states:

> Being violently tossed about by the waves of delusion and
>   karma,
> And tormented by the many sea monsters of the three
>   sufferings,
> I seek your blessing to generate a fierce and powerful wish
>   for liberation
> From the limitless and fearful great ocean of samsara.

---

186. This is the highest meditative stabilization possible within samsara.

Through this very powerful supplication a stream of five-colored light rays and nectar descends from the bodies of the guru and assembly of deities and enters the body and mind of yourself and all other living beings, whereby the particular obstructions are purified and, in particular, the various realizations are developed in the minds of yourself and all living beings.

How to Train in the Path Leading to Liberation

While remaining in a state of meditation on the guru and assembly of deities, summon a mental experience by contemplating how samsara is the nature of suffering. From there, once you develop an extremely powerful wish for liberation, you will begin to wonder, "Just what is the root of this samsara that is the nature of suffering?" When you do, you should consider the verse from the *Commentary on Valid Cognition* that states:

> If the self exists, one knows other;
> From self and other come grasping and hatred;
> Through the association with these
> All faults emerge.

Thus, all these sufferings of samsara emerge through the force of karma and afflictive emotions. The ultimate root of all karma and afflictive emotions is the innate self-grasping. Therefore, understand that the root of samsara is self-grasping and that you must develop the wisdom realizing the mode of existence that refutes the root of this apprehended object and overcomes this self-grasping; for that to occur, you must have a mind of stable concentration that can abide on its object single-pointedly; for that to occur, you must have pure moral discipline; and for that to occur, you must perfectly prevent the four doors that give rise to downfalls, which are (1) not knowing, (2) lack of respect, (3) nonconscientiousness, and (4) a multitude of afflictive emotions. You must also employ introspection, modesty, and shame with undistracted attention, which must be protected by never allowing even for a moment the harmful thieves of the afflictive emotions to rob your wealth of moral discipline. Therefore, think, "Guru-deity, please grant your blessings so that I may be able to conduct myself in this way."

Make extremely powerful supplications by reciting the verse from the
ritual text that states:

> Forsaking a mind that views as a joyous garden
> This unbearable prison, the net of samsara,
> I seek your blessing to uphold the victory banner of liberation
> By maintaining the riches of the aryas' three trainings.

Through this very powerful supplication a stream of five-colored light
rays and nectar descends from the bodies of the guru and assembly of deities and enters the body and mind of yourself and all other living beings,
whereby the particular obstructions are purified and, in particular, the
various realizations are developed in the minds of yourself and all living
beings.

The phrase that states, "By maintaining the riches of the aryas' three
trainings" accords with the three higher trainings that I have already
explained, while "the riches of the aryas" refers to the following seven
qualities: (1) faith, (2) moral discipline, (3) listening, (4) giving, (5) modesty,
(6) shame, and (7) wisdom. Apply each of these when practicing what
should be done and so forth. Although these are extremely important, I
am not going to elaborate on them further.

These two verses reveal the path of a person of the middle scope by
contemplating the faults of samsara as the truth of suffering, and the
stages of entering samsara, which are the true origins, and the way of
training in true paths for the sake of attaining liberation, which is the
true cessation. This is the way to train in the structure and nature of the
three higher trainings. Within that, at this point the means of training in
the moral discipline are what are primarily being emphasized, which is
the true intent of Omniscient Je [Tsongkhapa]. This has been presented in
very few words; however, if it were explained in detail its meaning would
be extremely vast.

**How to Train the Mind in the Path Common to a Being of Great
Capacity** has two sections:

1. **How to Generate Bodhichitta**
2. **How to Train in the Deeds [of a Bodhisattva] following the
   Generation of Bodhichitta**

How to Generate Bodhichitta has four sections:

1. How to Generate Great Compassion, Which Is the Root of the Mahayana
2. An Extensive Explanation of How to Meditate on Equalizing and Exchanging Self with Others according to the Seven-Point Mind Training
3. How to Meditate on Superior Intention and Bodhichitta
4. How to Take the Vows of Aspiring Bodhichitta and Engaging Bodhichitta

How to Generate Great Compassion, Which Is the Root of the Mahayana

The lord of oral instructions for training in bodhichitta is Jowo Je Glorious Atisha. Glorious Atisha revealed two special oral instructions for training in bodhichitta that came from the two great charioteers:[187] (1) how to train in bodhichitta in conjunction with the seven oral instructions of cause and effect, and (2) how to train in bodhichitta in conjunction with equalizing and exchanging self with others. It is stated in numerous sutras taught by the conqueror that great compassion is the root of the Mahayana path and can be practiced by utilizing either of these two systems. It is stated that great compassion is the life of the Mahayana path, which is similar to the life-force of a person. Great compassion dwells in all Mahayana paths; great compassion is their root. It is said that if you don't have great compassion, any of the Mahayana paths is without a foundation, which is just how it is explained in the sutras. This has also been stated in numerous texts of the glorious protector Arya Nagarjuna. Master Chandrakirti, in his text *Entering the Middle Way*, also states the great importance of great compassion at the beginning, middle, and end for progressing through the path, which in no way contradicts the intention of all the great charioteers.

To be able to develop great compassion you definitely must have affectionate love, which is also in agreement with the intention of all the great

187. The two great charioteers are Nagarjuna and Asanga. Nagarjuna is the source of equalizing and exchanging self with others and Asanga is the source of the sevenfold cause-and-effect method, both of which are in turn based on the perfection of wisdom sutras and were revealed by Manjushri and Maitreya, respectively.

charioteers. There arose distinct oral instructions utilizing two different techniques for the cultivation of affectionate love. Furthermore, it is stated in the perfection of wisdom sutras that one develops affectionate love by meditating on living beings as being your loved ones. Following that system, the great master Chandrakirti, Chandragomin, and the supreme scholar Kamalashila advised developing affectionate love by meditating on all living beings as having been your mother and remembering their kindness. In particular, Master Kamalashila gave extensive explanations on how to cultivate these paths in your mental continuum in his *Second Stages of Meditation*. Another system explains the faults of self-cherishing and the benefits of cherishing others by using many lines of reasoning. Once you produce affectionate love, the way to cultivate great compassion is explained in the *Avatamsaka Sutra*. Following that system, the bodhisattva Shantideva provides an explicit explanation in his two texts entitled *Compendium of Trainings* and *Guide to the Bodhisattva's Way of Life*. This method is also taught in Protector Nagarjuna's texts entitled *The Jeweled Garland of the Middle Way*,[188] *Commentary on Bodhichitta*,[189] and *Discourse of the Wish-Fulfilling Dream of a Jewel*.[190] In this way both oral instructions of these great charioteers were blended together in this practice as a single oral instruction by Vajradhara Losang Chökyi Gyaltsen and as a single body of practice.

You begin by recognizing [all beings] as your mother, recalling their kindness, and wishing to repay it. In dependence upon these three you develop affectionate love and great compassion. Next, you accomplish affectionate love and great compassion through contemplating the faults of self-cherishing and the benefits of cherishing others, which produces these in a way that is more powerful and stable than before, and you meditate through numerous avenues on equalizing and exchanging self with others. Next, he reveals the way to produce superior intention and bodhichitta through the force of the previous rounds of contemplation. These pith instructions of the path were explained by the great charioteers in accordance with the intention of the conqueror and are extremely difficult to realize. Vajradhara Losang Chökyi Gyaltsen thoroughly examined

188. *Rin chen phreng ba*; *Ratnāvalī*.
189. *Byang chub sems 'grel*; *Bodhicittavivaraṇa*.
190. *rMi lam yid bzhin nor bu'i gtam*; *Svapnacintāmaṇiparikathā*.

the oral instructions of the great charioteers and combined them with the oral instructions of the Hearing Lineage of Conqueror Tsongkhapa the Great; therefore, having discovered this system, you should develop confidence in these uncommon oral instructions.

For that reason, with regard to the way to carry out this contemplation, while remaining in a state of meditation on the guru-deity, contemplate:

> If I properly train in the three higher trainings by evoking renunciation within my mental continuum and then overcome my attachment for samsara in its entirety through contemplating the difficulty in finding the leisure and endowments, death and impermanence, cause and effects, and the faults of samsara, I will indeed be capable of liberating myself from samsara. However, my kind mothers, who have nurtured me with kindness since beginningless time, are being tormented in the prison of samsara. Seeing this, if I abandon them and strive to attain liberation for myself alone, this would be a total disgrace as well as malicious, not to mention that I would not bring an end to my own faults or attain a state endowed with all good qualities due to having fallen into a lower path. It is also said that although we may be urged by the light rays of the Buddha's compassion, it is still difficult to enter the Mahayana.

Contemplating in this way determine, "Since [despite my progress in the Hinayana] I must enter the Mahayana from the very beginning so that I can accomplish the welfare of myself and others, I should enter the Mahayana right now."

The gateway to entering the Mahayana is the precious mind of bodhichitta, and to generate that mind you must cultivate great compassion; to generate that you need affectionate love; the ultimate loved one is your mother; therefore, you must develop the recognition of [all beings] as your mother; to generate that you need equanimity; therefore, you should initially meditate on equanimity. To develop equanimity that regards all beings equally, practice viewing all beings as being equally friendly, practice contemplating how there is no certainty between enemies and friends, practice by contemplating how living beings are equally tormented, and so on as you see fit. These oral instructions state that you should accomplish equanimity by primarily contemplating how they are equally tormented in the phrase that states, "all these tormented migrating beings." Furthermore, the *Compendium of Trainings* states:

> Self and others are constantly rooted in misery.
> Migrating beings suffer equally
> Along the path of many abysses
> As they slip and fall with each step.

By contemplating in accordance with these teachings on the torment of migrating beings, you should have equanimity without acting out of attachment or hatred. Clearly imagine yourself surrounded by all living beings and meditate on equanimity by thinking:

> When I observe their situation, I understand that they are blind to wisdom through the dense cataracts of ignorance that they have accumulated since beginningless time and they are completely lost with no idea where they are going. They have become insane through the malevolent influence of the afflictive emotions as they head toward the great abyss without any peace and they are oppressed by numerous sufferings numbering in the hundreds of thousands. When I think about their pitiful situations such as these, I hold some of them dear while others I keep at a distance, yet it makes no sense to act out of attachment and hatred; therefore, I should meditate on equanimity without partiality.

You should meditate on equanimity by thinking, "I should not abandon these living beings, and why shouldn't I help these beings for they have been nothing but my old mothers." Furthermore, a sutra states, "Monks, if you classify sentient beings, since beginningless time they have been your loved ones hundreds of times; there is no one whatsoever that has not been your father and mother." The scriptures also state that in dependence upon reasoning we can establish that there are no limits to the bounds of samsara; therefore, you should recognize all living beings as your own mother. Next, these mothers have repeatedly acted as your mother since beginningless time. When each of them acted as your mother, you were cared for by their kindness in the same way as your mother in this life cared for you with kindness; therefore, it is extremely important for you to repay their kindness. Therefore, meditate on repaying their kindness by thinking, "I must liberate these kind old mothers from this miserable precipice of samsara."

By meditating on equanimity, recognizing all beings as your mother, remembering their kindness, and wishing to repay their kindness in this way, you will come to cherish them from the depths of your heart like your only child. And by generating however much affectionate love and compassion you can in this way, you will not treat all living beings with partiality and will come to cherish them dearly and see them as beloved through your spontaneous love. It is taught that if you generate love in this way, you should once again repeatedly contemplate the suffering of living beings abiding in samsara and cultivate great compassion, and in this way imagine that you are requesting the blessings of the guru-deity to generate it in your mental continuum by reciting the verse from the ritual text that states:

> Contemplating how all these pitiful living beings are my mothers
> Who have cherished me with kindness again and again,
> I seek your blessing that I may generate uncontrived compassion,
> Like the love of a mother for her precious child.

Through making this extremely powerful supplication a stream of five-colored light rays and nectars descends from the bodies of the guru and assembly of deities and enters the body and mind of yourself and all other living beings, whereby the particular obstructions are purified and, in particular, the various realizations are developed in the minds of yourself and all living beings.

The phrase that contains "precious child" and "uncontrived compassion" reveals the degree of cultivating love and compassion. Thus, the *Stages of Meditation* also states, "When you focus on the suffering of all living beings with affection as though they were your unhappy child and you have a spontaneous and equal sense of compassion that wishes to purify them, you have completed great compassion." The omniscient Je [Tsongkhapa] also proclaimed:

> Please grant your blessings that through recognizing
> All embodied beings as my mother, recalling the sufferings
> Of these tormented beings, and overcoming the mind wishing to
> Accomplish my happiness alone, I may generate effortless
>   compassion.

An Extensive Explanation of How to Meditate on Equalizing and Exchanging Self with Others according to the Seven-Point Mind Training

I will not be able to compose a detailed presentation of each of the seven points because I am concerned that this text would become too verbose, yet I will give a concise explanation by combining the root verses of these oral instructions without corrupting their essential meaning. This instruction of mind training relies upon the oral instructions of Protector Manjushri that he bestowed upon Shantideva by making a comparative study of the meaning of numerous Mahayana sutras, such as the *Avatamsaka Sutra* and so forth, that directly reveal the methods for meditating on equalizing self and others. It was [to receive] these oral instructions that Glorious Atisha crossed the ocean in a ship to meet Serlingpa, from whom he received numerous teachings. For twelve long years he received teachings from Serlingpa, which entered and filled the vase of his mind. After traveling to Tibet, [Atisha] bestowed these teachings upon Drom Rinpoche in secret, which became renowned as the "Concealed Dharma of the Forefather." Geshe Chekawa[191] propagated these teachings widely by composing an outline to these seven topics and spread them far and wide as the famed *Seven-Point Mind Training*.

As for these seven points, they are (1) an explanation of the preliminaries as a foundation, (2) training in the two bodhichittas as the actual practice, (3) transforming unfavorable conditions into the path to enlight-

---

191. Geshe Chekawa received these teachings from Geshe Sharawa, who in turn received them from Dromtonpa's disciple, Geshe Potowa.

enment, (4) an explanation of integrating the practices into a single lifetime, (5) the measure of having trained the mind, (6) the commitments of mind training, and (7) the precepts of training the mind.

An explanation of the preliminaries as a foundation: For this you contemplate the difficulty of obtaining a human life of leisure and endowments, death and impermanence, the cause and effect of karma, and the faults of samsara. These are renowned as the "four preliminary Dharmas." These have already been explained in the sections on the beings of the small and middling scope.

Training in the two bodhichittas as the actual practice: In many of the previous mind-training texts meditating on the ultimate bodhichitta is presented as a preliminary, after which the way to meditate on the conventional bodhichitta is taught, which is in accordance with the teachings of the *Ornament of the Middle Way*.[192] Although it is acceptable for those few persons of the Mahayana lineage with sharp faculties to meditate on the view of emptiness as a preliminary, and then subsequently meditate on the conventional bodhichitta, if the disciples of this day and age meditate on the view of emptiness without already having a stable foundation in the method aspect, it will prove to be difficult and dangerous and it will not strike the essential point. In the *Lamp for the Path* Jowo Atisha proclaimed:

> Whoever is governed by their familiarization with
> Skillful means should then meditate on emptiness.

The *Root Verses of Mind Training* states:

> Teach the secret once they attain stability.

Thus, this is stating that you should first become stable in skillful means and then meditate on the fundamental nature of reality. The *Guide to the Bodhisattva's Way of Life* provides extensive explanations on how to

---

192. *dBu ma rgyan*; *Madhyamakālaṃkāra*. This is a famous text composed by Shantarakshita in the eighth century.

meditate on the wisdom section of the six perfections once stability has been accomplished in the preliminaries from the leisure and endowments up to concentration. The omniscient Je [Tsongkhapa] also advises that you meditate in the same sequence. Therefore, following the same intended meaning as those [previous statements], these oral instructions also do not advocate meditating on the view of emptiness as the preliminary and instead state that you teach the method aspects as the preliminary followed by how to meditate on the view of emptiness, which I will explain later. The stages of other sections are clearly laid out according to the words of the text. Therefore, at this point, with regard to how to meditate on equalizing and exchanging self with others, there are two sections: (1) how to meditate on equalizing self and others, and (2) how to meditate on exchanging self with others.

With regard to how to meditate on equalizing self and others, the ritual text states, "No one desires even the most subtle suffering." For equalizing self and others there are two systems: (1) how to equalize them conventionally, and (2) how to equalize them ultimately. Both of these systems are explained in the *Compendium of Trainings* and *Guide to the Bodhisattva's Way of Life*. The *Ornament for Clear Realization*[193] repeatedly teaches how to equalize ultimately and how to conventionally exchange self and others during the chapter on "culmination of clear realization."[194] The *Ornament for Mahayana Sutras* presents five ways of equalizing self and others. I am concerned that if I comment on these points in detail it would become too verbose; therefore, I will not elaborate further.

These oral instructions contain the concise presentation of the points of the great trailblazers. With regard to how to carry out these contemplations, while remaining absorbed in the meditation on the guru-deity, visualize that you are surrounded by all living beings and undertake the following contemplations: "Myself and all these old mother sentient beings are all equal in only wishing for happiness and not wishing for suffering; even if they absolutely do not wish to suffer it is as though they live in a completely mistaken dream where, despite desiring only happiness and not wishing for even the slightest suffering, they are never satisfied with

193. *mNgon rtogs rgyan*; *Abhisamayālaṃkāra*.
194. The full title in Tibetan is *rTse mor phyin pa'i sbyor ba*. Of the seventy topics of the perfection of wisdom presented in the *Ornament for Clear Realization*, this chapter contains eight topics.

the happiness they receive. Thus, although they do not wish to suffer and desire happiness, it is as though they have gone mad due to the demon of extreme ignorance and afflictive emotions, whereby they are not creating the causes of happiness and are only creating the causes of suffering." By contemplating this situation, whenever you see your old mother sentient beings creating even the slightest virtuous causes or the resultant happiness, develop a mind of extreme joy. Think, "How wonderful it would be if all of these old mothers came to possess complete happiness and the causes of happiness; guru-deity, please grant your blessings that this may come to pass."

The ritual text states:

> In that no one desires even the most subtle suffering
> Or is ever content with the happiness they have,
> There is no difference between myself and others;
> Seeing this, I seek your blessing that I may delight in the
>   happiness of others.

Through making this extremely powerful supplication a stream of five-colored light rays and nectars descends from the bodies of the guru and assembly of deities and enters the body and mind of yourself and all other living beings, whereby the unique obstructions are purified and, in particular, the various realizations are developed in the minds of yourself and all living beings.

Next is meditating on exchanging self with others. For this you begin by **contemplating the faults of self-cherishing.** Remain absorbed in meditation on the guru-deity and contemplate in accordance with the following verse from the *Commentary on Valid Cognition*, which states:

> Whoever perceives the self ascribes
> An "I" to that which he constantly grasps.
> Through grasping comes attachment for happiness.
> Through attachment the obscuring faults are produced.

> One perceives it as a good quality, whereby all of existence
>   [is produced].
> Ascribing "I," you accept it as being evidence of its existence,
> Whereby you form attachments to the self,
> And through its existence samsara is produced.

Because of this great demon of self-cherishing you have been united with suffering from beginningless time until the present. If you continue to come under the influence of this demon you will once again wander endlessly in samsara and never be able to transcend the experience of suffering. All the suffering from remaining in samsara emerges solely through the force of this self-grasping. Whatever undesired things occur in this life all stem solely from this great demon of self-grasping. In short, through this mind that grasps and cherishes a self all nonvirtue and suffering are produced and all of your virtuous actions will be ruined, like mixing poison with food. Through the force of this evil mind's grasp, whatever virtuous roots you accumulate will only become the cause of samsara, and although you may wish to be liberated from the faults of samsara, through the influence of this self-cherishing whatever virtuous roots you engage in are lost into inferior paths. The previous holy beings have called this evil mind of self-cherishing "the owl-headed cause of disaster." Thus, we should make a strong promise by thinking, "In this and all future lives I will not, even for a moment, come under the influence of this evil mind that brings disaster." And think, "Guru-deity, please grant me your blessing that I may be able to succeed in this." The ritual text states:

> Seeing that this chronic disease of maintaining self-cherishing
> Gives rise to all unwanted suffering,
> I seek your blessing to destroy this great demon of
>   self-cherishing
> By despising it as the object of blame.

Through making this extremely powerful supplication a stream of five-colored light rays and nectars descends from the bodies of the guru and assembly of deities and enters the body and mind of yourself and all other living beings, whereby the unique obstructions are purified and in particular the various realizations are developed in the minds of yourself and all living beings.

With regard to **the benefits of cherishing others**, while remaining absorbed in meditation on the guru-deity, think, "All the temporary and ultimate happiness comes from cherishing living beings; therefore, from this moment on I will not come under the influence of self-cherishing but maintain the mind cherishing these old mother sentient beings even more than my life." If you wonder how all happiness comes from cherishing all living beings, consider how even the temporary body of a human rebirth must be attained solely through the kindness of living beings. All of your enjoyments, such as food, clothing, and so forth, also come solely through the kindness of living beings. All of the best things in samsara, such as an excellent body, great power, and so forth, come solely from the kindness of living beings.

Following the same reasoning, when you harm your old mother sentient beings through killing and so forth, you will be reborn in hell. When you are free from that state and attain a human body, you will be plagued by unwanted things, such as a short life, numerous illnesses, great harm and injury, and so forth. Freeing your old mother living beings from being killed will produce only joy and happiness, and you will attain a happy rebirth, long life, excellent body, and so forth. Likewise, through stealing from living beings due to miserliness you will not be able to find possessions [in a future life] and you will be reborn as a hungry ghost, and when you do attain a human body you will experience only suffering through being poor, destitute, and so forth. Benefiting your old mother living beings with possessions will produce only happiness and well-being, such as enjoyments, vast resources, and so forth. Through proclaiming the faults of living beings only suffering will come your way; you will be reborn as an animal, and although you [eventually] attain a human body, you will be of low social standing, be despised by all, have little power, be tormented, and so forth. By cultivating a happy mind toward living beings and meditating on patience, only well-being and happiness will arise, and you will attain an excellent form, high social standing, great power, be venerated by all, and so forth. In short, all the suffering of samsara comes from forsaking living beings because of your self-cherishing. Not only do all things excellent come from the kindness of living beings, but even the resultant state of enlightenment comes from the kindness of living beings.

Once you visualize your old mothers, generate bodhichitta, and train in the deeds of a bodhisattva, such as generosity and so forth, you will attain enlightenment. By abandoning living beings there is no possibility of attaining enlightenment. Take this point into consideration! The *Guide to the Bodhisattva's Way of Life* states:

> The Buddhadharma is accomplished equally
> Through living beings and the conqueror;
> Why would you not show the same respect
> To living beings as you do to the conqueror?

Protector Nagarjuna also states in his *Commentary on Bodhichitta*:

> Since you attain the unsurpassed state of enlightenment
> In dependence upon living beings,
> What is so surprising that whatever
> Enjoyments of gods and men there may be,
> Including Brahma, Indra, and Raudra,
> And the worldly protectors in the three realms,
> Come from benefiting living beings?

Therefore, these mother sentient beings are the agents bestowing your entire temporary and ultimate purposes; therefore, they are superior to even a wish-granting jewel and you must generate a mind that deeply cherishes and values them by thinking, "They are similar to my guru and supreme deity." Protector Nagarjuna stated:

> They are wish-fulfilling jewels,
> And excellent vases, and a wish-fulfilling cow.
> For that reason they are like your deity and guru
> And they are to be relied upon.

> By seeing this thoroughly through scripture and reasoning
> All virtue and excellence is held in a holy being

That has concern for all living beings,
And all good qualities will arise before too long.

Geshe Langri Tangpa's *Eight Verses of Mind Training* states:

With the intention to accomplish
The highest welfare for all living beings,
Who surpass a wish-fulfilling jewel,
May I eternally cherish them.

Think, "I must cherish all these mother living beings even more than my own life. Guru-deity, please bestow your blessing that I may be able to act in this way." Recite the verse from the ritual text that states:

Seeing that the mind that cherishes my mothers
And accomplishes their happiness
Is the gateway and source of limitless good qualities,
I seek your blessing to cherish these beings
More than my life, even if they rise up as my enemies.

Through making this extremely powerful supplication a stream of five-colored light rays and nectars descends from the bodies of the guru and assembly of deities and enters the body and mind of yourself and all other living beings, whereby the unique obstructions are purified and, in particular, the various realizations are developed in the minds of yourself and all living beings.

By contemplating the faults of self-cherishing and the benefits of cherishing others through many avenues, in this way you will develop extremely powerful love and compassion for old mother sentient beings. With regard to this, you should examine the situation by thinking, "Although I should generate the thought to exchange self with others if I am to liberate these kind mother sentient beings from the abodes of samsara, when I consider whether or not I am capable of generating such an attitude, I must determine whether or not I am unable. If I am unable to [exchange self with others] despite my efforts, I won't obtain any results from my hardships, whereas if I am able [to exchange self with others], I should generate it."

Fools claim the great benefits [attributed to exchanging self with others] are mere words whereas the wise engage in it with everything they do and don't pursue it with mere words. You should engage in this practice by considering whether or not it is necessary to carry out your actions in that way, and when you decide that, although it is necessary you must determine whether or not you are capable of accomplishing it. If you examine the situation in this way, you will see that you can definitely exchange self with others. For example, although you generate strong aversion to merely seeing or hearing your enemy, if you subsequently reconcile, he or she will seem like a great friend. If you can change your attitude in this way with someone you couldn't even stand to associate with, you can certainly cultivate an experience of a mind that cherishes [others].

With regard to the meaning of exchanging self with others, it does not mean that you exchange your body with others or that you exchange your mind with others, for something like this is not even possible. Therefore, it means that you are exchanging positions of the mind of self-cherishing and the mind that forsakes others with developing a mind that cherishes others through forsaking yourself. In short, our teacher engaged in exchanging self with others out of his great compassion, whereby he perfected the aims of himself and others. We childish beings abandon others and cherish ourselves, whereby we experience continuous suffering through our unending samsara. Therefore, think, "Guru-deity, please grant your blessing that I may be able to exchange self with others just as the compassionate teacher did." Recite the verse from the ritual text that states:

> In short, since the childish work for their own welfare
> Whereas the buddhas work for the welfare of others,
> I seek your blessing to be able to realize
> The faults and qualities and thereby exchange myself for others.

Through making this extremely powerful supplication a stream of five-colored light rays and nectars descends from the bodies of the guru and assembly of deities and enters the body and mind of yourself and all other living beings, whereby the unique obstructions are purified and, in particular, the various realizations are developed in the minds of yourself and all living beings.

This method is revealed in the *Guide to the Bodhisattva's Way of Life*, which states:

> Whatever happiness there is in this world
> All comes from wishing others to be happy.
> Whatever suffering there is in the world
> All comes from wishing for one's own happiness.

> What need is there to say any more?
> The childish work for their own welfare
> And the Buddha works for the welfare of others;
> Just look at the difference between these two!

> If I do not exchange my happiness
> For the suffering of others,
> I will not attain enlightenment
> And there will never be any happiness in samsara.

Thus, by contemplating the benefits of exchanging self with others and the faults of not exchanging them you will meditate on equalizing self and others with powerful delight. By seeing that you will definitely be able to generate such thoughts once you become familiar with them, you will develop an unbelievably powerful aspiration determined to meditate on equalizing and exchanging self with others. Remain with such thoughts while absorbed in a meditation on the guru-deity.

Contemplate:

> If I do not wish to suffer and desire happiness, I must recog-
> nize that the source of all my suffering is this self-cherishing
> and the basis of all good qualities is cherishing living beings.
> I am not free even for an instant from the control of this
> demon of self-cherishing, which is like a demon lurking in

my heart. I will not newly generate my previously generated self-cherishing. I will cut the continuity of that which has been generated. I will newly generate the mind of cherishing mother living beings that has not been previously generated. Once it has been generated, I will continuously increase this yoga of exchanging self with others. Guru-deity, please grant your blessing that I may be able to act accordingly.

Recite the verse from the ritual text that states:

> Since self-cherishing is the door to all faults
> And cherishing mother beings is the basis of all good qualities,
> I seek your blessing to take as my heart practice
> The yoga of exchanging self with others.

Through making this extremely powerful supplication a stream of five-colored light rays and nectars descends from the bodies of the guru and assembly of deities and enters the body and mind of yourself and all other living beings, whereby the particular obstructions are purified and, in particular, the various realizations are developed in the minds of yourself and all living beings.

This method is revealed in the *Seven-Point Mind Training*, which states:

> Banish the one to blame for everything
> And meditate on the great kindness of all.

By contemplating the meaning of this you will come to deeply cherish mother sentient beings and see them as very dear, whereby you will develop a mind of affectionate love much more powerfully than before. Contemplate, "If I [practice exchanging self with others] in whatever I do, I will be able to liberate these mother sentient beings from the suffering of samsara. From their side, it is extremely difficult for sentient beings to generate the slightest virtuous thoughts; therefore, it is as though there will never come a time when they are liberated from samsara. I must remove the sufferings of all these living beings and liberate all these mother sentient beings from the suffering of samsara. For that purpose I should meditate on taking and giving (*tonglen*). Guru-deity, please bestow your blessing that I may be able to conduct myself in that way."

The ritual text states:

> Therefore, great compassionate venerable guru,
> I seek your blessing that all the negative karma, obscurations,
> And suffering of all mother living beings without exception
> May ripen upon me right now and may all
> My happiness and virtue be delivered to others
> So that all living beings may be endowed with happiness.

Through making this extremely powerful supplication a stream of five-colored light rays and nectars descends from the bodies of the guru and assembly of deities and enters the body and mind of yourself and all other living beings, whereby the unique obstructions are purified and, in particular, the various realizations are developed in the minds of yourself and all living beings.

This mind of exchanging self with others is the very heart essence of Mahayana mind training; therefore, you should sincerely apply yourself to developing it and summon whatever human strength and capacity you possess and put it all into this. For the sake of [increasing] your understanding you should prepare with these verses as a plaintive call to your guru as a way of evoking his compassion and make supplications to develop this "heart of the path" in your mental continuum. Furthermore, it is said that you should recite the supplication at least three times. To this day the tradition continues among the hermits to make this supplication three times.

With regard to how to meditate on taking and giving at this point, while remaining in a state of meditation on the guru-deity you clearly visualize yourself surrounded by mother living beings and then contemplate, "These old mothers of mine are tormented by suffering and each one is worthy of my compassion," and then meditate on taking and giving through your extremely powerful love and compassion. If, due to lack of familiarity, you develop fear and trepidation that thinks, "Right now I cannot even bear my own suffering; therefore, how could I possibly take on the suffering of others?" you should take on your own future suffering for the sake of familiarizing your mind with this practice. To do this you begin by taking the suffering that may occur later in the afternoon right now during the earlier part of the day. Then take on tomorrow's experience of suffering today. In the same way you continue to take on the experience of the month, year, the end of your life, and then all your future lives into the present. When your courage increases through your familiarity with that, you meditate on taking and giving by first imagining your mother of this life before you. Simultaneously with your exhalation through your right nostril you imagine that all of your happiness and virtue exists in the aspect of white light rays and enters the left nostril of your mother, whereby she becomes endowed with your happiness and the causes of happiness; then you should meditate on joy. Simultaneously with your inhalation you imagine that all of her negative karma and suffering emerges from your mother's right nostril as completely black shavings similar to hair trimmings. You draw them in with your breath and they enter through your left nostril and descend to your heart, where your self-cherishing dwells, whereby your self-cherishing is immediately destroyed. You should meditate on joy that feels, "My mother has been freed from all of her suffering and the causes of her suffering." Once you have perfected that thought, you should meditate on taking and giving in the same way with your other loved ones, such as your father and so forth.

Next, sequentially increase the scope of your practice until you are meditating on taking and giving for all living beings as pervasive as space. Next, simultaneously give away your one body and enjoyments of the three times together with your virtues to all living beings pervading space in the aspect of white light rays and simultaneously take on all the negative karma, obscurations, and suffering of all living beings, whereby all living beings are liberated from all of their negative karma, obscurations, and suffering and imagine they are enlightened. Next, practice giving to all worldly realms and taking all of their faults, whereby all environments transform into nothing but pure lands, such as Sukhavati. At this point you should meditate with great delight by thinking, "How wonderful it would be if I were able to liberate all living beings from samsara." Here I have set forth just a small portion of the essential points. The way to practice taking and giving through the extensive mental scope of exchanging self with others is an extremely vast oral instruction. For this there are numerous essential points of visualization through which there are numerous ways to present offerings to the buddhas and bodhisattvas. There are also numerous extremely important essential oral instructions, such as how to visualize for the long life of your holy guru and so forth. As explained earlier, these methods for meditating on taking and giving are in the root verses for *Seven-Point Mind Training*, which state:

> Train by alternating taking and giving.
> Begin by sequentially taking from yourself
> And mount these two upon the breath.

With regard to the third point of mind training, **transforming unfavorable conditions into the path,** while remaining in a state of meditation on the guru-deity contemplate how the worldly environment is filled with extreme proliferation of the ripened results from the ten nonvirtues and how thoughts of living beings that are its inhabitants have not transcended the causes of afflictive emotions, nor have their actions transcended the causes of bad actions, and so forth. Through the force of these the power of gods, nagas, evil spirits, and so forth who delight in these nonvirtues increases. In general, there are a wide range of beings that inflict harm on the practice of Dharma. In particular, if you don't practice something like this mind training in times like these, as you are struggling with unfavorable circumstances from various avenues to entering the gateway of the Mahayana Dharma, it will be very difficult to complete your Dharma practice. Through this mind training you can transform unfavorable conditions into favorable conditions, transform all obstacles into assistants, and once we can think of all harmful agents as your spiritual guides that urge you to practice Dharma, you will know how to take them into the spiritual path. When this happens, all unfavorable circumstances will arise as assistants to accomplishing enlightenment; therefore, it is extremely important that you understand how to take unfavorable conditions into the spiritual path. Therefore, for this practice of transforming adverse conditions there are two: transforming through thought and transforming through deeds. Transforming [adverse conditions] through thought has two sections: (1) transforming them into the path through bodhichitta, and (2) transforming them into the path through the view.

With regard to **transforming adverse conditions into the path through bodhichitta**, consider how there is nowhere else to direct the blame for whatever harm and suffering befalls you other than the demon of self-grasping. However, all these undesired circumstances are not without a cause and are solely the result of your bad actions from previous lives; therefore, [these adverse conditions] are a means of exhausting your bad karma. For that reason you should think that since the results of these bad actions are exhausted in this life, they are blessings from your compassionate guru for the sake of closing the door of rebirth in the lower realms. Furthermore, meditate on taking and giving by thinking, "Limitless living beings experience harm and suffering such as this; therefore, may all the harm and suffering of living beings ripen within my mental continuum." Furthermore, meditate on taking and giving by contemplating, "These humans and nonhumans that are causing me harm have been nothing but kind to me throughout my previous lives and are being propelled by my own bad karma that is causing them to engage in these negative actions, whereby they will be going to hell. As for me, they inspire me to engage in virtuous actions, whereby it becomes an aid to developing my good qualities; therefore, they are not in fact causing me any harm. May the negative karma and obscurations of these beings that are harming me, who are worthy of my compassion and are my old mothers, ripen upon me and may all of my happiness and virtue ripen upon them." Furthermore, completely dedicate your body mentally to the nonhuman beings who are engaged in these harmful actions by reciting, "In general, I dedicate this corporeal body of flesh, blood, and bones to the nonhuman beings as a substitute for all living beings, and specifically to those engaged in the practice of Dharma, and particularly the holy body of the glorious guru. For those who like flesh, eat my flesh; for those who like blood, drink my blood; for those who like bones, eat my bones; take whatever you desire!" Recite this and continuously mentally dedicate yourself to these nonhuman beings. With all your heart recite, "Through your great kindness you have assisted me in my meditation on bodhichitta. What's more, cause all the harm and suffering of all living beings to ripen upon my self-cherishing and [annihilate it]!"

Furthermore, the way to stop seeing whatever suffering befalls you as a fault and perceiving it as a good quality is expressed in the *Guide to the Bodhisattva's Way of Life*, which states:

> Moreover, suffering has good qualities:
> Through despair arrogance is dispelled,
> One generates compassion for those in samsara,
> Negative karma is destroyed, and one delights in virtue.

Once you contemplate the numerous teachings such as these you should transform adverse conditions into the aids to enlightenment to the best of your ability.

With regard to **transforming them into the path through the view**, the oral instructions of Jetsun Losang Chökyi Gyaltsen state:

> By harboring this demon in your heart
> From beginningless time until the present
> You apprehend a selfless object as having a self
> That functions to deceive you through tricking you with
>   its immediate benefit;
> Now you burn in hell for an innumerable time,
> Yet today, through the kindness of my guru,
> I have recognized this evil hidden spirit of the enemy,
>   self-grasping.
> Having seen the nature of the primordial mind free from
>   elaboration,
> I encountered the youthful son of the self-emergent awareness
>   and
> The beautiful sphere of reality of the objective clear light—
> The union of method and wisdom as the inseparable space
>   and awareness
> Collected inseparably here as the best assistants.

And:

All phenomena arise in dependence upon the Father
And are perceived as the illusory display of mere appearance,
Yet one is bound by seeing them as truly existent.

By viewing all the various appearances that arise, such as happiness and suffering, good and bad, and so forth, as illusory-like and not truly existent, you should perceive all appearances as manifestations of dependent arising to the best of your ability. In short:

Whether living and dying, success and failure,
Happiness and suffering, high and low, pleasant and unpleasant,
    and so forth,
Whatever happens is the blessing of your guru;
A la la, whatever happens is perfect!

Thus, once you know how to bring whatever happens, whether good circumstances or bad, into an impetus for virtuous practices and as aids to the practice of Dharma, these good and bad circumstances will not be able to shake your self-confidence and you will quickly progress along the path of the Mahayana.

With regard to **how to transform [adverse conditions] into the path through deeds**, you practice the four deeds mentioned in the ritual text where it states, "With the skillful means endowed with the four preparations." Thus, there are four deeds:

1. Accumulating merit
2. Purifying negative karma
3. Giving tormas to the obstructing spirits
4. Requesting the enlightened actions of the Dharma
    protectors

With regard to how to bring adverse conditions into the path through those four, if you don't desire suffering and wish for happiness you should assemble the various causes of happiness. And when adverse conditions, such as sickness, harm from spirits, and so forth, emerge, you should contemplate by thinking, "These are signs from my guru." Present offerings and a mandala to your guru and the assembly of deities and make supplications such as "Please grant your blessings that if it is best that I am sick, may I be ill. Grant your blessings that if it is best that I live, may I live. Grant your blessings that if it is best that I die, may I die." By doing this you will put a stop to your hopes and fears.

With regard to **transforming [adverse conditions] into the path through the purification of negative karma**, if you don't desire suffering you should consider it a sign from your guru that you should forsake negative actions that are its cause and sincerely apply yourself to confession and restraint through the four opponent powers. With regard to **transforming [adverse conditions] into the path through giving tormas to the obstructing spirits**, you should think, "Once I am distracted by the things of this life, I forget about the Dharma; therefore, accept this torma and encourage me in my virtuous practices through your great kindness. What's more, may you cause all the unwanted conditions of all living beings to ripen upon my self-cherishing and continue to encourage me in my virtuous practices until enlightenment." With regard to **requesting the enlightened action of the Dharma protectors**, you offer them a torma and request their enlightened actions by requesting them to put an end to your hopes and fears in the same way you supplicated the guru and assembly of deities earlier.

Thus, if you are unable to do that because you are not familiar with these ways of transforming adverse conditions into the path through either thought or deed, or if you have little courage, you should make a sincere effort in accumulating merit and purification by understanding that all favorable and unfavorable conditions are the result of your karma and request the [Dharma protectors] to not allow any obstacles to occur that would interfere with your Dharma practice.

These oral instructions for transforming adverse conditions into the path were taught by numerous holy beings of the past in the land of snows and were given titles such as "Instructions for Equalizing Flavor," "Bringing Happiness and Suffering into the Path," "Bringing Whatever You Encounter into the Path," and so forth, which contain numerous highly praised and profound instructions. If you wish to sincerely practice this Hearing Lineage of the second conqueror, Je [Tsongkhapa], you should have deep heartfelt conviction in this oral instruction.

With regard to the **explanation of integrating the practices into a single lifetime,** the ritual text states:

> In short, I seek your blessing so that whether good or evil
>   appearances arise
> I may transform them into the path of increasing the two
>   bodhichittas
> By practicing the five forces, the essence of all Dharma,
> And cultivate a happy mind alone.

For this there are (1) practices done during your entire life, and (2) practices at the moment of death. The practices at the moment of death will come later. With regard to the practices while living, we combine them with the five forces:

1. The force of the intention
2. The force of familiarity
3. The force of the white seed
4. The force of destruction or atonement
5. The force of prayer

With regard to the *force of the intention*, you repeatedly set your intention by thinking, "From today until enlightenment and particularly before I die and especially on this very day, I will not come under the influence of my enemy, this demon of self-grasping, for even an instant, and will conjoin my meditation with the two types of precious bodhichitta."

With regard to the *force of familiarity*, once you attain confidence in these oral instructions of Glorious Atisha and Conqueror Tsongkhapa the Great that contain the complete body of the stages of the path to enlightenment, you should strive to cultivate familiarity with them at all times.

As for the *force of the white seed*, for the sake of generating the precious bodhichitta that has not been generated and continually increasing the bodhichitta that has already been generated, you should make a sincere effort in accumulating merit and purifying negative karma.

Regarding the *force of destruction or atonement*, you should work to crush your self-cherishing, which is an impediment to the precious mind of bodhichitta.

As for the *force of prayer*, you should make dedications, prayers, and supplications so that whatever virtuous actions you undertake become the cause of increasing the precious mind of bodhichitta.

Regarding these five forces, it is said, "These instructions can all be subsumed into a single syllable, HUM, for a lifetime's practice." What it means is that from today until enlightenment, since there is nothing superior to these instructions, which embody the complete path in its entirety, you will not look anywhere else but instead will work with single-pointed determination to bring them into a unified practice.

Regarding the fifth point of mind training, **the measure of having trained the mind**, the ritual text states:

> I seek your blessing to transform them into the path of
>   increasing the two bodhichittas
> By practicing the five forces, the essence of all Dharma,
> And cultivate a happy mind alone.

The *Root Verses of Mind Training* states:

> Integrate all the teachings into a single purpose,
> Hold the two witnesses as of primary importance,
> Rely solely upon a constantly happy mind,
> If you can [practice] even while distracted you are trained.

If we condense the meaning of this verse, it means that even if you are unable to transform good and bad circumstances by properly practicing the Mahayana mind training, you should not let your familiarity with bodhichitta deteriorate throughout all circumstances. Furthermore, we see such things in the biography of the omniscient foremost being [Tsongkhapa] where he says, "Furthermore, when others set out excellent cushions for me, honor me with respect, and so forth, I don't need to give it much thought at all. Instead, I feel that these are all impermanent and are untrustworthy and are like illusory deceptive seductions. I have extremely powerful thoughts of aversion from the depths of my heart as though they were insignificant appearances. I have naturally felt this way since the time of my birth." Thus, this is saying that you should make a sincere effort not to rely upon whatever appearances arise such as happiness and suffering, good and bad, and so forth, and instead learn to naturally use them as aids to your mind-training practice.

With regard to the phrase from the ritual text that states, "Immediately applying meditation to all interactions," the *Root Verses of Mind Training* states:

> The three objects, three poisons, and three virtuous roots—
> Train through words in all your daily actions and
> Conjoin with meditation whatever you meet.

What I have composed here accords with these oral instructions and, as for how to put them into practice, they also contain the entire meaning for how to transform adverse conditions into the path through the four preparations and are in accordance with the true intent of both the mind training and these oral instructions.

Regarding the way to put them into practice, when any fleeting favorable or unfavorable outer and inner conditions arise, such as the inner afflictive emotions like attachment and so forth, as well as the outer harms from humans and nonhumans, you should not come under their influence for even an instant, but turn them into aids for virtuous practices to the best of your ability in general, and in particular you should work to transform them into the means and aids for increasing the precious mind of bodhichitta that cherishes others.

Furthermore, if you develop attachment through pleasing objects by suddenly encountering the right conditions, you should identify them immediately and meditate on taking and giving by thinking, "May all the attachment of however many mother sentient beings there are in the three realms who have come under the influence of attachment (as well as the suffering they experience under its influence and all of the suffering they create through it) ripen within my mental continuum. I shall give all of my virtue and happiness to all of my mother living beings!"

Furthermore, when you encounter unpleasant objects, such as when others suddenly speak to you with harsh language and so forth, and you become angry or are concerned you may become angry, you should not come under the influence of such circumstances even for an instant, and instead meditate on taking and giving by taking all the anger and suffering of all your mother living beings as extensive as space within your mental continuum and giving all of your happiness and virtue to all your mother living beings.

Furthermore, once you observe neutral objects and you come under the influence of ignorance that lacks clarity about the nature of reality, you should summon forth the ignorance of all living beings as extensive as space, as well as all the suffering generated through it, and send out all of your happiness and virtue. In the same way, whatever circumstances suddenly emerge, you should transform them all into aids to increasing your bodhichitta. This way of transforming circumstances into the path comes from the *Perfection of Wisdom Sutra in Eight Thousand Lines*.

You should not become frightened whenever any adverse conditions, such as sickness, harm from spirits, famine, precipices, wild animals, and so forth, suddenly arise, but instead happily accept them without any fear. Because such adverse conditions suddenly arise in the worldly realms, there are limitless harmful things; therefore, feel, "Although there are all these harms and sufferings, may I learn to transform them into something positive. Although this body may be eaten at this very moment by wild animals, since I wish to train in the practices of a bodhisattva I will offer my body with joy." Also, wear the armor of intention and send forth prayers by contemplating, "When I become enlightened in a buddha's pure land, faults such as wild animals, famine, precipices, and so forth will not occur; therefore, I must definitely accomplish this state endowed with all good qualities and an absolutely perfect environment and beings." These [prayers] are the concise meaning of the teachings set forth in the sutras. You should learn the details from the sutras themselves. Further, all of your daily actions, such as traveling and sleeping, should not slip into those of ordinary beings but should be transformed into methods for increasing your bodhichitta in dependence upon the oral instructions of skillful means to the best of your ability. The complete set of extensive oral instructions for maintaining a pure sphere of activity in your daily actions appears in the sutras, and such things are taught in the *Cloud of Jewels Sutra*, which states:

> Whether offering a flower to a stupa of the tathagata or a
> statue of the tathagata, or presenting incense or perfume,

you should make dedications that it may dispel the bad scent of the damaged moral discipline of all living beings and that they may come to possess the scent of moral discipline of the tathagatas. If you are sweeping and cleaning or spreading plaster, you should make thorough dedications that the unpleasant daily actions of all living beings may become nonexistent and their daily actions may become beautiful. When you apply a flower parasol, you should thoroughly dedicate so that all living beings may be free from the torments of the afflictive emotions and secondary afflictive emotions. When you enter a temple, you should generate bodhichitta by thinking, "In this way may all living beings enter the supreme city of nirvana." Generate bodhichitta by thinking, "In that way may all living beings be released from the prison of samsara." When you open the door to your home, you should generate bodhichitta by thinking, "I shall open the door to all happy migrations through the supramundane exalted wisdom." When shutting the door, you should generate bodhichitta by thinking, "I am shutting the door to all lower realms." When you sit down, you should generate bodhichitta by thinking, "I am establishing all living beings in the essence of enlightenment." When you lie down on your right side, you should generate bodhichitta by thinking, "May I thoroughly liberate all living beings through the liberation of full enlightenment." When you rise from that, you should generate bodhichitta by thinking, "I shall raise all living beings by lifting them out of every afflicted state." When you move your body, you should generate bodhichitta by thinking, "May my movements become like those of a great being for all living beings." When you sit down, you should generate bodhichitta by thinking, "In the same way may I expel the pain and torment of attachment, hatred, and ignorance of all living beings." When you wash your face, you should generate bodhichitta by thinking, "In the same way may I cleanse the faults of the stains of afflictive emotions from all living beings." When you wash your hands, generate bodhichitta by thinking, "In the same way may I dispel the foul scent of the afflictive emotions of all living beings." When you wash your feet, you should generate bodhichitta by thinking, "May I dispel the various particles of the afflictions of all living beings." When you brush your teeth, generate bodhichitta by thinking, "In the same way may I remove all the various stains of all living beings." In this way dedicate all the movements of your body for the benefit and happiness of all living beings.

In the same way, when you make prostrations to a stupa of the tathagata you should generate bodhichitta by thinking, "In the same way may all living beings, together with worldly gods, make prostrations." Child of the lineage, acting in this way is the skillful means of thorough dedication of a bodhisattva.

There are other such extensive teachings that you should learn in detail from the sutras themselves.

The sixth point of mind training is **the eighteen commitments of mind training:**[195] (1) mind training should not contradict your other commitments, (2) do not become reckless, (3) do not fall into partiality, (4) maintain a mind cherishing others while keeping the actions of your body and speech in accordance with the accepted modes of behavior, (5) do not speak of others' faults, (6) although you may perceive the faults of others, do not fixate on them, (7) rely upon the principal antidotes whenever an afflictive emotion surfaces, (8) forsake all hopes of your own benefit, such as respect and honor, for being a mind-training practitioner, (9) do not let your virtuous practices mix the signs of inherent existence and self-cherishing, (10) do not hold a grudge against those who harm you, (11) do not respond to scolding with harsh words and so forth, (12) do not respond to harm, (13) do not engage in actions that would harm the body and minds of others, (14) do not load upon others the blame for your own faults, (15) forsake thoughts and deeds of gaining dominance over communal enjoyments for your purposes, (16) do not engage in mind

195. What follows is a description of each of the eighteen commitments using slightly different language than Geshe Chekawa's *Seven-Point Mind Training*.

training merely to receive benefit from harmful spirits (i.e., misuse mind training as a means to avoid harm from spirits), (17) do not be proud or arrogant because of your practice of mind training, and (18) abandon negative thoughts wishing happiness for yourself and suffering for others.

The seventh point of mind training is **the twenty-two precepts of mind training**: (1) train yourself to undertake all of your yoga practices, such as the yoga of eating and so forth, solely with the intention to benefit others, (2) train in this mind of equalizing and exchanging self with others in all practices of enhancement and expelling obstructing spirits, (3) train in bodhichitta prior to any virtuous action you undertake and seal the conclusion with dedication, (4) train in bringing whatever arises, be it happiness or suffering, to be an aid to your mind training, (5) train in protecting all of your commitments as you would your life in general, but your commitments of mind training in particular, (6) train in severing the continuity of your afflictive emotions the moment they arise through relying upon the appropriate antidotes, (7) train in relying primarily upon the guru as the cause of accomplishing the Dharma, in making your mind serviceable, and accomplishing the favorable conditions that are absolutely necessary for practicing Dharma, (8) train in not letting your faith and devotion in your guru deteriorate, not letting your delight in mind train- ing deteriorate, and protecting your three sets of vows so that they do not deteriorate, (9) train in applying yourself so that your three doors are never separated from virtue, (10) train in mind training without any partiality toward all, (11) train so that your mind training pervades every- thing that arises, (12) train in meditating on love and compassion for those for whom it is difficult to generate this, such as your competitors and so forth, (13) train in meditating on mind training at all times without regard to good or bad circumstances, (14) train in practicing primarily the con- densed essential meaning, (15) train in abandoning the six mistakes that make you incapable of practicing virtue and that bring great suffering in this life and so forth,[196] (16) train in continually striving in your practice without being inconsistent, (17) train in practicing with single-pointed focus without wavering, (18) train in abandoning the afflictive emotions

---

196. The six mistakes are (1) mistaken patience, (2) mistaken aspiration, (3) mistaken experi- ence, (4) mistaken compassion, (5) mistaken benefit, and (6) mistaken rejoicing.

through repeated analysis, (19) train in not boasting to others, (20) train in not becoming irritated by the slightest harsh words, (21) train in not coming under the influence of expecting praise and fame for your practice of Dharma, and (22) train in being constantly steady in your Dharma practice without the slightest fluctuation in your practice with starts and fits because of the novelty of your virtuous practices.

Thus, you should become well acquainted with taking and giving through equalizing and exchanging self with others and perfect your mind training through these seven points without wasting this life of leisure and endowments that you have obtained this one time and that is so very meaningful. Think that you are requesting the guru-deity for his blessing to be able to practice in this way and recite the following verses from the ritual prayer:

> When the world and its beings are completely filled with
> The results of nonvirtue and unwanted suffering pours down
>   like rain,
> I seek your blessing that I may see this
> As a cause to exhaust the results of bad actions
> And transform adverse conditions into the path.
>
> In short, whether good or evil appearances arise,
> I seek your blessing to transform them into the path of increasing
>   the two bodhichittas
> By practicing the five forces, the essence of all Dharma,
> And cultivate a happy mind alone.
>
> I seek your blessing that I may extract great meaning from this
>   life of freedom and endowment
> With the skillful means endowed with the four preparations
> By immediately applying meditation to all interactions
> And practicing the commitments and precepts of mind
>   training.

Through this extremely powerful supplication a stream of five-colored light rays and nectars descends from the bodies of the guru and assembly of deities and enters the body and mind of yourself and all other living beings, whereby the various obstructions [to succeeding in mind training] are cleansed and special realizations are generated in the minds of yourself and all other living beings.

How to Meditate on Superior Intention and Bodhichitta

Thinking in this way, meditate properly on the guru-deity. Thus, you generate affectionate love through meditating on recognizing all beings as your mother, recalling their kindness, and wishing to repay their kindness, as well as contemplating, through numerous avenues, the faults of self-cherishing and the benefits of cherishing others, so that you cherish and care for mother sentient beings as though they were a wish-fulfilling jewel. Also, meditate on taking and giving by way of great compassion that is unable to bear [their suffering] by contemplating the situation of your old mothers. Because of this, if you are moved by uncontrollable love and compassion, meditate on superior intention by thinking, "I must liberate these old mother sentient beings of mine from all the sorrows of samsara and peace and establish them in the state of enlightenment." You may then wonder if you are capable of establishing all living beings in the state of complete enlightenment when right now you are not even capable of establishing just one living being in the state of complete enlightenment. Not only that, although you may attain the state of the two types of arhat, with the exception of accomplishing some limited benefit for living beings, you will not be capable of establishing all living beings in the state of complete enlightenment. If you wonder who is capable of accomplishing such a thing, it is a completely perfect buddha. His body is adorned with all the good qualities, complete with the signs and indications. The good qualities of his speech are such that it is effortlessly endowed with sixty qualities and is capable of teaching Dharma in the individual languages of each and every living being. The good qualities of his mind directly perceive all ultimate and conventional objects of knowledge. His compassion regards all living beings like that of a mother for her only child and his great compassion is utterly unbiased, whereby it does not go beyond the proper time to subdue [living beings], even for an instant. His enlightened actions are spontaneously accomplished and even each light ray radiated from his body, speech, and mind is capable of establishing limitless living beings in the state of omniscience and so forth. In short, he is endowed with every type of good quality and is free from every fault, which are qualities possessed only by completely perfect buddhas. For that reason, if you are going to perfect the aims of both yourself and others, you must obtain the state of such an enlightened being. For that reason, come what may, you should attain the state of precious completely perfect enlightenment as quickly as possible for the welfare of all living beings. Imagine that you are requesting the guru-deity for his blessing to be able to accomplish such a state while reciting the following verse from the ritual text:

> I seek your blessing that I may [generate] perfect bodhichitta by
> Dispatching the wind mounted by taking and giving,
> And liberate living beings from the great ocean of existence
> With the mind of love, compassion, and superior intention.

Through making this extremely powerful supplication a stream of five-colored light rays and nectars descends from the bodies of the guru and assembly of deities and enters the body and mind of yourself and all other living beings, whereby the unique obstructions are purified and, in particular, the various realizations are developed in the minds of yourself and all living beings.

How to Take the Vows of Aspiring Bodhichitta and Engaging Bodhichitta

Thus, if you evoke a powerful experience of the mind of bodhichitta through the oral instructions of sevenfold cause and effect and equalizing and exchanging self with others, you should perform the ritual for taking the vows of aspiring bodhichitta. For that you should supplicate a fully qualified Mahayana spiritual guide. Once you have arranged as many offerings as you can afford, you should engage in the common preliminary of going for refuge and then accept the sacred promises of aspiring bodhichitta. With regard to how such a ritual should be performed, this is explained in the *Great Exposition on the Stages of the Path to Enlightenment*[197] and should be done according to the observed lineage of practice. Once you accept the aspiring bodhichitta, you should recall its benefits for the purpose of increasing your deep appreciation for generating bodhichitta and generate bodhichitta six times each day for the sake of increasing your actual bodhichitta. You should train in the mind of not abandoning living beings, accumulating the two collections [of merit and wisdom] and the four causes of not letting your bodhichitta deteriorate in this life, and abandoning the four nonvirtuous Dharmas[198] so that you won't be separated from bodhichitta in your future lives, while relying on the four virtuous Dharmas.[199] You should also train in the eight precepts uncommon to the aspiring bodhichitta.

Jowo Je [Atisha] stated:

> For those wishing to enter the gateway of the Mahayana
>   Dharma
> Bodhichitta is like the sun and the moon
> That pacify suffering and dispel darkness;
> It is appropriate to strive for an eon to produce it.

The holy beings rely upon the encouragement of conduct of the bodhisattvas and texts on the path of the Mahayana. You should strive in whatever way possible with all your might to continually increase your precious mind of bodhichitta, without letting it deteriorate, as the uncommon skillful cause of enlightenment.

Next, if you are capable of carrying the responsibility of the bodhisattva vows, you should properly train in the precepts through accepting the

---

197. Tsong-kha-pa, *The Great Treatise on the Stages of the Path to Enlightenment*, vol. 2 (Ithaca, NY: Snow Lion Publications, 2004), 61–68.

198. The four nonvirtuous practices are (1) deceiving abbots, masters, gurus, and those worthy of offerings, (2) making others feel regret about something that is not regrettable, (3) speaking disparagingly, etc., to beings who have correctly entered the Mahayana, and (4) in an absence of sincerity, using deceit and misrepresentation to get the service of others.

199. The four virtuous practices are (1) forsaking consciously lying to any living being whatsoever even in jest or even for the sake of your life, (2) not deceiving but remaining sincere to all living beings, (3) developing the idea that all bodhisattvas are the teacher, and (4) causing the living beings that you are helping to mature so as not to desire the Hinayana but to adhere to perfect enlightenment.

vows of engaging bodhichitta for the sake of greatly increasing and expanding the power of your bodhichitta. There are numerous divergent rituals, both extensive and concise, for accepting the vows of engaging bodhichitta. There are two different ways for receiving them: there are the extensive teachings in the chapter of pure moral discipline [in Asanga's *Bodhisattva Bhumi*] and the concise teachings of verses in the *Guide to the Bodhisattva's Way of Life*. The *Heap of Jewels Sutra* explains how in the past Venerable Manjushri generated bodhichitta when he was the king of space, and the ritual presented in *A Lamp for the Path* is in accordance with this teaching. Moreover, many of the scholars and pandits of India taught a variety of extensive and concise [methods for taking the bodhisattva vows] that are similar in meaning with the exception of some differences in the wording. Whatever way you train as a bodhisattva, they are all the same in the precepts they accept.

For that reason, the conquerors and bodhisattvas bear witness and your training becomes just like the buddhas and bodhisattvas of the past, just like the buddhas and bodhisattvas of the future, and just like the training of the buddhas and bodhisattvas currently residing in the ten directions. Make a promise by stating, "For the sake of quickly liberating all of my old mother sentient beings I will train in all of the practices of a bodhisattva from this very moment." And once you accept the vows of engaging bodhichitta you should perfectly train in all of the precepts of the bodhisattva vows by not becoming defiled by the eighteen root downfalls or the forty-six infractions.

If you condense all of the practices of a bodhisattva they are (1) the moral discipline of restraint, (2) the moral discipline of assembling virtuous Dharmas, and (3) the moral discipline of working for the welfare of living beings; therefore, we should make every effort to train in these. Thus, we should imagine that we are requesting the guru-deity for his blessing to be successful in accomplishing them. Recite the following verse from the ritual text, which states:

> I seek your blessing to earnestly engage in the sole path
> Traversed by all the conquerors of the three times:
> To restrain my mind with pure bodhisattva vows and
> Practice the three moral disciplines of the Mahayana.

Through making this extremely powerful supplication a stream of five-colored light rays and nectars descends from the bodies of the guru and assembly of deities and enters the body and mind of yourself and all other living beings, whereby the unique obstructions are purified and, in particular, the various realizations are developed in the minds of yourself and all living beings.

For those wishing to enter the Mahayana, whether they are entering the gateway of either sutra or tantra, they absolutely must take the bodhisattva vows. The moment all of the buddhas of the three times accepted these vows they trained in their precepts, so if you want to become a buddha, it is only through these oral instructions that you will succeed, and this is why [the ritual text] refers to this as "the sole path traversed by all the conquerors of the three times." These vows are extremely vast; therefore, you should train by reading the Mahayana sutras. For those intelligent beings endowed with great determination, they should listen to and contemplate the sutras of the Mahayana together with their commentaries and learn all of the trainings and disciplines from the outset. If you are not able to manage that, you should train once you have made a thorough examination of the foremost great being [Tsongkhapa's] *Commentary on the Chapter of Moral Discipline.*[200]

How to Train in the Deeds [of a Bodhisattva] following the Generation of Bodhichitta has two sections:
1. How to Train in the General Deeds of a Bodhisattva
2. How to Train in the Profound View of the Middle Way in Particular

How to Train in the General Deeds of a Bodhisattva has six sections:
1. How to Practice the Perfection of Generosity
2. How to Practice the Perfection of Moral Discipline
3. How to Practice the Perfection of Patience
4. How to Practice Enthusiastic Perseverance
5. How to Meditate on the Perfection of Concentration
6. How to Attain the Perfection of Wisdom

200. *Tshul khrims le'u'i rnam bshad.*

How to Train in the General Deeds of a Bodhisattva

If you do not train in the path of the bodhisattva's deeds once you generate aspiring and engaging bodhichitta, it will not be possible to accomplish the resultant state of enlightenment, not to mention the fact that you made a promise by stating, "I will quickly liberate all living beings" with all the buddhas and bodhisattvas as your witness. You also promised, "Just as all the buddhas and bodhisattvas trained, so will I also train in the same way"; therefore, it would be an utter disgrace if you were to abandon training in the deeds of a bodhisattva. The *Guide to the Bodhisattva's Way of Life* states:

> Since I have vowed myself in that way,
> If I do not practice with my deeds
> I will be deceiving all these living beings;
> Therefore, what sort of rebirth will I have?

There are a wide variety of teachings similar to what has just been stated. Therefore, although there are limitless bodhisattva deeds, when condensed they are subsumed under the six perfections, which have been extensively explained in the *Ornament of Mahayana Sutras* by the Venerable Protector Maitreya. The bodhisattva Shantideva subsumed all of the bodhisattva deeds into giving away your body, enjoyments, and roots of virtue. He has also explained [the bodhisattva deeds in relation to] protecting, purifying, and increasing, which have four aspects each, making twelve in all. With regard to their meaning, they are the very means of engaging in the practice of the six perfections. In these oral instructions [of Lama Chöpa] as well, all of the bodhisattva deeds are subsumed under the six perfections. Here, there is also an inner subdivision of each of the perfections into six, and you should learn in detail how to engage in each of the perfections so that each one is endowed with all six perfections. With regard to some who state that gaining experience in the Mahayana teachings looks as easy as shooting an arrow, for most people this appears to be similar to how easy the words and meaning of these instructions are to understand, yet with regard to the teachings that state, "You should train in accordance with the complete body of the path that accords with the meaning of the sutras and the commentaries of the great charioteers," most of the [aspiring trainees] become disheartened and discouraged; therefore, the holy beings have propagated far and wide these essential instructions of the Mahayana.

How to Practice the Perfection of Generosity

Thus, once you reach a degree of certainty with regard to the aforementioned instructions, you should engage in the practice of generosity and contemplate in this way while remaining absorbed in the state of meditation on the guru-deity by thinking, "I shall swiftly obtain the state of perfect complete enlightenment for the welfare of all mother living beings. For that purpose I shall train properly in the practice of the three types of generosity." Furthermore, with regard to the practice of generosity, you have not perfected the perfection of generosity by merely abandoning miserliness or giving some substance to another. The perfection of generosity is complete when you have perfected the strength of the mind of giving; therefore, you should train in the oral instruction for increasing the mind of generosity. For that, there is giving your body, giving your enjoyments, and giving your roots of virtue.

With regard to giving your body, once you have transformed your body into a wish-fulfilling body, you train in imagining that you send forth limitless emanations from that body that directly fulfill the various wishes of all living beings. Furthermore, you send forth cooling water to those in the hot hells, as well as pleasing food, clothing, dwellings, and so forth, and once you emanate these things their suffering is purified by your act of generosity. You can also transform yourself into pleasing friends for the harmful lords of death. Imagine that once their bodies become absolutely perfect, they become endowed with supreme bliss. In the same way, send forth emanations of whatever it is that living beings desire from your wish-fulfilling body to all those in the cold hells, and to hungry ghosts, animals, demigods, gods, and humans, whereby their respective sufferings are purified. Imagine that [their bodies] transform into the absolutely perfect bodies for the practice of Dharma.

Next, with regard to how to give your enjoyments, send forth limitless enjoyments of material possessions in accordance with whatever [living beings] desire, whereby they are satiated by the enjoyments that accord with the mental dispositions of each and every living being. To give your roots of virtue, imagine that you give away all of your virtuous roots of the three times to all living beings in the six realms, whereby each of their negative karma and obscurations, together with their imprints, are purified, after which their mental continuums are liberated and they attain the truth body. Regarding this practice, the *Guide to the Bodhisattva's Way of Life* states:

> Without any sense of loss
> I shall give away my body and likewise my wealth
> As well as all my virtues of the three times
> For the sake of accomplishing the welfare of living beings.
>
> Through giving everything I transcend suffering
> And my mind will accomplish liberation.
> I shall simultaneously give everything
> To living beings, which is the supreme giving.

These verses contain all three types of giving. The generosity of material things is giving your body and wealth. For the giving of fearlessness, you imagine you pacify their individual sufferings of fear and trepidation. And for giving Dharma, you imagine giving your roots of virtue. With regard to emanating countless enjoyments from the bodhisattva grounds, it is taught that the way to do this is to have the bodhisattvas possessing wisdom engage in acts of generosity of skillful means. These methods of meditation on giving are extensively praised in the *Compendium of Trainings* and *Guide to the Bodhisattva's Way of Life*, which contain indispensable oral instructions for quickly completing the great wave of the bodhisattva's conduct. Thus, you quickly complete the perfection of generosity in dependence upon the magical oral instructions for increasing the mind of giving. Imagine you are supplicating the guru-deity to be able to practice in that way while reciting the verse from the ritual text that states:

> I seek your blessing to complete the perfection of generosity
> Through the oral instructions of increasing the mind of giving
>   without attachment

And thus transform my body, enjoyments, and virtues accumulated throughout the three times
Into the things that each living being desires.

Through making this extremely powerful supplication a stream of five-
colored light rays and nectars descends from the bodies of the guru and
assembly of deities and enters the body and mind of yourself and all other
living beings, whereby the unique obstructions are purified and, in particular, the various realizations are developed in the minds of yourself and
all living beings.

How to Practice the Perfection of Moral Discipline

While remaining absorbed in this state of meditation on the guru-deity
you should contemplate, "I shall quickly attain the state of complete
enlightenment for the welfare of all mother sentient beings. For that purpose I shall properly train in the three types of moral discipline." With
regard to the three moral disciplines, they are (1) the moral discipline of
restraint, (2) the moral discipline of accumulating virtuous Dharmas, and
(3) the moral discipline of striving for the welfare of living beings. For
the moral discipline of restraint there is the moral discipline of restraint
of the pratimoksha, the moral discipline of restraint of the bodhisattva,
and the moral discipline of restraint of secret mantra. With regard to the
moral discipline of restraint of the pratimoksha, there are the seven types
to be abandoned, together with their attendant vows.[201]

Furthermore, there is the moral discipline of restraint of properly protecting vows of a novice monk, such as the thirty-three transcendences
of acceptance (together with the congruent faults), and the 253 rules
included within the vows of a fully ordained monk. Moreover, there are
limitless subtle and coarse downfalls subsumed in the basis, together with

---

201. The seven types of pratimoksha vows are those taken by (1) a fully ordained monk, (2) a fully
ordained nun, (3) a novice monk, (4) a novice nun, (5) a female novice in training, (6) a male lay
practitioner, and (7) a female lay practitioner. There are also seven types for lay practitioners:
(1) promising to keep just one vow, (2) promising to keep some of the vows, (3) promising to
keep most of them, (4) promising to keep all five, (5) promising to keep all five as well as celibacy,
(6) promising to keep all five, maintain celibacy, and wear the robes of a monk or nun and act in
accordance with the monk's or nun's vows, and (7) a mere lay follower of refuge.

what to cease, accomplish, and perform, which should all be properly protected just as they are described. For the bodhisattva vows there are the eighteen root downfalls and forty-six secondary downfalls. Moreover, there are limitless subtle and coarse downfalls that are incompatible with the three types of moral discipline in accordance with what has been taught by the conqueror. More about the moral discipline of mantra will come later.[202]

Thus, with regard to properly protecting the rules of the three sets of vows as you would your life without letting them lapse, there is the moral discipline of restraint; with regard to properly training in the six perfections, there is the moral discipline of gathering virtuous Dharmas; and with regard to training in accordance with the teachings of the conqueror of working for the welfare of living beings once you have focused on the eleven ways of working for their welfare, there is the moral discipline of working for the welfare of living beings.

You should complete the perfection of moral discipline by training in all three of these types of moral discipline. Think that you are supplicating the guru-deity to be able to practice in this way while reciting the following verse from the ritual text:

> I seek your blessing to complete the perfection of moral discipline
> By never transgressing, even at the cost of my life,
> The boundaries of the pratimoksha, bodhisattva, and secret
>   mantra vows,
> While collecting virtuous Dharmas and accomplishing the welfare
>   of living beings.

Through making this extremely powerful supplication a stream of five-colored light rays and nectars descends from the bodies of the guru and assembly of deities and enters the body and mind of yourself and all other living beings, whereby the unique obstructions are purified and, in particular, the various realizations are developed in the minds of yourself and all living beings.

---

202. For a brilliant exposition on the three sets of vows, see Jamgön Kongtrul Lodrö Tayé, *Buddhist Ethics* (Ithaca, NY: Snow Lion Publications, 1998).

How to Practice the Perfection of Patience

While remaining absorbed in this state of meditation on the guru-deity you should contemplate, "I shall quickly attain the state of complete enlightenment for the welfare of all mother sentient beings. For that purpose I shall properly train in the perfection of patience." With regard to the three types of patience, there are (1) the patience disregarding harm done to you, (2) the patience of accepting suffering, and (3) the patience of gaining certainty about Dharma. When you meditate on these types of patience, once you have contemplated well the benefits of patience and the faults of anger, you will meditate with great delight; therefore, I will present the benefits of patience. Regarding these, temporarily you will gain a special body in the happy realms, that body will have an excellent form, you will have superior lineage, all will find you pleasing, and so forth. Most of the excellences of higher rebirth stem from patience. The resultant body of complete enlightenment that is adorned with the signs and indications, for which we are never satisfied no matter how much we look at it, and when we see it there is nothing that is disagreeable, all come from the power of patience. If you don't practice patience, there is no way you will perfect the great wave of the bodhisattva's deeds.

With regard to the faults of anger, if you are overwhelmed with strong anger, you will be afflicted by sickness and harm from spirits, and through their power you will have a short life and your merit will deteriorate, and once you die you will fall into hell and so forth. Thus, there are limitless shortcomings [of anger] and, in particular, if you become angry, your precious mind of bodhichitta will deteriorate. What's more, if you come under the influence of anger, you will have no basis for training in the deeds of a bodhisattva.

With regard to meditating on patience through contemplating these points, you accumulate the causes that are indispensable for accomplishing the state of enlightenment. You should generate great courage to prevent anger and meditate on patience by thinking, "Although all living beings in the three realms may arise as my enemies and will criticize me, commit faults against me, engage in nonvirtuous actions, cut off each of my fingernails, threaten to beat me, or even kill me, through the power of joy

I will not generate even an instant of anger toward them and I will not let my love and compassion for living beings deteriorate. Also, if through the power of joy I will not let my practice of bodhichitta deteriorate, what need is there to mention that I will not generate anger toward the most subtle harms and suffering?" Furthermore, think, "I will not become angry with the agents of harm," and you should develop courage in dependence upon the magical practice of skillful means without falling into any extreme mindsets. With regard to this method, whatever harmful agents toward your body, life, or riches emerge, you should think over them in this way.

For example, if through spirit possession your own aged mother were to become insane and agitated without any memory and she was harming those who had been especially kind to her, not only would her own son not become angry toward his old mother when she is speaking extremely unpleasant things, threatening to beat him, and so forth, but he would generate compassion in particular and wonder, "How can I free my old mother from this demonic illness?" and apply whatever method he can. In the same way, you should make sincere effort in the means of accomplishing the benefit of living beings by thinking:

> Right now, although these living beings appear to be the agents of harm, they are in fact only my old mothers. These old mothers are engaged in such bad actions because they are plagued by the spirit possession of the afflictive emotions and act without control. Therefore, how could it be okay for me to become angry? In particular, I shall dwell in a state of compassion and use whatever skillful means I possess to liberate these mothers of mine from the spirit possession of the afflictive emotions. What's more, because they are harming me, in the future they will experience suffering. However, because of this, my previous negative karma will be extinguished and because I am able to bear this harm and suffering, I will swiftly complete my accumulations for my enlightenment; therefore, they are in fact the cause of my purification of nonvirtue and obscurations while completing my accumulation of merit. It is for these reasons that these harmful agents that are now appearing are in fact emanations of my guru and are actually my spiritual

masters. For me, these are in fact agents of benevolence, while I am the one harming them.

With regard to meditating in this way, the *Four Hundred Stanzas*[203] states:

> Just as a physician does not quarrel
> With those angry when seized by demons,
> The Buddha perceives the afflictive emotions
> And not the person possessed by afflictive emotions.

Master Chandrakirti stated:

> The wise analyze and state,
> "This is not the fault of living beings,
> This is the fault of the afflictive emotions,"
> And do not quarrel with living beings.

The *Jataka Tales*[204] states:

> I do not consider that this person is ruining his virtue
> Or that it is as though he is purifying my nonvirtue,
> Yet if I am not patient with one such as this,
> How could there be anyone more cruel than me?

Further, you should think, "If those harming me cause my honor and respect to decline, not only should I not get mad at them, but since they are liberating me from the fetters of honor and respect's grip, I will quickly be liberated from the wheel of samsara; therefore, they are my spiritual masters and are extremely kind to me." With regard to this, the *Guide to the Bodhisattva's Way of Life* states:

> Therefore, those who conspire to
> Prevent me from being praised and so forth

203. *bsTan bcos bzhi brgya pa; Catuḥśatakaśāstra.* A famous text by Aryadeva, translated into English by Ruth Sonam as *Yogic Deeds of a Bodhisattva* (Ithaca, NY: Snow Lion Publications, 1994).
204. *sKyes pa rabs kyi gleng gzhi; Jātakanidāna.*

Are actually acting to protect me
From falling into the lower realms.

I who strive for liberation have no need for
Wealth or reputation since they keep me bound in samsara.
How could I get angry with someone
Who works to liberate me from such bondage?

Those who wish to cause me suffering are
Like buddhas bestowing their blessings.
Since they prevent me from lower rebirth
How could I possibly be angry with them?

Having contemplated in this way, you should determine to quickly complete the perfection of patience by generating altruism and an extraordinarily brave mind by thinking:

I will not develop an angry mind toward my old mother living beings for even an instant, and no matter what harm they cause me I will cherish them as though they were a wish-fulfilling jewel, and viewing them as my spiritual guides, I will make offerings to them and respond to their harm by accomplishing their benefit. I will take upon myself all the negative karma, obscurations, and suffering of my old mothers. I will give all my old mothers my virtue and happiness, and just as Buddha Shakyamuni did in the past with the five *yaksha* brothers[205] and so forth, I will cherish the agents of harm most of all and cause them every type of happiness. And when I finally become a buddha, I shall give them the nectar [of Dharma] first of all.

---

205. This is in reference to Buddha Shakyamuni's first five disciples, who in a previous life of his were five *yaksha*s who came to the Buddha when he was King Bala Maitreya and asked for his blood. King Bala Maitreya offered them the blood from his own body and prayed that he would be able to lead them to the state of enlightenment. Due to this act, when in a future life the Buddha attained enlightenment, the five *yaksha*s were born as humans and became his first five disciples.

Imagine that you are requesting the blessings of the guru-deity to be able to act in this way while reciting the following verse from the ritual text, which states:

> I seek your blessing to complete the perfection of patience
> So that even if the myriad of beings of the three realms
> Become angry, humiliate, criticize, threaten, or even kill me,
> I will not become discouraged but will respond to their harm
>   with benevolence.

Through making this extremely powerful supplication a stream of five-colored light rays and nectars descends from the bodies of the guru and assembly of deities and enters the body and mind of yourself and all other living beings, whereby the unique obstructions are purified and, in particular, the various realizations are developed in the minds of yourself and all living beings.

With regard to the phrase "the myriad of beings of the three realms," the three realms are (1) those (a) between the desire realm up to and including the form realm, (b) the formless realm, and (c) the desire realm itself; (2) the three realms from the form realm; and (3) the three realms from the formless realms. These three ways of rebirth in the three realms amount to nine. This is how the previous holy beings have explained it. Alternatively, they are the three realms of samsara that are like a whirling firebrand and a circling waterwheel that you have been circling through since beginningless time without rest and constantly taking rebirth in; therefore, it is called "myriad of births" and is used in the plural.

Although they don't actually enumerate and name the three types of patience in these oral instructions, the meaning contains them all by evoking a great wave of courage generated in this way through meditating on the patience of a bodhisattva. The patience disregarding harm done to you and the patience of accepting suffering are extremely clear. With regard to the patience of gaining certainty about Dharma, this means generating devotion for the good qualities of the Three Jewels, cause and effect of virtue and nonvirtue, and the wondrous powers of the buddhas and bodhisattvas, which are also contained in the previous modes of practice.

How to Practice Enthusiastic Perseverance

While remaining absorbed in this state of meditation on the guru-deity you should contemplate, "I shall quickly attain the state of complete enlightenment for the welfare of all mother sentient beings. For that purpose I shall properly train in the three types of enthusiastic perseverance." With regard to the three types of enthusiastic perseverance, they are (1) the armor-like enthusiastic perseverance, (2) the enthusiastic perseverance of collecting virtue, and (3) the enthusiastic perseverance of delighting in the welfare of living beings.

Develop powerful enthusiasm by meditating on enthusiastic perseverance through contemplating its benefits and faults by thinking, "All virtuous qualities follow after enthusiastic perseverance, and if I come under the influence of laziness I will not accomplish the purpose of this life; therefore, how could I possibly train and perfect the great wave of the bodhisattva's deeds?"

With regard to the actual meditation, you should put on the armor of enthusiastic perseverance by thinking:

> To attain the state of enlightenment, even if I must remain in the hell realms for 1,003 countless great eons, where the length of one day is equal to a thousand great eons, for the sake of dispelling the suffering of one living being, I will gladly do so by applying enthusiastic perseverance for the sake of complete enlightenment. If I am willing to refuse to forsake enthusiastic perseverance for that length of time, what need is there to mention the various sufferings for a length of time shorter than that?

The above is how the armor-like enthusiastic perseverance is described in the *Bodhisattva Bhumi* as well as how it is taught in the *Sutra of Inexhaustible Intellect*.[206] Think, "I shall perfect enthusiastic perseverance. If the period since beginningless time in samsara until the present makes one day,

---

206. *bLo gros mi zad pas bstan pa'i mdo*; *Akṣayamatinirdeśasūtra*..

and thirty of those days make a month, and twelve of those months make a year, and it takes a hundred thousand of those years to generate bodhichitta once and see one buddha, and it takes as many of those [hundred-thousand-year periods] as there are grains of sand in the Ganges River to understand the mind and deeds of one living being, in this way I will learn all of the dispositions and deeds of all living beings without becoming discouraged for even an instant."

The *Concise Perfection of Wisdom Sutra* states:

> If it takes as many eons as there are drops of water in
>   the ocean,
> With years composed of days and nights
> Of extremely long measure
> That are equal to the extent of samsara,
>
> To produce the supreme bodhichitta once,
> Even if you must accomplish the other accumulations in the
>   same way,
> Still, your compassion prevents you from becoming weary
> And you produce the sacred bodhichitta without
>   discouragement.

You should contemplate along these lines and develop armor and courage. If you have the idea that this is too difficult and the idea that it is a very long period of time, you will not be capable of perfecting such courage and you will become discouraged or weary. Instead, without thinking about the hardships, you should be extremely delighted, like an elephant tormented by the heat entering a lotus garden.

With regard to the brief conceptions that you should generate, they are expounded in the *Compendium of Precious Qualities*,[207] which states:

> The wise bodhisattva thinks, "I will suffer
> For ten million eons to accomplish enlightenment,"

---

207. *Yon tan rin po che sdud pa*; *Prajñāpāramitāratnaguṇasaṃcayagāthā*.

And strives to accomplish the pure Dharma for a long time;
Therefore, the lazy defile the perfection of enthusiastic
  perseverance.

Generate the supreme bodhichitta and sustain it from the
  outset
Until you attain the unsurpassed enlightenment.
Those with clear wisdom will commence with enthusiastic
  perseverance and
Will strive to generate this mind for the length of even one
  day and night.

If someone said, "I will destroy Mount Meru
In this instant and afterward attain supreme enlightenment,"
Even for the length of time they generated such a thought
At that time such a bodhisattva has become lazy.

When he develops the thought, "I have no concern for the
  degree of hardship,"
A mere instant of such bodhichitta grinds Mount Meru to dust.
The wise bodhisattva sets forth with enthusiastic perseverance
And attains supreme enlightenment as a guide without
  a long wait.

You should think about the meaning of this, and if you feel, "I must endure numerous hardships and austerities" and become disheartened and discouraged, you should realize that in actuality you will not experience suffering and instead develop joy from within yourself and a mind of great bliss. The *Guide to the Bodhisattva's Way of Life* states:

Having mounted the steed of bodhichitta,
Which dispels discouragement and weariness,
You proceed from joy to joy;
What wise person would ever become discouraged?

The *Precious Garland* states:

> If it is difficult to endure suffering for even a short while,
> What need is there to mention a long time?
> What could bring harm even over limitless time
> To those happy and without suffering?
>
> Since they are without physical suffering
> How could they have mental suffering?
> Through their compassion they suffer
> For the world and therefore remain a long time.
>
> Do not become disheartened thinking,
> "Buddhahood is such a long way off";
> Instead, you should continuously strive to
> Remove your faults and attain good qualities.

If you are able to develop such determined great courage in that way, you will not suffer but instead will give rise to bliss, and by sequentially increasing that [courage] you will attain the first *bhumi* and attain the concentration called "the suppression of all phenomena through bliss." *Entering the Middle Way* states:

> If, from hearing and contemplating the word "give,"
> The bodhisattvas develop bliss that is a bliss that not even
> The buddhas experience through abiding in peace,
> What need is there to mention giving away everything?

Even if you ask for the head of a bodhisattva who is on the first bhumi onward, their mind will experience a bliss that far exceeds even the bliss that shravaka and pratyeka buddhas experience while absorbed in the meditation of nirvana.

Thus, once you develop such armor and great courage, you should complete the limb of skillful means in dependence upon the magical oral instruction for undertaking your enthusiastic perseverance. Although you may strive solely at enthusiastic perseverance, if you don't have the essential points of the oral instructions or are without the complete set of the method's components, you will never cover much ground. For example, once you think, "It is extremely important that I subdue my mind through the practice of Dharma," however you pretend to apply yourself, you are doubtful in how to proceed because you don't understand the afflictive emotions; therefore, you can't identify any of the prescribed boundaries of the three types of vows and your mind becomes ruined by the faults and downfalls. Therefore, this is similar to kings who engage in battle with their four types of troops[208] and apply the methods of destroying their enemies who are far away while not harming life and limb of those close to them.

When bodhisattvas commence their enthusiastic perseverance, they rely upon the four powers: (1) the power of aspiration, (2) the power of dependability, (3) the power of joy, and (4) the power of abandonment; and they are endowed with the two ways of destroying the enemies of the afflictions, such as laziness, anger, and so forth, as well as not harming others through even the most subtle afflictive emotions and faulty conduct.

At that time, once they generate a mind of great delight, they prevent discouragement and weariness. And because of their compassion they never become distracted from the welfare of living beings and produce the complete collection of causes for accomplishing enlightenment by making a great effort in perseverance. Feel "I must quickly accomplish the perfection of enthusiastic perseverance." Imagine that you are requesting the blessings of the guru-deity to be able to act in this way while reciting the following verse from the ritual text, which states:

> I seek your blessing to complete the perfection of effort
> By striving for supreme enlightenment with unwavering
>   compassion
> Even if I must remain for an ocean of eons dwelling within the
>   flames
> Of the lowest hell for the sake of each living being.

Through making this extremely powerful supplication a stream of five-colored light rays and nectars descends from the bodies of the guru and

---

208. Cavalry, elephants, chariots, and infantry.

assembly of deities and enters the body and mind of yourself and all other living beings, whereby the unique obstructions are purified and, in particular, the various realizations are developed in the minds of yourself and all living beings.

In this way as well, although the words that are used here as the principal way of developing the great wave of the bodhisattva's courage do not include the other types of enthusiastic perseverance, they contain the entire meaning.

As for "gathering virtue," this is enthusiastic perseverance that completes all the accumulations that are the cause of supreme enlightenment, and the fact that it works for the welfare of living beings is extremely clear. In these teachings there are three types of laziness that are incompatible with enthusiastic perseverance. They are (1) the laziness of procrastination, (2) the laziness of attachment to bad actions, and (3) the laziness of discouragement and weariness. The way to put an end to these is through delight and compassion and so forth. These [aforementioned qualities] are extremely important and contain numerous points that are difficult to realize. Because you may have doubts concerning much of what has been said here, the wise should remove such doubts by examining these oral instructions and the texts of the great charioteers.

How to Meditate on the Perfection of Concentration

While remaining absorbed in this state of meditation on the guru-deity you should contemplate, "I shall quickly attain the state of complete enlightenment for the welfare of all mother sentient beings. For that purpose I shall properly train in all aspects of concentration of the bodhisattvas."

As mentioned earlier, during the preliminary discourse, there is the place where you will meditate, the dwelling in which you meditate, the essential features of bodily posture, and so forth. Although the conqueror taught numerous divisions of the objects of observation of concentration, in brief they can be subsumed under ultimate objects of observation and conventional objects of observation. We absolutely must ultimately settle upon a single object of observation for concentration and it may be any appropriate object of observation. Furthermore, the object of observation is an internal basis of visualization that appears to the mind and not an external object of observation that is set out in front of you as a visual object, such as a small stone, piece of wood, and so forth.

Concentration is the nature of the mental factor of mindfulness; therefore, it is an object of observation created by the mind. The object of observation for concentration is not an object that appears to the sense consciousness. Therefore, regarding the object of concentration that should be the focus of your meditation, it is the natural state of emptiness and not mental constructs or the mere emptiness of the ephemeral; instead, you should focus on the natural state of emptiness that is the true nature of all phenomena.

With regard to concentrative meditation, once you have focused on the mode of existence of the object of observation, it must have two special characteristics: it must (1) not be content with [merely] abiding single-pointedly, and (2) possess extremely vivid clarity. These two factors will be interrupted by the occurrence of mental sinking and excitement. Single-pointed nonconceptuality is impeded by mental excitement and extremely intense clarity, and vividness is impeded by mental sinking.

With regard to mental sinking, although the mind can sustain itself single-pointedly on the meaning of the fundamental nature of reality with intense clarity supported by a factor of stability, when the intense clarity diminishes slightly you have been affected by subtle mental sinking. And although you may have a slight factor of lucidity, if you don't have intense clarity, you have coarse mental sinking. If you don't have even a slight amount of lucidity, you have become impeded by severe mental sinking.

With regard to mental excitement, the *Compendium of Abhidharma*[209] states, "What is mental excitement? It is a mind without peace that is regarded as a derivative of attachment that pursues pleasant objects and functions to obstruct the development of tranquil abiding." Once you become attached to the good qualities of pleasing objects, such as forms, sounds, and so forth, your mind is drawn to those objects. Thus, most of the texts of the great charioteers, such as [Asanga's] *Discrimination of the Middle and the Extremes*, [Maitreya's] *Ornament for Mahayana Sutras*, and so forth, state that to accomplish completely perfect concentration you must employ the means of eliminating the two obstacles of mental sinking

209. *mNgon pa kun btus*; *Abhidharmasamuccaya*.

and excitement. The omniscient foremost great being [Tsongkhapa] also addresses these in his great and small *Treatises on the Stages of the Path*. In these oral instructions of Vajradhara Losang Chökyi Gyaltsen he refers to "the faults of sinking, excitement, and wandering" and lists "wandering" as being separate from mental sinking and excitement, which is an uncommon oral instruction given to the omniscient foremost great being [Tsongkhapa] by Manjushri and is the method used in the Ganden mahamudra teachings for stabilizing the mind and sustaining it; however, at this point [Panchen Losang Chökyi Gyaltsen] gives little more than a hint about it. For that [wandering], when you are sustaining a stabilized mind, you directly apply the means of stopping discursive wandering.

You may ask, "What is the distinction between the means of stopping mental excitement and the means of stopping mental wandering?" Mental excitement itself is scattering; therefore, you may wonder, "How is scattering different from excitement?" There is a vast discrepancy between these two! Although mental excitement is scattering, there are numerous distinctions between scattering and excitement; therefore, they are vastly different. Furthermore, in accordance with my previous explanation of mental excitement, it belongs to the category of the mental factor of attachment. Not only does mere scattering wander to an object of attachment, but it scatters through anger, it scatters through pride, jealousy, and so forth. Further, it scatters to virtuous objects that are nonafflictive; it also scatters to neutral objects that are neither virtuous nor nonvirtuous; and it also scatters to the objects of the six senses and so forth. Since they are all obstructions to single-pointed concentration, you should learn the antidotes that will stop them all. That is the intended meaning during the mental stability of the uncommon Ganden mahamudra of the Ganden Hearing Lineage. Although this system is also repeatedly referred to by the omniscient foremost great being [Tsongkhapa], he uses little more than subtle hints at the end of the teachings on identifying mental excitement in the *Great Exposition on the Stages of the Path to Enlightenment*, which states:

> *Query*: "Well then, since it is scattering if it causes wandering to things other than the object of observation, is excitement likewise scattering from the object of observation to virtuous things?" *Reply*: Excitement is a single aspect of attachment;

therefore, mental wandering through other afflictive emotions is not mental excitement. Mental wandering is classified as a mental factor among the twenty secondary afflictive emotions. Scattering to a virtuous visualization can be affected by any virtuous mind or mental factor; therefore, not all scattering is mental excitement.

Also, in the *Questions of Pure Superior Intention*[210] [Tsongkhapa poses the question]:

Query: Are excitement and scattering the same or not the same? If they are not one, what is the difference between them?

In *Losang's Melodious Laughter: Questions and Answers of Pure Superior Intention* [the First Panchen Lama replies]:

Reply:
Scattering and excitement are not the same.
Excitement is disquiet and belongs to attachment, as is
Taught in the *Compendium of Abhidharma*.

Scattering is an expansion of that;
Therefore, it scatters through anger and so forth.
Both interfere not only with placement meditation
But with analytical meditation as well.

I have already written about the uncommon oral instructions regarding how to stop scattering in my instruction manual for Ganden mahamudra; therefore, I will not elaborate on it here.

Thus, think:

I shall completely forsake mental sinking, excitement, and wandering and remain in a state of mindfulness on the mode

---

210. *Dri ba lhag bsam rab dkar.*

of existence of emptiness endowed with the special characteristics and ascend progressively higher through the nine
stages of settling the mind: (1) placement, (2) continual placement, (3) replacement, (4) close placement, (5) controlling,
(6) pacified, (7) completely pacified, (8) single-pointed, and
(9) placement in equipoise. Guru-deity, please bestow your
blessing that I may be able to accomplish that.

While remaining in that state, make the following request from the ritual
prayer:

I seek your blessing to complete the perfection of concentration
By abandoning the faults of sinking, excitement, and wandering,
While concentrating with single-pointed mental stabilization
On the ultimate nature of reality—the truth of all phenomena.

Through making this extremely powerful supplication a stream of five-
colored light rays and nectars descends from the bodies of the guru and
assembly of deities and enters the body and mind of yourself and all other
living beings, whereby the unique obstructions are purified and, in particular, the various realizations are developed in the minds of yourself and
all living beings.

There are three types of concentration: (1) the concentration of this
life that is a concentration abiding in the blissful state of body and mind,
(2) the concentration that acts as a support for good qualities [of spiritual
realization], and (3) the concentration that works for the welfare of living
beings. They also have two types of entity: (1) mundane, and (2) supramundane. Although there are also three divisions through perspective and
so forth, I am not going to enumerate them here. The teachings of these
oral instructions are according to the uncommon nature of concentration
and this concentration functions as all three types [of concentration], such
as the concentration that causes bliss to the body and mind and so forth.
With regard to the division of mundane and supramundane concentrations, there is a distinction between whether or not the meditator has
attained the path of an arya; therefore, both cannot be carried out at the
same time by one yogi.

How to Attain the Perfection of Wisdom has two sections:
1. How to Meditate on the Space-Like Meditative Equipoise of Emptiness
2. How to Meditate on the Emptiness of Illusory-Like Subsequent Attainment

How to Meditate on the Space-Like Meditative Equipoise of Emptiness

While remaining absorbed in this state of meditation on the guru-deity you should contemplate, "I shall quickly attain the state of complete enlightenment for the welfare of all mother sentient beings. For that purpose I shall properly train in the concentration of the union of special insight and tranquil abiding."

Furthermore, once you focus single-pointedly upon emptiness as the nature of reality of all phenomena in accordance with the previous explanation on how to meditate on the concentration that "results from abandoning the five faults and employing the eight recognitions," you should sequentially accomplish the nine mental abidings through meditating properly via relying upon the eight recognitions that abandon the five faults that obstruct concentration, such as mental sinking, excitement, and so on. Finally, you attain a special concentration accompanied by physical and mental pliancy. With regard to that, although tranquil abiding may be observing the nature of reality, that alone will not be capable of severing the root of samsara; therefore, you must repeatedly employ the wisdom of individual examination and accomplish special insight. Furthermore, if you only perform analysis, once the mind becomes distracted you need to once again accomplish a factor of stability. If you don't have a fresh factor of stability, your tranquil abiding will deteriorate and you won't attain the union of tranquil abiding and special insight. Further, if you only strive to establish single-pointedness on the meaning of reality by continuously sustaining tranquil abiding, you will not have the means of accomplishing special insight. Therefore, no matter how much continuity you have [in single-pointed placement], it will not be possible to accomplish special insight and you will not attain the union of tranquil abiding and special insight.

Therefore, as explained earlier, to accomplish the union of tranquil abiding and special insight you remain in a state of stability without letting it deteriorate, and analyze the meaning of reality with the wisdom of individual investigation, like a small fish that swims without disturbing the surface of the water, and establish a slight degree of stability with a definitive mode of apprehension of ultimate analysis. Again you analyze and alternate between analysis and placement [meditation]. Thus, once you can continuously sustain that you will be able to induce a factor of stability through the natural force of analysis. Soon after that, you will naturally be able to carry out analysis simultaneously with stability, which will induce pliancy. In that way you will come to possess a special physical and mental bliss of pliancy and a concentration that is called "the concentration on the union of tranquil abiding and special insight." It is highly praised if you understand how to accomplish the union of tranquil abiding and special insight in that way.

Je [Tsongkhapa's] *Songs of Spiritual Experience* states:

> Mere single-pointed concentration is not sufficient
> To cut the root of samsara;
> And no matter how much you analyze your delusions,
> If tranquil abiding is divorced from wisdom,
> You will not be able to overcome your delusions.
> Yet wisdom searching for ultimate truth,
> Riding the horse of unwavering tranquil abiding,
> Wielding the sharp weapon of the Madhyamaka reasoning,
> Will completely destroy the view holding extremes.
> With vast wisdom examining in this way
> Expand your knowledge realizing suchness.

And:

> Merely accomplishing the concentration of single-pointed
>   meditation,
> That is beyond description, will not do!

Instead, you must engage in individual investigation into the
mode of existence
And then remain extremely steady without wavering.
Therefore, generate the concentration of tranquil abiding and
special insight
And make great effort at unifying these two.
I, the yogi, practiced in this way;
You who seek liberation should do the same.

Therefore, carrying out this yoga of space-like meditative stabilization is
a special concentration that is the union of tranquil abiding and special
insight and is the ultimate antidote that severs the root of samsara and is
praised by the omniscient foremost great being [Tsongkhapa]; therefore,
you should think, "Guru-deity, please grant your blessing that I be able to
quickly accomplish such a [concentration]" and recite the verse from the
ritual text that states:

I seek your blessing to complete the perfection of wisdom
Through the yoga of space-like mental stabilization on ultimate
reality
Conjoined with the great bliss of pliancy induced by
The wisdom of the individual analysis of suchness.

Through making this extremely powerful supplication a stream of five-
colored light rays and nectars descends from the bodies of the guru and
assembly of deities and enters the body and mind of yourself and all other
living beings, whereby the unique obstructions are purified and, in particular, the various realizations are developed in the minds of yourself and
all living beings.

How to Meditate on the Emptiness of Illusory-Like
Subsequent Attainment

While remaining absorbed in this state of meditation on the guru-deity
you should contemplate, "I shall quickly attain the state of complete
enlightenment for the welfare of all mother sentient beings. For that pur-

pose I shall properly train in the practice of illusory-like collections of appearance and emptiness."

Furthermore, when you arise from a state of meditation that has assembled together and is sustaining (1) a pure vacuity that is a space-like meditative stabilization that does not perceive even an atom of conventional phenomena as the factor of appearance, together with (2) an ascertaining consciousness that has a mode of apprehension realizing the nontrue existence of phenomena as the ascertaining factor, you will naturally perceive whatever appears, both outwardly and inwardly, such as mountains, houses, and so forth, as well as people, animals, and so forth, as being false appearances that are illusory-like; or if you are not able to [instinctively view them in that way], you should train in seeing them that way.

There are numerous classifications that can be used as examples of such false illusory appearances, such as an illusion, a mirage, a city of smell eaters, an echo, a reflection in a mirror, a dream, and so forth. Among these, in this oral instruction, we use illusions, dreams, and reflections in a mirror. Among these three, the examples of a dream and a reflection are the most important. In addition to these examples we need some personal experience, and for us here in Tibet, we don't have any experience of seeing things such as illusions other than following the words of our guru's teaching.[211] Yet, we can relate to dreams and reflections according to our own experience; therefore, these will be easy if we contemplate them. With regard to contemplating a reflection in particular, it is praised numerous times by Master Chandrakirti in his *Entering the Middle Way* for inducing certainty about the collection of appearances and emptiness as well as in his commentary on *Four Hundred Stanzas* and so forth. Also, the omniscient foremost great being [Tsongkhapa] states that once you understand its meaning, it is very special, and Vajradhara Losang Chökyi Gyaltsen also uses a reflection as his primary example. Therefore, without a doubt, all inner and outer phenomena are like reflections in a lake, and if you examine appearances in this way, you will discover a consciousness ascertaining the illusory-like falsity of appearances that appear yet

211. In ancient India it was relatively common to have street magicians that could conjure apparitions (i.e., create illusions).

lack true existence. Think, "Guru-deity, please grant your blessing that I may perfect the illusory-like concentration" and recite the verse from the ritual prayer that states:

> I seek your blessing to complete the illusory concentration,
> Realizing that outer and inner phenomena are like illusions, dreams,
> And like reflections of the moon in a pure lake,
> Which, although they appear, have no true existence.

Through making this extremely powerful supplication a stream of five-colored light rays and nectars descends from the bodies of the guru and assembly of deities and enters the body and mind of yourself and all other living beings, whereby the unique obstructions are purified and, in particular, the various realizations are developed in the minds of yourself and all living beings.

How to Train in the Profound View of the Middle Way in Particular

While remaining absorbed in this state of meditation on the guru-deity you should contemplate, "I shall quickly attain the state of complete enlightenment for the welfare of all mother sentient beings. For that purpose I shall strive to meditate properly on the nonmistaken ultimate view of the profound Middle Way."

Furthermore, *Guide to the Bodhisattva's Way of Life* states:

> All of these limbs were taught by the
> Muni for the sake of wisdom.

All of the eighty-four thousand heaps of Dharma teachings of the conqueror were taught solely as a means to realize this profound dependent arising as the nature of reality.

> The teachings in harmony with the heaps of Dharma
> Are the antidotes to the types of [afflicted] conduct.

With regard to the eighty-four thousand heaps of Dharma, they were taught as an antidote to the eighty-four thousand afflictive emotions, and the ultimate root of all afflictive emotions is this ignorance grasping at true existence. If you destroy ignorance you will naturally put an end to all other afflictive emotions. Yet, by destroying one of the other afflictive emotions you will not destroy their other counterparts. By relying on the antidote for desirous attachment, you will not destroy anger. By relying upon the antidote to anger you will not destroy desirous attachment, which is clearly explained in *Clear Words*.[212] By meditating on dependent relationship as the antidote to ignorance you are able to destroy all the afflictive emotions, which is expressed by Aryadeva [in his *Four Hundred Stanzas*] that states:

> Just as the body sense power depends on the body,
> All [afflictive emotions] are brought about by ignorance;
> Therefore, by destroying ignorance
> You will destroy all the afflictions.

This profound dependent relationship of the nature of reality is the sole means of realization and accords with the true intent of all the scriptures and their commentaries. Although this profound dependent relationship of the nature of reality is taught through limitless types of classification in the precious perfection of wisdom sutras taught by the conqueror, it is extremely difficult to realize; therefore, the conqueror himself has said that its realization is very rare. For that reason you should strive in the meaning of this perfection of wisdom in dependence upon the path of reasoning of the great charioteer Nagarjuna, who was prophesied by the conqueror himself in numerous sutras and tantras, which state that he would perfectly comment upon the conqueror's own true intent regarding the meaning of this profound teaching. Although you may try to, through some other means that does not rely upon the path of reasoning set forth by Protector Nagarjuna and his spiritual heirs, you will not be able to discover this profound meaning. Glorious Chandrakirti stated:

---

212. *Tshig gsal*; *Prasannapadā*; Chandrakirti's commentary on Nagarjuna's *Fundamental Treatise on the Middle Way Called "Wisdom."*

There is no means of peace outside of
The path of Master Nagarjuna.
These [mistaken paths] defile the conventional and ultimate truths;
Through these defilements there is no attainment of liberation.

Although you may have heard some supposedly profound instruction, if it is incompatible with the system of Protector Nagarjuna, you will not be able to realize this profound dependent relationship that is the ultimate intention of the conqueror. *Losang's Melodious Laughter: Questions and Answers of Pure Superior Intention* also states:

In short, if the view contradicts the
Excellent view of Nagarjuna's system,
No matter how you describe it with words such as
"It is endowed with a hundred perfect qualities,"
Forget about omniscience; you will
Not even attain liberation.

You, Protector, joined your hands and commanded,
"The perfect teachings are in
Accordance with Chandrakirti's pronouncements."

Although Protector Nagarjuna commented on the profound perfection of wisdom with limitless types of reasoning, such as the reasoning of "the absence of being one or many" examining the nature, the reasoning of the "diamond slivers" examining the cause, the reasoning of "the production and cessation of existence and nonexistence," and so forth, the principal among them all, the one that is the king of reasoning, is the reasoning of dependent arising. By relying on the reasoning of dependent arising you will reach absolute certainty about the mode of existence of emptiness that is free from all extremes of conceptual elaboration; therefore, it receives the highest praise. Once you gain confidence in the workings of cause and effect through inducing certainty about the dependent arising of appearances, you will also make a special effort in the method aspects. And through inducing certainty about emptiness, although you perceive things as possessing inherent attributes, this perception will be incapable of binding you with its negative influence. And that is not even the full extent of its positive effects, for if you induce certainty about dependent arising, you will be free from all extremes of conceptual elaboration, such as permanence, annihilation, and so forth. Emptiness will dawn of its own accord, and through inducing a consciousness ascertaining emptiness appearances will naturally appear as dependent arisings. Emptiness will dawn as dependent arising and dependent arising will dawn as emptiness. Appearances will dispel the extreme of existence and emptiness will dispel the extreme of nonexistence.

For such a profound presentation as this, our father, the omniscient foremost great being [Tsongkhapa], offered limitless outer, inner, and secret offerings to Protector Manjushri, and by making extremely powerful supplications for a long time he had a direct vision of Protector Manjushri, who taught him the entire path of sutra and tantra and, in particular, he taught him the ultimate view of the profound Middle Way through this profound method of dependent arising that dispels the extreme of existence through appearances and dispels the extreme of nonexistence through emptiness in dependence upon Protector Nagarjuna's path of reasoning. Through this, once Je Rinpoche perfectly grasped the meaning of this in his mind, he taught the view [of emptiness] in the same way it was taught to him by Venerable Manjushri, by composing the following verses [in his *Three Principal Aspects of the Path*] that state:

> Whoever has eliminated the perception of inherent existence
> Yet sees the infallibility of cause and effect
> Of all phenomena in samsara and nirvana
> Has entered the path that pleases the buddhas.

> If nondeceptive dependent-related appearance is
> Accepted as being separate from emptiness and
> For as long as their existence is seen as being separate,
> You have not realized the true intent of the muni.

> When they arise as one, simultaneously without alternating,
> And by merely perceiving nondeceptive dependent relationship

You destroy all modes of apprehension grasping at truly existent
objects,
You have completed your analysis of the view of emptiness.

Moreover, the extreme of existence is dispelled through
appearances
And the extreme of nonexistence is dispelled through emptiness;
While understanding the way in which cause and effect operate
through emptiness,
You will not be captivated by grasping at extremes.

Moreover, his *Essence of Eloquence Praising the Buddha*[213] states:

Ignorance is the root of whatever faults
There are in the world.
They are all overcome by anyone who perceives
The dependent relationship that you have taught.

At that time, how could the wise
Not comprehend the path of
The dependent arising
That you have taught?

[Lama Tsongkhapa] has immense praise for those who have grasped
from the depths of their hearts the profound system of dependent relationship. The conqueror also extensively praised dependent arising and
emptiness appearing as noncontradictory in the *Perfection of Wisdom Sutra.*
Protector Nagarjuna also said:

Those who understand the emptiness of phenomena
See cause and effect as valid;
This is more amazing than the amazing,
More wondrous than the wondrous.

213. *Thub pa'i dbang po la bstod pa legs par bshad pa'i snying po.*

And:

> Through which dependent relationship emerge . . .

And:

> I prostrate to the Buddha
> Whose incomparable supreme teachings
> State that emptiness and dependent origination
> Are synonymous with the path of the Middle Way.

Among all the teachings of Buddha Shakyamuni, these very teachings on dependent arising are praised as the very best, the most sublime, and the most supreme. For that reason, if you examine all phenomena of samsara and nirvana, you will see that they do not possess even an atom of inherent existence. However, when not examined, the dependent relationship of cause and effect infallibly functions. Furthermore, it is not that it is fabricated by the mind or merely empty for a short while; all phenomena from form up to omniscience are empty of true existence and are simultaneously compatible with the existence of conventional phenomena, and appearances and emptiness are not contradictory but instead assist one another. When this thought arises you have discovered the true intent of the conqueror. Imagine you are supplicating the guru-deity by thinking, "Please grant me your blessing that I may quickly generate within my mental continuum the ultimate profound view of the Middle Way just as it was explained by the great being Nagarjuna." While contemplating in this way, recite the verse from the ritual prayer that states:

> I seek your blessing that I may realize the meaning of Nagarjuna's
>   true intent,
> That samsara and nirvana lack even an atom of inherent
>   existence,
> And that the nondeceptive dependent relationship of cause and
>   effect
> Complement each other without contradiction.

Through making this extremely powerful supplication a stream of five-colored light rays and nectars descends from the bodies of the guru and assembly of deities and enters the body and mind of yourself and all other living beings, whereby the unique obstructions are purified and, in particular, the various realizations are developed in the minds of yourself and all living beings.

Thus, the profound view of the Middle Way is extremely difficult to realize, and if you don't realize it, you won't discover the life of the path during any of the practices of either sutra or tantra. You will also not be able to progress upon the path of the great deeds of the bodhisattva, despite sacrificing your eyes, no matter how much you train. Although these oral instructions possess such profound meaning that has been explained by Nagarjuna and reveal the true intent of the conqueror, they merely open your eyes to the vastness of the six perfections and encourage you to strive for the view of emptiness. Yet other than striving, they don't clearly explain how to meditate [on emptiness]. However, the oral tradition of the root text of mahamudra of the precious Ganden Oral Lineage does clearly explain the ultimate oral instructions of the view on the path of the conqueror. Once you combine [the above-mentioned instructions] with the oral instructions of Lama Chöpa, you will perfectly understand how to meditate on the view of the Middle Way.

Thus, through the words of these oral instructions you will be able to evoke an experience of the vital points of the path from how to properly rely upon your spiritual master up to either tranquil abiding and special insight or the view of the Middle Way; this is arranged with few words according to the lineage of oral instructions. You should learn about the extensive points of these paths from the *Great Exposition on the Stages of the Path to Enlightenment*, which is the lamp of the three worlds.

How to Train the Mind in the Uncommon Path of the Vajrayana has three sections:
1. **Becoming a Suitable Vessel for the Profound Path of Mantra**
2. **How to Maintain Pure Vows and Commitments once You Have Become a Suitable Vessel**
3. **How to Meditate on the Two Stages of the Path**

Becoming a Suitable Vessel for the Profound Path of Mantra

The ritual text states:

> And through the kindness of the captain—the vajra holder—
> I may cross the intricate ocean of the tantras.[214]

Having trained your mind in the common path, from the proper reliance upon your spiritual master up to the tranquil abiding and special insight, you should perceive all of existence like a pit of blazing fire without developing the desire to be something as exalted as the lord of the earth even in your dreams and overcome your attachment to all of the so-called wonders of samsara. And with a very powerful intention strive all day and night to attain liberation. Once you have perceived all living beings equaling space as being your mother—while thinking over your own experience—contemplate the situation of living beings and, by seeing how your old mothers are oppressed by unbearable sufferings while being stuck in the prison of samsara, you will become involuntarily moved by great compassion that finds their suffering unbearable. Through this you greatly increase your mind of enlightenment that cherishes others, through which you develop the intention, "I must train in all the practices of a bodhisattva, and for the sake of each and every living being, from my side I will develop great courage that will not become discouraged and will never give up trying, even if I must remain in the hell realms for innumerable eons. And when I consider things from the perspective of living beings, in each passing moment I have great longing for enlightenment so that I may liberate all my mother living beings from the prison of samsara as quickly as possible. For that purpose I am going to enter the unsurpassed Vajrayana."

The gateway to entering the unsurpassed [highest yoga tantra] vehicle is a completely pure empowerment; therefore, you must receive a completely pure empowerment from a fully qualified vajra master. If you don't

---

214. There is a disparity between the English translation and original Tibetan with regard to the order of the lines in the verse.

receive an empowerment, despite the fact that you may develop an understanding of tantra, meditate on the two stages, and so forth, not only will you not accomplish supreme attainments, but without an empowerment in the profound secret mantra [vehicle] you will be going to the lowest hell through the faults of carelessly partaking of enjoyments, which has been explained in numerous tantras and texts of the mahasiddhas. To obtain a pure empowerment you need a fully qualified vajra master; therefore, you must initially seek a fully qualified vajra master with great diligence. If you must examine someone carefully to decide whether or not you can rely on or follow them to a terrifying place for even one day, what need is there to mention that [such careful examination is necessary] to be free from all the fears of samsara and peace? And not just any guru will do to lead you to the ground of buddhahood! In the same way, just as you must rely

KHEDRUP SANGYE YESHE

upon a trusted and able captain who has great courage, knows the way, and is skilled in the means of extracting jewels from a great ocean, so you must also rely upon a trusted and able vajra master who is nondeceptive in all ways, has great compassion, possesses the oral instructions, knows the way of mantra, and possesses a lineage of blessing that has not deteriorated in order to extract the wish-fulfilling jewel of union from within the great ocean of great secret tantra.

If you find such a guru, conduct yourself in accordance with your previous training in the common path and, even more importantly, in accordance with the section on how to properly rely upon the spiritual master, and then make supplications to receive an empowerment. Although the vajra master may be pleased, he will still examine the disciple well to see if he or she is a suitable vessel or not; if he finds that they are a suitable vessel, [the guru] will take him or her under his care. Initially, the guru will give instructions on the *Fifty Verses of Guru Devotion*.[215] While that disciple is listening to the *Fifty Verses of Guru Devotion* he should retain the words and contemplate their meaning. Next, he should sincerely apply himself to the explanation of how to properly rely upon the spiritual master. Next, the empowerment is bestowed. Furthermore, from the beginning of the empowerment, the disciple must take the bodhisattva vows and commitments of the five buddha families. By protecting the vows and commitments you have promised to maintain and entering the mandala, you receive the vase empowerment that places special potentialities within you and empowers you to meditate on the generation stage, attain the resultant emanation body, a pure land, mandala, and so forth. Next, you are sequentially bestowed the later empowerments that empower you to meditate on the completion stage in its entirety and establish a special potentiality in your mental continuum to accomplish the resultant complete enjoyment body, truth body, and nature truth body, or in other words, the body of union. Moreover, during all four empowerments you are purifying massive obscurations, purifying outer and inner obstructions and interferences, receiving the blessings of all the buddhas and

215. For a translation and commentary to this practice, see https://www.lamayeshe.com/sites/default/files/pdf/373_pdf_copy1.PDF.

bodhisattvas, and creating special power of merit to meditate on the two stages. They also function to establish a complete set of dependent-related conditions that will quickly develop within your mental continuum all the essential features of the two stages.

Therefore, bestowing empowerment should not be thought of as merely a preliminary to the path. Instead, during a complete empowerment, a complete foundation of all the essential points of the two stages, together with results, is laid out; therefore, once the door to mantra is initially opened until the complete union of enlightenment you must extract the innermost meaning of the empowerment that contains all the essential points of the path. Thus, once you receive a pure empowerment, and you establish the basis of properly protecting your commitments and vows, you should listen to and contemplate the meaning of tantra and strive in the essential points of the two stages.

With regard to the place where all the essential points of the two stages of the path exist, in Guhyasamaja, for instance, they are in the *Guhyasamaja Root Tantra*, and although the *Guhyasamaja Root Tantra* contains all the essential points of the two stages in their entirety, if you don't rely upon the guru's oral instructions on topics such as the six limits and the four modes,[216] even if you are a jewel-like disciple, you will not discover the essential points of the path in dependence upon the *Root Tantra*. Therefore, what need is there to mention other [less qualified] disciples? For that reason, the conqueror himself opened the door of the root tantra by teaching the explanatory tantras such as the *Subsequent Tantra*[217] and the *Vajramala* for the sake of clearly revealing the essential points of the root tantra. Although there are these explanatory tantras, still, the subsequent generations of disciples were not able to discover the essential points of the path; therefore, they must rely upon the instructions of the oral lineage to understand the explanations of the root tantra. For that reason, if there is a special oral instruction of the Hearing Lineage, by training in that oral instruction you will be able to develop a special understanding of the sutras and tantras taught by the conqueror, as well as their commentaries

216. See footnote 194.

217. *rGyud phyi ma*; *Guhyasamāja Uttaratantra*. This is the eighteenth (and final) chapter of the *Guhyasamaja Root Tantra* that was taught subsequent to his exposition of the first seventeen chapters and serves as a summary.

as set forth in the texts of the great charioteers. Otherwise, if you don't have the words of the conqueror or the texts of the great charioteers yet you possess the oral lineage of the guru, you will understand. However, if you grasp on to some oral instruction that is incompatible with the words [of the conqueror] and its valid commentaries, even if you think, "This is the greatest oral instruction," not only will you be incapable of progressing along the profound path, it will serve as a powerful factor leading to the decline of the essential teachings of the conqueror. Therefore, those with discriminating wisdom should never rely upon some well-known instruction that is incompatible with the conqueror's teachings. Instead, they should rely upon the oral instructions of a holy guru that combine the root and explanatory tantras and hold these as the supreme instructions of the conqueror himself.

For that reason, the foremost great being [Tsongkhapa] stated:

> With regard to seeing some supplementary Dharma for cutting through mere external explanations of tantras and the great texts that serve as commentaries to them, and holding on to a view that thinks there is some really profound separate hidden instruction that is not taught [in the tantras], this person does not have the proper regard for ultimate Dharma that is taught in the great texts of mantra. Once you create these obstacles to the emergence of these oral instructions, it is a major factor in their quick deterioration; therefore, you should abandon it like a poison. Instead, you should sincerely apply yourself to the methods that appear in the instructions on the great texts in dependence upon the oral instructions of a holy guru.

And:

> With regard to the location of these profound ultimate instructions, they are in the root tantras of the precious class of tantra. These are not easy to understand; therefore, you need a lama, and the lama cannot just say whatever comes to his mind, but the lama should understand them through the root

and explanatory tantras by following the explanatory tantras. The way for a disciple to easily develop an understanding in their mental continuum is to receive an unmistaken explanation based on the explanatory tantras that reveal the meaning of the root tantras. Therefore, you should come to understand them in this way by learning them orally. Once you forsake the writings in the tantras, and think that you can learn everything orally without relying upon the written tantras, this is incorrect. For that reason, merely through training in the supreme oral instructions for a long time, when you then see the valid texts of the four classes of tantra, you will be unable to come to a definite understanding about the meaning of the tantras by carrying over the oral precepts. With such a view, when you then analyze the meaning of the tantras you will feel that you will not be able to discover any certainty whatsoever, which is evident in your utterly mistaken understanding and the mistaken meaning. In that way, whatever system of either mantra or sutra, it should be just like preparing the race track prior to having a horse race. In the same way, you should understand the causal factors for whatever you are going to practice by listening and contemplating. Once you do, not only must you definitely undertake your practice by reaching absolute certainty in that way, but since you wish to undertake your practice from the depths of your heart, if you examine the great texts of mantra, you will view [having the wish to practice without proper study] as a subject of laughter. When it appears that, no matter how much or how little you study, nothing comes from it, through either training in numerous tantras, or not training, those wishing for liberation should carefully examine [the tantras].

Further, through the force of his great compassion [Tsongkhapa] urges the great meditators of Tibet in the *Questions of Pure Superior Intention*, by stating, "Those engaged in meditation should seek an unmistaken path," and presents the question, "What should be done if there is a famous instruction that is in disagreement with the conqueror's teaching?" This question was responded to in *Losang's Melodious Laughter*, which states:

> If the famous oral instructions are in accordance with
> The meaning of all of the scriptures of the conqueror
> And the commentaries of the scholars and siddhas,
> We should not wish to forsake them even in our dreams.
>
> However, although they may be famous,
> When they are incompatible, we should
> Abandon such oral instructions.

For that reason, with regard to the ultimate oral instructions, which make it easy to discover the meaning of the root tantras in dependence upon the explanatory tantras, these are texts such as Protector Nagarjuna's two texts that reveal the generation stage, namely the *Condensed Sadhana*[218] and *Performance Incorporating the [Guhyasamaja] Sutra*,[219] and his text revealing the completion stage entitled *The Five Stages*,[220] which contain the ultimate oral instructions on texts of the arya [tradition]. Arya Aryadeva composed a text entitled *A Lamp for a Summary of Conducts*,[221] Chandrakirti composed *The Illuminating Lamp Commentary*,[222] and so forth. Je [Tsongkhapa] in his *Lamp Illuminating the Five Stages* and *Great Exposition on the Stages of the Path of Mantra*, which contain all of the oral instructions in their entirety and were composed so as to be easy for disciples of this day and age to be able to understand, are the sole lamps of the three worlds. In the *Great Exposition on the Stages of the Path of Mantra* [Tsongkhapa] states:

> With regard to those who wish to engage in the practice of the path of highest yoga tantra from the depths of their hearts, they should rely upon such supreme oral instructions. Just as anyone who wishes to extract a precious wish-fulfilling jewel

218. *sGrub pa'i thabs mdor byas pa*; *Piṇḍīkṛtasādhana*.
219. *mDo bsres*; *Śrīguhyasamājamahāyogatantrotpādakramasādhanasūtramelāpaka*.
220. *Rim pa lnga pa*; *Pañcakrama*.
221. *sPyod pa bsdus pa'i sgron ma*; *Caryāmelāpakapradīpa*.
222. *Sgron ma gsal bar byed pa'i rgya cher bshad pa*; *Pradīpodyotanāmaṭīkā*.

from the great ocean must rely upon a captain who knows the way, those who wish to strive in the jewel of the profound two stages must strive to engage in listening and contemplating the ocean of great secret tantras in dependence upon a wise holy guru.

Next, recite the verse from the ritual prayer that states:

> And through the kindness of the captain—the vajra holder—
> I may cross the intricate ocean of the tantras.

This is stating that you must obtain a pure empowerment into a mandala with an authentic tantra as its source in dependence upon a fully qualified vajra master and that you must have reached absolute certainty through theoretical knowledge stemming from listening and contemplating the pith instructions concerning the meaning of the two stages of the tantras in dependence upon a holy guru skilled in the meaning of tantra.

For that reason, you should not only grasp the meaning of each and every one of these vajra words of Vajradhara Losang Chökyi Gyaltsen, but you should strive to attain complete stability in these methods coming down through the oral instructions of the Hearing Lineage of the omniscient foremost being [Tsongkhapa] that reveal the great essential points of the path.

How to Maintain Pure Vows and Commitments once You Have Become a Suitable Vessel

Recite the lines from the ritual text that state:

> Therefore, I seek your blessing that I may cherish more than
>   my life
> The vows and commitments, the root of attainments.[223]

---

223. These two lines appear first in the English translation of the ritual text. Here they are presented as the second half of the verse whose first two lines appeared in the previous section.

Once you have trained your mind in the common path and entered mantra by receiving a completely pure empowerment, you must strive sincerely to keep your commitments and vows pure, as this is the root of the path. If you properly protect your commitments and vows, you will definitely be able to produce attainments. With regard to this, the *Fourteen Root Downfalls*[224] states:

> If you abandon [downfalls] through mantra,
> You will definitely reach attainments.

Furthermore, if you meditate on the path on the basis of pure commitments and vows, the best will accomplish enlightenment in this life without having to wait too long, the middling in the intermediate state, and the least over a series of rebirths. Even if you don't meditate to any great degree on the two stages in this life, it is said that if you maintain your commitments and vows properly without letting them deteriorate, you will definitely attain enlightenment within sixteen lifetimes.

As Saraha states in his *Commentary to the Difficult Points of the* Buddhakapala Tantra *Called Jnanavati*,[225] when he quotes the *Treasury of Secrets*:[226]

> If they are perfectly bestowed an empowerment,
> They will receive an empowerment life after life.
> Through that they will accomplish attainments
> Within seven lives even without meditating.

> For those who meditate, if they
> Maintain their commitments and vows
> Yet don't become accomplished in this life,
> Through the force of their karma
> They will reach attainments in another life.

---

224. *rTsa ltung bcu bzhi pa.*
225. *dPal sangs rgyas thod pa'i rgyud kyi dka' 'grel ye shes ldan pa zhes bya ba; Śrībuddhakapālatantra syapañjikājñānavatīnāma.*
226. *gSang ba'i mdzod kyi rgyud.*

If someone defiles their commitments,
Not only will they not reach attainments,
But they will find it difficult to attain a human rebirth.

Also, the *Fifth Commitment*[227] states:

If one is without downfalls,
They will accomplish purity in sixteen lives.

And the *Liberating Moon*[228] states:

Even without meditation, if you are without downfalls,
You will accomplish purity within sixteen lives.

The same thing has been stated in numerous tantras and texts of the mahasiddhas.

With regard to abandoning your vows and commitments by not protecting them properly, not only will you not accomplish attainments, but all of your future lives will be a disaster. The *Fourteen Root Downfalls* states:

Otherwise, if you defile your commitments,
The defiled are seized by mara.
Next, they will experience suffering
As they go headfirst into hell.

If you defile your commitments, in this life you will be harmed by numerous demons, misleading spirits, and so forth and when you die you will immediately be tormented by a multitude of terrifying sights and, once you die, you will fall into the lowest of hells. Although those who defile their commitments make offerings to the personal deities, the [deities] will not accept them. With regard to this, the *Secret Moon Drop Tantra*[229] states:

---

227. *Dam tshig lnga pa; Samayapañca.*
228. *rNam grol zla ba.*
229. *Zla gsang thig le'i rgyud; Candraguhyatilakatantra.*

Those who desire the attainments of mantra
Should strive to protect their commitments.
If the practitioners of mantra act otherwise,
They will not accomplish the purpose of mantra and so forth.

Even though they are supplicated by those with commitments,
The deities will still not accept them.[230]
They will have great suffering in this life
And the hells beyond this world.

Those who transgress their commitment-conducts
Will only accomplish the state of ignorance.

Regardless of how much you may meditate on mantra, if you abandon your commitments and vows, there is no way that deities and protectors will be pleased. Those who defile their commitments will experience numerous sufferings at the hands of the dakinis and flesh-eaters, and even the deities will not protect them.

The *Heruka Root Tantra* states:

The one who destroys the commitments
And engages in bad actions
Without a doubt is killing Brahmins.
This confused and wicked being,
This evil one, will become ransom
And will be eaten by the dakinis.
I will not protect you from that.

Among the secret beings,
The practitioner who damages the guru's commitments
Is like a sacrificial animal
And has fallen from the world of the Buddha.

---

230. This means that even if a very pure practitioner makes supplications to the deities on behalf of someone with defiled commitments, the deities will not assist them.

Likewise, the seventh chapter of the *Yamantaka Tantra* says much of the same thing.

As explained in the *Cluster of Oral Instructions*,[231] if you practice secret mantra yet do not properly protect your commitments, although you may be beautiful on the outside, you will be like a rotten piece of fruit on the inside. Master Jnanabodhi states, "With regard to those who undertake a variety of ritual actions of accumulating secret manta yet don't properly protect their commitments and vows, they are like a leper rotting on the inside while outwardly draped in clothes and ornaments and are objects of disgrace." This same sentiment is stated in all the tantras and texts of the mahasiddhas. Once you understand the faults of not protecting every aspect of your commitments you will definitely develop high praise for keeping all aspects of your commitments and you will come to cherish your commitments more than even your life. The *Samvarodaya Tantra* states:

> So, if you wish supreme attainments,
> You should always protect your commitments,
> Even at the risk of losing your life,
> Even at the time of your death.

Thus, this states that you should risk your life to protect your commitments and vows. You should protect your [vows and commitments] more than even cherishing your own life. Yet if you don't understand the commitments and vows, it will be impossible for you to keep them; therefore, you should properly rely upon a holy guru who is skilled in the meaning of tantra and learn the commitments of mantra from him. Here I shall settle for nothing more than the concise meaning. With regard to the phrase "the commitments and vows," Vajradhara stated, "Those who have entered the door of mantra should practice in these ways with the conduct of their three doors," and, "It is unacceptable to act in these various ways," and in this way established that the vows refer to the faults that are meant to be transcended by protecting and abandoning. The commitments are whatever Vajradhara stated that are not to be violated.

---

231. *Man ngag snye ma.*

Therefore, they are distinguished by what is overcome, but they do not have a separate nature [from the vows].

There are two types of commitments: (1) the general commitments of the five buddha families, and (2) their individual commitments. Although there are limitless commitments of the five buddha families in general, if their meaning is condensed, there are either two—(1) the root, and (2) the branch commitments—or three—(1) the commitment of eating, (2) the commitment of protecting, and (3) the commitment of reliance. From the perspective of the concise meaning of these three, the commitment of eating is blessing your food and drink once you imagine them to be the five meats and five nectars. You then offer them to the deity and partake of them yourself, as is commonly explained in the tantras on the yoga of eating and so forth. The "commitment of protecting" is protecting [your commitments] and abandoning the limitless faults that violate the precepts of mantra, such as the fourteen root downfalls, the eight secondary downfalls, and so forth. Furthermore, once you identify each of the transgressions, you should examine your mental continuum in the six daily sessions and evaluate whether or not you have become defiled by these transgressions and rely on a mind of restraint. In particular, rely upon introspection as to whoever are your closest associates according to the situation.

With regard to the way to prevent yourself from becoming defiled by a downfall, the *Fourteen Root Downfalls* states:

> Therefore, to destroy pride you
> Should not deceive yourself and [you should] gain
>   knowledge.

You should protect yourself by closing the four doors through which downfalls occur, which are (1) not knowing, (2) lack of respect, (3) carelessness, and (4) a multitude of afflictive emotions.

With regard to the commitments of reliance, these are the commitment substances that are to be upheld and are taught in the tantras, such as a vajra, bell, rosary, hand drum, *katvanga*, skull cup, ritual ladle and funnel [for burnt offerings], vase, the six bone ornaments, and so forth. It is best if you can actually produce all of these. At the very least you should definitely have a vajra, bell, and rosary, and for the other commitment substances you should definitely keep at least a drawing of them. This was taught by my holy guru.

Among these general commitments of the five buddha families, the most important things to abandon from the very beginning are the fourteen root downfalls. Regarding the root downfalls, they are a "defeat" that destroys the vows of mantra; therefore, you should be very careful not to be defiled by them from the moment you receive an empowerment. Regarding this point, the *Fifty Verses of Guru Devotion* states:

> Next, having been made a suitable vessel for the holy Dharma
> Through being given mantra and so forth,
> You should read and memorize
> The fourteen root downfalls.

And the *Fourteen Root Downfalls* also states:

> The mantra practitioner who wishes to benefit themselves
> Should strive to maintain [their vows].

This is stating that in case you do become defiled, you should immediately confess it and take your vows once again. Of all those root downfalls you should be especially cautious about not becoming defiled by the first, which is not to disparage your guru. Among all the commitments, the commitment of the guru is the main one, and the guru is the root of all attainments; therefore, you should apply yourself with whatever human capacity and strength you have not to blunder when it comes to this direct dependent relationship.

The *Great Exposition on the Stages of the Path of Mantra* states:

> You should strive sincerely according to the teachings, which state that you should protect your vows and commitments as you would your life. In particular, it is said that if you are defiled by a root downfall, your mental continuum becomes ruined and it will be very difficult to develop good qualities; therefore, you should sincerely attempt to not become defiled

by them. You should also strive sincerely not to be defiled by
the other downfalls as well. If you do, you should once again
repair them through confession and restraint in accordance
with the Dharma.

And:

It is stated repeatedly in the tantras and their commentaries
that the guru is the root of all attainments; therefore, the
previous holy beings have said that it is extremely important
that you meditate on guru yoga from the very outset. Furthermore, there are extensive discourses regarding the first root
downfall that are summarized in protecting the commitments
in *Fifty Verses of Guru Devotion*, and it is also the most important
of all the precepts.

Although there are limitless classifications of the individual commitments
of the five buddha families, all the vows can be subsumed under nineteen,
which I have already explained during the previous section on taking the
vows.

Thus, these ways of guarding the general and individual commitments
of the five buddha families are presented here in these oral instructions
of Lama Chöpa and contain all the most important points.[232] With regard
to going for refuge and generating bodhichitta at the beginning [of the
ritual text], this maintains the precept that we should go for refuge six
times a day and uphold the commitments of Vairochana to maintain the
three refuges, as well as to train in aspiring bodhichitta and generate
bodhichitta six times a day. This is how you protect your promise to
maintain bodhichitta by upholding the vows of the five buddha families.
Next, with regard to equanimity and love as the meditation on the four
immeasurables, this accomplishes giving fearlessness and love from among
the teachings of the four types of giving as part of the commitment of
Ratnasambhava. As for [the other two commitments of Ratnasambhava],
giving material things and Dharma, they occur during giving refuge as

232. In the following section Kachen Yeshe Gyaltsen gives a more or less sequential outline of
the Lama Chöpa ritual and explains how each section of the ritual fulfills the various nineteen
commitments of the five buddha families.

part of the six perfections [later in the ritual]. Next, generating yourself as the desire deities in the aspect of the father and mother and holding a vajra and bell, guard the three commitments of Akshobya of the vajra, bell, and mudra. As for meditating on Guru-Vajradhara, this upholds the commitment of the master as part of the commitment of Akshobya and is how you protect the principal commitment of the *Fifty Verses of Guru Devotion*. Next, you make prostrations with your three doors to the guru and assembly of deities and present offerings, which is how you guard the precept of going for refuge, [which states that you must] make offerings to the Three Jewels every day; the precept of aspiring bodhichitta, [which states that you must] accumulate merit through making prostrations, offerings, and so forth; and the commitment to make offerings as part of the commitment of Amoghasiddhi of the five buddha families. Next, the practice of upholding the vows fulfills the commitment of the five buddha families to enumerate your vows. Next, enumerating your precepts of each of the three sets of vows fulfills the commitments of Amoghasiddhi, the precepts of the bodhisattva vows, and in particular enumerating the root and branch commitments. With regard to reciting the general confession, *Guide to the Bodhisattva's Way of Life* states:

> Three times during the day and night
> You should recite the *Sutra of the Three Heaps*,
> And in dependence upon the conqueror and bodhichitta
> Purify the remaining downfalls.

Thus, you accomplish the precepts of bodhichitta.

With regard to offering a mandala to the guru and assembly of deities, the *Fifty Verses of Guru Devotion* states:

> With a mandala and flowers in the palm of your hands
> Respectfully honor your teacher-guru.

This fulfills the precept of offering a mandala to your guru and your personal deity. Making supplications through recalling his good qualities and kindness operates in accordance with numerous teachings from the *Fifty Verses of Guru Devotion* concerning the need to supplicate the guru. Entreating him to turn the wheel of outer, inner, and secret Dharmas, meditating on the deities of the four classes of tantra, and training the mind in the complete path that is embodied in the three vehicles and the four classes of tantra fulfill the training in the commitments of Amitabha.[233] Training in the three types of moral discipline accomplishes [the commitment] to protect your bodhisattva vows and the commitment of Vairochana to train in the three types of moral discipline. Meditating on the empty nature of reality accomplishes numerous commitments of mantra, the main one being the commitment of mind, as well as not being defiled by the eleventh root downfall and so forth.

The primary way to protect the commitments is to realize that the commitments and vows themselves are the root of all common and supreme attainments and to act with the pure intention that thinks, "I shall protect them more than my life," and make supplications to be able to perfect them in this way. Thus, when the holy beings that are well versed in the meaning of the tantras examine these teachings, they will see that these oral instructions contain all the primary essential points that receive extensive praise in the tantras and texts of the mahasiddhas. Through this you will generate great faith in these teachings and be uncontrollably swept away by a mind of extreme wonderment.

Concerning what was mentioned above with regard to the way of protecting the practice of mantra as explained in the tantras vis-à-vis the general and individual commitments of the five buddha families, some people claim that you primarily need to protect the commitments through the six-session [guru yoga], yet even the famous "golden Dharmas" of Tibet cannot compare to these uncommon oral instructions of this incomparable oral lineage of the omniscient Je [Tsongkhapa] that sets an unprecedented standard here in the land of snows. You should train in the bodhichitta through the entire body of the oral instruction of Lama Chöpa.

Because I fear that this text would become too verbose if I were to reveal all the essential points and extensively explain how to protect the commitments and how to identify each and every one and how [Lama Chöpa] possesses extraordinary exalted features for those wishing to tra-

233. The three commitments of Amitabha to rely upon (1) the teachings of sutra, (2) the teachings of the two lower tantras, and (3) the two higher classes of tantra.

verse the path through these oral instructions, I have not exhaustively explained the commitments of mantra. Therefore, those possessing intelligence should study the tantras and texts of the mahasiddhas in dependence upon the teachings of the omniscient Je [Tsongkhapa] concerning the instructions on the commitments of mantra. You should undertake an exhaustive search and reach a definite conclusion induced by the path of scripture and reason and not through mere devotion.

In short, you should think, "For the welfare of all living beings I shall quickly attain the state of a perfectly complete buddha. For that purpose I shall perfectly obtain an empowerment in dependence upon a fully qualified vajra master. I shall protect and cherish the commitments and vows I have promised to maintain while receiving the empowerment more than my own life. Guru-deity, please grant me your blessing so that I may be able to conduct myself in this way." Thinking in this way, recite the verse from the ritual text that states:

> Therefore, I seek your blessing that I may cherish more than my life
> The vows and commitments, the root of attainments,
> And through the kindness of the captain—the vajra holder—
> I may cross the intricate ocean of the tantras.

Through making this extremely powerful supplication a stream of five-colored light rays and nectars descends from the bodies of the guru and assembly of deities and enters the body and mind of yourself and all other living beings, whereby the unique obstructions are purified and, in particular, the various realizations are developed in the minds of yourself and all living beings.

How to Meditate on the Two Stages of the Path has three sections:
1. How to Actually Meditate on the Two Stages
2. How to Practice Transference of Consciousness if You Have Not Reached a State of Realization despite Having Meditated
3. How to Pray to Come under the Care of Your Guru throughout All of Your Lives and How to Withdraw the Field of Merit for the Sake of Receiving His Blessings in Your Mental Continuum

How to Actually Meditate on the Two Stages has two sections:
1. How to Train in the Generation Stage
2. How to Train in the Completion Stage

How to Train in the Generation Stage

The ritual text states:

> And through the yoga of the first stage may I transform
> Birth, death, and the intermediate state into the three bodies
>   of the conqueror.

Having received a pure empowerment and abiding in perfectly pure commitments and vows, you must then train in the two stages of the path so that you can accomplish the state of enlightenment. If either one [of the two stages] is incomplete, there is no way you can accomplish supreme attainments. Furthermore, you strive to perfect your training in the generation stage, after which you should meditate on the completion stage. Without the generation stage as a preliminary, it will be impossible to generate even the most insignificant facsimile of the realization despite meditating on the completion stage, and it will not be possible to develop a complete and thorough realization of the completion stage. The completion stage is of primary importance for the three bodies during the path, yet you will have no way of accomplishing all three of those bodies during the path without bringing the three bodies into the path during the generation stage as a preliminary. The *Explanatory Tantra Vajramala* explains that you should meditate on the completion stage once you have performed the generation stage as a preliminary. In Protector Nagarjuna's *Five Stages* he states:

> Those who desire to be completion-stage practitioners
> Perfectly abide on the generation stage.
> This method is taught by the complete buddhas
> As being like the steps of a ladder.

This very clearly states that just as you must sequentially ascend the steps from the first step onward when climbing the steps of a ladder, so you must sequentially meditate on the two stages. In Aryadeva's *Compendium of Conducts* he states:

> You should train in the common path (from proper reliance upon your spiritual master up to tranquil abiding and special insight) entitled "the Buddha vehicle." Once you gain experience of that, you should train in the coarse generation stage entitled "single recollection." Once you gain experience of that, train in the subtle generation stage entitled "the enduring yoga." Once you gain experience of that, you should progress through the stages of the path from training in isolated body up to the final union. If you don't go through each of the previous paths, there is no way you will progress through the latter [stages], which is extensively explained citing the paths of scripture and reasoning. In the same way, you should train in at least a concise sadhana and the first concentration of the generation stage.

For that reason, in these instructions it states that you should first train in the generation stage and you should come to a great certainty about the sequence of the path by making a detailed analysis first through the force of the written word.

With regard to the enumerations and sequence of the path, it is a source of difficulty that is a place of great error and is difficult to understand. Therefore, you should learn them through studying the *Great Exposition on the Stages of the Path of Mantra*. Thus, from among the two stages, you should initially meditate on the generation stage and, what's more, it is not called "the generation stage" if you are merely generating the body of a single deity. Instead, you should understand how to perform a complete mandala of deities, together with the supporting and supported mandala that is concordant with the basis of purification and correlates with the stages of birth and disintegration. Additionally, initially you practice bringing death into the path as the truth body by meditating on emptiness through the stages of withdrawal that are congruent with the sequence of destruction and empty state of the environment and its beings. Next, you bring the intermediate state into the path as the enjoyment body and bring rebirth into the path as the emanation body and blend the meditations with your mental continuum with a degree of certainty. You generate the complete supporting and supported mandala that is congruent with the stages of the formation of the world and its beings and then seal it with the bestowal of empowerment. You should then complete the offerings and praises as well as mantra recitation. For this there are also extensive and concise systems. The extensive is explained in the twelfth chapter of the *Guhyasamaja Root Tantra*, which presents the detailed system for meditating on the generation through the four limbs of approach and accomplishment. The concise system is explained in that same chapter, which states:

> Alternatively, you should approach by
> Stable conduct through the four vajras.

This explains that the concise generation stage is carried out through generating the four vajras. There are limitless benefits because of the generation stage, such as your mental continuum is blessed by the conquerors and bodhisattvas; you come under the care of the supreme deity throughout all of your lives, and so forth, a little of which I already explained during the preliminary discourse. Moreover, by offering limitless outer, inner, secret, and suchness offerings to the guru, who is inseparable from the mandala deity, you complete a massive collection of merit to quickly generate the profound path of the completion stage in your mental continuum. Also, since the cause of those outer, inner, and secret offerings correlates to the result, the practitioner spontaneously accomplishes dependent-related outer, inner, and secret networks for training in the completion stage in the future. Primarily during the completion stage you should accomplish the three bodies at the time of the path by transforming birth, death, and the intermediate state into the actual three bodies. For that you must perfect your practice of bringing the three bodies into the path of the generation stage by mentally transforming birth, death, and the intermediate state into the three bodies. During the generation stage the complete set of dependent arising—between the basis of purification and the purifying agent—is completely mapped out.

You absolutely must mentally evoke the experience of the three bodies so that you can quickly accomplish the three bodies of the completion stage. From the very beginning of the generation stage you generate yourself as the male and female desire deities and train in the secret offering and so forth through stable divine pride and clear appearance and generate a stable imagination of bliss and emptiness, whereby you will be able to quickly induce a special simultaneously born [bliss] of the completion stage. Also during the generation stage, you prevent ordinary appearances and conceptions and strive to perfect stable divine pride and clear appearance on the complete supporting and supported mandala, which will be greatly increased during the completion stage. During the ultimate union of body at the time of enlightenment you will arise in the complete supporting and supported mandala.

Here I have explained just a fraction of this system for generating an understanding that is compatible with the teachings of these instructions; yet even if Conqueror Vajradhara himself were to appear and give a detailed discourse on the two stages with regard to enumerations, sequence, and so forth, they would not be of any more benefit than these teachings; therefore, you should study the great treatises on mantra composed by the omniscient Je [Tsongkhapa].

In short, you should think, "For the welfare of all living beings I must attain the state of a completely perfect buddha. For that purpose I shall sincerely apply myself to the yoga of the first stage by working to transform birth, death, and the intermediate state into the three bodies of the conqueror. Therefore, may I receive the blessings of the buddhas and bodhisattvas within my mental continuum and may all outer and inner unfavorable conditions be pacified so that I may generate the profound path of mantra within my mental continuum. May the guru-deity please bestow his blessing so that I may be able to prevent ordinary appearances and conceptions through the entire environment appearing as a celestial mansion, all beings appearing as nothing other than gods and goddesses, which will ripen my roots of virtue so that I may generate the completion stage in its entirety within my mental continuum." With this in mind, recite the verse from the ritual prayer that states:

> I seek your blessing that I may purify all the stains of ordinary
>   appearances and conceptions
> So that whatever appears may manifest as the body of the deity
> And through the yoga of the first stage may I transform
> Birth, death, and the intermediate state into the three bodies
>   of the conqueror.

Through making this extremely powerful supplication a stream of five-colored light rays and nectars descends from the bodies of the guru and assembly of deities and enters the body and mind of yourself and all other living beings, whereby the unique obstructions are purified and, in particular, the various realizations are developed in the minds of yourself and all living beings.

How to Train in the Completion Stage

This is revealed in the verse that ends, "Upon the eight-petaled lotus within the central channel in my heart." This embodies all of the points of the various tantric systems of the completion stage and, in accordance with that, the mahasiddha composed various systems that contain various numbers of points. Although there are various numbers of points, such as the collection of five stages, the collection of four yogas, the collection of four joys, the collection of the six limbs of yoga, and so forth, they all contain the same essential meaning.

With regard to these instructions [of Lama Chöpa], they are revealed in the five stages of the arya tradition. These five stages are revealed in the sixth chapter of the *Guhyasamaja Root Tantra*, which explains the five stages of the completion stage by stating:

> Through visualizing the body in mantra [practice],
> Being aroused through speech and mind,
> Through the joy and satisfaction of the mind
> You should accomplish supreme attainments.

These are vajra words and are very difficult to discern; therefore, ordinary beings will not be able to understand their meaning through mere verbal conventions. Because of that, the conqueror himself revealed them in detail through the explanatory tantras, such as the *Vajramala*, where he identified the five stages. In conjunction with the explanatory tantras Protector Nagarjuna subsequently composed a text on the five stages that clearly reveals how to practice the completion stage, which became famed as *The Five Stages of the Arya Tradition of Guhyasamaja*. With regard to these five stages, they are (1) the stage of vajra recitation, (2) the stage of observing the mind, (3) the stage of self-blessing, (4) the stage of manifest enlightenment, and (5) the stage of union. These instructions reveal all five of these stages in their entirety. The stage of vajra recitation is speech isolation. Furthermore, it is equally nominally imputed as "restraining vitality and exertion" (or *pranayama* in Sanskrit). With regard to restraining pranayama of speech isolation, this is revealed in the lines [from Lama Chöpa] that state:

> And that you, Protector, may arrange your feet
> Upon the eight-petaled lotus within the central channel in
>   my heart.

Restraining vitality and exertion of speech isolation is the means of practicing the completion stage by penetrating the vital points at the heart. The words of these oral instructions clearly reveal the essential point of the heart and the object of observation there. They also reveal the four later stages by stating, "The path of the clear light, illusory body, and union." For the clear light there is both the example of clear light and meaning of clear light. The way to generate the clear light of isolated mind is "the stage of observing the mind." The illusory body is "self-blessing." The meaning clear light is "the stage of manifest enlightenment" and "union"; this clearly reveals the five stages. Aryadeva's *Compendium of Conducts* lists the body isolation separately. There you meditate on body isolation by penetrating the vital point of the lower door [of the central channel] as a preliminary for the sake of easily generating realization of pranayama of speech isolation. Next, you become accustomed to the heart. Some of the previous lamas of this oral instruction are in accordance with the intention of the *Compendium of Conducts*, for which you train in isolated body by meditating on the subtle lower door as a preliminary. Next, you meditate on the mantra drop at the heart. This accords with the general stages of the arya system and has a strong relationship with the system of engaging in the completion stage in dependence upon the subtle generation stage as well as making it easy [to generate completion-stage realizations] and so forth. Although this is certainly an excellent way to proceed, the teachings of these oral instructions don't state that you focus your attention on the lower door as a preliminary. When you comprehend the meaning of these teachings, you see that it is also not inappropriate to penetrate the vital point at the heart.

Gyalwa Ensapa also taught this very method of penetrating the vital point of the heart from the beginning when meditating on the completion stage through this guru yoga. It is also taught in the completion stage of Jnanapada's tradition of Guhyasamaja that you penetrate the vital point of the heart from the outset. Mahasiddha Ghantapa also explains in his *Five Stages of Heruka* that you begin by penetrating the vital point of the heart, and accomplished practitioners as limitless as particles of this earth have appeared in dependence upon these oral instructions. Therefore, based on the oral instructions stemming from the tantras and mahasiddhas there have arisen a multitude of various doors within the body to penetrate.

The intended meaning that is the essential point of all [these various tantric systems] is to open the door of the central channel and collect the winds of the right and left channels into the central channel, whereby you generate the exalted wisdom of simultaneously born bliss and emptiness and accomplish the clear light illusory body of union from that very exalted wisdom and its mount [the very subtle wind]; this is what the ultimate point of all these instructions comes down to. Therefore, if you understand this method, it is said that you will achieve fearlessness with regard to the meaning of the tantras, and the tantras and texts of the mahasiddhas will arise as personal instructions. Omniscient Je [Tsongkhapa] stated:

> You should meditate by learning the uncommon oral instructions for the system of meditation that meditates on an object of observation of the important points of the body, such as a syllable, drop, and so forth, within the center of your body or the lower end of the central channel. Through this, if you focus the mind, although you are not directly meditating on

the wind, because the wind and mind have the same object of engagement, it will become a way for the winds to enter the central channel. If you understand this excellent causal process, once you understand that the essential points of the numerous texts of the completion stage are authentic, you will come to a point of absolute certainty with regard to them.

Thus, from the multitude of different doors for penetrating the vital points of the vajra body, in these oral instructions Vajradhara Losang Chökyi Gyaltsen teaches penetrating the vital point of the heart. With regard to this, from among all the multitude of various teachings for penetrating the vital points of the vajra body, he is revealing that this is the ultimate pith instruction from among them all.

With regard to the completion stages, they are the foundation of whatever skillful means of that path that there are and they function to quickly accomplish supreme attainments. At the time of base, during formation of the body of living (human) beings, the heart [channel wheel] is formed first, and after that the limbs of the body sequentially develop. Finally, when you die, once the winds and consciousness absorb in the heart, you die, and from that clear light of death you accomplish the intermediate-state body. From that intermediate state you take rebirth in a coarse body. Similar to whatever exists on the basis, although there are a multitude of various doors of visualization during the path of the completion stage, they should all work toward the heart; and once you collect the wind and mind into the heart, the clear light dawns. From that comes the illusory body, and from that body you assume a coarse body and transform the three bodies of the basis into the three bodies at the time of the path. Once you identify the three bodies amid your own continuum, these instructions function to accomplish supreme attainments in one short life of this degenerate age and are the ultimate oral instructions that explain the true intent of the great being Nagarjuna's commentary on tantra and are the instructions that extract the heart essence of Conqueror Tsong-khapa the Great; thus, in the *Lamp Illuminating the Five Stages* he states:

Therefore, with regard to the most excellent place to penetrate the vital point of the body explained in the arya tradition, it is the center of the heart channel and should be held as the most significant instruction. Through a string of birth, death, and intermediate state at the time of the base, you continuously circle through samsara. Yet this is the ultimate skillful means to transform death into the truth body, the intermediate state into the enjoyment body, and rebirth into the emanation body. Another method is the oral instructions that identify the innate inhalation and exhalation of wind that abides in each living being. This is acceptable because it is similar to the "king of pranayama"; this is the oral instruction of the great Vajradhara Nagarjuna for introducing us to how to recognize the three buddha bodies.[234]

Therefore, regarding the way to penetrate the essential point of the heart as presented in these oral instructions, while remaining in a state of Vajradhara Father and Mother as the sole lineage of the great secret, directly in the center of your body are the three channels [right, left, and central] in the manner of a life-tree.[235] The right and left channels wrap around the central channel to form knots at each of the channels. Furthermore, there are four channel wheels: (1) the wheel of great bliss at the crown has thirty-two channels, (2) the wheel of enjoyment at the throat has sixteen channels, (3) the wheel of Dharma at the heart has eight channels, and (4) the emanation wheel at the navel has sixty-four channels. Visualize those four channel wheels. If you wish to expand it, you can also visualize the lesser channel wheels below and above. Thus, you should accomplish as much clear appearance of the three channels and four channel wheels as you can by repeatedly visualizing them. Fur-

234. The "king of pranayama" is in reference to vajra recitation. In the practice of vajra recitation, the practitioner combines the inhalation, exhalation, and the period of refrain between the two with the three syllables HUM, OM, and AH, which are the seed-syllables of the mind, body, and speech of the buddhas, respectively. By combining the natural flow of the breath with the three syllables, the winds are unified with the body, speech, and mind of all the buddhas, which are truth body (HUM), emanation body (OM), and enjoyment body (AH), respectively. In this way, the natural flow of the winds is identified as the three buddha bodies.
235. This is in reference to a wooden pole that is carved with mantras, consecrated, and then placed in the center of a stupa and is considered the "life" of the stupa, similar to one's own life channel.

thermore, most of the tantras and texts of the mahasiddhas state that you enter the completion stage once you have perfected the generation stage. Therefore, if you are going to practice in that way, at this point you take guru yoga as the life of the path and combine it with the visualizations for the completion stage. Yet in this day and age most disciples will not be capable of realizing the two stages by practicing exactly in this way. Therefore, those who wish to establish imprints for the path of mantra should meditate on the generation stage in the first part of the session and then train a little in the completion stage on the basis of guru yoga.

Thus, once you visualize the channels and you attain some slight degree of clear appearance, you should strive to penetrate the essential point of the object of visualization. The *Concise Five Stages*[236] states:

> You should know the four essential aspects of
> Object, time, body, and wind.

This is stating that you should have all four essential features for meditation on the completion stage. Therefore, if you don't find the essential object of concentration, you will not have a foundation for meditating on the completion stage. As for that essential object, the mind focuses on the body of Guru-Vajradhara in the center of the central channel at the eight channel petals of the Dharma wheel at your heart. This teaching focusing on a single body comes from the foremost omniscient being Losang Yeshe [the Second Panchen Lama] in the lineage of Lama Donyo Khedrup. From that foremost being emerged a lineage of Dorje Zinpa Losang Rigdrol that states that you focus your mind on a short AH within the heart of that body [of Vajradhara]. In general, if you are not mistaken with your visualization, there are various objects that you can focus your mind on, such as a syllable, body, or drop. Focusing your mind on the short AH is also the teaching of Gyalwa Ensapa the Great and is the intention of the *Compendium of Conducts*. Therefore, the omniscient foremost great being [Tsongkhapa] also taught that you should focus your attention on the short AH at this point. You should learn the details about this essential point orally from your guru.

236. *Rim lnga bsdus pa.*

Having focused your mind in this way, you stop the flow [of the winds] in the right and left channels and cause them to enter, abide, and dissolve into the central channel. The sign that they have entered is that the movement [of the winds through the nostrils] becomes of equal force. The sign that they are abiding is that they stop. The sign that they have dissolved is that the various signs of mirage-like, smoke, fireflies, and candle flame emerge. Next, the minds of appearance, increase, and near-attainment dissolve, whereby white, red, and black appearances emerge. When they are withdrawn, [the three minds are also called], empty, very-empty, and great-empty, respectively. In addition to the state of near-attainment, its second half is without mindfulness, and when that is cleared away, the all-empty clear light dawns that is like space free from the three faults of contaminants.[237] At that point, you should place your mind in a state of meditative equipoise on the clear light of bliss and emptiness to the best of your ability.

When you arise from that state, you should imagine you are arising in the illusory body called "self-blessing" and place your mind in a state of meditative equipoise upon it to the best of your ability. Next, you once again assume the coarse aggregates; these are the three mixings during waking.[238] Likewise, you practice the three mixings during sleep and the three mixings during death. In this way you sincerely apply yourself to the nine rounds of mixing.

Thus, once you are able to focus on the mantra drop, if you loosen the channel knots a little, you should train in vajra recitation with the winds inseparable from mantra, which is the king of pranayama and is the ultimate oral instruction of the arya tradition of Glorious Guhyasamaja. When you attain a very good experience through sincerely applying your-

237. There are three external contaminants and three internal contaminants. The three internal contaminants are the minds of white appearance, red increase, and black near-attainment. The three external contaminants are the sky being pervaded by moonlight, sunlight, and darkness.
238. There are nine mixings: three during waking, three during sleeping, and three during dying. To practice the first three you mix the clear light of waking with the truth body, the illusory body with the enjoyment body, and the coarse aggregates with the emanation body. To practice the second set of three you mix the clear light of sleep with the truth body, dreaming with the enjoyment body, and awakening with the emanation body. To practice the third set of three you mix the clear light of death with the truth body, the intermediate state with the enjoyment body, and rebirth with the emanation body.

self to that [vajra recitation], you practice the two stages of dissolution[239] and vajra recitation in conjunction with the pervasive winds and so forth. Through applying yourself in this way you will be able to collect every one of the root and branch winds directly into the indestructible drop at your heart exactly the same as during the stages of death. Through applying yourself in this way, when you are close to attaining the example clear light of isolated mind, you should once again make a special effort in guru yoga and present a ganachakra and so forth to your guru, whereby you receive special oral instructions, and through training in these causal accumulations you will accomplish example clear light. When you arise from that clear light you will arise in the actual illusory body of the third stage as the enjoyment body of the path with wind of five-colored light functioning as the substantial cause and the mind of simultaneously born great bliss functioning as the cooperative condition that is accomplished in the exact same way as the intermediate state is accomplished from the basic clear light of becoming. In that way, just as you assume a coarse body from the intermediate state of the base, once that illusory body enters the heart of the old aggregates you engage in practices such as guru yoga and the two types of dissolution.

Through practicing in that way, when you perceive the signs that you are close to attaining meaning clear light, you present a ganachakra as well as outer, inner, and secret offerings to your guru, and once you listen to his oral instructions on the clear light, you actualize meaning clear light of the fourth stage as the internal enlightenment that accords with the external enlightenment where all appearances, as well as grasping at the outer and inner signs of true existence, have subsided, just like clouds dissipating into the sphere of space. At that time all the conceptual elaborations of dualistic appearances are purified and you attain the exalted wisdom that directly perceives the ultimate mode of existence of the mind. That exalted wisdom functions to remove, from its very root,

---

239. There are two types of dissolution: (1) holding the body entirely, and (2) subsequent destruction. For the first your body dissolves from above and below into the indestructible drop at your heart, and for the second the world and its beings dissolve into your body, after which your body dissolves as before. They are practiced in conjunction with vajra recitation on the pervasive winds. For more information, see *The Roar of Thunder* (Ithaca, NY: Snow Lion Publications, 2012).

self-grasping together with its seeds, which are the root of samsara. That is also called "the yoga of completely pure exalted wisdom."

With regard to such a body, the *Guhyasamaja Root Tantra* states:

> Its blazing vajra-light rays
> Cover a hundred leagues.
> It is adorned with all ornaments
> And appears in a pure nature.
>
> Gods such as Brahma, Raudra, and so forth
> Are incapable of even seeing it.

Thus, it is adorned with the thirty-two noble signs and the eighty minor adornments and its light rays fill all worldly realms. Its limitless emanations are capable of working for the welfare of migrating beings. Once you attain that body, you do not need to accomplish a new body because it is sustained by a similar type of continuity.[240] With regard to this, Protector Nagarjuna stated:

> Through abiding in the concentration of union
> There are no new objects of training.

Through familiarizing yourself with the similar type of continuity as that [pure illusory] body you will receive signs that you are close to accomplishing the union of no more learning. Because of that, in the very same way as Bhagavan Buddha Shakyamuni subdued Mara in the past, similar things will happen to you, and all the abodes of the demons will be stirred up and the demons will strive to terrorize you and so forth, which has been stated in numerous tantras, such as *Samputa* and so forth. Therefore, once those signs emerge, you engage in the uncommon stages of practice as the secondary cause for actualizing the union of no more learning, and during the special time of external purification you attain the completely

---

240. This means that the very subtle wind that is the substantial cause for the pure illusory body is the very same wind that will become the substantial cause for the enjoyment body at the time of your enlightenment. Therefore, there is no new object of attainment, merely improving and purifying the illusory body that one already has attained.

pure body of Vajradhara's union with the seven limbs of embrace. You never again stir from that body and abide with the five certainties[241] while continuously enjoying Dharma teachings, after which you send forth countless trillions of emanation bodies.

In this way, these teachings on the essential point of the five stages of the path are more secret than even the greatest secrets and are the pure extracted essence of the ocean of the great secret tantras. Yet I am like a fool who, through my own power, is incapable of recognizing even a fragment of the ultimate secrets. However, I have written a mere portion of the teachings of the omniscient Je [Tsongkhapa] and Mahasiddha Ensapa, as well as the teachings that I learned orally from my own holy guru. With regard to these ultimate secrets depending solely upon the kindness of the guru, the *Explanatory Tantra Vajramala* states:

> For that reason, with faith you should
> Train in the oral instructions from
> The lineage of the guru with all your effort.

> Therefore, strive in the abode through the tantra's stages
> Pervaded by the transmission of tantra.
> You should train in the supreme suchness
> By striving in the oral instructions that come from
> Yogini's instructions as well as guru's instructions.

And Protector Nagarjuna's *Five Stages* states:

> The tantra of Glorious Guhyasamaja
> Is the sealed abode of these suchnesses.
> You should realize them from the mouth of your guru
> By following the explanatory tantras.

As these state, you should learn these ultimate secrets from the mouth of your guru. Therefore, to actualize the meaning of tantra, and through

---

241. These are the attributes of the enjoyment body of no more learning and are (1) excellent teacher, (2) teaching, (3) retinue, (4) place, and (5) time.

the force of their great compassion, the holy beings have set these forth in detail for those who wish to practice from the depths of their heart and have composed the prayer that states:

> Directly reveal the five stages of these oral instructions
> And grant your blessing that I may actualize them in this life.

Although they composed prayers to actualize the higher stages of the actual completion stage, they also reveal the way to actualize the result.

Therefore, they made themselves a suitable vessel for the profound path of mantra through a completely pure empowerment, and once they became a pure vessel, they protected their commitments and vows as they would their life, after which they meditated on the two stages, together with their limbs. And, in dependence upon that, they collected the meaning of all the tantras into methods for actualizing the final result and wrote compositions. Although there are numerous ways of collecting the meaning of the tantras that come from the tantras and texts of the mahasiddhas, once the omniscient Je [Tsongkhapa] saw the amazing collected compositions, such as the *Compendium of Vajra Wisdom*,[242] he compiled the meaning of the tantras and assembled them by composing commentaries that serve as the proper condition for a single individual to attain enlightenment. Therefore, this method is the ultimate intention of Je [Tsongkhapa], and when those with great intelligence contemplate these methods, they develop faith and their minds are uncontrollably captivated by these oral instructions of Vajradhara Losang Chökyi Gyaltsen.

With regard to this being the true intent of Je [Tsongkhapa], the *Great Exposition on the Stages of the Path of Mantra* states, "Thus, although any of the different systems for compiling the stages of the path is certainly acceptable, this should be explained according to the intention of the *Compendium of Vajra Wisdom*." And:

> With regard to the general theme for combining the [points of the] path, because the order of the teachings set forth in the tantras is necessarily out of sequence, I looked over the

---

242. *Ye shes rdo rje kun las btus pa*; *Vajrajñānasamuccayatantra*.

tantras and their commentaries through the lens of my understanding of combining the meaning of all the tantras into a
factor for a single individual's enlightenment. It is a means
of having the supreme instructions dawn as completely pure
precepts; therefore, it is extremely important for someone to
understand that all the meaning of all the tantras has been
condensed and arranged into the stages of the path by assembling them as points of practice.

In short, think, "I must quickly attain the state of a complete perfect
buddha for the welfare of all mother sentient beings. For that purpose,
once I ripen my mental continuum through the first stage, when I enter
the second stage I am going to meditate with extreme intensity on the
yoga of the guru-deity and request the guru-deity to come to the center
of my heart at which point I will meditate single-pointedly. The ultimate
recitation that evokes my guru's mental continuum is the profound vajra
recitation. In dependence upon its power, the winds will enter, abide,
and dissolve into my central channel and the clear light will dawn. From
that clear light I will arise in the illusory body of the third stage, and by
attaining the clear light of the fourth stage and the union of the fifth stage
I will attain the state of the union of Vajradhara. Guru-deity, please bless
my mental continuum to accomplish this." Contemplating in this way,
recite the verse from the ritual prayer that states:

> I seek your blessing that I may manifest in this life
> The path of the clear light, illusory body, and union.
> And that you, Protector, may arrange your feet
> Upon the eight-petaled lotus within the center of the central
>   channel in my heart.

Through making this extremely powerful supplication a stream of five-
colored light rays and nectars descends from the bodies of the guru and
assembly of deities and enters the body and mind of yourself and all other
living beings, whereby the particular obstructions are purified and, in
particular, the various realizations are developed in the minds of yourself
and all living beings.

How to Practice Transference of Consciousness if You Have Not Reached a State of Realization despite Having Meditated

The ritual text states:

> If by the time of my death I have not completed the points
> of the path . . .

Although the previous holy gurus have taught numerous classifications of transference of consciousness and imputed them with different names, if their meaning is abridged, according to these oral instructions, there are two ways to practice transference of consciousness: (1) the common way, to practice at the time of death through Mahayana mind training, and (2) the uncommon way, to practice transference of consciousness through mantra. They have also taught the common transference of consciousness through the five forces and how to practice transference of consciousness through the yoga of the guru-deity that is established upon the basis of practicing the five forces. From among these two practices at the moment of death, for most disciples in this day and age, this way of practicing at the time of death as set forth in Mahayana mind training is of extraordinary great benefit. Regarding this method, the *Kadam Mind Training* states:

> The five forces are the crucial conduct for
> The instructions of Mahayana mind training.

In accordance with this, you should undertake the transference of consciousness through the five forces.

With regard to how to do this, when the time of death is approaching you should offer all of your belongings to your guru, the Sangha, and so forth without any attachment whatsoever, which constitutes the *force of the white seed*.

Next, you restore your commitments and vows and, after making perfect supplications in the presence of your guru and the assembly of deities, you should offer the seven-limb prayer and a mandala offering. Then, you make prayers that at the time of death, the intermediate state, and in your future lives you will train in the two bodhichittas, you will never forget this guru yoga and will actualize it, and through all your lives you will always come under the care of the guru, which is *the force of prayer*.

Next, you think, "From beginningless time until the present, this self-cherishing has brought me ruin and even now, if I still come under its influence, it will cast me into the lower realms," and once you see this self-cherishing as the enemy it is, you should do whatever you can to get rid of it, which is *the force of destruction*.

Next, think, "Whatever may come, in every situation I will never be separated from guru yoga and my meditation on the two bodhichittas," which is *the force of intention*.

Finally, cultivating whatever strength of mind you possess to meditate on the two precious bodhichittas is *the force of meditation*.

Meditate on taking and giving in conjunction with love, compassion, and the two bodhichittas from within the state of all five of these forces and think, "All phenomena are merely imputed by the mind, and other than this they do not possess even an atom of inherent existence," and within a state of operating with confidence in the view, you practice transference of consciousness to the best of your ability.

With regard to what sort of lying posture you should undertake at that time, you lie down on your right side and place your right hand under your cheek and use its ring finger to block the right nostril. Your legs are outstretched with the left upon the right and with your left hand on top of the [left leg]. At this time, recall the liberating life story of our teacher and think, "This is similar to the way our compassionate teacher lay down in the past to reveal his passing into the state of nirvana," and through the force of this it will be impossible for you to fall into the lower realms. In short, you should strive to die within a state of practicing renunciation, bodhichitta, and the profound view of the Middle Way, which are the essential practices of the common path. It would be highly commendable if you were able to [die in this way], and your subtle mind at the time of death will be transformed into a virtuous state, which is mentioned in the higher and lower Abhidharma texts;[243] these state that if you die

---

243. The "higher" are those Abhidharma texts of the Mahayana and the "lower" are those of the Hinayana.

within that state you will not fall into the lower realms. Since this is so, what need is there to mention not falling into the lower realms if you die with such splendid thoughts [as the three principal aspects of the path]? Although you should absolutely rely upon these special postures, because the result is similar to the cause, if you die within a powerful state of the precious mind of bodhichitta, by attaining this special human body it will definitely awaken quickly your imprints for the path of the Mahayana, and even if you do fall into the lower realms, while you are there you will recall bodhichitta and immediately be liberated from the lower realms, which is similar to the teachings in the *Jataka Tales* as to when [Buddha was born in the hell realms]. For that reason, what need is there to mention that you won't fall into the lower realms if you recall a particularly powerful precious bodhichitta at the moment of your death?

As for becoming an object of worship for migrating beings, including the gods, the *Guide to the Bodhisattva's Way of Life* states:

> I prostrate to whomever has generated
> That precious holy mind
> And go for refuge to those sources of happiness,
> Who respond with happiness to even those who cause harm.

All the buddhas and bodhisattvas have extended such praise more than once.

With regard to how to practice transference of consciousness through the uncommon yoga of mantra, although you don't need [transference of consciousness] if you have attained mastery through your training in the two stages of the path, if you haven't attained such independence you should practice the yoga of transference of consciousness when the signs of death arise; therefore, prior to this you should learn what the signs of death are. Once you do, when they arise you should apply the methods for reversal through "cheating death"[244] rituals. There are numerous teachings on how to recognize the signs [of impending death] in the tantras and texts of the mahasiddhas, such as the *Samvarodaya Tantra*, *Vajradaka Tantra*, the *Chatuhpitha Tantra*, and so forth, which contain ways of identifying

244. Tib. *'chi blu*.

the signs that emerge, such as how to recognize the various signs and shapes, the shadow of your body, and so forth, as well as how to identify the signs that arise in the mind and signs that come through dreams. However, the most important teaching among them all is how to observe the signs of the winds. Therefore, you should learn the teachings in the *Samvarodaya Tantra*, which contains special teachings on how the wind moves from the right to the left nostril during the waxing moon of each month. Once you learn them, and you observe the winds that indicate impending death, you should sincerely apply yourself to cheating death practices and, if despite your efforts, they are not overcome and the signs of death are still definitely appearing, you should practice transference of consciousness by ascertaining the correct time according to the oral instructions you receive from your guru.[245] If you practice transference of consciousness before the time is right, it is a serious misdeed. The *Vajradaka Tantra* states:

> Perform transference when the time comes.
> The wrong time becomes killing the deities;
> By merely killing the deities
> You will burn in hell. Therefore, the signs of death
> Should be learned in earnest from the wise.

The same thing has been stated in numerous tantras and texts of the mahasiddhas.

Once the time has come, the way to practice transference of consciousness has been stated by the previous lamas who have labeled it with the terms "the transference of consciousness of the truth body," "the transference of consciousness of the enjoyment body," and "the transference of consciousness of the emanation body." The meaning is that you should practice visualizing transference of consciousness through meditating on mixing through bringing [death] into the path as the truth body, as well as visualizing a pure land through deity yoga and so forth. With regard to meditating through mixing by bringing [death] into the path as the

---

245. See *The Extremely Secret Dakini of Naropa* (Ithaca, NY: Snow Lion Publications, 2011) for a detailed presentation on transference of consciousness.

truth body, if you have gained experience of the completion stage through previously completing the generation stage, you should actualize the three empties[246] through the stages of the winds withdrawing during death and sustain the meditative equipoise of mixing the mother and son clear lights to the best of your ability.[247] When you arise from that, arise in either the actual enjoyment body at the time of the path, or if you are unable to do that, imagine you arise [as the enjoyment body] and assume rebirth with a special body in the pure dakini land and so on.

If you have no experience in the completion stage and are a person training in the generation stage, you should think, "I shall identify the dissolution of the twenty-five coarse elements at the time of death and sustain my meditation on bliss and emptiness to the best of my ability. Next, when [the minds] of appearance, increase, and near-attainment arise, the clear light will soon dawn," and when those appearances arise, you should place your mind in a state of bliss and emptiness through thoughts of great joy. Next, when the clear light dawns, you should place your mind in a state of bliss and emptiness to the best of your ability. When you arise from that, you should imagine you arise as the primordial protector [Vajradhara]. Next, you should strive to assume a rebirth with a special body for the practice of mantra. Other than being nominally imputed as "transference of consciousness," in actuality they are meditations for bringing the three bodies into the path and mixing.

As for training in the actual transference of consciousness through deity yoga, in addition to appearing in detail in the *Samvarodaya Tantra*, the *Vajradaka*, and *Chatuhpitha Tantra*, they also appear in the *Oral Instructions of Manjushri* of the Jnanapada tradition of Guhyasamaja. This transference of consciousness is highly praised in those tantras. The *Vajradaka Tantra* states:

> Killing a Brahmin every day,
> Performing the five actions of immediate retribution,
> Stealing, pillaging, and even rape
> Will be liberated through this path.

246. These are the three empties associated with the minds of white appearance, red increase, and black near-attainment mentioned earlier.
247. For further details on this practice, see *The Extremely Secret Dakini of Naropa*, 239.

You will not be defiled by these nonvirtues
And will far transcend the faults of samsara.

The same thing also appears in the other tantras such as the *Chatuhpitha Tantra* and so forth. The *Oral Instructions of Manjushri* also states:

Through this ritual any sentient being
Who has committed the five heinous actions and
Out of ignorance has killed Brahmins and so forth
Will not lack any attainment on that account.

Yet once you receive these excellent oral instructions,
By protecting your vows and commitments
There is no doubt you will attain the three bodies.
If you don't attain the three bodies,
You will mainly become a knowledge holder
And accomplish mahamudra through the path.

Thus, this is saying that in dependence upon the yoga of transference of consciousness, although you may be an extremely nonvirtuous person who has committed the five heinous actions and so forth, it will not be possible for you to be harmed by them, you will close the door to rebirth in the lower realms, and you will attain a special body in the happy realms, and with that body you will progress along the path and attain enlightenment.

With regard to how to undertake transference of consciousness, you should practice as explained above and, in particular, you should restore your two higher sets of vows and try to have a completely pure and happy mind without any regrets whatsoever and then make extremely powerful supplications to your guru on the crown of your head. With strong devotion you should repeatedly contemplate the good qualities of the environment and of beings of the pure land to which you wish to transfer your consciousness, such as Sukhavati. Train with a very strong aspiration to quickly go to that pure land. Next, in accordance with the actual explanation of transference of consciousness in the tantras, there are nine doors through which your consciousness can depart; therefore, with the exception of the "golden door" at the crown of your head, you should properly block the other eight doors. You should train in transference of consciousness by opening the golden door. For those who aren't familiar with such practices through routine practice, they can prove to be very difficult at the time of death; therefore, Vajradhara Losang Chökyi Gyaltsen composed commentaries on transference of consciousness entitled *The Hero Engaging in Battle.*[248] Visualize the central channel in the center of your body, an opening at the Brahmin aperture at the crown of your head, and no other opening at any other place. In the very center of your heart your consciousness appears in the aspect of either a deity or a drop. Direct your mind toward either visualization and focus your attention. You should be someone who is capable of practicing transference of consciousness through the force of wind by holding the vase breath. At the very least you should be someone who is capable of practicing transference of consciousness through the force of aspiration; therefore, you should have a very strong aspiration to practice transference of consciousness. Light rays radiate from the heart of the guru [on the crown of your head] as a hook that enters through the Brahmin aperture at the crown of your head and enters into your central channel. Once you visualize your mind as either the deity-body or drop, it is seized by the hook and by combining the [recitation of] the mantra HIK and pulling the winds upward, [your mind] is transferred to the heart of your guru. Next, your consciousness is transferred to Sukhavati! Still, you should learn the essential points of this orally from your guru. If you wish to be transferred to Tushita, you should practice by learning separately the oral instructions of Vajradhara Losang Chökyi Gyaltsen for performing transference of consciousness to that [pure land].

In short, you should think, "I must quickly attain the state of perfect complete enlightenment for the welfare of living beings. For that purpose I shall perfect the yoga of the two stages with this vajra body complete with leisure and endowments. If I must die before I achieve mastery, I will practice the common and uncommon practices for transference of consciousness and attain a body of a knowledge holder in the pure dakini land, or I will travel to another pure land, or I will take a body of leisure and endowments endowed with the three trainings and abide in the pure conduct of celibacy. In dependence upon this, I shall perfect my meditation on the two stages. Guru-deity, please bless my mental continuum that

248. *dPa' bo gyul 'jug.*

I am able to succeed in such practices." With these thoughts recite the verse from the ritual prayer that states:

> If by the time of my death I have not completed the points
>   of the path,
> I seek your blessing to travel to the pure land
> Through the powerful perfect method of the guru's transference
>   of consciousness
> And by perfectly applying the oral instructions of the five forces.

Through making this extremely powerful supplication a stream of five-colored light rays and nectars descends from the bodies of the guru and assembly of deities and enters the body and mind of yourself and all other living beings, whereby the unique obstructions are purified and, in particular, the various realizations are developed in the minds of yourself and all living beings.

How to Pray to Come under the Care of Your Guru throughout All of Your Lives and How to Withdraw the Field of Merit for the Sake of Receiving His Blessings in Your Mental Continuum has two sections:
1. Making Prayers to Be Cared for by Your Guru throughout All of Your Lives and Offering a Torma
2. Withdrawing the Field of Merit for the Sake of Blessing Your Mental Continuum

Making Prayers to Be Cared for by Your Guru throughout All of Your Lives and Offering a Torma

This is revealed in the verse that begins:

> In short, I seek your blessing that throughout every life . . .

Thus, once you have established whatever imprints you can through scanning meditation on the complete path and have earnestly invoked the guru to hold you with his compassion and grant his blessing, if you haven't actualized the complete path in this life, you should set your determination by thinking, "I must attain the state of enlightenment in one life, three lives, seven, or at the very most sixteen. Until that time, may the guru-buddha continuously reveal to me the profound instructions and may there never be any unfavorable conditions, even for an instant. Guru-deity, please grant your blessing that through the force of this I may quickly complete all of the good qualities of the grounds and paths, after which I may quickly attain the state of Vajradhara the Great."

You should also think, "My kind root guru, Tubwang Dorje Chang the Great, although you have already attained enlightenment countless eons ago, still you unceasingly engage in your enlightened actions until samsara is empty without a moment's break. Therefore, in some pure lands you reveal the aspect of passing into the sphere of peace. In some you take rebirth. In some you become ordained. In some you reveal the way to actualize perfect and complete enlightenment and so forth. You perform these simultaneously, and in each and every instant you reveal them in limitless universal pure lands. Please grant your blessings that in no matter which pure land you display the deeds of a completely enlightened being, I may also become the first in your retinue and, as your chief disciple, maintain all the secrets of your body, speech, and mind." With these thoughts, recite the verses from the ritual prayer that state:

> In short, I seek your blessing that throughout every life I
>   may never
> Be separated from you, Protector, but always come under
>   your care,
> Uphold all the secrets of your body, speech, and mind,
> And become your seniormost disciple.
>
> Protector, wherever you manifest as a buddha,
> May I be the first in your retinue and
> May there be the auspiciousness of spontaneously accomplishing
>   without effort
> All of my temporary and ultimate needs and wishes.

Because of this very powerful supplication, an inconceivable stream of nectar descends from the bodies of the guru and assembly of deities. It enters your body and mind, whereby all the negative karma and obscurations you have accumulated since beginningless time, and in particular all of the negative karma and obscurations, together with their imprints that interfere with the commitments of the guru's body, speech, and mind, are all purified. You should imagine that through receiving his blessing you will become his foremost disciple through all of your lives.

Next, at this point you should offer a torma. The torma is used in both sutra and tantra to pacify obstacles and is praised as being very important for accomplishing your desired aims. In particular, in highest yoga tantra and the sadhanas composed by the mahasiddhas it is stated that a torma is absolutely necessary to accomplish any action. The best is to offer a torma at the beginning and end of the session, but if you are not able, you should at least offer it at the end of each session. It is said that if you are unable to offer it at the end of each session, you should definitely offer it at the end of the last session. Whatever torma substance and vessel you use, it should be done according to the ritual of generation and properly offered to mundane and supramundane guests, and it is suitable to be performed according to most highest yoga tantra sadhanas. As for the extensive method, this should be learned in detail through Master Abhyakara's two texts entitled *The Rosary* and *Cluster of Oral Instructions*.

With regard to the uncommon particulars of each personal deity, they should be extracted from their individual tantras and sadhanas. Furthermore, if we take Guhyasamaja as an example, the [way the] inner offering [is blessed] is unique to Guhyasamaja, as is the ritual for generating the torma, together with its visualization; it would be excellent if you took these from the arrangements in the *Subsequent Tantra* and the *Vajramala*. Likewise, you should follow the teachings from the sadhana *The Stages of Yoga*.[249] Each father tantra and mother tantra has its own unique significant points; therefore, if you take something from one sadhana and amend it to others, you will lose the significant points and uncommon unique features; therefore, you shouldn't do this. Thus, if you are abiding in the yoga of Vajrabhairava, you should bless the inner offering and torma offerings according to Yamantaka. You should do the same thing for the rituals of each of the other deities, such as Guhyasamaja.

---

249. *rNal 'byor dag rim*. This is a self-generation sadhana of Guhyasamaja composed by the second Changkya rinpoche, Ngawang Losang Choden.

It is not necessary to invoke the guests of the torma. Once you are abiding in the yoga of Vajrabhairava, it is completely appropriate to offer the torma to all the deities of the four classes of tantra, which is something that you should also learn from the section within each of their sadhanas with regard to how to present the offerings. In these oral instructions the inner offering and offering torma are blessed according to abiding in either the yoga of Heruka, Yamantaka, or Guhyasamaja. You present the torma offering to all the gurus, personal deities, buddhas, bodhisattvas, heroes, dakinis, Dharma protectors, and guardians that you visualized earlier. With regard to the extensive and concise wording for offering the torma, this should be determined by your circumstances. Moreover, there are numerous diverse unique explanations, such as how to offer the torma, generating the guests, and so forth that are influenced by the degree of the practitioner's realizations. However, I am not going to write more on the subject.

Thus, once you offer the torma, you should make supplications that you may perfect your practice and that there not be any obstacles to your practice of mind training as a way of completing the entire body of the path through the yoga of the guru-deity as well as entrusting [the guests of the torma offering] with performing their enlightened actions and so forth.

Withdrawing the Field of Merit for the Sake of Blessing Your Mental Continuum

Recite the verse from the ritual prayer that states:

> Thus, through requesting the supreme guru in this way,
> May you be delighted, come to the crown of my head, bestow
>   your blessing,
> And once again place your radiant feet firmly
> Upon the anthers of the lotus at my heart.

As explained earlier, you present outer, inner, secret, and suchness offerings to Lama Tubwang Dorje Chang and the assembly of deities and make extraordinarily powerful supplications to generate each one of those paths in your mental continuum. Next, you should evoke as much clear appearance of your guru and the assembly of deities as you are able and meditate with extremely powerful faith and devotion, whereby light rays radiate from the heart of your kind root guru, Lama Tubwang Dorje Chang the Great, and strike the limitless peaceful and wrathful deities in his retinue, whereby they sequentially melt into light and dissolve into your kind root guru. Your kind root guru, Lama Tubwang Dorje Chang the Great, is delighted and comes to the crown of your head. He enters your central channel through the crown of your head and descends to the center of your heart, where he dissolves into your mind, whereby the mind of the guru, the mind of the supreme deity, and your mind all mix inseparably and you place your mind in a state of stable divine pride to the best of your ability. It is from within that state that you meditate on either the Ganden mahamudra or the profound yoga of the completion stage. This section also has a special relationship with the practice of withdrawing the field of merit through the "sequential withdrawal of subsequent destruction" during the practice of the completion stage. This is one of the most profound secrets and is the ultimate essential oral instruction for accomplishing union in one life; therefore, you should learn about this in detail orally from your guru.

Thus, this guru yoga contains the complete essential instructions of the paths of sutra and mantra and embodies the practices of the maha-siddhas that are the heart essence of the tantras and are extraordinarily powerful. As I have already explained above, this lineage has come down through a lineage of holy beings who have attained complete realizations of this path that stems from the omniscient Je [Tsongkhapa]. In particular, Mahasiddha Dharmavajra had a direct vision of Conqueror Tsongkhapa the Great and received limitless oral instructions on sutra and tantra and, in particular, this guru yoga with the three nested beings. Mahasiddha Dharmavajra also took this guru yoga as his heart practice and attained the vajra body as the rainbow body. Gyalwa Losang Dondrup [Ensapa] also relied upon this guru yoga and attained the body of union. This was repeatedly stated while the omniscient Panchen Losang Chökyi Gyaltsen Palsangpo was giving the profound commentary to this guru yoga; I heard this directly from the mouth of my guru, Drubpai Wangpo the Great.[250]

250. This is a reference to Drubwang Losang Namgyal (1670–1741).

How to End the Session

If you have created the Lama Chöpa field of merit, once you have withdrawn the field of merit you should recite the *Root Text on the Precious
Oral Lineage of Ganden Mahamudra That Is the Main Path of the Conquerors.*[251]
The way to carry out the visualizations when you are by yourself should
be done as explained earlier, and whether you carry them out alone or
recite them in a group, you should end with *The King of Prayers of Good
Deeds,*[252] the dedication prayers of Guhyasamaja, the prayers of Ganden
mahamudra, and so forth and perform extensive dedication prayers with
a powerful aspiration for your temporary and ultimate wishes. If you are
making concise prayers, you should recite the dedication verses from the
ritual prayer, which state:

> I dedicate the pure virtue that I have created in this way
> So that I might be able to uphold the pure Dharma of scripture
>   and realization,
> And accomplish all the prayers and deeds
> Of all the sugatas and their children of the three times.

> By the force of this in all my lives may I
> Never be separated from the four wheels of the Supreme Vehicle,
> And thus complete the paths of renunciation, bodhichitta,
> Correct view of emptiness, and the two stages.

> Through the virtues I and others have accumulated and will
>   accumulate
> From now until I and others attain enlightenment,
> May there be the auspiciousness of the Venerable Guru's
> Holy form body abiding like an immutable vajra.

> In all my lives may I never be separated from the perfect guru
> Or the glorious enjoyments of the Dharma,

---

251. *dGa' ldan bka' rgyud rin po che'i bka' srol phyag chen rtsa ba rgyal ba'i bzhung lam.* This is the
famous root text on Ganden mahamudra composed by the First Panchen Lama.
252. *bZang po spyod pa.*

And by completing the good qualities of the grounds and paths
May I quickly attain the state of Vajradhara.[253]

This dedication prayer composed by Vajradhara Losang Chökyi Gyalt-sen is extremely vast. Although there are limitless ways of performing dedications and prayers within all the limitless teachings from the sutras, the supreme among them all is the *King of Prayers*, which contains all the essential points of the prayers, such as the million prayers of the buddhas and bodhisattvas, which are all in the *King of Prayers*. The concise essential point of all the prayers in the *King of Prayers* is as follows:

> Just as the hero Manjushri and likewise Samantabhadra
> Realize the nature of reality,
> To follow their perfect example
> I dedicate my training and all of this virtue.

> I thoroughly dedicate all of my roots of virtue
> With the dedication that is praised as supreme
> By all the conquerors of the three times:
> For the sake of performing these noble deeds.

Both of these verses are taught in Master Chandrakirti's autocommentary to *Entering the Middle Way*. These oral instructions contain the essential points condensed from these two verses that are the heart of the *King of Prayers*, which are revealed in our verse that states:

> I dedicate the pure virtues I have created
> So that I might be able to uphold the pure Dharma of scripture
>   and realization,
> And accomplish all the prayers and deeds
> Of all the sugatas and their children of the three times.

Also, the omniscient Je [Tsongkhapa] stated:

---

253. These four lines do not appear in either the ganachakra or Lama Chöpa ritual texts. They appear as the final verse in Lama Tsongkhapa's lamrim poem entitled "The Foundation of All Good Qualities."

> The dedications of the buddhas and bodhisattvas that are like
>   streams of the Ganges
> Are contained within the prayer to uphold the holy Dharma.
> Therefore, whatever roots of virtue I have accumulated,
> I also dedicate them all for the sake of propagating the teachings
>   of the Buddha.

> Contemplate this method and develop a good aspiration
> Through the great kindness of the treasury of wisdom,
>   the venerable guru.

As this states, among all the dedication prayers, the prayer to uphold the holy Dharma is praised as supreme. These oral instructions also state:

> I dedicate the pure virtues I have created
> So that I might be able to uphold the pure Dharma of scripture
>   and realization.

This is making a dedication prayer to uphold the holy Dharma.

Also, there is no dedication prayer whatsoever that is superior to collecting all scriptures of sutra and tantra in one individual as the causal factors for enlightenment and likewise accomplishing them. This is a dedication prayer that delights the buddhas and bodhisattvas from the very depths of their hearts.

As for how it is composed in these oral instructions, it states:

> By the force of this in all my lives may I
> Never be separated from the four wheels of the Supreme
>   Vehicle,
> And thus complete the paths of renunciation, bodhichitta,
> Correct view of emptiness, and the two stages.

The "four wheels" are explained by Nagarjuna when he states:

> Abiding in a land that is conducive [to practice],
> Relying upon a holy being,

Having merit through making prayers of excellent nature—
You are empowered by these four wheels.[254]

Therefore, those intelligent beings should have stable faith and confidence in each and every vajra word of Vajradhara Losang Chökyi Gyaltsen as elucidating the core of all the sutras and tantras.

How to Engage in the Session Breaks

The text of this oral instruction states, "Whatever appears to you throughout each of your daily actions should be seen as the manifestation of gods and goddesses that are the nature of bliss and emptiness and so forth while performing the yoga unifying the generation and completion stage. Also, you should strive in your practice inseparably with the lamrim or the practices for training the mind that have the complete pith instructions of Mahayana mind training."

Furthermore, while remaining in a state of continuously recalling renunciation, bodhichitta, and the correct view of emptiness, which are the essence of the path to enlightenment, you restrain the doors of your senses, eat the proper amount of food, and strive in the yoga of not sleeping but when you do, do so properly, and strive in the yogas of eating and washing as explained in the commentaries on the lamrim. Once you establish a solid foundation of the proper ways to undertake these practices according to the common path, you should train in the uncommon methods of practice for the session breaks according to highest yoga tantra. When your body and mind become tired through striving sincerely in the common path and the two stages of the uncommon path, you rest and continue with the yoga of reinvigoration. Regarding this practice, the *Guhyasamaja Root Tantra* states:

You should analyze the mandala about one
Hand-span above your crown.

---

254. Thus, the four wheels are (1) a conducive environment, (2) meeting a holy being, (3) making excellent prayers, and (4) having extensive merit.

Once you imagine an OM in its center,
All five nectars should descend.

Through this yoga of the vajra
You will become radiant in an instant
And your body and mind will abide in bliss;
You should have no doubts that this will come to pass.

In accordance with this, while visualizing yourself clearly as the deity, imagine that in the sky, about one hand-span from above the crown of your head, is a VA from which emerges a moon mandala with every aspect the nature of light. Below the moon mandala emerges a white inverted OM the nature of light. Imagine the moon and OM are radiating light to the ten directions, which invokes all the buddhas and bodhisattvas in the ten directions in the aspect of the fathers and mothers of the five buddha families, which dissolve into the OM and moon. An immeasurable stream of nectar descends from that and enters through the crown of your head whereby your entire deity body is filled from the crown of your head to the soles of your feet. The father and mother buddhas bestow empowerment and you receive their blessing, whereby your body and mind develop an extraordinary bliss. The strength of your body and mind increases and your life, merit, and good qualities of scripture and realization increase and you receive the attainment of immortality while you hold [the winds] in embrace through the vase breath for a short while. If you meditate continuously in this way, the strength of your body and mind will increase and you will not develop gray hair, wrinkles, and so forth. You will have a youthful appearance, the strength of your virtuous practices will develop, your body will not become tired, you will have a long life, and so forth. Moreover, if you digest your food a little and then bring the vase breath down to the navel while holding it there for a little while, it will help to digest your food and you will not develop illnesses. Through long familiarity with that you will receive numerous benefits, such as a long life and so forth. These are the means of resting and reinvigorating your body and mind while carrying them out in conjunction with your virtuous practices.

The primary practice during the session breaks is to restrain the doors of your senses through the uncommon practices. For this you should stop ordinary appearances and conceptions while remaining in a state of divine pride as Vajradhara Father and Mother as the [lord] of the sole lineage of the great secret. Train yourself in perceiving whatever objects of the six senses appear as bliss and emptiness appearing as deities. Furthermore, from the outset you should train in perceiving whatever appears as all being the manifestation of emptiness. Once you are well acquainted with that, you should train in perceiving all objects that appear as manifestations of bliss and emptiness appearing in the aspect of deities. Regarding this method of training in perceiving whatever appears as all appearing as deities, the *Guhyasamaja Root Tantra* states:

> Through mantra always meditate on
> Forms, sounds, scents, and so on as the deity.
> As an alternative to meditating on that,
> Meditate on them as aspects that accord with their lineage.

Thus, you should train in perceiving the various objects that appear in the aspect of deities by seeing whatever forms that appear are all Vairochana, whatever sounds that appear are all Ratnasambhava, whatever scents that appear are all Amitabha, whatever tastes that appear are all Amoghasiddhi, and whatever tactile objects that appear are all Akshobya. Although they also have an inner classification as the hundred lineages and so forth that you train in, because I am concerned this will become too verbose I am not to write more on the subject.

Further, sometimes once you perceive whatever objects appear to your six senses as all being offering goddesses, you visualize yourself as Vajradhara and imagine you are enjoying them as offerings. Furthermore, whatever forms there are all appear as Rupavajra goddesses, whatever sounds there are all appear as Shaptavajra goddesses, all scents appear as Ghandarvavajra goddesses, all tactile objects appear as Sparshavajra goddesses, and all cognitive objects appear as Dharmadhatuvajra goddesses. Having perceived them in this way, and with the clear appearance of yourself as Vajradhara, imagine that they function as offerings for the six senses, such as the eyes and so forth, which nurtures and increases even further your experience of bliss and emptiness. These methods are the heart practice of the mahasiddhas and are the heart of highest yoga tantra, which is even more secret than the greatest secrets. The omniscient Je [Tsongkhapa] has repeatedly stated that although you may not have such insights, after receiving a highest yoga tantra empowerment you should make supplications and prayers to succeed in such a profound path as this.

Moreover, you should prevent all of your daily actions, such as walking, lying down, and sleeping, from becoming ordinary by transforming them into the path through the skillful means of highest yoga tantra. For this method as well, while remaining in the state of stable divine pride of being the lord of the sole lineage of the great secret [Vajradhara], you should transform whatever physical daily actions you undertake, such as walking, lying down, and sitting, and transform them into mudras to the best of your ability and train in manifesting all verbal expressions as the mantra to the best of your ability. Once you become familiar with this process, when you reach higher stages of the path all of your physical and verbal actions will actually transform into mantra and mudra. The *Adorning the Essence of the Vajra Tantra* relates this to Guhyasamaja when it states:

> If you abide in a state of equanimity,
> Whatever bodily movement you make,
> And whatever words perfectly flow,
> Will be transformed into mantra and mudra.

With regard to the uncommon yoga of eating, whatever food and drink you partake of should all be blessed as the five meats and five nectars and offered to yourself as the deity. As it states in the concise sadhana, you should cleanse and bless your tongue, throat, and heart and imagine that your hands are the funnel and ladle and your food and drink are the burning substances, which you partake of as an inner burnt offering. While you are partaking of them, you imagine that the main portion of your food and drink is offered to the guru-deity in the center of your heart. If you practice in this way, you will purify receiving alms and you will not incur a karmic debt and, instead, whatever food and drink you enjoy will become a means of amassing a great collection of merit. These and many other benefits have been taught in the tantras and texts of the mahasiddhas. Likewise, when you put on your clothes they should also be offered to the guru-deity. In the three lower classes of tantra these are called "the yoga of the three enjoyments." These are common to all four classes of tantra. Here, we should carry these out by learning how to do the yogas in conjunction with the generation and completion stages unique to highest yoga tantra. When you become familiar with that, something like eating and drinking, which would have otherwise been meaningless and have many shortcomings, will become highly meaningful by transforming them through the path of skillful means. Those serious practitioners who wish to practice should take these important pith instructions of Vajradhara to heart.

With regard to the uncommon yoga of sleeping, as appearances are withdrawn through the dissolution of the twenty-five coarse elements you should imagine that you abide in the state of the clear light of great bliss and meditate on mixing at the time of sleep. As for the uncommon yoga of rising, you should imagine that the four heart-yoginis urge you to rise from the clear light in the body of the deity through singing vajra songs, the sound of *damarus*, and so forth. For the uncommon yoga of rising you should imagine that goddesses such as Lochana and so forth as well as Rupavajra goddesses and so forth sing auspicious songs and the sound of music bestows empowerment with the vase water. In addition to these practices for the session breaks mentioned above, you should rely on mindfulness during the session breaks and restrain your three doors in general, and in particular rely upon mindfulness with regard to your commitments and vows of mantra. With that as a foundation, you should understand how to apply that to all the other limbs as well. Forsaking your high regard for maintaining your commitments and vows and merely working on clear appearance and divine pride will be like throwing away the root and hoping for the branches and you will make little to no progress. Although you may be careful to perfectly protect your commitments and vows, if your commitments become broken and defiled because of numerous afflictive emotions and so forth, you should immediately make a sincere effort to restore them. Furthermore, if you are affected by a root downfall, you should first make confession and then supplicate your guru and receive another empowerment. If that is not possible due to circumstances, you should restore them through self-initiation. There are numerous methods taught in the tantras and texts of the mahasiddhas that explain how to restore the other defiled commitments through practices of eating, protecting, and reliance. You can also restore them through accomplishing and presenting offerings to a mandala; restore them through a feast of heroes; restore them through the torma ritual; and purify them through reading profound scriptures, such as the perfection of wisdom sutras. You can purify negative karma and downfalls in dependence upon [ritual] bathing and reciting profound mantras and *dharanis*. You can purify them through the ritual of *Summoning and Separating from the Lower Realms.*[255] You can purify them through the burnt offering of Vajradaka. You can purify negative karma and obscurations, as well as restore your commitments, through meditation and recitation of Vajrasattva. You can restore and purify through the recitation of Samayavajra. There have been numerous means of purification taught.

Among all of these, the last three, as well as purification through accomplishing and making offerings to a mandala, are the most important. If you recite a hundred thousand of the hundred-syllable mantra through the meditation and recitation of Vajrasattva, you will be able to purify even root downfalls, and if you recite it twenty-one times each day, you will prevent your negative karma and downfalls from increasing. With regard to the meditation and recitation of Samayavajra, in the *Guhyasamaja Root Tantra* as well as numerous texts it states, "the tathagata Amoghasiddhi as the deity Samayavajra," "the deity of summoning commitments," and "there is no doubt about accomplishing the commitments," which reveal that it is extremely high praise for this deity to purify defiled commitments. With regard to the way in which to practice the recitation of Samayavajra, in the heart of yourself appearing clearly as the deity is a variegated lotus and moon mandala upon which is a HA, from which emerges a sword with its handle marked by a HA. That completely transforms into Samayavajra, who has a green-colored body, three faces, and six arms while embracing the mother. His three places are blessed [by the three syllables]. The wisdom beings are invoked and dissolved. He is bestowed empowerment, and the father is sealed with Akshobya and the mother by Amoghasiddhi. At his heart is a moon upon which is a variegated vajra, in the center of which is a green HA surrounded by the mantra rosary.

255. *Ngan 'gro dgug bral.*

Recite the mantra OM AH PRAJNA DHRIK HA HUM as many times as you are able, such as a hundred times, a thousand times, and so forth. A stream of nectar descends from the mantra and seed syllable, whereby your entire body is filled. All of your defiled commitments are expelled and drip out through the doors of your senses and all of your pores. Your body becomes clear and luminous and the nature of light and you are satiated by an uncontaminated great bliss. You should practice the burnt offering of Vajradaka by observing how it is practiced in accordance with the lineage.

Moreover, you should sincerely apply yourself to accumulating merit and purifying negative karma through numerous avenues. You should examine the scriptures of our teacher and their commentaries that reveal the essential points of the path for these instructions and listen to the instructions repeatedly from a spiritual master who can teach this path, and you should always associate with special companions who practice this path. It is extremely important that you forsake bad companions that have no faith in this path and who have done away with their commitments to the guru of the close lineage of blessing. You should sincerely strive to assemble all the causes for generating this path in your mental continuum.

Geshe Dolpa said, "In your spare time accumulate merit and purify negative karma and sincerely contemplate with perseverance. If you do, although you may think, 'I will not generate [realizations] in a hundred years,' you will generate them because there are no composite phenomena that remain static." When Protector Manjushri gave these instructions to the omniscient Je [Tsongkhapa] he said, "You should supplicate the guru by making him inseparable from the supreme deity, strive sincerely in accumulating a vast collection of merit, and analyze the texts of the great pioneers. Once you combine these three, you should practice for a prolonged period of time." In accordance with this, the former holy beings of this oral lineage have undertaken their practice in the same way. Therefore, those who wish to uphold the excellent tradition of the Ganden Hearing Lineage should practice this way and without placing their efforts in anything else, and carry on with the [example they set] with their lives. The followers of some Tibetan meditators have claimed, "Other than taming my mind through practice, it is inappropriate to engage in conceptual elaborations, such as looking at scriptures and so forth." With regard to these proclamations, these are not the supreme instructions in the authoritative texts of the great charioteers that are the heart of the conqueror's teachings and are merely fabrications from the teachings of non-Buddhists. Therefore, such [statements] are not in this oral lineage of the omniscient Je [Tsongkhapa] and are wrong views.

Moreover, those practicing the essence of these oral instructions should train in regarding whatever appears as all being the manifestations of the three secrets of the guru-deity, and whatever actions one undertakes should be done with the guru resting in the center of your heart as a witness while you should try your best to transform all objects that appear into offerings to the guru and so forth. This will then become an aid to your guru yoga that you carry out during the four actual sessions.

Thus, here is the concise meaning of these extensive explanations on the oral instructions of the Lama Chöpa ritual in accordance with the instructions that are vajra words composed by Vajradhara Losang Chökyi Gyaltsen. First, you must absolutely gain experience of training your mind in the common path in dependence upon a holy protector. Next, moved by great confidence through your great compassion, so that you can quickly become enlightened, you receive a completely pure empowerment. Once you establish a solid foundation of protection for your commitments and vows that you promised to maintain during the empowerment, you should meditate on the quick path of mantra and take guru yoga as the life of the path. Therefore, from within a particularly virtuous mind you most certainly should subdue your mind through the common and uncommon refuge and bodhichitta. Next, meditate on the yoga of the first stage. Next, bless the environment and its beings as well as the offerings. Next, visualize the field of merit and imagine it is the nature embodying all Three Jewels, through which you offer the seven-limb prayer and the mandala. At that time, while remaining in that state and viewing everything that appears as being the nature of bliss and emptiness, you should establish special imprints that come from repeatedly contemplating the definitive meaning unique to highest yoga tantra. Next, you make supplications to your kind root guru, who is kind in the three ways and embodies all three objects of refuge, and by making such extremely powerful supplications a hundred times, a thousand times, and so on you contemplate his good qualities, and by recalling his great kindness you make powerful supplications for a long time and then receive the blessing of the four empowerments. Next, you should summon the guru's mind by reciting his name mantra for a long time. Next, while remaining in a state of meditation on the guru and assembly of deities, you should engage in scanning meditation on the complete body of the path of both sutra and tantra. Begin by establishing the root of the path by developing extremely powerful faith and devotion through scanning meditation on the proper way to rely upon the spiritual master as the root of the path. Next, you should turn your mind away from thoughts of this life by contemplating the great value of this life of leisure and endowment, how difficult it is to obtain, and how it doesn't last for long. Next, sincerely apply yourself to the welfare of your future lives by contemplating going for refuge and karma and its effects. Next, you should turn your mind away from all of samsara by contemplating the general sufferings of samsara. Train in the means of liberation through the path of the three higher trainings. Next, sincerely apply yourself with whatever human strength and capacity you possess to generate the precious mind of bodhichitta that cherishes others more than yourself and is the root and life-pillar of all the paths of the Mahayana. Next, motivated by that precious mind [of bodhichitta], train in the six perfections, which are the embodiment of all the essential instructions of the vast activities of the bodhisattva's deeds and, in particular, make extremely powerful prayers to be able to train in the profound view of the Middle Way and to quickly generate it in your mental continuum. Next, you should become a suitable vessel for meditating on the path of mantra through a perfectly pure empowerment. Having become a proper vessel, once you establish your pure commitments and vows as the foundation, you should train in the yoga of the first stage that serves to ripen your roots of virtue for developing the completion stage in its entirety. Next, you should make extremely powerful prayers to be able to train sequentially in the five stages of the path up to the union and to be able to generate those paths quickly in your mental continuum.

With these stages of the path the jewel-like disciple has a complete and unmistaken method for attaining enlightenment in one short life of this degenerate age. Even if you are not such a supreme disciple, you should establish as many imprints as you can for the complete path and make very earnest prayers. The great pioneer Arya Asanga has repeatedly stated that you should train in the entire body of the path without ever being satisfied by merely the fine branches of the path. In particular, Glorious Atisha and Conqueror Tsongkhapa both share the same intention that you train in the complete path. Drom Rinpoche said, "It is my guru's tradition and no other that knows how to bring all the teachings within a four-sided path," which means that Jowo Atisha knows how to train in the complete body of the path, and it is solely through his kindness that these teachings have come to Tibet. This aspiration was shared by the omniscient Je [Tsongkhapa] and is repeatedly stated in Je Rinpoche's own teachings. The *Lamp Illuminating the Five Stages* states:

> With regard to practicing, once you develop a good understanding of the entire body of the path through the teachings on the path from the proper reliance upon your spiritual master up to the resultant union, this contains the layout of the entire basis for progressing along the path, making it different from other [incomplete paths].

The *Great Exposition on the Stages of the Path of Mantra* also states:

> All of the teachings in their entirety are covered, from the initial training in the path up to how to actualize the final result. Therefore, if your mental continuum becomes fit through initially training your mind in the common path, strive to please your guru, and once you recognize you are capable of practicing, you should take the commitments and vows in dependence upon the profound path of a completely pure empowerment. Next, you should hold as extremely precious the three types of vows that include those [taken] during [the empowerment] as well as others you have taken. Once you have established a proper foundation through properly protecting [your vows and commitments], you should meditate on the first stage through the yoga of the four sessions, which functions to ripen your mental continuum for develop-

ing special realizations of the completion stage. Next, if you accomplish the body of union in dependence upon the special stages of the completion stage, you will have assembled the causal factors for complete enlightenment within a single person that contain all the essential points of sutra and tantra. Once you have gained certainty in that, you will uphold the complete teachings of the Buddha and you will be capable of propagating them to others as well.

The *Songs of Spiritual Experience* states:

> You need both supreme paths of the Mahayana,
> Namely the causal and the resultant.
> Therefore, once you have generated the common path,
> Rely upon a protector as a skilled captain
> And enter into the great ocean of tantra.
> Having entered, rely upon the complete oral instructions
> And make this life of leisure and endowments meaningful.
> The venerable guru practiced in this way;
> You who seek liberation should do the same.

Therefore, although these teachings that were received by the omniscient Je [Tsongkhapa] were taught in the past, there are no teachings superior to these. Therefore, those with intelligence should develop conviction from the depths of their hearts for the oral instructions of Vajradhara Losang Chökyi Gyaltsen that are the heart essence of the omniscient Je [Tsongkhapa] and contain the complete body of the paths of sutra and tantra. These oral instructions also received high praise from Vajradhara Losang Chökyi Gyaltsen himself when he stated, "If you are going to practice this yoga on a daily basis, you will be practicing the essence of all sutra and tantra teachings, which will become the stable root of all prosperity and well-being in this life." And [the colophon to Lama Chöpa states]:

> Churning the sea of milk of sutra and tantra's sacred
> Oral instructions with the intellect of Mount Meru,

The pitcher's nectar of unprecedented eloquent explanations
Is assembled as well-written verses accomplishing the fortunate's
    spiritual life.

This [commentary] is filled by the all-devout disciples as
    a lamp that
Dispels all the darkness in their hearts and is
Also a hook that quickly summons all the
Mundane and supramundane perfections.

Thus, this is stating that [the teachings of Lama Chöpa] embody the essential instructions of all the sutra and tantra, and if you practice with an understanding of these key instructions, you will accomplish the practices of all the sutras and tantras and this is the supreme method that leads you to the Buddha-ground much more quickly than even the quickest practices. At the very least, you should sincerely strive with the prayers of the stages of this path. The *Explanatory Tantra Vajramala* states:

The yogi should strive sincerely in this.

And Jnanapada's text the *Oral Instructions of Manjushri* states:

The practitioner should put all their strength into
This supreme secret of the highest secret
By at the very least practicing through prayer.

When you train in these complete paths, you will develop a
strong desire to attain the higher paths when you practice the
lower paths. Also, when you listen to the higher, you develop
a strong desire to accomplish the lower.

Moreover, it is stated, "When you practice [Lama Chöpa] you should complete it through examining and analyzing the Kadam mind training, and you should begin by purifying whichever afflictive emotion is the strongest."

Those with discriminating wisdom should practice once they have repeatedly examined these teachings. Furthermore, if you have little faith in your spiritual master, you will have severed the root of all prosperity and well-being, whereby you will not make any progress in your virtuous endeavors no matter how hard you try; therefore, you should make extremely powerful supplications through recalling his good qualities and his kindness and recite this guru yoga with great diligence. Also, when, because of your powerful craving for the things of this life, you have strong attachment to your relatives, country, friends, companions, siblings, food, drink, and so forth, you should primarily meditate with great diligence on this precious human life of leisure and endowments and on impermanence and try your very best to overcome craving for the things of this life. When you are overcome by your craving for the things of this life, it is because you are not remembering your future lives, whereby you will have no desire to practice Dharma, you will not develop sincere faith, you will not develop a mind of faith in the objects of refuge, and if you do not develop a wholehearted conviction in cause and effect and the acceptance and abandonment of actions, you will have no way of developing the higher good qualities. At times such as these, you should create as many imprints as possible through engaging in scanning meditation at the very least so that although you may meditate on the higher subjects, you will not mentally abandon them, and you absolutely must make prayers to generate each one of [those realizations] in your mental continuum. Through this you will not fall sway to the path of appearances and bias. Once you train your mind in the complete path, you will have [in your mental continuum] numerous profound points of great importance that are necessary for the practitioner. You should learn them in detail orally from your spiritual master.

With a method such as this you should carry out this practice on guru yoga that combines the complete body of the path in either four or six sessions. At the very least you should do it once [a day] and evoke some experience that will transform your mind, which will then become the supreme method for extracting the essence of your life of leisure and endowments.

Thus, you should undertake this practice of precious teaching of the Ganden Hearing Lineage and propagate it to other fortunate beings.

Colophon

The foremost incomparable Shakyamuni, who is the sole refuge and protector of beings during the age of strife, who is praised like an incomparable white lotus in limitless pure lands,

Glorious Vajradhara the Pervasive Lord, every part of your body is all the mandalas of the four classes of tantra;

Losang Drakpa, the king of the Dharma of the gentle protector [Manjushri] that is a lamp for the teachings as factors of enlightenment, who is the sole embodiment of the exalted wisdom of all the infinite conquerors,

May you eternally sit upon the anthers of the lotus of my heart with your feet radiating white light in the form of the supreme guru who embodies all the limitless conquerors. In the bottomless ocean of sutra and tantra

It is difficult to see even a portion of the jewel of profound meaning
With a blinded mind and inferior training.
How can someone like me find the jewel of the noble path?

Like a weak bee trying to stir up a great
Treasure from the water by fluttering his feeble wings,
A foolish feeble being like me has attempted to compose a text
Of profound teachings based on the scholars' commentaries.

Just as the sound of Dharma arises from the
Mindless wish-fulfilling tree through the blessings of the conqueror,
A few ordinary gods and men also abide in the profound [teachings]
And carry out discussions that emerge from the teachings
     of the conqueror.

From Palden Yeshe, the radiant light and blessing and speech
Of the day-maker of the teachings,[256]

256. Palden Yeshe is the third Panchen Lama. Although there is an attempt by the Chinese government to extend the lineage of the Panchen Lamas by adding some of the previous lives

Emerges the flower of the Hearing Lineage's oral instructions
And the foliage of scripture and realization bloom.

The thousand petals of the complete path blossom
As the wish-fulfilling tree of eloquence
In the joyous garden for the bees seeking liberation
And produces a beautiful ornament for the pleasure garden
    of the muni's teachings.

Now the collection of Tibetan bees with clear minds
Drinks this essence of nectar of the Hearing Lineage,
Their voices humming with a thousand eloquent melodies,
As a vast treasure that extracts the essence of the ear in all
    directions.

Although I supplicated the guru-deity for a long time
With confidence in the teachings and stainless reasoning
Combined with perfect analysis,
If I erred, I make confession to the guru-deity.

Although I am an inferior infant who has become crazed by
    a mistaken path,
While I have not been forsaken by my compassionate father
    and mother as
The guru and assembly of deities, the great treasures of compassion,
Have cleansed me of my faults together with their causes.

Although I have met such a perfect and complete
Unmistaken path as this, still I am attached to this life.
The compassionate guru sees this heartless being that I am
And blesses me so that my life may come to have higher meaning.

---

of the first Panchen Lama, Losang Chökyi Gyaltsen, to the list, throughout the history of the
Ganden Hearing Lineage the lineage of the Panchen Lamas begins with Losang Chökyi Gyaltsen.

What use are the activities of this life when it
Will be difficult to meet an excellent path such as this in
   a future life?
Without becoming distracted, may I perfect my practice in one life
In the isolated forests of mantra taught by the conqueror.

Through whatever perfectly pure merit I accumulate
By striving like a conch and lotus in this method,
May I endure in sustaining my old mothers with kindness
And ripen and liberate them through this noble path.

For as long as whatever treasures that exist in this world
Are illuminated by the day-maker,
May I perceive the appearance of this noble path
That liberates countless beings through these excellent teachings.

May the oath-bound sons who have heard numerous teachings,
Quick-acting Mahakala, Kalarupa, and the Lord of Secrets [Vajrapani],
As well as the collection of heroes and dakinis of the three places
Accomplish their enlightened actions to accomplish this Dharma
   without remaining idle.

May there be the auspiciousness of the sutra and tantra
Teachings of Losang Dorje Chang spreading in
Every direction as the foundation for all benefit and happiness
And establish all beings in bliss.

This completes the commentary on Lama Chöpa entitled "A Treasury of
Oral Instructions from the Hearing Lineage Revealing the Innermost
Secret." The holy guide of the deities, including all beings, the lord of the
lineage and all mandalas, the omniscient Panchen Jetsun Losang Palden
Yeshe Palsangpo gave me the command to compose this by stating, "You
must compose an extensive commentary on Lama Chöpa entitled *Inseparable Bliss and Emptiness* that is the essence of the oral instructions of
the Ensa Hearing Lineage that reveals the essential oral instructions." In
accordance with his command I regarded this injunction as a supreme

offering of practice and received it on the crown of my head, and I joyously accepted the words of the foremost being. This Dharma comes from the holy guru, who has attained supreme attainments in dependence upon this path. I, Gelong Yeshe Gyaltsen, based this commentary on the oral instructions that I received from the mouth of my holy guru. The primary sources for these oral instructions are the root and explanatory tantras of Guhyasamaja and the texts of the mahasiddhas as well as the teaching of the omniscient Je [Tsongkhapa] that I examined in detail, which is called *Subduing All in the Ways of Faith*. It was composed in the year of the Fire Female Pig during the waxing moon on the day of the second conqueror [Tsongkhapa] in the Tibetan district Mangyul in the isolated forest in the mountains called Tashi Samten Ling.

Outline of the Commentary

1. An Explanation of the Source of These Instructions
2. An Explanation of the Greatness of These Instructions
3. How to Practice the Actual Instructions

How to Practice the Actual Instructions has two sections:
1. How to Engage in the Actual Session
2. How to Engage in the Session Breaks

How to Engage in the Actual Session has three sections:
1. The Preliminaries
2. The Actual Session
3. How to End the Session

The Preliminaries has two sections:
1. The General Preliminaries
2. The Extraordinary Preliminaries

The General Preliminaries has two sections:
1. How to Correct Your Motivation
2. How to Go for Refuge and Generate Bodhichitta

The Extraordinary Preliminaries has three sections:
1. Generating Yourself as the Deity
2. Purifying the World and Its Beings
3. Blessing the Offerings

Blessing the Offerings has two sections:
1. Blessing the Inner Offering
2. Blessing the Other Offering Substances

Blessing the Inner Offering has four sections:
1. Clearing
2. Purifying
3. Generating
4. Blessing

The Actual Session has four sections:
1. Meditating on the Assembly of Guru-Deities in the Field of Merit
2. Presenting Them with the Offerings of the Seven Limbs and the Mandala
3. Making Supplications by Way of Your Great Faith and Devotion
4. Training the Mind and Receiving Blessings by Way of Scanning Meditation on the Complete Body of the Path of Sutra and Tantra

Meditating on the Assembly of Guru-Deities in the Field of Merit has two sections:
1. The Actual Way to Visualize the Assembly of Guru-Deities
2. The Way to Invoke the Wisdom Beings and Make Them Inseparable

Presenting Them with the Offerings has two sections:
1. Contemplating the Reasons for the Greatness of Lama Chöpa
2. The Actual Way of Presenting Offerings to the Guru [and Assembly of Deities]

The Actual Way of Presenting Offerings to the Guru [and Assembly of Deities] has three sections:
1. Making Prostrations
2. Presenting Offerings
3. How to Perform the Remaining Limbs

Making Prostrations has five sections:

1. Making Praises and Prostrations by Seeing the Guru as the Complete Enjoyment Body
2. Making Praises and Prostrations by Seeing the Guru as the Emanation Body
3. Making Praises and Prostrations by Seeing the Guru as the Truth Body
4. Making Praises and Prostrations by Seeing the Guru as the Nature Embodying All Three Jewels
5. Making Praises and Prostrations to All the Buddhas and Bodhisattvas in the Ten Directions by Seeing Them as Emanations of the Guru

The Way of Presenting Offerings to the Guru and Assembly of Deities has five sections:

1. Outer Offerings Related to the Vase Empowerment
2. Inner Offering Related to the Secret Empowerment
3. Secret Offering Related to the Wisdom Empowerment
4. Suchness Offering Related to the Word Empowerment
5. The Way to Offer Medicine, Oneself as a Servant, and Uphold the Vows

Outer Offerings Related to the Vase Empowerment has five sections:

1. Offering the Four Waters
2. Offering the Close Enjoyment Offerings
3. Offering the Objects of Desire
4. Offering the Mandala
5. Offering Your Practice

Confession and the Remaining Limbs has five sections:

1. How to Perform Confession
2. How to Rejoice
3. How to Request Them to Turn the Wheel of Dharma
4. How to Request Them Not to Pass into Nirvana
5. How to Perform Dedication

Making Supplications by Way of Your Great Faith and Devotion has four sections:

1. How to Make Supplications through Contemplating the Faults and Benefits and Evoking His Mental Continuum through Reciting His Name Mantra
2. How to Make Supplications through Recollecting His Good Qualities and Kindness
3. How to Make Supplications through Recollecting His Outer, Inner, Secret, and Suchness Qualities
4. How to Make the Supplication of Planting the Stake and Taking the Four Empowerments of Concentration

How to Make Supplications through Recollecting His Good Qualities and Kindness has two sections:

1. Making Supplications by Training in Faith as the Root by Contemplating His Good Qualities
2. Making Supplications through Recalling His Kindness

Making Supplications by Training in Faith as the Root by Contemplating His Good Qualities has three sections:

1. Making Supplications by Contemplating the Good Qualities of Your Guru as Explained in the Vinaya
2. Making Supplications by Contemplating the Good Qualities of Your Guru as Explained in the Common Mahayana
3. Making Supplications by Contemplating the Good Qualities of Your Guru as Explained in the Vajrayana

How to Make Supplications through Recollecting His Outer, Inner, Secret, and Suchness Qualities has four sections:

1. How to Make Supplications by Proclaiming His Outer Qualities
2. How to Make Supplications by Proclaiming His Inner Qualities
3. How to Make Supplications by Proclaiming His Secret Qualities
4. How to Make Supplications by Proclaiming His Qualities of Suchness

Training the Mind and Receiving Blessings by Way of Scanning Meditation on the Complete Body of the Path of Sutra and Tantra has two sections:
1. The Way to Rely upon the Spiritual Master as the Basis of the Path
2. How to Train the Mind through Such Reliance

How to Train the Mind through Such Reliance has two sections:
1. How to Train the Mind in the Common Path
2. How to Train the Mind in the Uncommon Path of the Vajrayana

How to Train the Mind in the Common Path has three sections:
1. How to Train the Mind in the Path Common to a Being of Small Capacity
2. How to Train the Mind in the Path Common to a Being of Medium Capacity
3. How to Train the Mind in the Path Common to a Being of Great Capacity

How to Train the Mind in the Path Common to a Being of Small Capacity has two sections:
1. Generating a Mind Striving for a Future Life in the World
2. An Explanation of the Method for Happiness in a Future Life in the World

How to Train the Mind in the Path Common to a Being of Medium Capacity has two sections:
1. Generating a Mind Striving for Liberation
2. How to Train in the Path Leading to Liberation

How to Train the Mind in the Path Common to a Being of Great Capacity has two sections:
1. How to Generate Bodhichitta
2. How to Train in the Deeds [of a Bodhisattva] following the Generation of Bodhichitta

How to Generate Bodhichitta has four sections:
1. How to Generate Great Compassion, Which Is the Root of the Mahayana
2. An Extensive Explanation of How to Meditate on Equalizing and Exchanging Self with Others according to the Seven-Point Mind Training
3. How to Meditate on Superior Intention and Bodhichitta
4. How to Take the Vows of Aspiring Bodhichitta and Engaging Bodhichitta

How to Train in the Deeds [of a Bodhisattva] following the Generation of Bodhichitta has two sections:
1. How to Train in the General Deeds of a Bodhisattva
2. How to Train in the Profound View of the Middle Way in Particular

How to Train in the General Deeds of a Bodhisattva has six sections:
1. How to Practice the Perfection of Generosity
2. How to Practice the Perfection of Moral Discipline
3. How to Practice the Perfection of Patience
4. How to Practice Enthusiastic Perseverance
5. How to Meditate on the Perfection of Concentration
6. How to Attain the Perfection of Wisdom

How to Attain the Perfection of Wisdom has two sections:
1. How to Meditate on the Space-Like Meditative Equipoise of Emptiness
2. How to Meditate on the Emptiness of Illusory-Like Subsequent Attainment

How to Train the Mind in the Uncommon Path of the Vajrayana has three sections:
1. Becoming a Suitable Vessel for the Profound Path of Mantra
2. How to Maintain Pure Vows and Commitments once You Have Become a Suitable Vessel
3. How to Meditate on the Two Stages of the Path

How to Meditate on the Two Stages of the Path has three sections:

1. How to Actually Meditate on the Two Stages
2. How to Practice Transference of Consciousness if You Have Not Reached a State of Realization despite Having Meditated
3. How to Pray to Come under the Care of Your Guru throughout All of Your Lives and How to Withdraw the Field of Merit for the Sake of Receiving His Blessings in Your Mental Continuum

How to Actually Meditate on the Two Stages has two sections:

1. How to Train in the Generation Stage
2. How to Train in the Completion Stage

How to Pray to Come under the Care of Your Guru throughout All of Your Lives and How to Withdraw the Field of Merit for the Sake of Receiving His Blessings in Your Mental Continuum has two sections:

1. Making Prayers to Be Cared for by Your Guru throughout All of Your Lives and Offering a Torma
2. Withdrawing the Field of Merit for the Sake of Blessing Your Mental Continuum

How to End the Session

How to Engage in the Session Breaks

Colophon

PART II

Ritual Texts

PANCHEN LOSANG CHÖKYI GYALTSEN

The Ritual of the Profound Path of Lama Chöpa
Entitled "Inseparable Bliss and Emptiness"

(Zab lam bla ma mchod pa'i cho ga bde stong dbyer med ma)

In Sanskrit: Guru Pujasya Kalpa Nama
In Tibetan: bLa ma mchod pa'i cho ga

*I prostrate and go for refuge to the feet of the holy gurus who have incomparable
kindness. Please care for me at all times and in every situation with your great
compassion.*

*The wish-fulfilling jewel instantly bestows supreme bliss
Together with the supreme attainments upon
Whoever relies upon your three bodies.
In an instant you bestow the supreme wishes we desire.*

*By respectfully bowing to the lotus feet of the vajra holder
You accomplish every benefit and happiness for fortunate disciples,
Which is not surpassed by any means whatsoever.
It has sprouted from the lotus garden of the sacred oral
Instructions of sutra and tantra as a beautiful
Necklace of delightful flower garlands.*

*Furthermore, this is the foundation for all of those wishing liberation, the root of
all the limitless common and supreme attainments and contains all the essential
oral instructions practiced by yogis of the Supreme Vehicle. It reveals the unmistaken path for oneself that revolves around proper reliance upon the virtuous
friend.*
     The Blue Udder *states:*

> *The primary embodiment of all instructions
> Is to not forsake the spiritual friend,
> From whom emerges faith, bodhichitta, and so forth—
> Who, as the source of all good qualities, bestows all.*

The foremost omniscient being [Tsongkhapa] also stated:

> *The root connecting all the excellent interdependence,*
> *Which accumulates excellence for this life and the next,*
> *Is striving with thought and action to properly rely upon the*
> *Holy virtuous friend who teaches the path.*
> *Seeing this, do not abandon him even at the cost of your life,*
> *And please him by offering your practice of the teachings.*
> *I, the yogi, practiced in that way;*
> *You, who seek liberation, should do the same.*

And:

> *Your kind guru is the root of all good qualities*
> *Of virtue and excellence of this world and beyond.*

The Fifty Verses of Guru Devotion *states:*

> *Vajradhara himself said that*
> *Attainments come from following the master.*
> *Realizing this, you should thoroughly delight your guru*
> *With all of your belongings.*

And [another scripture states]:

> *Surpassing the qualities possessed by a jewel,*
> *Good disciples should have devotion for their gurus*
> *And they should always rely upon their wise gurus.*
> *Why? Because the wise are the source of good qualities.*
>
> *They will subsequently reveal the perfection of wisdom;*
> *Therefore, rely upon the virtuous friends of the Buddhadharma.*
> *The conqueror promised they are the foremost of all good qualities.*

For that reason the vajra master surpasses even all the buddhas as the field within which the disciple is to accumulate merit and purify obscurations.

The Samvarodaya Tantra *states:*

> He is the self-arisen bhagavan,
> One with the supreme deity.
> Because he is the best treasure for instructions
> The vajra master surpasses [the deity].

In accordance with that reasoning, [Khedrup Sangye Yeshe] stated:

> *Meditating on guru yoga contains all the essentials of the path and
> is the supreme means of taking the essence of this life of leisure and
> endowments. Therefore, we should practice in accordance with this.*

> *Furthermore, from within a particularly virtuous state of mind you
> should begin by going for refuge, generating bodhichitta, and medi-
> tating on the four immeasurables. You should engage in the yoga of
> whatever deities is most suitable, such as Guhyasamaja, Heruka, or
> Yamantaka, and then radiate rays of light from your body, whereby
> all worlds and their beings are cleansed of impurities. All environ-
> ments are the celestial mansion and all beings are gods and goddesses
> and everything is the nature of limitless purity.*

*In accordance with this, we begin by reciting the verses for going for refuge and
generating bodhichitta in accordance with Khedrup Sangye Yeshe's lineage for
recitation:*

Going for Refuge and Generating Bodhichitta

From the state of great bliss I arise as the guru-deity.

Light rays emerge from my body appearing clearly [as the guru-deity]
and radiate out to the ten directions, blessing all worlds and beings. With
limitless purity and unique good qualities they become a perfect display
of all things excellent.

From within a completely pure mind of great virtue I and all mother sentient beings as extensive as space, from now until [we reach] the essence of enlightenment, go for refuge to the guru and Three Precious Jewels.

Recite three times:

Namo Guru Bhä
Namo Buddha Ya
Namo Dharma Ya
Namo Sangha Ya

Recite three times:

For the welfare of all mother sentient beings I will become the guru-deity and lead all living beings to the supreme state of the guru-deity.

Recite three times:

For the welfare of all mother sentient beings, in this very life I shall quickly, quickly become the primordial Buddha, the guru-deity, and then liberate all mother sentient beings from their suffering and establish them in the great bliss of the Buddha-ground. For that purpose I will undertake the practice of the profound path of the yoga of the guru-deity.

You should bless the inner offering and offering substances according to any appropriate highest yoga tantra ritual. If you are blessing them in a brief fashion, continue as follows:

OM AH HUM (3x)

The nature of exalted wisdom appearing as the inner offering and the individual offering substances that operate as objects of the six senses and generate a unique exalted wisdom of bliss and emptiness; an inconceivable cloud of outer, inner, and secret offerings, commitment substances, and priceless offerings completely pervade all of space and cover the whole ground.

If you are reciting these actual verses, they are easy to put into practice; therefore you should recite them without being distracted, and engage in the practice while meditating on its meaning.

Visualizing the Field of Merit

In the expansive heaven of inseparable bliss and emptiness in the center of a vast cloud of Samantabhadra's offerings on the peak of a wish-fulfilling tree with beautiful leaves, flowers, and fruit is a lion throne blazing with jewels upon which is an extensive lotus-, sun-, and moon-seat. Upon this is my root guru, who is kind in the three ways, the very nature of every buddha. He is in the aspect of a fully ordained monk with one face and two hands with a radiant expression. His right hand is in the aspect of expounding Dharma and his left in the mudra of meditative equipoise holding a begging bowl filled with nectar. He wears the three saffron robes of a monk and his head is adorned with a golden pandit's hat.

Alternatively, you can skip from "the very nature of every buddha . . ." and continue:

At his heart is the pervasive lord Vajradhara with one face, two hands, and a blue-colored body. He holds a vajra and bell and embraces Vajradhatu Ishvari while delighting in the play of spontaneously born bliss and emptiness. He is adorned with a variety of jeweled ornaments and is draped in heavenly silken garments.

Once you have arranged it [i.e., the wording of the ritual text] according to your disposition, continue with the following regardless of which of the two systems you used:

Adorned with the signs and indications and blazing with a thousand rays of light, he sits in the vajra posture enveloped by five-colored rainbow lights. His aggregates are the five sugatas, his four elements are the four mothers, his senses, channels, and joints are in actuality bodhisattvas. His pores are the twenty-one thousand arhats. His limbs are the wrathful lords. His light rays are directional guardians and harm-givers. The worldly beings are cushions for his feet.

Sitting amid an ocean, he is surrounded in sequence by the lineage gurus, personal deities, a collection of mandala deities, buddhas, bodhisattvas, heroes, dakinis, and Dharma protectors.

Invoking the Wisdom Beings

Their three places are marked by the three vajras. Hooking light rays radiate from the HUM and invoke the wisdom beings from their natural abodes in the same aspect as those visualized.

Although the nature of all phenomena is free from coming and going,
You manifest your enlightened actions of wisdom and compassion
According to the minds of those to be subdued;
Holy refuge and protector, please come to this place together with
    your retinue.

You are the source of all excellence, bliss, and everything supreme
    in the three times,
The root and lineage gurus, Three Precious Jewels,
And a collection of heroes, dakinis, Dharma protectors, and guardians;
Please come to this place through the power of your great compassion
    and remain firm.

OM GURU BUDDHA BODHISATTVA DHARMAPALA
SAPARIWARA EH HAYA HI / DZA HUM BAM HO

The wisdom beings and commitment beings become nondual.

It is the intention of many tantras to perceive your guru inseparable from Vajradhara in that way. In the Fifty Verses of Guru Devotion *it states:*

> [For that reason, a disciple with good qualities,
> Such as compassion, generosity, moral discipline, and patience,]
> Should never regard his master and
> Vajradhara as being separate.

With regard to meditation on his aggregates as the five buddha families, the Vajramala *states:*

> The body of the conqueror abides in sequence
> Within the body of the vajra master.

Thus, this accords with the intention of this and other teachings.

You should visualize the field of merit, summon and absorb the wisdom beings, and effortlessly imagine him to be the nature embodying the Three Jewels.

Then, as Protector Nagarjuna's Five Stages *states:*

> You should completely forsake all [other] offerings
> And commence with perfect offerings to the guru.
> By pleasing him you will obtain the
> Supreme exalted wisdom of omniscience.

Once you have induced absolute certainty in these teachings, which state that making offerings to the guru is superior to making offerings to all other buddhas and bodhisattvas, you should offer the seven limbs, beginning with prostration:

Prostration

Making Praises and Prostrations by Seeing the Guru as the Complete Enjoyment Body

I prostrate to the lotus feet of my jewel-like guru,
The vajra holder, whose compassion
Can bestow in an instant even the supreme state of
The three bodies, the sphere of great bliss.

Making Praises and Prostrations by Seeing the Guru as the Emanation Body

I prostrate at the feet of the holy refuge and protector.
As the exalted wisdom of all the infinite conquerors

Displaying the aspect of a saffron-robed monk,
Your skillful means appear according to the needs of your disciples.

Making Praises and Prostrations by Seeing the Guru as the Truth Body

I prostrate at the feet of the foremost supreme guru.
Having uprooted all faults together with their imprints, you are
An abundant treasure of precious good qualities
And the sole gateway to all benefit and happiness.

Making Praises and Prostrations by Seeing the Guru as the Nature Embodying All Three Jewels

I prostrate to the kind gurus.
In reality you are all buddhas and teachers, including the deities,
The source of all eighty-four thousand pure Dharmas,
Radiant amid the entire assembly of aryas.

Making Praises and Prostrations to All the Buddhas and Bodhisattvas in the Ten Directions by Seeing Them as Emanations of the Guru

With faith and devotion I sing a melodious ocean of praise
And prostrate with emanated bodies equaling atoms of the world
To all those worthy of prostration in the three times and the ten
    directions,
Such as the guru and Three Precious Jewels.

*Once you have prostrated with your three doors, you should present offerings once
you have sealed the three circles of the offerings in the nature of the nonconceptual
wisdom of inseparable bliss and emptiness.*

Offerings

Offering the Four Waters

My refuge and protector, my guru together with your retinue,
I offer this ocean of clouds of various offerings;

From extensive radiant jeweled vessels perfectly arrayed
The purifying nectars of the four waters gently flow.

Offering the Close Enjoyment Offerings

Beautiful flowers finely arranged as blossoming trees,
Petals, and garlands filling the earth and sky.

The lapis-colored smoke of sweet-smelling incense
Filling the heavens like blue summer clouds.

Light from the sun and moon, glittering jewels,
And a mass of joyfully frolicking lamps
Dispelling the darkness in a billion worlds.

A vast ocean of scented water with the sweet scent of saffron,
Sandalwood, and camphor swirling out to the horizon.

A massive heap of delicacies of gods and men
As food and drink endowed with a hundred flavors.

From an endless variety of musical instruments
Emerges a symphony that fills the three worlds.

Offering the Five Objects of Desire

An abundance of outer and inner goddesses as the objects of desire
Holding forms, sounds, scents, tastes, and objects of touch that
    pervade every direction.

Mandala Offering

My refuge and protector, great treasure of compassion,
The supreme field of merit, I offer to you with a mind of faith
A hundred million of the four continents, Mount Meru, and
The seven major and minor precious possessions of a king—
A collection of perfect worlds and beings that generate every joy
As a great treasure of desired enjoyments of gods and men.

Offering Your Spiritual Practice

From the purity of samsara and nirvana, both set out and imagined,
I offer this delightful garden to please the venerable guru.
On the banks of an ocean are offering substances that arise
With a broad thousand-petaled lotus—the source and
Nature of all mundane and supramundane joy,
Blooming with flowers that are the virtues of the three doors of
    myself and others,
With a hundred thousand scents of Samantabhadra's offerings and
Endowed with the fruits of the three trainings, the two stages,
    and five paths.

The Inner Offering Related to the Secret Empowerment

I offer this drink of China tea endowed with the glories
Of a hundred flavors and with an excellent scent as
The five hooks, the five lamps, and so forth,
Purified, transformed, and increased into an ocean of nectar.

Secret Offering Related to the Wisdom Mudra Empowerment

I offer beautiful, voluptuous, illusory-like consorts,
A host of messengers born from mantra, places, and spontaneously
    born,
With slender figures, in the bloom of youth,
And skilled in the sixty-four arts of love.

Suchness Offering Related to the Word Empowerment

I offer you the supreme ultimate bodhichitta
Beyond words, thoughts, and expressions;
The sphere of reality; all phenomena free from the
Elaborations of inherent existence as the great exalted wisdom of
Spontaneous bliss liberated from obstruction.

Offering Medicine and Oneself as a Servant

I offer numerous types of excellent medicine
That destroy the illness of the 404 delusions,
And to please you, I offer myself as your servant;
Please hold me as your disciple for as long as space exists.

You should offer medicine and yourself as a servant together with the visualization.

Now, continue by offering the remaining limbs, such as confession and so forth:

Confession

In the presence of the greatly compassionate ones I confess with regret
The nonvirtues and negative actions I have accumulated
Since beginningless time, caused others to do, or have rejoiced in,
And promise to refrain from such actions again in the future.

Rejoicing

Although dreamlike phenomena are free from
The signs of inherent existence,
We sincerely rejoice in all the pure white virtues and
Whatever bliss and joy that arise for ordinary and arya beings.

Requesting Them to Turn the Wheel of the Dharma

Please send down a rain of vast and profound Dharmas
From the multitude of clouds of your wisdom and compassion

So that the jasmine garden may nurture, sustain, and propagate
The benefit and happiness for limitless sentient beings.

Requesting Them Not to Pass into Nirvana

Although your vajra body knows neither birth nor death
But is a vessel of the powerful conqueror's union,
Please remain according to our wishes
Without passing away until samsara ends.

Dedication

I dedicate this collection of pure white virtue that I have produced
So that throughout all my lives I may never be separated
From the venerable guru who is kind in the three ways;
May I always come under his care and attain the union of
    powerful Vajradhara.

If you have the time during the [verse] for confession, you should confess your [downfalls] for each of your three sets of vows through practices such as Lama Dorzinma,[257] *the* Confession of Bodhisattva Downfalls,[258] *and so forth.*

Next, the Vajrapani Empowerment Tantra *states:*

> *Apprehend your master's good qualities.*
> *Never focus upon his [apparent] faults.*
> *If you apprehend his qualities, you receive attainments.*
> *If you focus on his faults, you will not accomplish attainments.*

Thus, you should repeatedly rely upon introspection by thinking, "I will not let my mind look for flaws in my guru." Once you do, you should properly contemplate the sacred teachings of the sutras and tantras that repeatedly discuss the benefits of

---

257. *bLa ma rdo 'dzin ma.* This is also known as the *General Confession.*
258. *Byang chub ltung bshags.*

relying upon the guru and the faults of not relying upon him or her. In particular, merely hearing the name of your root guru robs the lower rebirth of its fear and merely contemplating him dispels the suffering of samsara. If you make requests to him, all attainments are bestowed with ease. Rely upon him with fervent devotion without placing your hopes in any other and contemplate that he is the very nature embodying the nondeceptive Three Jewels. While contemplating in this way, make as many requests as you can with prayers such as the Migtsema *and so forth, after which you should make the following request:*

Making Supplications through the Guru's Qualities of the Vinaya

I make requests to the foremost second buddha,
A great ocean of moral discipline, the source of all good qualities,
Replete with a treasury of much learning,
In saffron robes, the elder and upholder of the Vinaya.

Making Supplications through the Guru's Qualities of the Mahayana

I make requests to you, the Mahayana virtuous friend,
Lord of the Dharma, successor of all the conquerors,
Endowed with the ten qualities required to
Teach the path of the sugatas.

Making Supplications through the Guru's Qualities of the Vajrayana

I make requests to you, principal holder of the vajra;
Your three doors are perfectly subdued, you have great wisdom
    and patience,
And without pretense or deceit, with knowledge of mantras
    and tantra,
You are endowed with the two sets of ten qualities
And are skilled in drawing [mandalas] and explaining them.

Making Supplications by Recalling the Kindness of Your Guru

I make requests to you, my compassionate refuge and protector;
You perfectly reveal the path of the sugatas for those
Migrators of these degenerate times so difficult to tame,
Who were not subdued by the countless buddhas of the past.

I make requests to you, my compassionate refuge and protector;
As the sun of the Buddha's teaching is setting
So many living beings are without a refuge or protector,
Yet you perfectly accomplish the deeds of the conquerors.
I make requests to you, my compassionate refuge and protector;

Even just one of your hair pores
Is praised as the perfect field of merit, superior to
All the conquerors of the three times and the ten directions.

Making Supplications by Proclaiming His Outer Qualities

I make requests to you, my compassionate refuge and protector;
From your charming, graceful web of magical emanations and skillful
     means
The ornamental wheels of your three sugata bodies
Manifest in ordinary forms to guide living beings.

Making Supplications by Proclaiming His Inner Qualities

I make requests to you, supreme guru, the nature of the Three Jewels;
Your aggregates, elements, sources, and limbs
Are the nature of the fathers and mothers of five buddha families,
The bodhisattvas, and the wrathful powerful deities.

Making Supplications by Proclaiming His Secret Qualities

I make requests to you, protector of the primordial union;
You are the ten million circles of mandalas,

The manifestation of omniscient exalted wisdom,
The principal vajra holder, pervasive lord of a hundred lineages.

Making Supplications by Proclaiming His Qualities of Suchness

I make requests to you, actual ultimate bodhichitta,
The manifestation of spontaneous joy free from obstruction,
The all-pervasive nature of all things stable and moving,
Free from beginning and end, the pure nature of Samantabhadra.

Making Supplications by Planting the Stake and Receiving the Four Empowerments

You are the guru, you are the yidam, and you are
The daka and Dharma protector.
From now until I attain enlightenment I will seek no refuge
   other than you.
In this life, the intermediate state, and in all future lives
Please hold me with the hook of your compassion,
Liberate me from all fears of samsara and nirvana,
Bestow all attainments, be my constant companion, and
Protect me from all obstacles. (3x)

Through the force of requesting three times in this way,
White, red, and blue light rays and nectars
Arise sequentially and collectively
From the guru's body, speech, and mind and
Descend sequentially and collectively into my three places.
My four obstructions are purified;
I receive the four empowerments and attain the four bodies.
My guru is pleased; a replica dissolves into me,
And I receive his blessings.

Next, for the sake of once again receiving his blessing and summoning his mental continuum, make prayers for one's own benefit.

Making Requests for the Path of the Great Vehicle Together with Mind Training

Through the force of having made respectful offerings and requests
To you, the venerable and holy guru, the supreme field of merit,
I seek your blessings, protector, the root of all bliss and excellence;
Please joyously take me into your loving care and grant me your
    blessing.

Having found this leisure and endowment just once,
And realizing how quickly it is destroyed and how difficult it is to find,
I seek your blessing that I may extract the essence of this endowment
Without becoming distracted by the meaningless activities of this life.

Being terrified by the blazing fire of the lower realms' suffering,
From the depths of my heart I go for refuge to the Three Jewels
And seek your blessing that I may strive earnestly to
Accomplish the complete collection of virtue and abandon negative
    actions.

Being violently tossed about by the waves of delusion and karma,
And tormented by the many sea monsters of the three sufferings,
I seek your blessing to generate a fierce and powerful wish for
    liberation
From the limitless and fearful great ocean of samsara.

Forsaking a mind that views as a joyous garden
This unbearable prison, the net of samsara,
I seek your blessing to uphold the victory banner of liberation
By maintaining the riches of the aryas' three trainings.

Contemplating how all these pitiful living beings are my mothers
Who have cherished me with kindness again and again,
I seek your blessing that I may generate uncontrived compassion,
Like the love of a mother for her precious child.

In that no one desires even the most subtle suffering
Or is ever content with the happiness they have,
There is no difference between myself and others;
Seeing this, I seek your blessing that I may delight in the happiness
    of others.

Seeing that this chronic disease of maintaining self-cherishing
Gives rise to all unwanted suffering,
I seek your blessing to destroy this great demon of self-cherishing
By despising it as the object of blame.

Seeing that the mind that cherishes my mothers
And accomplishes their happiness
Is the gateway and source of limitless good qualities,
I seek your blessing to cherish these beings
More than my life, even if they rise up as my enemies.

In short, since the childish work for their own welfare
Whereas the buddhas work for the welfare of others,
I seek your blessing to be able to realize
The faults and qualities and thereby exchange myself for others.

Since self-cherishing is the door to all faults
And cherishing mother beings is the basis of all good qualities,
I seek your blessing to take as my heart practice
The yoga of exchanging self with others.

Therefore, great compassionate venerable guru,
I seek your blessing that all the negative karma, obscurations,
And suffering of mother living beings without exception
May ripen upon me right now and may all
My happiness and virtue be delivered to others,
So that all living beings may be endowed with happiness.

Recite the [above verse] three times as a practice of recitation.

When the world and its beings are completely filled with
The results of nonvirtue and unwanted sufferings pour down
   like rain,
I seek your blessing that I may see this
As a cause to exhaust the results of bad actions
And transform adverse conditions into the path.

In short, whether good or evil appearances arise,
I seek your blessing to transform them into the path of increasing
   the two bodhichittas
By practicing the five forces, the essence of all Dharma,
And cultivate a happy mind alone.

I seek your blessing that I may extract great meaning from this life
   of freedom and endowment
With the skillful means endowed with the four preparations
By immediately applying meditation to all interactions
And practicing the commitments and precepts of mind training.

I seek your blessing that I may [generate] perfect bodhichitta by
Dispatching the wind mounted by taking and giving,
And liberate living beings from the great ocean of existence
With the mind of love, compassion, and superior intention.

I seek your blessing to earnestly engage in the sole path
Traversed by all the conquerors of the three times:
To restrain my mind with pure bodhisattva vows and
Practice the three moral disciplines of the Mahayana.

I seek your blessing to complete the perfection of generosity
Through the oral instructions of increasing the mind of giving
   without attachment
And thus transform my body, enjoyments, and virtues accumulated
   throughout the three times
Into the things that each living being desires.

I seek your blessing to complete the perfection of moral discipline
By never transgressing, even at the cost of my life,
The boundaries of the pratimoksha, bodhisattva, and secret mantra
vows,
While collecting virtuous Dharma and accomplishing the welfare
of living beings.

I seek your blessing to complete the perfection of patience
So that even if the myriad of beings of the three realms
Become angry, humiliate, criticize, threaten, or even kill me,
I will not become discouraged but will respond to their harm with
benevolence.

I seek your blessing to complete the perfection of effort
By striving for supreme enlightenment with unwavering compassion
Even if I must remain for an ocean of eons dwelling within the flames
Of the lowest hell for the sake of each living being.

I seek your blessing to complete the perfection of concentration
By abandoning the faults of sinking, excitement, and wandering,
While concentrating with single-pointed mental stabilization
On the ultimate nature of reality—the truth of all phenomena.

I seek your blessing to complete the perfection of wisdom
Through the yoga of space-like mental stabilization on ultimate reality
Conjoined with the great bliss of pliancy induced by
The wisdom of the individual analysis of suchness.

I seek your blessing to complete the illusory concentration,
Realizing that outer and inner phenomena are like illusions, dreams,
And like reflections of the moon in a pure lake,
Which, although they appear, have no true existence.

I seek your blessing that I may realize the meaning of Nagarjuna's
true intent,
That samsara and nirvana lack even an atom of inherent existence,

And that the nondeceptive dependent relationship of cause
   and effect
Complement each other without contradiction.

Therefore, I seek your blessing that I may cherish more than my life
The vows and commitments, the root of attainments,
And through the kindness of the captain—the vajra holder—
I may cross the intricate ocean of the tantras.

I seek your blessing that I may purify all the stains of ordinary
   appearances and conceptions
So that whatever appears may manifest as the body of the deity,
And through the yoga of the first stage may I transform
Birth, death, and the intermediate state into the three bodies
   of the conqueror.

I seek your blessing that I may manifest in this life
The path of the clear light, illusory body, and union.
And that you, Protector, may arrange your feet
Upon the eight-petaled lotus within the central channel
   in my heart.

If by the time of my death I have not completed the points
   of the path,
I seek your blessing to travel to the pure land
Through the powerful perfect method of the guru's transference
   of consciousness
And by perfectly applying the oral instructions of the five forces.

In short, I seek your blessing that throughout every life I may never
Be separated from you, Protector, but always come under your care,
Uphold all the secrets of your body, speech, and mind,
And become your seniormost disciple.

Protector, wherever you manifest as a buddha,
May I be the first in your retinue and

May there be the auspiciousness of spontaneously accomplishing
    without effort
All of my temporary and ultimate needs and wishes.

Thus, through requesting the supreme guru in this way,
May you be delighted, come to the crown of my head, bestow your
    blessing,
And once again place your radiant feet firmly
Upon the anthers of the lotus at my heart.

Recite this verse and imagine that the guru's mind, the mind of the supreme deity, and your mind have become inseparable in nature. Throughout all of your daily actions view whatever appears as the nature of bliss and emptiness manifesting as goddesses. Engage in the combined practices of the yoga of the generation and completion stages as well as the pith instructions for training the mind with all the essential features of the stages of the path or the Mahayana mind training. At the conclusion you should seal it by making dedication prayers for your virtuous conduct. If you wish to make a concise [dedication], proceed as follows:

Dedication

I dedicate the pure virtue that I have created in this way
So that I might be able to uphold the pure Dharma of scripture and
    realization,
And accomplish all the prayers and deeds
Of all the sugatas and their children of the three times.

By the force of this in all my lives may I
Never be separated from the four wheels of the Supreme Vehicle,
And thus complete the paths of renunciation, bodhichitta,
Correct view of emptiness, and the two stages.

You should also learn some of the essential instructions orally. If you are going to practice this yoga on a daily basis, you will be practicing the essence of all sutra and tantra teachings and it will become the stable root of all prosperity and well-being in this life.

Colophon

Churning the sea of milk of sutra and tantra's sacred
Oral instructions with the intellect of Mount Meru
The pitcher's nectar of unprecedented eloquent explanations
Is assembled as well-written verses accomplishing the fortunate's
    spiritual life.

This [commentary] is filled by the all-devout disciples as a lamp that
Dispels all the darkness in their hearts and is
Also a hook that quickly summons all the
Mundane and supramundane perfections.

Whoever practices this system, which is the source of virtuous
Accumulations, will accumulate merit white like the moon.
I pray that it may become the cause of all living beings to be cared for
By the holy protectors, who are the root of perfection.

This ritual, Lama Chöpa, was based on repeated requests of Dulwa Zinpa Chökyi Drakpa and Losang Phustog, who said they needed something like this. It was composed by the Shakya monk Losang Chökyi Gyaltsen. It was based on the guru yoga practice of Drubchen Ling, the guru yoga practices composed by Panglo Chenpo, the guru yoga practices composed by the great spiritual friends of the Sakya tradition, the guru practice composed by the omniscient Gendun Gyatso, and the guru yoga practices composed by the great Khenpo Rinpoche Khedrup Sangye Yeshe. Furthermore, I examined numerous guru yoga practices composed by lamas of various statuses among their individual traditions. By coming to a complete understanding of the intent of their expressed meaning, I combined all their best parts in perfect accordance with the sacred oral instructions of the sutras and tantras while leaving out other sections so that it is easy to understand. It was composed in the upper story of Gyaltsen room at the great monastery Tashi Lhunpo.

The Ganachakra Offering for Lama Chöpa

(bLa ma mchod pa'i tshogs mchod bzhugs so)

OM AH HUM (3x)

The nature, exalted wisdom, appearing as the inner offering and the individual offering substances, generates a unique exalted wisdom of bliss and emptiness within the range of the six senses. Since it completely pervades the entire area of the ground and the space above, they become filled with the inconceivable cloud of outer, inner, and secret offerings, commitment substances, [and] priceless offerings.

This should be done in conjunction with deity yoga.

EH MA HO: Great manifestation of exalted wisdom,
All lands are vajra-lands
And all abodes are great vajra-palaces with
A radiant ocean of clouds of Samantabhadra's offerings.

An abundance of glorious enjoyments,
All beings are actual heroes and heroines.
Without even the mistaken imputation "impurity"
There is only limitless purity.

HUM: All elaborations are pacified in the state of the truth body.
Upon a moving wind and blazing fire is
A grate of three human heads.
AH: Within a qualified skull cup
OM: The individual substances are set ablaze.

Upon them are OM, AH, HUM
Blazing with the brilliance of their respective colors.
The wind blows, the fire blazes, and the substances melt.
Boiling, a great vapor billows forth whereby

A collection of light rays radiates from the three syllables.
Going to the ten directions, they summon the
Three vajras together with their nectars,
Which dissolve separately into the three syllables, whereby

They melt into nectar and mix with the substances, which
Are purified, transformed, and increased. EH MA HO.
They transform into an ocean of desired enjoyments.
OM AH HUM (3x)

I invoke the root and lineage gurus, yidams, collection of deities,
The Three Jewels as the objects of refuge,
The heroes, dakinis, Dharma protectors, and guardians—
Please come to this place of offering out of your great compassion.

Sit upon this beautiful throne made of jewels
Amid this ocean of clouds of outer, inner, and secret offerings.
Please bestow upon me the supreme attainments I wish for
And remain firm with light radiating even from your feet.

*Next, with respect to offering the ganachakra, the action-vajra should collect the
first select portion and place it in the container, after which he should set it upon a
support. Make three prostrations, after which you recite: "Great Hero, please bless
this first portion of tsok." Likewise, offer the remaining tsok offering. With the
master acting as the principal, the knowledge holders should all recite in unison.*

HO: This ocean of tsok offering of uncontaminated nectar
Blessed by concentration, mantra, and mudra
I offer to delight the assembly of root and lineage gurus.
OM AH HUM
Satiated by this glorious display of all that is desired,
EH MA HO
Please send down a great rain of blessings.

HO: This ocean of tsok offering of uncontaminated nectar
Blessed by concentration, mantra, and mudra

I offer to delight the assembly of yidams and mandala deities.
OM AH HUM
Satiated by this glorious display of all that is desired,
EH MA HO
Please send down a great rain of attainments.

HO: This ocean of tsok offering of uncontaminated nectar
Blessed by concentration, mantra, and mudra
I offer to delight the assembly of Three Precious Jewels.
OM AH HUM
Satiated by this glorious display of all that is desired,
EH MA HO
Please send down a great rain of holy Dharma.

HO: This ocean of tsok offering of uncontaminated nectar
Blessed by concentration, mantra, and mudra
I offer to delight the assembly of dakinis and Dharma protectors.
OM AH HUM
Satiated by this glorious display of all that is desired,
EH MA HO
Please send down a great rain of enlightened actions.

HO: This ocean of tsok offering of uncontaminated nectar
Blessed by concentration, mantra, and mudra
I offer to delight the assembly of mother sentient beings.
OM AH HUM
Satiated by this glorious display of all that is desired,
EH MA HO
Please pacify mistaken impure appearances.

Next, take the special first portion of tsok with the torma. Then, the action-vajra
offers it to the vajra master with the following:

EH MA HO
You who have followed the path of the sugatas of the three times,
By realizing that you, the great hero,

Are the source of all attainments,
I forsake the mind of conceptualization;
Continuously partake in this circle of tsok.
A LA LA HO

Thus offer to the master. The master replies:

OM: With a nature inseparable from the three vajras
I appear clearly as the guru-deity.
AH: This uncontaminated nectar of exalted wisdom,
HUM: Without wavering from the mind of enlightenment,
I partake to satiate the deities dwelling in my body.

AH HO MAHA SUKHA

If you have the time and inclination, you should sing the "Song of the Spring Queen":

HUM Deshin Shekpa Tamchay Dang
Pawo Dang Ni Naljor Ma
Kandro Dang Ni Kandro Ma
Kun La Dak Ni Sol Wa Deb
De Wa Che La Gye Pa Herukay
Dewai Rab Nyo Ma La Nyen Che Nay
Chok Ka Shin Tu Long Cho Pa Yi Ni
Lhen Kye De Wai Chor Wa La Shuk So.

AL LA LA: LA LA HO: A LI AH: A RA LI HO:

Dri Me Kandroi Tsok Nam Kyi
Tse Wai Jik La Lay Kun Dzo.

HUM Deshin Shekpa Tamchay Dang
Pawo Dang Ni Naljor Ma
Kandro Dang Ni Kandro Ma
Kun La Dak Ni Sol Wa Deb
De Wa Chen Po Yi Ni Rab Kyo Pay

Lu Ni Kun Tu Yo Wai Kar Kyi Ni
Chak Gyai Pema Rol Pai De Wa Che
Naljor Ma Chok Nam La Cho Par Dzo.

AL LA LA: LA LA HO: A LI AH: A RA LI HO:

Dri Me Kandroi Tsok Nam Kyi
Tse Wai Jik La Lay Kun Dzo.

HUM Deshin Shekpa Tamchay Dang
Pawo Dang Ni Naljor Ma
Kandro Dang Ni Kandro Ma
Kun La Dak Ni Sol Wa Deb
Yi Ong Shi Wai Nyam Kyi Kar Dze Pa
Rab Gye Kon Po Kyo Dang Kandroi Tsok
Dak Kyi Dun Tu Shuk Te Jin Lob La
Lyen Kye De Chen Dak La Tsal Du Tsol.

AL LA LA: LA LA HO: A LI AH: A RA LI HO:

Dri Me Kandroi Tsok Nam Kyi
Tse Wai Jik La Lay Kun Dzo.

HUM Deshin Shekpa Tamchay Dang
Pawo Dang Ni Naljor Ma
Kandro Dang Ni Kandro Ma
Kun La Dak Ni Sol Wa Deb
De Chen Thar Pai Tsen Nyi Den Pa Kyo
De Chen Pang Pai Ka Tub Tu Ma Yi
Tse Chig Drol Par Mi She De Chen Kyang
Chu Kye Chok Kyi U Na Nay Pa Yin.

AL LA LA: LA LA HO: A LI AH: A RA LI HO:

Dri Me Kandroi Tsok Nam Kyi
Tse Wai Jik La Lay Kun Dzo.

HUM Deshin Shekpa Tamchay Dang
Pawo Dang Ni Naljor Ma
Kandro Dang Ni Kandro Ma
Kun La Dak Ni Sol Wa Deb
Dam Gyi U Su Kye Pai Pema Shin
Chak Lay Kye Kyang Chak Pai Kyon Ma Go
Naljor Ma Chok Pemai De Wa Yi
Si Pai Ching Wa Nyur Du Drol War Dzo.

AL LA LA: LA LA HO: A LI AH: A RA LI HO:

Dri Me Kandroi Tsok Nam Kyi
Tse Wai Jik La Lay Kun Dzo.

HUM Deshin Shekpa Tamchay Dang
Pawo Dang Ni Naljor Ma
Kandro Dang Ni Kandro Ma
Kun La Dak Ni Sol Wa Deb
Drang Tsi Chung Nay Nam Kyi Drang Tsi Chu
Pung Wai Tsok Kyi Kun Nay Tung Wa Tar
Tsen Nyi Druk Den Tso Kye Gye Pa Yi
Chu Ching Pa Yi Ro Yi Tsim Par Dzo.

AL LA LA: LA LA HO: A LI AH: A RA LI HO:

Dri Me Kandroi Tsok Nam Kyi
Tse Wai Jik La Lay Kun Dzo.

Next, send out the leftover tsok:

HUM: Mistaken impure appearances are purified in the sphere of
    emptiness.
AH: Great nectar accomplished from exalted wisdom,
OM: It transforms into a great ocean of desired enjoyments.
OM AH HUM (3x)

HO: This ocean of remaining tsok offering of uncontaminated nectar
Blessed by concentration, mantra, and mudra
I offer to delight the assembly of oath-bound field protectors.
OM AH HUM
Satiated by this glorious display of all that is desired,
EH MA HO
Please accomplish appropriate actions for the yogi.

HO: By offering this ocean of remaining tsok offering
To the remaining guests and their retinue,
May the precious teachings flourish.

May the holders of the teachings, the benefactors, and
I, the yogi, and those in my retinue
Be free of sickness, obtain a long life, power, glory, fame, good fortune,
Vast enjoyments, and all attainments.
Please bestow the attainments of
The actions, such as pacifying, increasing, and so forth.
Those who possess the commitments, please protect me,
Bestow assistance in all attainments,
Eliminate bad times, death and sickness, and
Harm from interfering and harmful spirits, and
Eradicate bad dreams, bad signs,
And bad actions.

May there be happiness in the world
And excellent years,
May our crops increase and the Dharma flourish,
And may peace and excellence and everything supreme
Arise according to my wishes.
By the power of this vast offering

May I become a buddha for the welfare of all living beings.
And may those not liberated by previous buddhas
Be liberated through my generosity.

This [tsok offering] was composed by Khedrup Sangye Yeshe.

Auspicious Verses

Through the signs of the pure virtue of samsara and peace
May I immediately be liberated from all inauspiciousness and
    misfortune.
May there be the auspiciousness of the display of glory and excellence,
And may there be a sky-treasure of temporary and ultimate virtue
    and excellence.

May the Dharma centers of the omniscient Losang Drakpa
Be completely filled with an assembly of yogis and Sangha
Making single-pointed effort in the three trainings, and thus
May there be the auspiciousness of the Buddha's teaching remaining
    for a long time.

Dwelling in the blessings of Losang Drakpa, who from
The time of his youth made requests to the collection of gurus
    and deities,
May we spontaneously accomplish the welfare of others and
May there be the auspiciousness of Losang Dorje Chang.

May there be the auspicious display of glory and excellence,
May desired enjoyments increase like a summer lake,
May there be an uninterrupted birth in a faultless lineage,
And may we spend day and night in Losang's sacred Dharma.

Through the virtues I and others have accumulated and will
    accumulate
From now until I and others attain enlightenment,
May there be the auspiciousness of the venerable guru's
Holy form body abiding like an immutable vajra.

SVATI

Appendix 1: *Fifty Verses of Guru Devotion* Composed by Ashvagosha

In Sanskrit: Guru Pantsa Shika
In Tibetan: bLa ma lnga bcu pa

I prostrate to the Bhagavan Vajrasattva.

1. And properly bow to the lotus feet of the guru,
   Who is the cause of attaining the state of Glorious Vajrasattva.
   Listen with devotion for I shall briefly explain what
   Has been expounded in numerous stainless tantras.

2. The tathagatas abiding in the worldly realms
   Of the ten directions prostrate to the vajra master
   From whom they received supreme empowerment
   Throughout the three times.

3. With a mandala and flowers in the palm of your hands
   Respectfully honor your teacher-guru
   And prostrate with his feet on your head
   With supreme faith throughout the three times.

4. For the sake of averting worldly criticism,
   If he is a layman or your junior,
   You should prostrate before the holy Dharma and so on
   While mentally maintaining the proper conduct.

5. You should perform all the proper conducts,
   Such as arranging his seat, rising,
   Accomplishing his wishes, and so on,
   Yet abandon prostrating and the inappropriate.

6. So that the samaya of either the guru or
   His disciples does not deteriorate,
   They should perform a mutual examination
   To insure they can brave a master-disciple relationship.

7. The wise disciple should not accept as a guru
   Someone who lacks compassion, is hostile and angry,
   Arrogant, attached,
   Lacking restraint, or boastful.

8. Stable, subdued, and wise,
   Patient, honest, and nondeceptive,
   Knowledge of mantras, tantras, and [ritual] actions,
   Compassionate and skilled in the treatises.

9. He possesses the two sets of ten qualities;
   He is skilled in drawing the mandalas
   And has knowledge of the activities of explaining mantra,
   Perfect faith, and subdued senses.

10. If a disciple comes under the care of such
    A protector and then despises him,
    They will be despising all the buddhas
    And they will continuously receive suffering.

11. If you are so stupid as to criticize your master,
    You will be plagued with infectious diseases,
    Afflictive illnesses, harm from spirits,
    Epidemics, and poisons, after which you will die.

12. You will be killed by kings, fire,
    Poisonous snakes, water, dakinis, thieves,
    Harmful spirits, and negative evil forces,
    After which you will go to hell.

13. You should never agitate the minds of
    Any of your masters.
    And if you are so stupid that you do,
    You will definitely roast in hell.

14. Whatever terrifying hells have been taught,
    Such as Avici and so forth,
    Are accurately explained to be the abode
    Of those who disparage their master.

15. For that reason, with all the energy you can muster,
    Never, under any circumstance,
    Disparage your wise vajra master,
    Who never boasts about his virtuous qualities.

16. You should respectfully present offerings
    To your guru and modify your behavior,
    Through which harms, such as infectious diseases and so on,
    Will not subsequently occur.

17. If it is taught that you should eternally attend to your
    Guru with whom you have samaya by offering
    Things such as your child, wife, and life, which are rarely
        offered,
    What need is there to mention your transient wealth?

18. In this way, the diligent can even attain
    Enlightenment in this very life, which is
    Otherwise difficult to attain even
    In countless millions of eons.

19. Always protect your samaya,
    Always make offerings to the tathagatas,
    Always present offerings to your guru as well,
    For he is equal to all the buddhas.

20. Desiring the inexhaustible,
    Whatever is even slightly pleasing
    Becomes the most special;
    It is what you should offer to the guru.

21. That generosity becomes an eternal
    Generosity to all the buddhas.
    That offering is the accumulation of merit;
    Through accumulation you accomplish supreme siddhis.

22. For that reason, a disciple with good qualities,
    Such as compassion, generosity, moral discipline, and patience,
    Should never regard his master and
    Vajradhara as being separate.

23. If you should never even step over his shadow
    Because you fear the negative karma, which is similar to
        destroying a stupa,
    What need is there to mention that you shouldn't step over his
    Shoes, seat, mount, and so on?

24. With enthusiastic determination
    Sincerely apply yourself to the instructions of your guru.
    If you are incapable, you should rationally
    Explain with [respectful] words why you are incapable.

25. Spiritual realizations come from the guru,
    As well as the attainment of higher status and happiness.
    For this reason you should make every effort to
    Not transgress the teachings of your guru.

26. Continuously reflect with single-pointed focus
    How you should protect the belongings of your guru as you
        do your life
    And honor your guru's retinue and even his
    Loved ones as you do your guru.

27. Do not sit on his seat or cushion nor walk ahead of him,
    Do not wear your hair in a topknot nor sit,
    Do not outstretch your limbs or place your hands on your hips,
    Nor should your wring your hands.

28. You should not lie down or sit
    If your guru is standing.
    You should always be ready to stand
    And serve him skillfully in the most excellent way.

29. While in the presence of your guru
    Do not expel things by spitting and so forth,
    Do not stretch out your legs when sitting,
    Do not walk around or argue.

30. While close enough for your guru to hear,
    Do not massage your limbs or dance,
    Do not sing or play music,
    And do not talk incessantly.

31. Rise from your seat and bow
    And then sit respectfully.
    You may proceed ahead of him
    At night, at rivers, or on frightening paths.

32. In the direct perception of your guru
    A wise [disciple] should not twist their body,
    Lean against a pillar, and so forth;
    Nor should they crack their knuckles.

33. When washing his feet, washing his body,
    Wrapping him [in a towel], massaging him, and so forth,
    You should begin by making a prostration, and
    After which you can do whatever you please.

34. If you need to address him by name,
    You should affix the title "In the presence of"
    So that others will treat him with respect
    And use other exalted words of reference as well.

35. When requesting advice from your guru
    You should listen carefully to your guru's instructions
    With your palms held in prayer at your heart without mental
        wandering
    And respond with "I shall do just as you have instructed."

36. If you laugh, smile, and so forth,
    Cover your mouth with your hand.
    You should let him know when you have completed
    Your task while using polite words.

37. Request the instructions you desire three times by
    Kneeling respectfully in his presence
    With your palms held in prayer while wearing the
    Appropriate attire and then sit respectfully.

38. All of your activities should be done with respect and veneration
    And not with an arrogant mind.
    You should be modest, timid, and
    Bashful like a newlywed bride.

39. You should abandon all actions such as
    Arrogance in the presence of your teacher.
    And after self-examination, you should
    Abandon all other similar actions as well.

40. If your guru is staying in the same area,
    You should not perform consecrations, mandala rituals,
    Burnt offerings, or gather disciples
    Without prior permission of your guru.

41. Whatever offerings you receive from consecrations and so on
    Should all be offered to your guru and,
    Once he accepts his portion of the offering,
    You can do whatever you like with the rest.

42. In the presence of his guru a disciple should not
    Act as a guru to his disciples and they should not treat him as a
      guru.
    They should cease acts of devotion, such as
    Rising, prostrating, and so forth.

43. Whenever making offerings to your master
    Or whenever your guru presents you with a gift,
    A wise disciple should bow and accept or
    Offer it with both hands.

44. You should diligently perform all of your actions
    With mindfulness that never forgets.
    Should your [vajra]-siblings transgress their behavior
    You should pleasantly correct each other.

45. Even without permission, if you are unable
    To bow to your guru because of illness and you must do
    What is prohibited, you will not incur any
    Negative karma if you have a virtuous mind.

46. What need is there to expound on this any further?
    You should sincerely apply yourself by
    Doing whatever pleases your guru
    And forsaking all that causes displeasure.

47. Vajradhara himself said that
Attainments come from following the master.
Realizing this, you should thoroughly delight your guru
With all of your actions.

48. A disciple with pure intention
Who has gone for refuge to the Three Jewels
Should be given this text to recite so that they
May properly follow their guru.

49. Next, having been made a suitable vessel for the holy Dharma
Through being given mantra and so forth,
You should read and memorize
The fourteen root downfalls.

50. Thus, may whatever limitless pure virtue I have accumulated
Through this faultless composition bring every benefit and happiness
To those disciples that are following their guru,
Through which all living beings may quickly become a conqueror.

Colophon

This text entitled *Fifty Verses of Guru Devotion* was composed by Master Ashvagosha.

Appendix 2: *The Root Text on the Precious Geden-Kagyu Mahamudra Entitled "The Main Path of the Conquerors"*

NAMO MAHAMUDRA

Respectfully I bow to the feet of the incomparable guru,
The lord of attainments, the pervasive lord who reveals the bare
Indescribable vajra-sphere of the mind as the
All-pervasive nature of mahamudra.

Promise to Compose

I shall compose the instructions that perfectly assemble the Geden and Kagyu instructions on mahamudra in the tradition of the supreme siddha Dharmavajra and his spiritual sons and embody the essence of the ocean of oral instruction on sutra and tantra.

The Preliminaries has three sections:
1. The Preparations
2. The Actual Instructions
3. The Conclusion

The Preparations

Because it is the gateway and life-pillar of the teachings and the Mahayana, you should sincerely go for refuge and generate bodhichitta without paying it mere lip service. As a preliminary to perceiving the ultimate nature[259] of

---

259. Tib. *chos nyid*; Skt. *dharmata*.

the mind you should also rely upon the accumulation of merit and the purification of obstructions by reciting a hundred thousand hundred-syllable mantras [of Vajrasattva] and the "Confession of Moral Downfalls,"[260] together with as many prostrations as possible. You should also make repeated heartfelt supplications to your root guru, who is inseparable from all the buddhas of the three times.

The Actual Instructions

Although there are numerous ways of describing mahamudra, there are two [primary] distinctions as sutra and tantra. The latter utilizes the skillful means of penetrating the essential points of the vajra body and so forth, from which emerges the clear light [mind] of great bliss. The mahamudra of Saraha, Nagarjuna, Naropa, and Maitripa is the very essence of highest yoga tantra as taught in the cycle of essential teachings of the mahasiddhas.[261]

The former (i.e., sutra tradition) refers to the extensive, middling, and concise perfection of wisdom sutras, which reveal the actual means of meditating on emptiness. The supreme arya Nagarjuna stated:

There is no path to liberation other than this.

Regarding this, I shall confer a commentary on mahamudra in accordance with this intention of [Nagarjuna] and shall describe it in accordance with the teachings of the lineage gurus that reveal the means of directly encountering mind.[262]

Although there are numerous nominal imputations for the individual [systems] such as "The Union of Simultaneously Born," "The Amulet Box," "The Fivefold [Mahamudra]," "The [Six Cycles] of Equal Taste," "The Four Syllables," "Pacifier," "The Object of Severance," "Dzogchen," "Guide to

---

260. Tib. *ltung bshags.*
261. Alex Berzin identifies these as "[The Seven Texts of the] Mahasiddhas" and "The [Three] Core Volumes." The Dalai Lama, *The Gelug/Kagyü Tradition of Mahamudra* (Ithaca, NY: Snow Lion Publications, 1997), 115.
262. Tib. *sems kyi ngo sprod.* In other traditions this is often translated as "pointing out instructions on the nature of mind," and so on.

the View of the Madhyamaka," and so forth,[263] when their definitive meanings are examined with scripture and reasoning by scholar-yogis with actual experience, they come down to a single intention. Therefore, there are two systems: (1) seeking meditation in addition to the view [of emptiness], and (2) seeking the view in addition to meditation. This commentary will be in accordance with the latter system.

Sit upon a comfortable seat for concentration with the seven essential bodily features. Cleanse the stale winds through the nine-round breathing. Properly differentiate the pure states of awareness from the defiled. With a completely pure mind of virtue, go for refuge and generate bodhichitta as a preliminary and then meditate on the profound path of guru yoga. Make one hundred or more very powerful supplications [to your guru], after which you dissolve your guru into yourself. Without engaging in any conceptual elaborations whatsoever, such as miscellaneous appearances, hopes, fears, and so forth, do not engage in any fabrication whatsoever. Remain in a state of meditative stabilization without the slightest wavering. It is not a ceasing of comprehension as though you have fainted or fallen asleep. Instead, you keep watch with unwavering mindfulness and expose any movement of awareness with introspection and firmly focus your attention on the nature of [mind] as awareness and clarity while perceiving it directly.[264]

Whenever you develop any conceptual elaborations, you should recognize them for what they are. Alternatively, completely sever whatever conceptual elaborations arise, just like a swordsman in a duel. When you have severed them in their place, relax at ease without losing mindfulness.

There are certain phrases such as "Maintain a relaxed state with tight apprehension and place the mind in that state." Moreover, as this quotation indicates, you should relax your mind without wavering in accordance with the quote that states:

> If you loosen the mind when it is bound in a tangle,
> Have no doubt you will be liberated.

263. Tib. *lhan cig skyes sbyor, ga'u, lnga sdan, ro snyoms, yi ge bzhi, zhi byed, gcod yul, rdzogs chen*, and *dbu ma'i lta khrid*, respectively.
264. Tib. *gcer gyis ltos*. An alternate translation would be "perceive it nakedly," which would imply that that clarity and awareness of the mind itself are being perceived without the overlay of conceptual elaborations.

Or another that states:

> When you examine the nature of whatever conceptions
>   you develop,
> They disappear on their own and arise as a pure vacuity.
> Likewise, if you also examine them when they are still,
> There is an unobscured vivid empty luminosity;
> Blend the perception of stillness and movement.

Whatever conceptions you develop, recognize them without [trying] to stop them. Instead, recognize their function and rest in their essential nature. It is similar to the example of a bird flying from its cage on a ship. In the same way, the [meditation manuals state], "If a raven sets flight from a ship, once he surveys the area, he will once again alight on the ship." By practicing in this way, no matter what, the essential nature of meditative stabilization is unobscured purity and clarity and is not established in any way whatsoever as having form. It is a pure vacuity like space, and anything at all will arise vividly [in the mind].

With regard to the ultimate nature of such a mind, although it is directly perceptible by superior seeing, it cannot be apprehended or revealed as being "this." With regard to "placing [your mind in a state] of relaxation without grasping at whatever arises," it is the sole intention of most of the great modern-day meditators of Tibet who proclaim that this is the oral instruction for delivering the state of enlightenment into the palm of your hand. Be that as it may, I, Chökyi Gyaltsen, state that this is the means of recognizing the conventional nature of the mind and is the most wondrous skillful means for beginners to accomplish mental quiescence.

Now I shall present the means of recognizing the true nature of the mind. This will be set forth according to the instructions of my root guru for dispelling the ignorance of my mind, who assumed the aspect of a saffron-robed monk and is the [embodiment] of every exalted wisdom of the buddhas.[265]

Without wavering from the previous state of meditative stabilization, meditate with a subtle awareness like a small fish swimming within pris-

265. This Tibetan phrase reads *sangs rgyas rnams kyi ye shes kun*, which contains *sangs rgyas* and *ye shes* (Sangye Yeshe), which is the name of the First Panchen Lama's root guru. Khedrup Sangye Yeshe was the lineage holder of the Ganden mahamudra lineage.

tine water, and skillfully analyze the nature of the person that is the meditator. The savior Arya Nagarjuna himself stated:

> If the person is not earth, not water,
> Not fire, not wind, not space,
> Not consciousness, and not all of them,
> Then what person is there other than these?
>
> Just as a person is not real
> Because the person is a collection of six elements,
> Likewise, each of the elements is also
> Not real because it is composite.

If you search in this way, you cannot find even an atom of [a truly existent] state of meditation, the person absorbed in a state of meditation, and so on. At that point, sustain the space-like meditative absorption single-pointedly and without wavering. Alternatively, within that state of meditative stabilization, uninterruptedly engage the mind in the unceasing continuity of clarity and awareness from which manifest and emanate various [phenomena] without obstruction and apprehend appearances and objects while not [inherently] depending upon them. Protector Shantideva states [in his *Guide to the Bodhisattva's Way of Life*]:

> The things we call "continuums" or "collections"
> Are false, similar to rosaries, armies, and so forth.

Place your mind in single-pointed meditative stabilization within the state of the absence of [inherent] existence according to the mode of appearance by relying upon scripture and reasoning. In short, [the aforementioned] accords with the oral instructions of my omniscient spiritual guide, Sangye Yeshe, which state:

> If you are thoroughly aware of your conceptual apprehensions
>   of whatever appears,
> They will dawn as the sphere of reality of ultimate reality without
>   depending upon anything else.

Place your mind in single-pointed absorption that
Abides in the state of awareness of this display. EH MA HO

Likewise, Padampa [Sangye] also stated:

The spear of awareness whirls in the state of emptiness;
People of Dingri, things are unobstructed in the view [of
emptiness].

These [previous two quotes] abide in the same intention.

Conclusion

With regard to subsequent [attainment], dedicate whatever pure virtue
has arisen from your meditation on mahamudra as well as from your
ocean of virtues accumulated throughout the three times toward unsurpassed great enlightenment.

Having meditated in this way, identify in detail the mode of appearance
of whatever appearances arise as objects of the collection of six [types of
consciousness], as well as the mode of existence that appears through vivid
bare perception and is the essential point of such recognition of whatever
appears.

In short, continually sustain an ascertainment of the mode of existence
of whatever various objects appear, such as your mind and so forth,
without grasping [at inherent existence]. Once you understand this point,
unify all phenomena within samsara and nirvana as having a single nature.
This was also expressed by Aryadeva when he proclaimed:

Whoever perceives one entity
Is said to perceive all entities.
Whoever perceives one emptiness
Perceives the emptiness of everything.

Thus, although from the perspective of correct meditative stabilization
on ultimate reality samsara and nirvana are free from the extreme conceptual elaborations of existence, nonexistence, and so forth, when you
investigate them upon arising from that state, there is without a doubt

the dependent relationship of action and agent that exist as nothing more than mere nominal imputations that manifest as illusory-like appearances as [phenomena] such as dreams, mirages, and the moon reflected in water. "Appearances do not obstruct emptiness and emptiness does not impede appearances" is realized as being synonymous with emptiness and dependent origination during the excellent path.

Colophon

Through the merit of myself, the renunciant
Losang Chökyi Gyaltsen, who heard many teachings,
May all migrating beings quickly become conquerors through
This path for which there is no other gateway to peace.

Nächu Rabjam[266] *Gedun Gyaltsen and Hotong Kachu Sherab Sengé, who, having perceived the crazy drama of the eight worldly concerns, dwell in isolated mountain retreats abiding in the conduct of an ascetic, made repeated requests for this very means of recognizing mahamudra for a long time so that they may use this as the heart of their practice of this path. Moreover, it was requested by numerous disciples who wish to implement this practice of definitive mahamudra.*

In particular, the foremost being, the lord of attainments, the omniscient Gyalwa Ensapa the Great stated:

> *In my songs of spiritual experience I have also composed the instructions from the proper reliance upon the spiritual guide up to tranquil abiding and superior seeing in accordance with the Kadam lamrim; however, in the end I was not able to explain this path. At present, the ultimate oral instructions on mahamudra are not well known in Tibet and at the moment I am unable to set them to writing.*

Thus, what at that time was not set forth due to the force of it being impermissible was therefore intended for a later time. For example, in the White Lotus Sutra *it states:*

---

266. Tib. *ngas bcu rab 'byams pa*. This is someone that completed the course of study from Tashi Lhunpo that is equivalent to a geshe degree.

> Because the object is perfectly realized by the exalted wisdom of the
>   Buddha[267]
> You could never say, "Those beings are enlightened"
> When they write about this method as a natural occurrence.
> Why? Because they see this as the time to protect it.

For the sake of fulfilling such prophecies that have been orally transmitted from
the incomparable teacher, the king of the Shakyas, up to my root guru, the
all-knowing and seeing Sangye Yeshe, I, the renunciant Losang Chökyi Gyaltsen, having upheld the sacred oral instructions of sutra and tantra, having not
remained with defiled commitments, and having not defiled the lineage of blessing according to the practice of actualizing this path, have compiled this text at
Geden Nampar Gyalwai Ling (Ganden Monastery).

---

267. This is seen as a prophecy of Sangye Yeshe, the First Panchen Lama's guru, whose name
means "the exalted wisdom of the Buddha" and appears clearly in this line from the Lotus Sutra.

KALARUPA

Appendix 3: *Supplication to the Mahamudra Lineage*

NAMO MAHAMUDRA

I supplicate you, the pervasive lord Vajradhara,
The glorious primordial buddha, principal of all lineages abiding
In the celestial mansion of the spontaneously accomplished
    three bodies;
Please grant your blessing that I may cut the entanglement of
    self-grasping within my mental continuum,
Train in love, compassion, and bodhichitta,
And swiftly attain the supreme mahamudra that is the path of union.

I supplicate you, wisdom-[buddha] Arya Manjushri,
The father of the conquerors of the three times
Abiding in the limitless pure lands in the worlds of the ten directions;
Please grant your blessing that I may cut the entanglement of
    self-grasping within my mental continuum,
Train in love, compassion, and bodhichitta,
And swiftly attain the supreme mahamudra that is the path of union.

I supplicate you, Venerable Losang Drakpa,
The lord and second buddha of the muni's teachings [appearing]
In the northern region of the land of snows;
Please grant your blessing that I may cut the entanglement
    of self-grasping within my mental continuum,
Train in love, compassion, and bodhichitta,
And swiftly attain the supreme mahamudra that is the path of union.

I supplicate you, Togden Jampal Gyatso,
The principal holder of the teachings of the lineage of practice
Of Manjushri's son, Tsongkhapa;
Please grant your blessing that I may cut the entanglement of
    self-grasping within my mental continuum,
Train in love, compassion, and bodhichitta,
And swiftly attain the supreme mahamudra that is the path of union.

I supplicate you, Baso Chökyi Gyaltsen,
Ripening fortunate disciples by opening
The treasury of instruction of the Hearing Lineage;
Please grant your blessing that I may cut the entanglement
    of self-grasping within my mental continuum,
Train in love, compassion, and bodhichitta,
And swiftly attain the supreme mahamudra that is the path of union.

I supplicate you, the supreme siddha Dharmavajra (Chökyi Dorje),
Who attained the immortal body of a knowledge holder
By perfecting the yogas of the two stages;
Please grant your blessing that I may cut the entanglement
    of self-grasping within my mental continuum,
Train in love, compassion, and bodhichitta,
And swiftly attain the supreme mahamudra that is the path of union.

I supplicate you, Losang Donyo Drupa (Ensapa),
Upholding the victory banner of teachings of definitive meaning,
Undefiled by bonds of the eight worldly concerns;
Please grant your blessing that I may cut the entanglement
    of self-grasping within my mental continuum,
Train in love, compassion, and bodhichitta,
And swiftly attain the supreme mahamudra that is the path of union.

I supplicate you, Khedrup Sangye Yeshe,
The guide of all beings in a dance of saffron robes
In the delightful palace of the three bodies;
Please grant your blessing that I may cut the entanglement
    of self-grasping within my mental continuum,

Train in love, compassion, and bodhichitta,
And swiftly attain the supreme mahamudra that is the path of union.

I supplicate you, Venerable Losang Chögyan (Panchen Lama),
Omniscient one inseparable from the protector of Conqueror Losang's
    teachings;
Please grant your blessing that I may cut the entanglement
    of self-grasping within my mental continuum,
Train in love, compassion, and bodhichitta,
And swiftly attain the supreme mahamudra that is the path of union.

I supplicate you, Mahasiddha Gendun Gyaltsen (Nächu Rabjampa),
Who perfected the practices contained in all commentaries on the
Teachings of sutra and tantra embodied in a single meaning;
Please grant your blessing that I may cut the entanglement
    of self-grasping within my mental continuum,
Train in love, compassion, and bodhichitta,
And swiftly attain the supreme mahamudra that is the path of union.

I supplicate you, Drupai Gyaltsen Dzinpa (Je Losang Tsondru
    Gyaltsen),[268]
Who attained the supreme state through experiencing
The essence of Conqueror Je Losang's teachings with great
    perseverance;
Please grant your blessing that I may cut the entanglement
    of self-grasping within my mental continuum,
Train in love, compassion, and bodhichitta,
And swiftly attain the supreme mahamudra that is the path of union.

I supplicate you, Gyuchen Konchog Gyaltsen,[269]
Skilled in instructing your fortunate disciples
In the essential nectar of the vast and profound holy Dharma;

268. There is a footnote in the Tibetan: "Tsondru Gyaltsen is the regent and direct disciple of
Panchen [Losang Chökyi Gyaltsen]."
269. There is a footnote in the Tibetan: "He is the great vajra holder of the tantric college of
Tashi Lhunpo."

Please grant your blessing that I may cut the entanglement
    of self-grasping within my mental continuum,
Train in love, compassion, and bodhichitta,
And swiftly attain the supreme mahamudra that is the path of union.

I supplicate you, Venerable Panchen Losang Yeshe;
You are Losang Chökyi Gyaltsen himself arriving once more
For the glory of migrating beings and the teachings;
Please grant your blessing that I may cut the entanglement
    of self-grasping within my mental continuum,
Train in love, compassion, and bodhichitta,
And swiftly attain the supreme mahamudra that is the path of union.

I supplicate you, Venerable Losang Trinlay (Lhapa Tulku),
The sovereign lord of the profound path of the Hearing Lineage
Who was directly blessed by the venerable buddhas;
Please grant your blessing that I may cut the entanglement
    of self-grasping within my mental continuum,
Train in love, compassion, and bodhichitta,
And swiftly attain the supreme mahamudra that is the path of union.

I supplicate you, the supreme siddha Drubwang Losang Namgyal,
Who perfected the practice of the essential meaning
Of Conqueror Je Losang's Hearing Lineage;
Please grant your blessing that I may cut the entanglement
    of self-grasping within my mental continuum,
Train in love, compassion, and bodhichitta,
And swiftly attain the supreme mahamudra that is the path of union.

I supplicate you, kind Kachen Yeshe Gyaltsen,
Who out of compassion gave instructions on the
Unmistaken meaning of Je Lama's instructions on the Hearing Lineage;
Please grant your blessing that I may cut the entanglement
    of self-grasping within my mental continuum,
Train in love, compassion, and bodhichitta,
And swiftly attain the supreme mahamudra that is the path of union.

I supplicate you, Venerable Phurchog Ngawang Jampa,
Who spread the essential teachings on the complete unmistaken path
Everywhere in the central and outlying regions;
Please grant your blessing that I may cut the entanglement
    of self-grasping within my mental continuum,
Train in love, compassion, and bodhichitta,
And swiftly attain the supreme mahamudra that is the path of union.

I supplicate you, Panchen Palden Yeshe,
The glorious primordial buddha in saffron robes
Who ripened all the lands of China and Tibet with the Dharma;
Please grant your blessing that I may cut the entanglement
    of self-grasping within my mental continuum,
Train in love, compassion, and bodhichitta,
And swiftly attain the supreme mahamudra that is the path of union.

I supplicate you, Khedrup Ngawang Dorje,
Who single-pointedly perfected the attainments in
The complete excellent paths of sutra and tantra;
Please grant your blessing that I may cut the entanglement
    of self-grasping within my mental continuum,
Train in love, compassion, and bodhichitta,
And swiftly attain the supreme mahamudra that is the path of union.

I supplicate you, Jetsun Ngulchu Dharmabhadra,
The protector who illuminated the conqueror's teachings through
    discourse and composition,
Who is learned and steadfast like a second buddha;
Please grant your blessing that I may cut the entanglement
    of self-grasping within my mental continuum,
Train in love, compassion, and bodhichitta,
And swiftly attain the supreme mahamudra that is the path of union.

I supplicate you, Yangchen Drupai Dorje,
Whose eyes of great unobservable compassion never close
And whose profound and extensive wisdom is like Manjushri's;

Please grant your blessing that I may cut the entanglement
of self-grasping within my mental continuum,
Train in love, compassion, and bodhichitta,
And swiftly attain the supreme mahamudra that is the path of union.

I supplicate you, Khedrup Tenzin Tsondru,[270]
Who perfected the yoga of bliss and emptiness and then
Directly traveled to the state of the conqueror's union;
Please grant your blessing that I may cut the entanglement
of self-grasping within my mental continuum,
Train in love, compassion, and bodhichitta,
And swiftly attain the supreme mahamudra that is the path of union.

(This is the beginning of another lineage.)

I supplicate you, Losang Tsondru Gyaltsen,[271]
Who perfected the realization of the profound path and then
Upheld the victory banner of the teachings of exposition and practice;
Please grant your blessing that I may cut the entanglement
of self-grasping within my mental continuum,
Train in love, compassion, and bodhichitta,
And swiftly attain the supreme mahamudra that is the path of union.

I supplicate you, Losang Donyo Drubpa,[272]
Who was not defiled by the stains of faults or downfalls and
Upheld the essence of the teachings of the three higher trainings;
Please grant your blessing that I may cut the entanglement
of self-grasping within my mental continuum,
Train in love, compassion, and bodhichitta,
And swiftly attain the supreme mahamudra that is the path of union.

---

270. There is a footnote in the Tibetan: "The former abbot of Sera Monastery's tantric college."
271. This is the beginning of another lineage that begins with another one of the First Panchen Lama's immediate disciples, Tsondru Gyaltsen. Both lineages were received by Pabongkha Rinpoche.
272. There is a footnote in the Tibetan: "He was a disciple of Dorje Dzinpa [Konchog Gyaltsen]."

I supplicate you, Venerable Drubkang Geleg Gyatso (1641–1713),
Displaying the aspect of a saffron-robed monk as though
The second conqueror, Je Losang Drag, had returned;
Please grant your blessing that I may cut the entanglement
    of self-grasping within my mental continuum,
Train in love, compassion, and bodhichitta,
And swiftly attain the supreme mahamudra that is the path of union.

I supplicate you, kind Phurchog Ngawang Jampa,
Who completely clarified the fortunate lineage
With a treasury of Dharma on the vast and profound paths;
Please grant your blessing that I may cut the entanglement
    of self-grasping within my mental continuum,
Train in love, compassion, and bodhichitta,
And swiftly attain the supreme mahamudra that is the path of union.

I supplicate you, the supreme scholar Jigmé Wangpo (Jamshay
    Konchog),
Who skillfully clarified the excellent path free from extremes
Through your far-reaching laughter of stainless reasoning;
Please grant your blessing that I may cut the entanglement
    of self-grasping within my mental continuum,
Train in love, compassion, and bodhichitta,
And swiftly attain the supreme mahamudra that is the path of union.

I supplicate you, Venerable Gungtang Tenpai Dronmé,
The incomparable propagator of exposition and practice
Of the supreme long-standing tradition of protector and conqueror
    Losang;
Please grant your blessing that I may cut the entanglement
    of self-grasping within my mental continuum,
Train in love, compassion, and bodhichitta,
And swiftly attain the supreme mahamudra that is the path of union.

I supplicate you, Venerable Konchog Gyaltsen (Amdo Palmang),
With your great bodily strength of experience and realization

Through tasting the nectar of Venerable Jamgon's Hearing Lineage;
Please grant your blessing that I may cut the entanglement
    of self-grasping within my mental continuum,
Train in love, compassion, and bodhichitta,
And swiftly attain the supreme mahamudra that is the path of union.

I supplicate you, Mahasiddha Ngodrup Rabten,
Who upheld the victory banner of the teaching lineage of practice
Abiding single-pointedly in the state of spontaneity;[273]
Please grant your blessing that I may cut the entanglement
    of self-grasping within my mental continuum,
Train in love, compassion, and bodhichitta,
And swiftly attain the supreme mahamudra that is the path of union.

I supplicate you, Yongzin Gendun Gyatso (Tasag),
Who perfected the good qualities of abandonment and realization and
Then sent down a rain of eloquent Dharma that was wished for;
Please grant your blessing that I may cut the entanglement
    of self-grasping within my mental continuum,
Train in love, compassion, and bodhichitta,
And swiftly attain the supreme mahamudra that is the path of union.

I supplicate you, Palden Tenpai Nyima (Gungtrul Khenrab),
Who was elevated to the state of the attainment of the two stages
And was the crowning jewel of the wisdom of all scholars;
Please grant your blessing that I may cut the entanglement
    of self-grasping within my mental continuum,
Train in love, compassion, and bodhichitta,
And swiftly attain the supreme mahamudra that is the path of union.

(The two lineages rejoin here:)

---

273. There is a footnote in the Tibetan: "This means remaining as a renunciant (literally, 'one who has abandoned activity') and a hidden yogi."

I supplicate you, Venerable Pabongkha Trinlay Gyatso,
Who upheld the victory banner of the teachings of sutra and tantra
Through the power of your love for all beings;
Please grant your blessing that I may cut the entanglement
    of self-grasping within my mental continuum,
Train in love, compassion, and bodhichitta,
And swiftly attain the supreme mahamudra that is the path of union.

I supplicate you, Yongzin Gatri Ling Chog,
Whose incomparable enlightened actions propagated the
Many aspects of the holy Dharma of the Buddha's teachings
Of scripture and realization according to the conqueror's intention;
Please grant your blessing that I may cut the entanglement
    of self-grasping within my mental continuum,
Train in love, compassion, and bodhichitta,
And swiftly attain the supreme mahamudra that is the path of union.[274]

I supplicate you, kind Losang Yeshe (Yongzin Kyabje Trijang Chog),
The guide who propagated the heart-essence of the
Venerable second conqueror for fortunate disciples;
Please grant your blessing that I may cut the entanglement
    of self-grasping within my mental continuum,
Train in love, compassion, and bodhichitta,
And swiftly attain the supreme mahamudra that is the path of union.

I supplicate you, my kind root guru,
Who gloriously appears on the seat of the previous
Venerable siddhas for the sake of faithful disciples;
Please grant your blessing that I may cut the entanglement
    of self-grasping within my mental continuum,
Train in love, compassion, and bodhichitta,
And swiftly attain the supreme mahamudra that is the path of union.

274. There is a footnote in the Tibetan: "This verse was composed by Kyabje Trijang Dorje Chang."

Please grant your blessing that I may see the venerable guru as
    a buddha,
Overcome attachment for abodes of samsara,
And, having assumed the responsibility of liberating all
    mother beings,
Swiftly attain the common and uncommon paths and
Attain the mahamudra of the glorious state of union.

My body and your body, O father,
My speech and your speech, O father,
My mind and your mind, O father;
Bless me that they may become inseparably one.

Colophon

Up to Yongzin Yeshe Gyaltsen [this prayer] is in accordance with Lama
Chöpa. The supplemental material was composed by Kyabje Pabongkha
Rinpoche. The names of each of the lineage gurus were added [in paren-
theses] for the sake of making it easy to understand. It was scribed by
Gelong Losang Dorje at Todrung Monastery. It was reprinted by Yongzin
Trijang Dorje Chang in 1968 and printed at Gangtok. The publication was
funded by Drepung Losal Ling Thubten Öser.

Glossary

Action mudra: A physical consort utilized to actualize the most subtle mind of clear light through completion-stage techniques of highest yoga tantra.

Action tantra: The first of the four classes of tantra, which emphasizes external actions and utilizes gazing at a physical consort as a means of generating a blissful subjective awareness used to penetrate the nature of reality.

Akshobya: One of the members of the five buddha families; he is blue in color and holds a vajra and bell. He is a physical representation of the purified aggregate of consciousness.

Amitabha: One of the members of the five buddha families; he is red in color and holds a lotus and bell. He is a physical representation of the purified aggregate of discrimination.

Amoghasiddhi: One of the members of the five buddha families; he is green in color and holds a sword and bell. He is a physical representation of the purified aggregate of compositional factors.

Arhat: Literally, "foe destroyer," which refers to someone who has attained liberation from samsara and can refer to both Hinayana and Mahayana arhats; however, it is most commonly used in reference to the former.

Avalokiteshvara: Known as "Chenrezig" in Tibetan, he is the manifestation of the compassion of all the buddhas appearing as a white deity in various aspects. The most common aspect has one face and four arms; another has eleven faces and one thousand arms.

Bodhichitta: The intention to become enlightened for the welfare of all living beings, which is motivated by love and the compassion that sees the suffering nature of samsara and seeks to liberate all living beings from it.

Bodhisattva: An individual who has generated bodhichitta and has entered the path to enlightenment.

Buddha Shakyamuni: The historical Buddha who lived approximately twenty-five hundred years ago and is the founder of the Buddhism practiced today.

Chakrasamvara: One of the three main deities of the Gelug lineage; also known as Heruka. The foremost deity of mother tantra. The teachings of Chakrasamvara reveal special methods for attaining the clear light and the practice of inner fire.

Channels: A channel is a passageway through which the winds and drops move. There are three primary channels: the central, right, and left. The ultimate goal of all highest yoga tantra practices is to bring the winds into the central channel and utilize the most subtle mind of clear light to realize the ultimate nature of reality.

Clear light: The extremely subtle mind that becomes manifest during the completion stage of highest yoga tantra and is utilized to realize emptiness.

Commitment being: A visualized buddha, either oneself generated as a buddha or a buddha visualized in the space before oneself, so named because it is a commitment of tantra to visualize the buddha. It is juxtaposed to the "wisdom being" that is invoked and dissolved into the commitment being, thus rendering them inseparable.

Completion stage: The second stage of highest yoga tantra, which utilizes channels, winds, and drops to cause the winds to enter, abide, and dissolve into the central channel, whereby one manifests subtle levels of consciousness while conjoining them with bliss.

Daka: A male enlightened being that assists tantric practitioners to accomplish realizations of secret mantra.

Dakini: A female enlightened being that assists tantric practitioners to accomplish realizations of secret mantra.

Deity: There are both mundane and supramundane deities. A mundane deity is any god or goddess that has not attained either liberation or enlightenment. A supramundane deity is either a bodhisattva on one of the three final grounds or a buddha visualized in the aspect of a particular deity.

Dependent arising: A phenomenon that exists only interdependently. All phenomena are dependent arisings and are thus noninherently existent since they require other phenomena for their existence.

Dharma: The teachings of the Buddha that lead one through spiritual paths that culminate in varying degrees of happiness, from the happiness of this life to the happiness of liberation and enlightenment.

Divine pride: The pride of being an enlightened being that is generated by dissolving one's ordinary aggregates and their sense of identity and replacing it with the "divine" pride of being the deity. This entire process is utilized to strengthen one's realization of emptiness by realizing that the "I" is merely imputed.

Drops: The drops are the subtle elements of our body that course through the channels within our body in dependence upon the movement of the inner energy that flows through the channels. The drops can be used to generate extraordinary blissful states of mind used to penetrate the nature of reality.

Emanation body: A coarse form body of an enlightened being that is emanated for the welfare of ordinary beings.

Empowerment: A ritual utilizing a mandala that transmits the blessing of a particular buddha in the aspect of a deity and establishes the imprints to attain the resultant body, speech, and mind of that deity.

Enjoyment body: The subtle body of an enlightened being that can be perceived only by bodhisattvas who have attained the path of seeing.

Equalizing and exchanging self with others: A method for generating bodhichitta consisting of the following five stages: (1) equalizing self and others, (2) recognizing the faults of self-cherishing, (3) recognizing the benefits of cherishing others, (4) taking and giving, (5) bodhichitta.

Field of merit: A visualization consisting of either a single or an assembly of enlightened beings. This is referred to as "a field of merit" because, just as we use a field of soil to plant seeds that will ripen as a harvest, the field of merit is a "field" in which we sow our virtuous actions, such as offerings and praises, which will ripen as the harvest of realizations.

Five stages of the completion stage: The natural progression that occurs as a person gains progressively higher realizations of the completion stage: isolated speech, isolated mind, clear light, illusory body, and union. It was arranged by Nagarjuna and is based on the Guhyasamaja tantra.

Four complete purities: The four factors that are essential for the practice of tantra: pure abode, pure body, pure enjoyment, and pure deeds.

Guhyasamaja: One of the three main deities of the Gelug lineage. It is the foremost father tantra that emphasizes the attainment of the illusory body.

Heroes and heroines: Male and female tantric deities that assist tantric practitioners to attain realizations.

Highest yoga tantra: The highest of the four classes of tantra, which emphasizes internal actions and utilizes embracing a physical consort as a means of generating the most subtle mind of clear light as a blissful subjective awareness that is capable of penetrating the nature of reality.

Illusory body: The third of the five stages of the completion stage of Guhyasamaja as presented by Nagarjuna; it refers to the subtle body that is actualized during the completion stage. There are two divisions of the illusory body: pure and impure. The impure illusory body, which is the third of the five stages of the completion stage, is attained after the attainment of ultimate example and is so called because the wind from which it is composed is still impure in the sense that the mind from which it arose has yet to directly realize emptiness. The pure illusory body is so called because it arises from meaning clear light that has directly realized emptiness.

Indestructible drop: The most subtle drop located within the heart-channel wheel. It is composed of the essence of red and white drops obtained from the mother and father at the time of conception. It is also the abode of the most subtle mind of clear light, which must be accessed to attain enlightenment.

Inner fire: Famous as "*tummo* meditation"; refers to the subtle red element that is the nature of heat that resides within the navel-channel wheel. Through causing the winds to enter, abide, and dissolve into the central channel, the inner fire blazes and melts the white element at the crown, causing an extremely blissful and subtle level of mind that is unprecedented for its power to realize emptiness, the ultimate nature of reality.

Intermediate state: The transitional state between the end of one life and the beginning of the next. The intermediate state can last up to forty-nine days and consists of seven minor transitional periods, each resulting in a "small death," after which one either takes rebirth or assumes another intermediate-state body.

Ishvara: A god dwelling in the highest state of existence within the desire realm. Buddha emanated the mandala of Heruka and Vajrayogini as a means of subjugating Ishvara and leading all living beings to enlightenment.

Isolated body: A preliminary to the five stages of the completion stage of Guhyasamaja as presented by Nagarjuna. It is so named because the wind that gives rise to the body as being ordinary is isolated from its movement by dissolving the wind into the central channel, which gives rise to the pure conceptions of the body as being the deity's body.

Isolated mind: The second of the five stages of the completion stage of Guhyasamaja as presented by Nagarjuna. It is so named because the wind that gives rise to the mind as being ordinary is isolated from its movement by dissolving the wind into the central channel, which gives rise to the pure conceptions of the mind as being the deity's mind.

Isolated speech: The first of the five stages of the completion stage of Guhyasamaja as presented by Nagarjuna. It is so named because the wind that gives rise to the speech as being ordinary is isolated from its movement by dissolving the wind into the central channel, which gives rise to the pure conceptions of the speech as being the deity's speech.

Karma: The cause-and-effect relationship between an action created and its corresponding result: whatever we experience is a result of our previous actions. Pleasant experiences stem from virtuous actions and painful experiences stem from nonvirtuous actions.

Knowledge goddess: A goddess that is either emanated from one's wisdom of bliss and emptiness or an actual woman with the realization of bliss and emptiness. In both cases, her function is to induce and increase the realization of bliss and emptiness in the mental continuum of either the practitioner or beings in the field of merit.

Losang Tubwang Dorje Chang: Also known as Lama Losang Tubwang Dorje Chang. This is a title given to the central figure of the Lama Chöpa field of merit. When prefaced with "Lama," this refers to one's personal guru. "Losang" is in reference to Tsongkhapa, whose proper name was Losang Drakpa. "Tubwang" is Tibetan for "powerful able one" and is an epithet for Buddha Shakyamuni. And "Dorje Chang" refers to Vajradhara. The title is given because the outer aspect of the central figure of the field of merit is in the aspect of Tsongkhapa with Buddha Shakyamuni in his heart, who in turn has Vajradhara in his heart. All three are seen as inseparable from your own root guru, hence the name "Lama Losang Tubwang Dorje Chang."

Madhyamaka: The "Middle Way" school of Mahayana philosophy founded by Nagarjuna. There are two primary divisions of the Madhyamaka: the Prasangika and the Svatantrika. The Prasangika utilizes consequential syllogisms and presents a slightly more subtle interpretation of emptiness than the Svatantrika. The Svatantrika utilizes autonomous syllogisms and presents emptiness in a slightly coarser interpretation than the Prasangika.

Mahasiddhas: Tantric adepts of varying degrees of realizations who have attained a degree of realization far beyond an ordinary being. They are most often associated with ancient India.

Milarepa: Tibet's most famous yogi, who lived from 1052 to 1135. Milarepa spent the earlier part of his life engaged in nonvirtuous actions and finally killed thirty-six people through the use of black magic. Repenting his nonvirtuous actions, he sought out his guru, Marpa, who famously put him through extreme hardships as a means of purifying Milarepa's negative karma. In the latter part of his life, Milarepa devoted himself to solitary retreat and eventually attained enlightenment and established numerous disciples on the path to enlightenment. His teachings were adopted by his disciple Gampopa, who combined them with the teachings of the Kadam lineage, resulting in the Kagyu lineage.

Mind Only: The Chittamatra school of philosophy within Mahayana Buddhism, which asserts that there are no external objects and that all phenomena are mere appearances to the mind.

Mixing: Generally classified under the heading "nine mixings," this term refers to mixing the basis, path, and result with the resultant truth body, enjoyment body, and emanation body during waking, sleeping, and meditation. For instance, a highest yoga tantra practitioner will mix death, intermediate state, and rebirth with the path as the truth body, enjoyment body, and emanation body during waking through the process outlined in their sadhana. The same process is applied to the clear light of sleep, dreaming, and awakening. It is finally applied at the end of one's life during the actual process of death.

Nagarjuna: The founder of Mahayana Buddhism, who is said to have traveled to the subterranean land of the *naga*s to obtain the perfection of wisdom sutras.

Nagas: Serpent-like beings who have varying degrees of power that can be either malevolent or benign.

Performance tantra: The second of the four classes of tantra, which places equal emphasis upon internal and external actions and utilizes exchanging glances with a physical consort as a means of generating a blissful subjective awareness used to penetrate the nature of reality.

Phenomena source: Either a single or double tetrahedral geometric object used throughout the Vajrayogini practice that symbolizes, among other things, emptiness and represents emptiness as the source of all phenomena.

Pratimoksha vows: Vows of individual liberation; a set of vows taken by Mahayana Buddhists with the motivation of attaining liberation from samsara.

Ratnasambhava: One of the members of the five buddha families; he is yellow in color and holds a jewel and bell. He is a physical representation of the purified aggregate of feeling.

Samsara: A cycle of uncontrolled rebirth through the force of afflicted actions and delusions.

Self-cherishing: An exaggerated sense of self-importance based on the mistaken interpretation of oneself as inherently existent that causes one to think of one's happiness as more important than everyone else's.

Self-grasping: Grasping at an inherently existent self based on a mistaken interpretation of the nature of reality, which is the cause of samsara and all the suffering within it.

Sevenfold cause and effect: A method for generating bodhichitta based on the following seven steps: (1) recognizing all beings as your mother; (2) remembering their kindness; (3) wishing to repay their kindness; (4) affectionate love; (5) great compassion; (6) superior intention; and (7) bodhichitta.

Sutra: The public discourses given by the historical Buddha.

Tsok offering: A tantric feast involving ritual music and sacred substances that is usually performed on the tenth day after the full moon and the tenth day after the new moon. It is a powerful way of redressing your commitments and solidifying your sacred relationship with the dakas and dakinis.

Tsongkhapa: A Tibetan lama who lived from 1357 to 1419. He was a great nonsectarian teacher who assembled various practices and lineages that resulted in the Gelug tradition.

Ultimate reality: The ultimate reality of all phenomena is their being empty of inherent existence.

Union: There are several types of union, such as the union of bliss and emptiness, the union of illusory and clear light, and the union of body and mind. When used in reference to the five stages of Guhyasamaja, it refers to the fifth stage, simply called "union." At this stage there is the union of meaning clear light and the pure illusory body, which is referred to as "a learner's union." At the resultant state of enlightenment it is called "the union of no more learning" or "the union of body and mind" and is synonymous with enlightenment.

Vairochana: One of the members of the five buddha families; he is white in color and holds a wheel and bell. He is a physical representation of the purified aggregate of form.

Vajra master: A highly realized lama who is skilled in tantric rituals.

Vajrabhairava: One of the three main deities of the Gelug lineage. Vajrabhairava, also known as Yamantaka, is both the "destroyer of the lord of death" and, as an emanation of Manjushri, functions to increase wisdom in his practitioners. See *The Roar of Thunder: Yamantaka Practice and Commentary* (Ithaca, NY: Snow Lion Publications, 2012).

Vajradhara: An emanation of Buddha Shakyamuni who appeared as a blue-colored deity and taught the various tantras.

Vajrayogini: A female enlightened being who is both the consort of Chakrasamvara and a tantric deity in her own right. Her practice is very simple yet profound and contains many unique instructions for attaining enlightenment in one life as well as traveling to the Kechara pure land. See *The Extremely Secret Dakini of Naropa: Vajrayogini Practice and Commentary* (Ithaca, NY: Snow Lion Publications, 2011).

Wisdom being: The actual mind of an enlightened being that is summoned to dissolve into the commitment being.

Yoga tantra: The third of the four classes of tantra, which places primary emphasis upon internal actions and utilizes holding hands with a physical consort as a means of generating a blissful subjective awareness used to penetrate the nature of reality.

Bibliography of Works in English

Āryadeva and Gyel-tsap. *The Yogic Deeds of Bodhisattvas.* Translated by Ruth Sonam. Ithaca, NY: Snow Lion Publications, 1994. (Reprinted as *Āryadeva's Four Hundred Stanzas on the Middle Way.*)

Atiśa and Dromtönpa. *The Book of Kadam: The Core Texts.* Translated by Thupten Jinpa. Boston: Wisdom Publications, 2008.

Buddha Shakyamuni. *Sutra of the Wise and the Foolish.* Translated by Stanley Frye. Dharamsala, India: Library of Tibetan Works and Archives, 1981.

Cozort, Daniel. *Highest Yoga Tantra: An Introduction to the Esoteric Buddhism of Tibet.* Ithaca, NY: Snow Lion Publications, 2005.

Dalai Lama. *The Gelug/Kagyü Tradition of Mahamudra.* Translated by Alexander Berzin. Ithaca, NY: Snow Lion Publications, 1997.

———. *The Union of Bliss and Emptiness: Teachings on the Practice of Guru Yoga.* Translated by Thupten Jinpa. Ithaca, NY: Snow Lion Publications, 2009.

Dharmarakshita. *Peacock in the Poison Grove: Two Buddhist Texts on Training the Mind.* Translated by Geshe Lhundrub Sopa with Michael Sweet and Leonard Zwilling. Boston: Wisdom Publications, 2001.

Gonsalez, David, trans. *The Chakrasamvara Root Tantra.* Seattle: Dechen Ling Press, 2010.

Gray, David, trans. *The Cakrasamvara Tantra (The Discourse of Śrī Heruka).* New York: American Institute of Buddhist Studies at Columbia University, 2007.

Jamgön Kongtrul Lodrö Tayé. *Buddhist Ethics.* Translated by Kalu Rinpoché Translation Group. Ithaca, NY: Snow Lion Publications, 1998. (Reprinted as *The Treasury of Knowledge. Book Five: Buddhist Ethics.*)

Kirti Tsenshap Rinpoché. *Principles of Buddhist Tantra: A Commentary on Chöjé Ngawang Palden's* Illumination of the Tantric Tradition: The Principles of the Grounds and Paths of the Four Great Secret Classes of Tantra. Translated and edited by Ian Coghlan and Voula Zarpani. Boston: Wisdom Publications, 2011.

Nagarjuna. *Nagarjuna's Letter to a Friend: With Commentary by Kyabje Kangyur Rinpoche.* Translated by Padmakara Translation Group. Ithaca, NY: Snow Lion Publications, 2005.

Nam-kha Pel. *Mind Training Like the Rays of the Sun.* Translated by Brian Beresford. Dharamsala, India: Library of Tibetan Works and Archives, 1992.

Ngulchu Dharmabhadra and the Fifth Ling Rinpoche, Losang Lungtog Tenzin Trinley. *The Roar of Thunder: Yamantaka Practice and Commentary.* Translated by David Gonsalez. Ithaca, NY: Snow Lion Publications, 2012.

Ngulchu Dharmabhadra and the First Panchen Lama, Losang Chökyi Gyaltsen. *Source of Supreme Bliss: Heruka Chakrasamvara Five Deity Practice and Commentary.* Translated by David Gonsalez. Ithaca, NY: Snow Lion Publications, 2010.

Pabongkha Dechen Nyingpo. *The Extremely Secret Dakini of Naropa: Vajrayogini Practice and Commentary.* Translated by David Gonsalez. Ithaca, NY: Snow Lion Publications, 2011.

———. *Lama Chopa Heruka Sadhana.* Translated by David Gonsalez. https://dechenlingpress.org/product/lama-chopa-heruka-sadhana/.

———. *Yamantaka Lama Chopa.* Translated by David Gonsalez. https://dechenlingpress.org/product/yamantaka-lama-chopa/.

Pabongkha Rinpoche. *Liberation in Our Hands.* 3 vols. Translated by Sermey Khensur Lobsang Tharchin with Artemus B. Engle. Howell, NJ: Mahayana Sutra and Tantra Press, 1990–2001.

Shönu Gyalchok and Könchok Gyaltsen, comps. *Mind Training: The Great Collection.* Translated and edited by Thupten Jinpa. Boston: Wisdom Publications, 2006.

Thubten Loden, Geshe Acharya. *The Fundamental Potential for Enlightenment.* Melbourne: Tushita Publications, 1996.

———. *Path to Enlightenment in Tibetan Buddhism.* Melbourne: Tushita Publications, 1993.

Tsong-kha-pa. *The Great Treatise on the Stages of the Path to Enlightenment*. 3 vols. Translated by the Lamrim Chenmo Translation Committee. Ithaca, NY: Snow Lion Publications, 2000–2004.

Tsongkhapa, Losang Drakpa. *A Lamp to Illuminate the Five Stages: Teachings on the Guhyasamāja Tantra*. Translated by Gavin Kilty. Boston: Wisdom Publications, 2013.

Index

Abhidhana Tantra, 92

Accomplishment of Exalted Wisdom, 99, 187–88

Accomplishment of Secrets, 77, 99, 104, 113, 155–56

accumulation of merit, 153, 176
  guru yoga and, 96–97, 184, 211
  offering of, 137–42
  during session breaks, 369
  transforming adverse conditions with, 268

Achala, 73, 83

action-vajra, 149

action vase, 64

Adorning the Essence of the Vajra Tantra, 85–86, 366

adverse conditions, transforming, 265–69, 410
  as measure of having trained, 271–74
  through bodhichitta, 266–67
  through deeds, 268–69
  through the view, 267–68

affectionate love, 247–48, 278

afflictive emotions
  of all beings, purifying, 52–53, 54, 231, 264–65
  as cause of suffering, 47–48, 54, 244, 245
  as demonic illness, 255, 289–90
  expelling and purifying, 44–45
  ignorance and, 307–8
  illnesses of, 162, 403
  mental wandering and, 300–301
  methods for abandoning, 153
  not relying on guru and, 188
  taking and giving of, 272

aggregates, nature of guru's, 70, 72, 79–80, 219

Akashagarbha, 73, 81, 82

Akshobya, 72, 80, 94, 227
  all tactile objects as, 365
  commitments of, 167, 329
  lineages of, 220

alcohol, inner offerings and, 145

Amitabha, 72, 80, 94
  all scents as, 365
  commitments of, 167, 330
  lineages of, 220

Amoghasiddhi, 72, 80
  all tastes as, 365
  commitments of, 167, 329
  lineages of, 220

Amrita Kundali, 73, 83

anger
  antidote to, 308
  contemplating faults of, 288–92
  taking and giving of, 272–73

Angulimala, 218

Aparajita, 73, 82

appearance
  as bliss and emptiness, 79
  as deities, 364–65
  dependent arising of, 309–13
  emptiness as nature of, 114–16
  extreme of existence and, 21, 310, 311
  false illusorylike, 306–307

arhats, 91
  guru's pores as, 70, 73, 84, 85
  two states of, 48, 278–79

Arrangement of the Three Commitments Tantra, 161–62

Array of Stalks Sutra, 209
Aryadeva, 186, 308, 320, 333, 337, 438
Asanga, 19, 43, 94, 247n, 281, 372
Atisha, 14, 20–21, 143, 174, 190, 197, 207, 247, 252, 253, 270, 280, 372
attachment
  antidote to, 308
  mental excitement and, 300, 301
  taking and giving of, 273
attainments
  empowerments and, 35–36
  EVAM and, 75
  guru yoga and, 31, 32, 102, 104, 186–88, 327
  making offerings and, 96–101, 144, 162–63
  protecting commitments and, 321–22, 325, 330, 331
Avalokiteshvara, 25, 81, 82, 191
Avatamsaka Sutra, 17, 79, 119, 139, 248, 252

Baso Chökyi Gyaltsen, 2, 22, 23, 24, 100, 444
Bhadracarya Pranidhana, 174
bhumis, 296
black near-attainment, 62, 342
blessing the offerings, 63–67
bliss, great
  clear light of, 58, 228–29, 434
  enthusiastic perseverance and, 295–96
  offering objects of desire and, 125–28
  offerings to guru and, 102–4
  secret offering and, 151–52, 157
  simultaneously born, 223–24
  truth body of, 221
bliss and emptiness, inseparable
  blessing offering substances and, 66, 67, 79, 114–16
  close enjoyment offerings and, 122, 123
  completion stage and, 79
  EVAM and, 76, 78
  exalted wisdom of, 75–79, 338
  mantra-water-for-drinking and, 118
  principal of assembly and, 69, 70, 73, 75
  secret and suchness mandala and, 136
  viewing all appearance as, 370
Blue Scripture (Geshe Potowa), 232

Blue Udder, 31, 393
bodhichitta
  aspiring and engaging, 52, 163–64, 279–82
  correcting motivation and, 44–45
  equalizing and exchanging self with others, 248, 254–65
  generating, 49, 52–55, 59, 153, 246–82, 371
  generating great compassion, 247–52
  meditating on superior intention and, 278–79
  meditating on ultimate, 253–54
  path of resultant, 53
  seven-point mind training, 252–78
  tantric vows and, 166–67
  transforming adverse conditions with, 265–66
  twenty-two types of, 141n
  uncommon method for generating, 55–57, 328–29, 395–97
  See also seven-point mind training; six perfections
Bodhisattva Bhumi (Asanga), 281, 293
bodhisattvas
  body mandala of guru and, 80–81, 85
  condensed practices of, 281–82
  perfection of wisdom as, 222
  Shantideva on deeds of, 283
  training in deeds of, 283–313, 314
  See also six perfections
Bodhisattva Section Sutra, 18
bodhisattva vows, 28n, 161, 329
  aspiring and engaging, 163–64, 279–82
  downfalls and, 169, 287
  tantric vows and, 166, 316
body
  generosity of wish-fulfilling, 284
  isolated body, 63, 337
  qualities of guru's, 213–16
  vase empowerment and, 226, 227
  See also vajra body
body mandala, of guru, 19, 70, 72–73, 74, 79–85
body of union, 179, 186, 220, 226, 229–30, 316, 334, 337, 344, 347, 373
"Bringing Happiness and Suffering into the Path," 269

bringing three bodies into the path. *See* three bodies

"Bringing Whatever You Encounter into the Path," 269

buddhas and bodhisattvas of the ten directions
abiding in body of guru, 73, 83–85, 95, 99, 184–85
collecting and summoning blessings of, 45, 65
emanation bodies of, 214
guru as embodiment of exalted wisdom of, 107–8, 219–20, 224
guru as surpassing, 211–12
making offerings to guru and, 98–99, 173, 184
rejoicing in virtue of, 174–75
seeing as emanations of guru, 110–13, 399–400

Buddha Shakyamuni, 72, 291, 344
age of strife and, 207–8
inconceivable emanations of, 105
mantra of, 232, 233
outer qualities of, 215–18
twelve deeds of, 105n–106n
See also conqueror's teachings

burnt offerings, 367

celestial mansion, 60, 132
transforming all environments into, 63, 67, 231

central channel
essential object of concentration in, 341
knots and channel wheels of, 339, 340
penetrating vital points of heart of, 337–40
transference of consciousness and, 353–54
winds collecting in, 220, 338, 339, 341, 347
See also channels

Chakrasamvara Root Tantra. See Heruka Root Tantra

Chakrasamvara tantra
blessing offerings for, 65
empowerments and, 34, 231
Lama Chöpa and, 1, 2, 3, 21
See also Heruka

Chandrakirti, 247, 248, 290, 306, 308–9, 320, 361

channels
in center of body, 340
nature of guru's, 71, 81
secret empowerment and, 224–25
See also central channel

channel wheels, 339, 340

Chapter That Focuses Completely on the Six Perfections, 222

charnel ground, 69

Chatuhpitha Tantra, 350, 352

Chayulwa, 95

"cheating death" rituals, 351

Chenga Drakpa Jangchub, 21

Chengawa, 190

Chöje Dondrup Rinpoche, 21

Chökyi Dorje (Chö Dorje, Dharmavajra), 2, 11, 24, 26, 29, 181, 359

Clear Illumination of All Hidden Meaning (Tsongkhapa), 97

Clear Lamp, 189

clear light
all-empty, 230, 342
of emptiness, 60, 230
example, 179, 220, 337, 343
of great bliss, 58, 103, 228, 229, 367, 436
of isolated mind, 153, 337, 343
of meaning, 109, 220, 337, 343, 347
mixing of mother and son, 352
wisdom empowerment and, 159n

Clear Words, 308

close enjoyment offerings, 118–25, 401

close lineage of blessings, 87

Cloud of Jewels Sutra, 273

Cluster of Oral Instructions, 94, 113, 144–45, 325, 357

Cluster of the Ultimate Meaning, 112, 205

Collection of Spiritual Grounds (Asanga), 43

Commentary on Bodhichitta (Nagarjuna), 248, 258

Commentary on the Chapter of Moral Discipline, 282

Commentary on the Kalachakra Empowerment Chapter, 206

Commentary on Valid Cognition, 177, 205, 245, 255–56

Commentary to the Difficult Points of the

Chandragomin, 248

Buddhakapala Tantra *Called Jnanavati*
(Saraha), 322
commitment beings, 94
commitments. *See* vows and commitments
commitment substances, 326
common path
of beings with great capacity, 246–313
of beings with medium capacity,
243–46
of beings with small capacity, 237–43
perfection of, 54
training in, 34, 37, 333
See also Mahayana; Vinaya
compassion
of Dharma teacher, 177, 198, 208
generating great, 247–52, 278, 314
toward harmful agents, 288–92
as root of Mahayana path, 247
Compendium of Abhidharma, 299, 301
Compendium of Conducts (Aryadeva),
333, 337, 341
Compendium of Conduct Tantra, 76, 113
Compendium of Precious Qualities, 294–95
Compendium of Sutras (Nagarjuna), 238
Compendium of Trainings (Shantideva), 238,
248, 250, 254, 285
Compendium of Vajra Wisdom, 346
completion stage
appearance as bliss and emptiness and,
79
empowerments and, 159n, 316
five stages of, 20, 63n, 178, 336–47
how to train in, 336–47
importance of preliminary stage for,
332–33
texts revealing, 320
three bodies of, 332, 334, 339
"Concealed Dharma of the Forefather,"
252
concentration
faults of sinking, excitement, and
wandering, 299–302
mandala offering and, 129
nine stages of settling the mind, 302
objects of observation, 298–99
perfection of, 298–302, 411
special characteristics of, 299
three types of, 302

See also meditation
conceptual elaborations dissolving, 221,
343
extremes of, 309–10
resting in essential nature of, 435–36
Concise Five Stages, 341
Concise Perfection of Wisdom Sutra, 294
Condensed Sadhana (Nagarjuna), 320
confession, 168–74, 403
four opponent powers, 171–72
of root and secondary downfalls,
169–70
confession buddhas, 91
Confession of Bodhisattva Downfalls, 404
"Confession of Moral Downfalls," 434
conqueror's teachings
on dependent arising, 307–13
on five stages, 336
guru yoga and, 13–19
limitless enumerations of, 16
oral instructions and, 13–15, 317–20
See also Dharma

daily actions
conduct during, 363–75
increasing bodhichitta during,
273–74
death
bringing into the path, 58, 59–60, 62,
333, 334, 335, 339, 351
clear light of, 339
contemplating, 253
eight stages of dissolution at, 61–62
learning signs of, 350
practices at moment of, 270
three mixings during, 342
See also transference of consciousness
dedication, of virtue, 180–82, 404,
413
dedication prayers, 360–62
definitive meaning guru, 222
degenerate age
accomplishing enlightenment in, 47, 76,
96, 97, 102, 339, 371
Buddha Shakyamuni and, 207–8
Heruka and, 97
deity/deities
all appearances as, 364–65

assembled retinue of, 87–91
  dwelling within body of guru, 72–73,
    79–85, 184
  generating complete mandala of, 334
  guru inseparable from, 18, 19, 21
deity yoga, 34
  generating self as deity, 57–63
  generating special bodhichitta, 55–57
  making offerings and, 96
  transference of consciousness through,
    352–55
  See also guru-deity assembly; guru yoga
dependent arising, 307–13, 334, 412
Dharma
  eighty-four thousand heaps of, 307–8
  request to turn wheel of, 176–78, 403–4
  See also conqueror's teachings; Three
    Jewels
Dharma protectors, 22, 91, 269
Dharmavajra. See Chökyi Dorje
Dharmodgata, 17, 18, 42, 189
Diamond Cutter Sutra, 222
directional protectors, 73, 84
Discourse of the Wish-Fulfilling Dream of a
  Jewel (Nagarjuna), 248
Discrimination of the Middle and the Extremes
  (Asanga), 299
dissolution, two stages of, 343
divine pride, 52, 53, 335
doha teachings, 20
Dorje Zinpa Konchog Gyaltsen, 30
Dorje Zinpa Losang Rigdrol, 30, 341
downfalls
  abandoning, and attainments, 322
  four doors of, 245, 326
  purifying, 171, 172
  results of, 323–25
  root and secondary, 169–70, 204, 281,
    287, 327
  subtle and coarse, 287
Drakor Khenchen, 21
Drom Rinpoche, 20, 174, 190, 199, 252,
  372
drop-elements, secret empowerment and,
  228
Drop of Exalted Wisdom Tantra, 185
Drop of Mahamudra, 36, 102–3, 173

eating
  commitment of, 167, 326
  yoga of, 326
eight powers, 71
Eight Verses of Mind Training (Geshe Langri
  Tangpa), 259
elements
  nature of guru's, 70, 72, 81, 219
  sequential dissolving of, 61, 352
emanation body
  bringing rebirth into the path as, 60, 62,
    333, 339–40
  of conquerors, 214
  seeing guru as, 105–109, 399–400
  supreme, 107
  transference of consciousness of, 351
  vase empowerment and, 226, 227, 316
Emanation Scripture. See Great Emanation
    Scripture
Empowerment of Vajrapani Tantra, 173
empowerments and blessings, 18, 407
  concise way of receiving, 225–26
  elaborate way of receiving, 226–31
  of highest yoga tantra, 34–37, 314–21,
    371
  inner offering related to secret, 142–51,
    402
  mantra recitation and, 231–34
  outer offering related to vase, 113–42
  secret offering related to wisdom,
    151–56, 402
  stages of path and, 159
  suchness offering related to word,
    157–59, 403
  uncommon method for, 230–31
emptiness
  dissolving into unobservable, 57, 60
  extreme of nonexistence and, 21, 310,
    311
  of illusory-like subsequent attainment,
    305–7
  of inherent existence, 153
  meditating on view of, 253–54
  Middle Way view of, 307–13
  as nature of appearances, 114–16
  as nature of selflessness, 58
  single-pointed focus upon, 299, 302,
    303, 304

emptiness (*continued*)
stages of withdrawal and, 58, 59–60, 333
transforming adverse conditions with view of, 266–69
See also bliss and emptiness, inseparable
ending the session, 360–63
enjoyment body
bringing intermediate state into the path as, 60, 62, 334, 339
of conquerors, 214
endowed with five certainties, 180, 220, 345n
secret empowerment and, 226, 228, 316
seeing guru as, 101–4, 399
transference of consciousness of, 351
enjoyments, giving away, 284–85
enlightenment
attaining, for benefiting beings, 48, 52, 278–79, 286
in one lifetime, 75, 76, 77, 96, 102, 186, 339
quickly accomplishing, 183, 322
See also attainments
Ensa lineage, 1
Entering the Middle Way (Chandrakirti), 14, 247, 296, 306, 361
equalizing self with others, 247, 252–53
equanimity, meditating on, 249–51
Essence of Eloquence Praising the Buddha (Tsongkhapa), 311
Essential Cycle of Teachings, 20
EVAM, 75–76, 78, 79
exalted wisdom
accomplishing, 20
of all the conquerors, 107–8, 220, 225
blessing offering substances and, 66
guru yoga and, 187–88
of inseparable bliss and emptiness, 76–79, 338
nature of the five, 145
as resultant perfection of wisdom, 222
Samantabhadra and, 79
of truth body, 112–13
yoga of pure, 344–45
exchanging self with others (tonglen), 248, 255–65

actual instruction, 263–64
afflictive emotions and, 272
benefits of cherishing others and, 257–65
faults of self-cherishing and, 255–63
meaning of, 260
perfection of patience and, 291
transforming adverse conditions with, 266
Explanatory Tantra Vajramala, 15–16, 19, 35–36, 37, 40, 43, 75, 79–84, 104, 109, 121, 123–24, 126, 128, 146, 147, 158, 160, 184, 203, 204–5, 206, 218, 332, 345, 374. See also *Vajramala*
Explanatory Tantra Vajra Mudra, 76
Explicit Commentary on Five Stages of the Completion Stage, 22
extremes of existence and nonexistence, 21, 309–10, 311

faith and devotion
in guru, 37, 100–101, 189–90, 211
receiving blessings and, 232–33
See also supplicating the guru
father and mother desire deities, 78, 136, 329
fear
generosity of pacifying, 285
overcoming, 273
field-born messengers, 151
field of merit
assembly of guru-deities in, 69–92
dissolving of, 57, 58
going for refuge in, 49–52
guru as perfect, 211–12
invoking the wisdom beings, 92–94, 398–99
offering substances for, 66–67
placement of guru in, 69, 91
visualizing, 397–98
withdrawing, for sake of blessings, 358–59
See also guru-deity assembly
Fifth Commitment, 323
Fifty Verses of Guru Devotion (Ashvagosha), 22, 32, 99–100, 111–12, 136, 162, 169, 200, 204–5, 316, 327, 328, 329, 394, 398, 425–32

five buddha families, 85
  as aggregates of guru, 72, 79–80, 219
  commitments of, 166, 167–68, 325–30
  empowerments and, 230, 316
  guru as nature of, 86
  hundred lineages and, 220
  request to turn wheel of Dharma of,
    178–79
five certainties, 180, 220, 345
five cow products, 41, 42, 129
five forces, 270, 410
  transference of consciousness through,
    348–49
five lamps and hooks, 144–45
five meats and nectars, 143–45, 146
Five Stages (Nagarjuna), 15, 96, 102,
  103–4, 108, 185, 320, 332, 345, 399
Five Stages of Heruka (Ghantapa), 338
*Five Stages of the Arya Tradition of
  Guhyasamaja, The*, 336, 337
flowers, offering, 119, 121–23, 124
food substances, offering, 120, 123
force of destruction, 270, 349
force of familiarity, 270
force of intention, 270, 349
force of meditation, 349
force of prayer, 270, 349
force of the white seed, 270, 348
four complete purities, 63
four empowerments. *See* empowerments
  and blessings
four fearlessnesses, 71
four great kings, 42
four greatnesses, 33
four great preliminary guides, 57, 137
Four Hundred Stanzas (Aryadeva), 290,
  306, 308
four immeasurables, 54–55, 57, 328
four joys, 228
four limbs of approaching and
  accomplishing, 62
four modes, 19, 221–22, 317
four opponent powers, 171, 172, 269
Fourteen Root Downfalls, 322, 323, 326,
  327
fourth empowerment. *See* precious word
  empowerment
Four Vajra Seats Tantra, 84

four vajras, generating, 62
four waters, offering, 113–18, 401
four ways of gathering, 52
four wheels, 360, 362–63, 413

ganachakra, 122, 146–51, 180, 343
Ganakchakra Offering, for Lama Chöpa,
  415–24
Ganden Hearing Lineage, 5, 6, 22, 31, 53,
  57, 87n, 300, 369, 375, 377n. *See also*
  oral instructions
Ganden mahamudra teachings, 45, 300,
  301, 313, 359. *See also* mahamudra
Gandhavajra, 73
General Confession, 170
General Secret Tantra, 206
generation stage
  appearance as deity in, 79
  bringing three bodies into the path, 58,
    59–62, 332–33, 334, 335, 336
  coarse and subtle, 59, 333, 337
  empowerments and, 159, 228, 316
  extensive and concise systems of,
    59–62, 332–33
  guru yoga as preliminary for, 58–59
  how to train in, 331–36
  texts revealing, 320
generosity, perfection of, 284–86, 411
Gen Losang Choephel, 3
Geshe Chekawa, 1n, 34n, 252
Geshe Khenrab Gajam, 3
Geshe Langri Tangpa, 259
Geshe Potowa, 129, 252, 252n
Ghandavajra, 82
Ghantapa, 338
*Glorious Guhyasamaja Explanatory Tantra
  That Prophesies Realization*, 154
Glorious Guhyasamaja Root Tantra, 107–8,
  112, 126, 157. See also *Guhyasamaja Root
  Tantra*
god realm, 47, 53. *See also* samsara
going for refuge, 16, 50–52, 371
  fear of lower realms and, 243
  uncommon method for, 55–57, 163,
    328–29, 395–97
Go Lotsawa, 21
Great Commentary Stainless Light, 206–7
Great Emanation Scripture, 22, 24, 25

Great Exposition on the Stages of the Path of Mantra (Tsongkhapa), 320, 327–28, 333, 346, 372–73

Great Exposition on the Stages of the Path to Enlightenment, 198–99, 207, 239, 280, 300–301, 313

great treasure vase, mandala offering and, 130, 131

Guhyasamaja
  arising as body of, 58, 59
  in assembled retinue, 87–88

Guhyasamaja Root Tantra, 19, 39, 42, 62, 75, 79, 112, 121, 126, 127–28, 136, 145–46, 157, 158, 172–73, 189, 211–12, 233, 317, 334, 336, 344, 363–64, 365, 368

Guhyasamaja tantra, 220, 221
  blessing offerings for, 65
  completion stages of, 63n, 179
  dedication prayers of, 360–61
  empowerments and, 34, 230
  Lama Chöpa and, 1, 2, 19, 20, 21
  mandala ritual of, 146
  torma offering and, 357

Guide to the Bodhisattva's Way of Life (Shantideva), 132, 161, 238, 248, 253, 254, 258, 261, 267, 281, 283, 285, 290–91, 295, 307, 329, 350, 437

guru
  in aspect of three nested beings, 24, 34, 74, 91, 93
  benefits of relying upon, 182–194
  body mandala of, 19, 70, 72–73, 74, 79–85
  buddhas and bodhisattvas abiding in body of, 73, 83–85, 95, 99, 184–85
  buddhas and bodhisattvas as emanations of, 110–13, 399–400
  as exalted wisdom of all conquerors, 107–108, 220, 225
  going for refuge in, 50–52
  good qualities of vajra master, 200–207, 315–16, 406
  how to view, 85–86
  as inseparable from deity, 18, 19, 21
  as inseparable from Vajradhara, 92, 95, 99, 224–25

  as nature of Three Jewels, 109–10, 188, 191, 219, 225, 400
  proper reliance upon, 16–19, 30–33, 234–36, 315–16
  purity of three vows of, 206–7
  recalling kindness of, 207–12, 406
  reciting name mantra of, 191–94, 231–33, 370
  recollecting good qualities of, 194–207, 235, 404–6
  as root of all attainments, 31–32, 102, 104, 185–89, 327
  seeing as the three bodies, 101–109, 399–400
  seeking blessings throughout all lives, 355–58
  as unsurpassed object of offering, 86, 102
  See also guru-deity assembly; offerings; supplicating the guru

guru-deity assembly, 69–92
  deities abiding in body of guru, 70, 72–73, 79–85
  exalted wisdom of bliss and emptiness and, 75–79
  invoking the wisdom beings, 93–95
  position of visualization, 69, 92
  retinue of deities, 87–91
  visualizing the principal, 69–87
  wish-fulfilling tree, 70–71
  withdrawing, for sake of blessings, 358–59
  worldly beings as cushions for feet of, 86–87
  See also field of merit

Guru-Vajradhara Father and Mother the Great, 228

guru yoga
  accumulation of merit and, 96–97, 184, 211–12
  contemplating benefits and faults of, 183–94
  deities dwelling in body of guru and, 184
  explanation of greatness of, 31–37, 96–100
  of Je Rinpoche's Hearing Lineage, 22–31
  as life of the path, 20–21, 173, 341

mahasiddhis of India and, 19–21
Mahayana teachings on, 17–18, 21–22
purification of obscurations and, 172–74
recitation of OM AH HUM and, 233
secret mantra and, 18–19
teachings of conqueror and, 13–19
uncommon oral lineage of, 21–22
See also deity yoga
Guru Yoga of the Profound Path That Completely Embodies the Path, The (The Ritual of Lama Chöpa), 13
Gyalwa Ensapa, 1, 2, 25–29, 43, 49, 53, 59, 74, 86–87, 91–92, 130, 190, 230, 231, 234, 338, 341, 359
Gyalwa Gendun Gyatso (Second Dalai Lama), 62

harmful agents
  practicing patience with, 288–92
  taking and giving with, 265–66
Hayagriva, 73, 83
Heap of Jewels Sutra, 112, 281
Hearing Lineage. *See* Ganden Hearing Lineage; oral instructions
heart
  mantra drop at, 338, 342
  penetrating vital points of, 338–40
Heart of Wisdom Sutra, 114
Hero Engaging in Battle, The (Losang Chökyi Gyaltsen), 354
heroes and heroines, 74, 91, 147, 148
Heruka
  abiding in body of guru, 97
  arising as body of, 58, 59, 62
  guru-deity assembly and, 74, 87, 89
  See also Chakrasamvara tantra
Heruka Explanatory Tantra Samvarodaya, 86, 110, 144, 147
Heruka Root Tantra, 96–97, 156, 160, 173, 184, 324
Hevajra, 88
Hevajra Tantra in Two Chapters Entitled "The Two Examinations," 218, 223
highest yoga tantra
  becoming suitable vessel for, 34–37, 314–21
  completion-stage training, 336–47
  empowerments of, 34–37, 314–17, 371

generation-stage training, 332–36
  good qualities of vajra master, 203–4, 315–16
  mahamudra as essence of, 434
  secrecy and, 34–37
  supplicating suchness qualities and, 221
holding the body entirely, 343n
human life
  formation of body for, 339
  of leisure and endowments, 238–43, 253
  See also sentient beings
hundred lineages, 220

ignorance
  as root of afflictions, 308, 311
  taking and giving of, 273
Ignorance Vajra, 74
illnesses
  of afflictive emotions, 161–62
  not relying on guru and, 189
Illuminating Lamp Commentary, The (Chandrakirti), 320
illusory body
  pure, 179
  secret empowerment and, 159n, 228
  of third stage, 109, 179, 337, 342, 343, 347
illusory-like subsequent attainment, 305–7, 411
impermanence
  contemplating, 238, 239, 241, 253
  seeing all appearance as, 272
incense, offering, 119, 122, 124
inner offering
  blessing and cleansing, 63–66, 143
  close enjoyment offerings, 123–25
  five meats and nectars, 143–45
  ganachakra and, 146–51
inner mandala offering, 135–36
  objects of desire, 126–27
  related to secret empowerment, 142–51, 402
  tea offerings, 142–43
inner qualities of guru, supplicating, 213, 219, 406
In Praise of the Praiseworthy, 217
"Instructions for Equalizing Flavor," 269

intention
force of, 270, 349
meditating on superior, 278–79
interfering spirits, 113, 114, 268
intermediate state, bringing into the path, 59, 61, 62, 334, 335, 336, 339
isolated body, 63, 337
isolated mind, 153, 343
isolated speech, 337

Jampal Gyatso, 22, 193
Jataka Tales, 290, 350
Jayulwa, 190
Jetsun Rendawa, 21
Jeweled Garland of the Middle Way, The (Nagarjuna), 248
Jnanapada, 156, 338, 352, 374
jointed grass seat, 42

Kachen Yeshe Gyaltsen, 2, 5–6
Kadam (Emanation) Scripture, 194
Kadam Mind Training, 348, 374
Kalachakra, 89
Kalachakra empowerment, 206
Kalachakra Tantra, 184
Kalarupa, 441
Kamalashila, 197, 248
karma
afflictive emotions and, 162
cause and effect of, 249, 253, 309, 310, 311, 312, 371
empowerments and, 226, 227, 228, 229
purifying negative, 50–51, 52, 54, 96, 168–74, 184, 192, 268, 369
suffering and, 47, 54, 245
Khedrup Je, 22–23, 193
Khedrup Sangye Yeshe, 29, 33, 53, 56, 111, 130, 143, 169, 177–78, 220, 232, 315, 395
King Indrabhuti, 19
king of pranayama, 340
King of Prayers of Good Deeds, The, 360–61
knowledge goddesses, 227, 229
Kshitigarbha, 73, 80, 81, 82

Lalita, 19
Lama Chöpa
contemplating greatness of, 96–100
as essence of sutra and tantra, 374
explanation of greatness of, 31–37
explanation of source of, 13–31
ganachakra offering for, 415–24
profoundness of, 1–3
Lama Donyo Khedrup, 341
Lama Dorzinma, 170, 404
Lama Kyungpo Lhäpa, 21
Lama Losang Tubwang Dorje Chang, 21, 31, 94, 160, 163, 192, 356, 358
establishing all beings as, 53
four empowerments and, 226–30
guru-deity assembly and, 73, 75, 77, 78
as object of refuge, 13, 34, 50, 57
secret offering and, 152
transforming into body of, 52
Lamp for a Summary of Conducts, A (Aryadeva), 320
Lamp for Compendium of Practice Elucidating the Meaning of the Five Stages, 153
Lamp for the Compendium of Practice, A, 156
Lamp for the Path (Atisha), 20, 253, 281
Lamp Illuminating the Excellent Path of the Hearing Lineage: A Literary Commentary to Ganden Mahamudra, 45
Lamp Illuminating the Five Stages (Tsongkhapa), 178, 320, 339, 372
lamps, offering, 119, 122–23
lamrim, 1, 2, 363
laziness, three types of, 298
leisure and endowments, contemplating, 47, 238–42, 253, 371, 408
Liberating Moon, 323
liberation
mind striving for, 243–45
training in path leading to, 245–46, 371–72
lifetime practices, 270–71
Lifetime Vows, 196
Lochana, 73, 74, 80, 227
Lodrak Drubchen, 21
lojong, 1, 2. *See also* seven-point mind training
Lokeshvara, 73
Losang Chökyi Gyaltsen, 13, 29–31, 69, 73, 75, 79, 91–92, 111, 113, 115–16, 135–36, 159, 180, 210–11, 223, 231, 239, 240, 248, 267–68, 300, 306, 321, 339, 346, 354, 359, 361, 363, 370, 373, 390

Losang Namgyal, 30
Losang's Melodious Laughter: Questions and Answers of Pure Superior Intention (Losang Chökyi Gyaltsen), 46, 69, 92, 301, 309, 320. See also *Questions of Pure Superior Intention*
Losang Yeshe (Second Panchen Lama), 30, 341
lower realms
  causes for rebirth in, 257
  contemplating rebirth in, 47, 242–43
  purifying, 52–53
  See also samsara
Luipa, 19
Luminous Great Bliss, 65

madhyamaka. *See* Middle Way
Mahabala, 73, 83, 84
mahamudra
  actual instructions for, 434–38
  concluding session, 438–39
  preliminaries for, 433–34
  relying upon the guru and, 188–89
  supplication to the lineage of, 442–52
  See also Ganden mahamudra teachings
Mahasiddha Mahasukha Nath, 19
Mahayana
  accumulating merit in, 96
  afflictive emotions and, 152–53
  bodhisattva vows, 163–64, 279–82
  compassion as root of, 247–52
  generating bodhichitta and, 49, 52–54, 246–82
  on good qualities of spiritual master, 197–200, 405
  guru yoga and, 17–18, 20–21
  offering roots of virtue and, 138–39
  practices for moment of death, 348–49
  seven limbs and, 182
  seven-point mind training, 252–78
  six perfections, 283–313
  three moral disciplines of, 281–82
  See also bodhichitta; seven limbs; seven-point mind training; six perfections
Maitreya, 12, 14, 19, 73, 81, 94, 283
Maitripa, 434
Mamaki, 73, 80
mandala offering, 128–37, 329, 370, 402
  continents and such, 130–31, 132
  inner mandala, 135
  kit for, 128
  outer mandala, 129–35
  secret and suchness mandala, 135, 136–37
  seven precious substances and possessions, 130, 131, 132–35
  six perfections and, 129–30
  twenty-three heap system, 130
mandala ritual, 146
Mandala Ritual Vajramala, 117
Manjushri, 1, 19, 21–22, 73, 81, 82, 87, 129, 193–94, 238, 252, 281, 310
Manjushri Root Tantra, 193, 197
mantra-born messengers, 151–52
mantra/mantra recitation of Buddha Shakyamuni, 232, 233
  close enjoyment offerings and, 122
  for confession, 170
  empowerments and, 231–33
  for generating self as deity, 58, 59
  invoking the wisdom beings, 94
  OM AH HUM, 232, 233, 340n
  reciting guru's name mantra, 191–94, 231–33, 370–71
  of Vajradhara, 231, 232, 233
  vase empowerment and, 227
mantra-water-for-drinking, 118
Marpa Lotsawa, 21, 44, 95, 174
Master Abhyakara, 130, 144–45, 164, 357
Master Jnanabodhi, 325
Master Kamalashila, 43, 248
Maudgalyayanaputra, 216
Mayajala Tantra, 95
medicine, offering special, 160, 403
meditation
  correcting motivation, 41–45
  dispelling impure winds, 43, 44
  on emptiness of illusory-like subsequent attainment, 305–7
  essential posture for, 43–44
  examining movement of breath, 44–45
  on mahamudra, 434–38
  place to practice, 39–41
  preparing place for, 41–42
  resting in sphere of awareness, 45
  seat for, 42–43

meditation (*continued*)
  on space-like meditative equipoise,
    303–5
  tranquil abiding, 298–302
  See also concentration, perfection of
Meeting of Father and Son Sutra, 106, 218
mental sinking, excitement, and
    wandering, 299–302
merit. *See* accumulation of merit; field of
    merit
messengers
  secret offering and, 151–52, 156
  suchness offering and, 157–59
Middle Way, profound view of, 21, 153,
    307–13, 371, 411–412
Migtsema, 183, 193n, 194n
Milarepa, 174
mind
  isolated mind, 153, 343
  qualities of guru's, 216–17
  recognizing true nature of, 434, 436–38
  wisdom empowerment and, 226,
    228–29
mindfulness
  during session breaks, 367
  of Vajrayana guru, 200
Mind Only school, 46
mind training, 1n, 34, 49, 374
  for beings of great capacity, 246–313
  for beings of medium capacity, 243–46
  for beings of small capacity, 238–243
  for daily actions, 363
  equalizing and exchanging self with
    others, 254–65
  generating bodhichitta, 246–82
  generating great compassion, 247–52
  generating mind striving for liberation,
    243–45
  on leisures and endowments, 238–42
  meditating on superior intention,
    278–79
  relying upon the spiritual master,
    234–36
  seven-point, 252–78
  six perfections, 283–313
  training in the path of liberation,
    245–46

  See also seven-point mind training; six
    perfections
moral discipline
  of beings, purifying, 274
  completely pure, 240, 245, 281
  mandala offering and, 128
  perfection of, 286–87, 411
  three types of, 165, 167, 281, 286–87,
    330
  of upholder of Vinaya, 195–97,
    286–87, 405
motivation, 41, 44–45, 52, 164
  bodhichitta, 48–49
  correcting, 39–49
Mount Jomo Lhari, 25
Mount Meru, mandala offering and, 130,
    131–32, 135
mudras
  close enjoyment offerings and, 122
  of Great King, 76
music, offering, 120–21, 122, 123

Nagarjuna, 19, 20, 21, 87, 95, 96, 102,
    112, 185, 238, 247, 248, 258, 308–13,
    320, 332, 337, 339, 344, 345, 362,
    434, 437
Naropa, 19, 21, 174, 434
nectar pills, 145
negative emotions. *See* afflictive emotions
Niladanda, 73, 83
nine-round breathing meditation, 44, 435
nine rounds of mixing, 342
nine stages of settling the mind, 302, 303
nirvana
  request to not pass into, 179–80
  winds as root of, 221
Nivarana Viskambin, 82
nonvirtues
  confessing and purifying, 169–74
  four nonvirtuous Dharmas, 280
  natural, 170, 172

Oath-Bound Dharmaraja, 21, 91
objects of desire, offering, 125–28, 401
objects of refuge. *See* field of merit; guru-
    deity assembly; Three Jewels
obscurations

empowerments and, 226, 227, 228,
    229–30, 316
purifying, 50–51, 52, 54, 96, 98,
    168–74, 184, 192–93
Ocean Cloud of Praises, 106
Ocean of Dakinis, 147
offering goddesses
    close enjoyment offerings and, 119–21,
        122–23
    four waters and, 116–17
    objects of desire and, 125–28
    sense objects as, 365
offerings
    anointing place for making, 41
    blessing inner, 63–65
    blessing offering substances, 66–67,
        113–14
    contemplating reasons for greatness of,
        96–100
    generation stage, 334
    inner offering, 142–51, 402
    making prostrations and praises, 101–113
    of oneself as servant, 159–63, 403
    outer offerings, 113–42, 401–2
    secret offering, 151–56, 402
    special medicine, 159
    suchness offering, 157–59, 403
    torma offering, 357–58
    understanding essential points of, 159
    vows and commitments, 163–68
    See also inner offering; outer offerings;
        seven limbs
OM AH HUM
    blessing offerings and, 66, 67
    four empowerments and, 225–26
    guru-deity assembly and, 91
    as three vajras, 94
    vajra recitation with, 232, 233, 340n
oral instructions
    of Je Rinpoche, 1–3, 20–31, 46, 67, 231,
        272, 269, 318–21
    Manjushri's bestowing of, 1, 21–22, 193,
        238–39
    teachings of conqueror and, 13–14,
        317–21
Oral Instructions of Manjushri (Jnanapada),
    98, 107, 156, 173, 184, 352–53, 374
ordinary appearances and conceptions

generation stage and, 335, 336
overcoming, 59, 65, 94
purifying, 118, 412
washing away stains of, 227
Ornament for Clear Realization, 254
Ornament for Mahayana Sutras (Maitreya),
    198, 254, 283, 299
Ornament of the Middle Way, 253
Öser Gyi Gyalpo (the King of Light Rays),
    216
Öser Gyi Gyaltsen (Victory Banner of
    Light Rays), 216
outer offerings
    blessing, 66–67, 113–16
    close enjoyment offerings, 118–25,
        401
    four waters, 113–18, 401
    interfering spirits and, 113
    as limitless offerings, 126
    mandala offering, 128–37, 402
    objects of desire, 125–28, 401
    offering your practice, 137–42, 402
    related to vase empowerment, 113–42
    See also mandala offering
outer qualities of guru
    inconceivable secrets of body, 214–16
    inconceivable secrets of mind, 216–17
    inconceivable secrets of speech, 216
    supplicating, 213–18, 406

Pabongkha Rinpoche, 3, 74n, 87n, 194n
Padma Shri Raja Garbha (the Essential
    King of the Glorious Lotus), 215–16
Pamtingpa brothers, 21
Pandaravasini, 73, 80
patience
    with harmful agents, 288–92
    mandala offering and, 128
    perfection of, 288–92, 411
    three types of, 200, 288
Perfect Joy, king of the smell eaters, 218
*Perfection of Wisdom Sutra in Eight Thousand
    Lines*, 17, 26, 273
perfection of wisdom sutras, 108, 109,
    175–76, 222, 247–48, 308, 311, 434
*Performance Incorporating the (Guhyasamaja)
    Sutra* (Nagarjuna), 320
perfume, offering, 120, 125

perseverance
  four powers and, 297
  mandala offering and, 129
  perfection of, 293–298, 411
  three types of, 293
phenomena, false illusory-like nature of,
  306–7
places to meditate, 39–43
planting the stake, 224–26, 407
Practical Commentary on the Complete Seat
  of the Five Stages of Guhyasamaja, A
  (Tsongkhapa), 74
Practice Manual on the Six Yogas (of Naropa
  Entitled) "The Three Convictions," 21
Praise to Dependent Relationship, 25
pratimoksha vows, 28n, 142, 154n, 169,
  206–7, 286–87, 411
Precious Garland, 296
precious word empowerment
  concise way of receiving, 226
  elaborate way of receiving, 229–30
  suchness offering related to, 157–59,
  403
preliminaries
  blessing the offerings, 63–67
  correcting motivation, 39–49
  extraordinary, 57–67
  general, 39–57
  generating bodhichitta, 52–57
  generating yourself as deity, 57–62
  going for refuge, 50–52
  for mahamudra, 433–34
  of mind training, 238–46, 253
  purifying world and all beings, 63
  special bodhichitta meditations, 55–57
prostrations and praises, 100–113, 329
purifying natural nonvirtues with, 170
  seeing buddhas and bodhisattvas as
    emanations of guru, 110–13, 400
  seeing guru as emanation body, 105–8,
    399
  seeing guru as enjoyment body, 101–4,
    399
  seeing guru as nature of Three Jewels,
    109–10, 400
  seeing guru as truth body, 108–9, 400
protector of primordial union, 219, 220,
  230, 231

Purchog Ngawang Jampa, 94
Pure Stages of Yoga, The, 65
Purification of Mental Obscurations
  (Aryadeva), 186–87

Questions of Pure Superior Intention
  (Tsongkhapa), 45–46, 69, 92,
  301, 319. See also Losang's Melodious
  Laughter: Questions and Answers of Pure
  Superior Intention

rainbow body, 179
Rasavajra goddess, 73, 82, 143
Ratnasambhava, 72, 80
  all sounds as, 365
  commitments of, 167, 328
  lineages of, 220
rebirth
  bringing into the path, 59, 60, 62, 333,
    334, 339–40
  higher, and patience, 288
  in lower realms, contemplating, 242
red increase, 61, 342
Red Yamari Tantra, 170
reflections, phenomena as, 306–7
refuge. See going for refuge
rejoicing, 174–76, 403
reliance
  commitments of, 167, 326–27
  power of, 172
renunciation, 59, 153, 238–43, 314
request to not pass into nirvana, 179–80,
  404
request to turn wheel of Dharma, 176–79,
  403–4
restraining pranayama of speech isolation,
  337
restraint, moral discipline of, 281,
  286–87
retreats
  boundary markers for, 42
  preparing place for, 41–42
Ribur Rinpoche, 3
rising, yoga of, 367
Ritual of the Profound Path of Lama Chöpa
  Entitled "Inseparable Bliss and Emptiness,"
  The, 391–414

Root Tantra of Glorious Guhyasamaja, 39. See also *Guhyasamaja Root Tantra*
Root Text on the Precious Geden-Kagyu Mahamudra Entitled "The Main Path of the Conquerors," The, 432–40
Root Text on the Precious Oral Lineage of Ganden Mahamudra That Is the Main Path of the Conquerors, 57, 170, 360
Root Verses of Mind Training, 253, 271–72
Rosary, The (Master Abhyakara), 357
Rupavajra, 81–82, 128, 227, 365, 367

Sadaprarudita, 17, 42, 189
Samantabhadra, 73, 81
  clouds of offerings of, 70, 71, 79, 126, 131, 148
  pure nature of, 221
Samayavajra, 368
Samputa Tantra, 168, 212, 344
samsara
  contemplating sufferings of, 46–48, 50, 53–54, 153, 244, 245, 253, 264–65, 371
  melting and dissolving of, 59
  mind striving for liberation from, 243–45
  purifying, 52–53, 54, 63, 231, 264
  self-grasping as root of, 221, 245, 255–62, 343–44
  three realms of, 292
  as world of unbearable suffering, 216
Samvarodaya Tantra, 32, 102, 107, 156, 325, 350, 351, 352, 395
Sandhi Vyakarana Tantra, 126
sangha. See Three Jewels
Saraha, 19, 20, 24n, 77–78, 104, 322, 434
Sarvanivarana-Viskambini, 73, 81
Sarvavid Vairochana, 90
scanning meditation, 49, 59, 355, 371, 375
Second Stages of Meditation (Kamalashila), 43, 248
Secret Accomplishment Clearly Revealing the Essential Meaning of the Root and Explanatory Tantras of Guhyasamaja, The, 19, 162–63, 186–87
secret empowerment
  concise way of receiving, 226

  elaborate way of receiving, 226–30
  illusory body and, 159n, 228
  inner offering related to, 142–51, 402
secret harm-givers, 84
secret mantra
  downfalls of, 170, 204, 286
  essential points of path of, 153
  generating special bodhichitta, 55–57
  on good qualities of guru, 200–207, 315, 406
  guru yoga and, 18–19
  protecting commitments and, 321–31
  results of intertwining faults with, 155–56
  tantric vows, 28n, 165–68
  transference of consciousness and, 350–55
  See also highest yoga tantra
Secret Moon Drop Tantra, 323–24
secret offering, 146, 158
  related to wisdom empowerment, 151–56, 402
secret mandala offering, 136–37
secret qualities of guru, supplicating, 213, 219–20, 406–7
Segyu lineage, 1
self-blessing stage, 337, 342
self-cherishing
  allowing all suffering to ripen upon, 266
  as cause of suffering, 54, 266
  contemplating faults of, 248, 255–63, 278, 409
  five forces and, 273
self-grasping
  recognizing evils of, 267
  as root of samsara, 221, 245, 343–44
sense offerings, 125–28
sense powers, nature of guru's, 80–81
senses, restraining doors of, 363, 364–65
sentient beings
  benefits of cherishing, 257–65, 278
  contemplating kindness of, 248–51, 258
  contemplating torment of, 249–50, 252–53

sentient beings (*continued*)
equalizing and exchanging self with, 252–65
going for refuge with, 50–52
melting and dissolving of, 59
purifying afflictions of, 52–53, 54, 63, 231, 264–65
as wish-fulfilling jewel, 258–59, 291
See also welfare of living beings
sequential withdrawal of subsequent destruction, 58, 59–60, 62, 333, 343n, 359
Serlingpa, 20, 252
servant, offering oneself as, 159–63, 403
session breaks, conduct during, 363–75
sessions, ending, 360–63
seven abandonments, 141
sevenfold cause and effect, 247, 279
seven limbs, 370
dedication, 180–82, 404
offerings, 117–72, 399–402,
performing confession, 169–74, 403
prostrations and praises, 101–13, 399–400
rejoicing, 174–76, 403
request to not pass into nirvana, 179–80, 404
request to turn wheel of Dharma, 176–79, 403–4
See also offerings; prostrations and praises
seven limbs of embrace, 62, 345
seven-point mind training, 252–78
eighteen commitments of, 275–76
equalizing and exchanging self with others, 254–65
integrating practices into single lifetime, 270–71
measure of having trained, 271–75
preliminaries as foundation of, 253
transforming adverse conditions, 265–69
twenty-two precepts of, 276–77
See also mind training
Seven-Point Mind Training, 34, 252, 262, 265
Shantarakshita, 253n

Shantideva, 238, 248, 252, 283, 437
Shantipa, 164
Shaptavajra, 73, 82
Shawari, 19, 24
simultaneously born joy, 228, 229–30
Six-Armed Mahakala, 21, 91
six limits, 221, 317
six perfections, 52, 283–313, 371
concentration, 298–302
generosity, 284–86
as guru and teacher, 222
inner subdivision of, 283
mandala offering and, 129–30
moral discipline, 286–87
patience, 288–92
perseverance, 293–98
wisdom, 303–13
sixty-four arts of love, 152
sleep
three mixings during, 342, 367
yoga of, 367–68
Sole Lineage of the Great Secret, 220
Songs of Spiritual Experience (Tsongkhapa), 239, 304, 373
space-like meditative equipoise, 303–5, 306
space vajra, 80
Sparshavajra, 58, 73, 82
special insight, 33, 303–5, 313
speech
isolated speech, 337–38
qualities of guru's, 216
secret empowerment and, 226, 230
spontaneously born messengers, 151
stage of self-blessing, 104, 185
Stages of Meditation, 251
Stages of the Path to Enlightenment, 33
Stages of Yoga, The, 357
subsequent destruction, 343n. *See also* sequential withdrawal of subsequent destruction
Subsequent Tantra, 317, 357
suchness
accomplishing, 21
ascertaining meaning of, 229–30
Mahayana accomplishment of, 198
suchness offering, 157–59, 403
suchness mandala offering, 136–37

suchness qualities of guru, supplicating, 213, 221–24, 407

suffering
contemplating samsara and, 46–48, 50, 53–54, 153, 245, 371
contemplating torment of migrating beings, 249–50, 252–53
good qualities of, 267
patience of accepting, 288–92
self-cherishing and, 255–63
taking and giving of, 263–65
three types of, 244
world of unbearable, 216

suitable vessel, for highest yoga tantra, 34–37, 314–21

Sumbaraja, 73, 83

Summoning and Separating from the Lower Realms, 368

supplicating the guru, 183–236, 329, 370, 405–7
contemplating benefits and faults of, 182–94
of mahamudra lineage, 443–52
mahamudra meditation and, 435
planting the stake, 224–26, 407
proclaiming inner qualities, 219, 406
proclaiming outer qualities, 213–18, 406
proclaiming secret qualities, 219–20, 406–7
proclaiming suchness qualities, 221–24, 407
qualities of elder of Vinaya, 195–197, 405
qualities of Mahayana spiritual master, 198–200, 405
qualities of Vajrayana guru, 200–7, 405
recalling guru's kindness, 207–12, 235, 406
receiving empowerments and, 225–30, 407
reciting guru's name mantra, 191–94
recollecting guru's good qualities, 194–207, 235

Supplication to the Mahamudra Lineage, 443–52

"Supreme Activity of the Conqueror," 63

Supreme Knowledge Tantra, 114

Sutra Declaring the Four Qualities, 171

Sutra Describing the Landscape of Sukhavati, 71

Sutra of Inexhaustible Intellect, 293

Sutra of King Prasenajit's Instructions, 138–39

Sutra of the Inconceivable Secret, 216

swastika, 42

taking and giving (tonglen), 263, 264–65
See also exchanging self with others

taking the essence, 63

Takkiraja, 73, 83

tantra. See highest yoga tantra; secret mantra

Tantra Requested by Subahu, 40–41, 114

tantric vows. See vows and commitments

Tara, 73, 80

tea offerings, 143

three baskets, 195, 197, 201

three bodies
bringing into the path, 58, 59–62, 331–32, 333, 334, 335, 339–40, 351–52, 412
seeing guru as, 101–10, 399–400
three sugata bodies, 213
transference of consciousness and, 351–52

three empties, 352

three faults of contaminants, 342

Three Hundred Verses of the Vinaya, 195

Three Jewels
going for refuge in, 50–52
guru as nature of, 109–10, 188, 191, 219, 225, 400
making offerings to, 329

three kindnesses, 72

three nested beings, 24, 34, 74, 91, 93, 359

Three Principal Aspects of the Path (Tsongkhapa), 238, 310

three realms, 288

three wisdoms, offering, 141–42

Tilopa, 19, 174

Togden Jampal Gyatso, 2, 68

tonglen. See exchanging self with others

torma offering, 268–69, 355–58

training the mind. See mind training; seven-point mind training

tranquil abiding, 33, 299–303, 313
  special insight and, 303–5
transference of consciousness, 348–55,
  412
  lying posture for, 349
  Mahayana practices for, 348–49
  secret mantra and, 350–55
Treasury of Secrets, 322
Treatise on the Middle Way, 115
Treatises on the Stages of the Path
  (Tsongkhapa), 300
Trisamayavyuharaja, 90
truth body
  bringing death into the path as, 58, 62,
    333, 339–40
  of conquerors, 214
  seeing guru as, 108–9, 222–23, 400
  transference of consciousness of, 351
  transforming all minds into, 53, 284
  wisdom empowerment and, 226, 228,
    229, 316
tsok offering, 147–51
Tsongkhapa, 23, 45–46, 69, 97, 117,
    121–22, 126–27, 129, 170, 229, 239,
    252, 254, 271, 306, 361–62, 372,
    373
  on completion stage, 340, 341, 342,
    346-47
  on generation stage, 62
  guru in aspect of, 72
  on guru yoga, 32, 92, 189
  Hearing Lineage of, 1, 13, 14, 21, 22–31,
    74, 359–60
  Manjushri and, 1, 21–22, 192–93,
    238
  on meditation, 300–301, 304
  name mantra of, 190–93
  on oral instructions, 318–20
  view of emptiness and, 310–11
Tubwang Dorje Chang. *See* Lama Losang
  Tubwang Dorje Chang
tummo, 124
twenty-four places, 74, 91

unfavorable conditions. *See* adverse
  conditions, transforming
union. *See* body of union
union of no more learning, 344

Ushnisha Chakravarti, 73, 83
Uttaratantra (Sublime Continuum), 105

Vairochana, 72, 79, 94
  all forms as, 365
  commitments of, 167, 328, 330
  lineages of, 220
  sitting posture of, 43–44
Vairochana Abhisambodhi, 90
Vairochana Abhisambodhi Tantra, 206
Vaishravana, 21, 91
Vajrabhairava
  arising as body of, 58, 60, 61, 64
  guru-deity assembly and, 73, 74, 87, 88
  Lama Chöpa and, 1, 2
  See also Yamantaka
vajra body, 79, 214
  accomplishing, 65
  explanation of, 179–80
  penetrating vital points of, 338–41, 434
Vajra Cutter Sutra, 109
Vajradaka Tantra, 85, 152, 156, 168, 350,
    351, 352
Vajradhara commitments, 325–26
  as essence of conquerors' mandalas, 111
  as essential object of concentration, 341
  guru as inseparable from, 92, 95, 99,
    224–25
  guru-deity assembly and, 68, 69, 70, 72,
    73, 74, 75
  mantra of, 232, 233–34
  transforming all bodies into, 53
Vajradhatu, 82
Vajradhatu Ishvari, 70, 72, 152, 228, 397
Vajra-Hatred, 58
Vajramala, 19, 75, 317, 337, 357. See also
  Explanatory Tantra Vajramala
Vajra Mandala Adornment Tantra, The, 201,
    204
vajra mind, 66, 80, 91, 94, 214
Vajra Nairatmya, 88–89
vajra of activities, 80
Vajrapani, 19, 37, 73, 81, 82, 193–94
Vajrapani Empowerment Tantra, 183, 404
Vajra Peak Tantra, 168
vajra recitation, 340n, 342–43
vajra recitation stage, 336–38
Vajra Rupini, 73

Vajrasattva, 83, 89, 90, 102, 103, 111, 144, 368, 434

Vajra Sparsha, 88

vajra speech, 66, 80, 91, 94, 214

Vajra Tent Tantra, 86, 97–98, 164, 203–4, 215

Vajravarahi, 58, 89

Vajra Vetali, 88

vase empowerment
  concise way of receiving, 226
  elaborate way of receiving, 226–28
  generation stage and, 159, 227, 316
  outer offering related to, 113–42

Vegadhari, 215

Verses about Friends, 199

Victory over the Enemy, 129

Vinaya
  on drinks of sages, 142–43
  on good qualities of guru, 195–97, 405
  moral discipline and, 195–97, 286–87
  on relying upon guru, 16–17
  skilled arts and, 152

virtue
  dedication of, 180–81, 404, 413
  offering roots of all, 137–42, 285
  perseverance of collecting, 293, 298
  rejoicing in, of others, 174–76

virtuous Dharmas four types of, 165, 280, 281, 286, 287

Vishvamata, 90

vows and commitments
  attainments and, 321–23, 325, 330, 331
  bodhisattva vows, 163–64, 279–82

  defilements and downfalls of, 34, 169–70, 189–90, 204, 281, 287, 323–25
  of five buddha families, 166, 167–68, 326–31
  ganachakra and, 146–47
  maintaining during session breaks, 367–68
  making confessions and, 168–74
  of mind training, 275–77
  pratimoksha vows, 16, 195–96, 286–87
  protecting, 18, 170, 317, 321–22, 370
  tantric vows, 165–68
  three sets of vows, 29, 170, 205–6, 207, 287, 372
  of Vajrayana guru, 205–7

waking, three mixings during, 342

water offerings, 113–18

Web of Illusion Tantra, 204

welfare of living beings
  attaining enlightenment for, 48, 52, 278–79, 286
  bodhichitta motivation for, 48–49
  compassion for beings as long as space exists, 178
  equalizing and exchanging self with others for, 254–65
  generating bodhichitta for, 52–57, 246–82
  moral discipline of working for, 281–82, 287
  offering oneself as servant to, 161
  perseverance in delighting in, 293, 298

What to Read Next from Wisdom Publications

Life and Teachings of Tsongkhapa
Robert Thurman

Discover the life and teachings of Je Tsongkhapa, the renowned founder of the Gelug school of Tibetan Buddhism.

Magical Play of Illusion
The Autobiography of Trijang Rinpoche
Trijang Rinpoche
Foreword by His Holiness the Dalai Lama

"Rinpoche's interests were varied and his field of mastery wide, ranging from classical philosophy to literature and poetry, and from traditional Tibetan healing sciences to the visual arts. The collection of his writings reflects his broad command of Tibetan cultural traditions . . . I feel fortunate to have been among the students of this great Tibetan master. I am profoundly grateful to Rinpoche for his kindness, for his teaching and transmissions, and for his personal friendship. It is a joy for me to add these few words of appreciation to the English translation of Trijang Rinpoche's autobiography."—from the foreword by His Holiness the Dalai Lama

Bliss of Inner Fire
Heart Practice of the Six Yogas of Naropa
Lama Thubten Yeshe
Foreword by Lama Zopa Rinpoche

"An impressive contribution to the growing body of Buddhist literature for an English-reading audience."—*The Midwest Book Review*

Introduction to Tantra
The Transformation of Desire
Lama Thubten Yeshe
Foreword by Philip Glass

"The best introductory work on Tibetan Buddhist tantra available today."—Janet Gyatso, Harvard University

Becoming Vajrasattva
The Tantric Path of Purification
Lama Thubten Yeshe
Foreword by Lama Zopa Rinpoche

"Lama Yeshe was capable of translating Tibetan Buddhist thought not only through language but by his presence, gestures, and way of life."—Gelek Rimpoche, author of *Good Life, Good Death*

Principles of Buddhist Tantra
Kirti Tsenshap Rinpoche

"Kirti Tsenshap Rinpoche was like the Kadam masters of the past in his profound renunciation. He showed not the slightest worldly activity, not a single one of the eight mundane concerns, and he had no self-cherishing thought. Everything he did, even talking, was utterly pleasing to the minds of sentient beings."—Lama Zopa Rinpoche

About Wisdom Publications

Wisdom Publications is the leading publisher of classic and contemporary Buddhist books and practical works on mindfulness. To learn more about us or to explore our other books, please visit our website at wisdompubs.org or contact us at the address below.

Wisdom Publications
199 Elm Street
Somerville, MA 02144 USA

We are a 501(c)(3) organization, and donations in support of our mission are tax deductible.

Wisdom Publications is affiliated with the Foundation for the Preservation of the Mahayana Tradition (FPMT).